The 151st Pennsylvania Volunteers at Gettysburg

The 151st Pennsylvania Volunteers at Gettysburg

Like Ripe Apples in a Storm

by
Michael A. Dreese

FOREWORD BY TIMOTHY H. SMITH

McFarland & Company, Inc., Publishers
Jefferson, North Carolina, and London

Library of Congress Cataloguing-in-Publication Data

Dreese, Michael A., 1963–
The 151st Pennsylvania volunteers at Gettysburg : Like ripe apples
in a storm / by Michael A. Dreese; foreword by Timothy H. Smith
p.   cm.
Includes bibliographical references and index.
ISBN 0-7864-0804-9 (illustrated case binding : 50# alkaline paper) ∞
1. United States — Army — Pennsylvania Infantry Regiment, 151st (1862–
1863).   2. Gettysburg (Pa.), Battle of, 1863.   3. Pennsylvania — History —
Civil War, 1861–1865 — Regimental Histories.   4. United States —
History — Civil War, 1861—1865 — Regimental Histories.   I. Title.
E475.53.D76   2000
973.7'349 — dc21

British Library Cataloguing-in-Publication data are available

Manufactured in the United States of America

*McFarland & Company, Inc., Publishers
Box 611, Jefferson, North Carolina 28640
www.mcfarlandpub.com*

For Heather, Brooke, and Shane,
who have been by my side through many storms

The apples are ripe in the orchard,
The work of the reaper is done,
And the golden woodlands redden
In the blood of the dying sun.

— *William Winter*

An army with banners … is not necessarily terrible. The whistling crowds preceding the military bands at the head of the regiments marching through a city's streets, the girls by the wayside waving handkerchiefs at the sight, the old men and women looking on approvingly, the world at large, dreams not for a moment of the anguish that lies hidden for all in the glittering display — the maimed bodies, the desolate homes, that lie in the wake of armies marching, whether in the cause of right or wrong. And yet, by a strange law, it is the noblest in peace who are ever so in war, and it would seem from the history of the world that only through bloodshed does mankind ever advance with a grand stride.

— *Richard Meade Bache*
(surgeon on the staff of General John F. Reynolds)

ACKNOWLEDGMENTS

From the gathering of source material through the editing of the final manuscript, one of the most satisfying aspects of writing this history has been the many new friendships that have developed throughout the long process. I also had ample opportunity to tap into the expertise of a number of old acquaintances. In fact, it is many ways an injustice that only my name appears on the cover, because this publication represents the contributions of a number of selfless individuals. As I list my many "co-authors" below, I apologize for any oversights or omissions. Of course, I assume full responsibility for the historical accuracy of the statements and material contained in this study.

My manuscript benefited immensely from the insights of several fellow historians, who took time from their own busy schedules to review my work. I am particularly indebted to my good friend Timothy Smith. As a long-time battlefield guide and award-winning author, Mr. Smith is widely known as one of the foremost authorities on the Battle of Gettysburg. Tim's eye for detail is uncanny, and his insights and suggestions for improvements were most welcome.

In a number of ways, historian Seward Osborne was the catalyst for this book. First, his excellent history of the 20th New York State Militia provided me with a wealth of information on the first day's fighting. Next, during a phone conversation, Seward firmly stated that the 151st Pennsylvania deserved a volume of their own, and he soon persuaded me to undertake the project. Finally, over the last several years, Mr. Osborne has graciously allowed me to review documents from his personal collection, and he has read over my entire manuscript. His influence and support, therefore, contributed much to the finished product.

I was indeed honored that Mr. Harry P. Pfanz offered to review my chapter devoted to July 1, 1863. At the time of this writing, Mr. Pfanz was completing his own manuscript for a book-length study of this phase of the battle. I greatly appreciated his kind comments and suggestions regarding my work.

Several descendants of the 151st also provided me with valuable advice. Joe Smith, M.D., John Hunt Walker, M.D., and Michael Straus deserve a great deal of credit for their assistance. Not only did these individuals allow me to publish photographs and written material regarding their ancestors, but they also provided genealogical and historical details that would otherwise have escaped my notice. Dr. Walker's *Appointment at Gettysburg* was an invaluable source for information on Sergeant George Heilig and other members of Company H.

As in my first book, the detailed maps of Garry Adelman grace the pages of this work. I greatly value Garry's historical knowledge, his cartographic skill, but above all, his friendship.

A very special thanks is due to Miss Carolyn Minguez for her extensive proofreading work. As I have always shunned the mechanics of writing for the more creative aspect, Carolyn's detailed analysis of the text for proper punctuation and syntax was much appreciated.

I also wish to make special mention of Ken and Sue Boardman for allowing me access to their extensive photographic collection and Civil War library.

The quality and uniqueness of this history would have been greatly diminished had it not been for the contributions of numerous descendants of the 151st. In addition to those mentioned above, the following individuals provided me with copies of documents and photographs from their personal collections for use in this volume: Polly Lauver, Mary Haney Arnold, Robert Kellogg Crane, Eric Michael, Richard Frecon, Robert and Sheryl Meyer, Robert Carichner, Rosemary McCorkel, Adah Sidon, Stewart P. Biehl, Florence Heydt, Sally Smith, the late

Helen Weidner, Ken Thomson, Jr., Roy Gehris, and Edward Ammarell.

A number of public institutions also provided significant contributions to this study. In particular, I wish to thank Rhonda Hoover, Edith Serkownek, and the staff of the Warren County Historical Society for bringing to my attention a number of invaluable collections pertaining to members of Company F.

The extensive manuscript collections, photo archives, and library of the United States Army Military History Institute (USAMHI), Carlisle Barracks, Pa., make it a particularly valuable repository for researchers. My frequent visits there were enhanced by the professionalism and courtesy of Michael J. Winey, Randy Hackenberg, Richard J. Sommers, and Louise Arnold-Friend.

Another rich source for historical material was the Adams County Historical Society, Gettysburg, Pa. I wish to thank Dr. Charles H. Glatfelter and Elwood H. Christ, director and assistant director, respectively, for their assistance.

Other helpful sources included D. Scott Hartwig, Gettysburg National Military Park Library; Robert Winder, Juniata County Historical Society; Ann Kenne, College Archivist and Special Collections Librarian, Franklin and Marshall College, Lancaster, Pa.; the staff of the William L. Clements Library, University of Michigan; and the National Archives and Library of Congress in Washington, D.C.

Thanks also to Dr. Richard Sauers, Jeffrey Wert, G. Craig Caba, Ronn Palm, the late John W. Heisey, James Pangburn, Mike Griffiths, Mark Troup, James Schmick, Austin Willi, and Larry Fryer.

Of course, I cannot close without acknowledging the sacrifices of my wife, Heather, and my two children, Brooke and Shane. They have shared alike the joys and frustrations of a Civil War author.

CONTENTS

FOREWORD

The Battle of Gettysburg was fought on the first three days of July 1863. Ever since the battle, individuals such as myself have catered to the large number of visitors to the town. As a licensed battlefield guide, I have conducted thousands of people over the field of the great battle. With the overwhelming number of monuments, markers, and tablets, it is impossible to tell the story of every unit that fought here. With so much to see, it is not surprising that the monument of the 151st Pennsylvania is rarely pointed out during tours of the field. As a matter of fact, on the rare occasion that the monument is noted, it is usually to tell the story of the schoolteachers who served in the unit.

There are several reasons that little attention has been paid to the regiment's role in the battle. Unfortunately, the 151st's monument is not in chronological order with the Gettysburg National Military Park's auto driving tour. Stop #1 of the official driving tour is located near the monument. But the unit saw action in the afternoon fighting, and this stop is reserved for a discussion of the morning action of the first day's battle and the death of General John F. Reynolds. This situation is not a recent development. It seems that the Northern veterans who administered the battlefield during its period of monumentation were much more interested in marking the positions of the units engaged in the morning action (a Northern victory) than in those of the afternoon action (a Northern defeat).

Another reason for their lack of fame is the fact that no history of the unit was ever published by its veterans. It should come as no surprise that the most popular units today are the ones that left behind a written record of their service. Many units who performed gallantly at Gettysburg are overshadowed by those who wrote extensively of their battle experiences. History is not written by the winners; it is written by whoever picks up the pen.

This lack of attention is unfortunate. The service of the 151st Pennsylvania Infantry at Gettysburg is deserving of our respect and of our continued study. The men of the 151st Pennsylvania were considered veterans in the Army of the Potomac. When the regiment arrived in Gettysburg, it was a nine-months unit near the end of its term of service with little combat experience to speak of. There was much uncertainty as to how these men would perform under fire.

Soon after their arrival to the field on the afternoon of July 1, 1863, the unit was placed in reserve near the Lutheran Theological Seminary. As the battle increased in size and fury, the 151st was called upon to slow the advance of the North Carolinians of General J. Johnson Pettigrew's Brigade. They engaged in a savage action which delayed the Southerners and allowed the other Northern units around them to fall back to a final defensive position along Seminary Ridge. Upon falling back itself, the 151st took position at a rail barricade directly in front of the Lutheran Seminary building. Eventually overwhelmed and driven back to Cemetery Hill, the 151st left their dead and dying scattered across the fields where they had fought. Although their loss was severe, the survivors rallied and participated in the repulse of Pickett's Charge on July 3rd.

But questions still linger. Much is made of the experience and leadership of the units that comprised the Iron Brigade, and how these factors contributed to their ability to withstand and sustain heavy losses under fire on July 1st. But what made the comparatively inexperienced men of the 151st stand and fight as they did?

The 151st Pennsylvania lost over 72 percent of its men, killed, wounded, captured, or missing at the battle. According to the definitive study of casualties, *Regimental Strengths and Losses at Gettysburg* by John W. Busey and David G. Martin, this figure is

1

the ninth highest percentage loss of any Northern regiment in the battle. Although they were involved in all three days of the fighting, the bulk of their casualties were taken in about an hour of fierce fighting, first at the edge of Herbst's woodlot, and then in front of the Lutheran Seminary.

The location of their regimental monument designates the spot where the 151st was thrown in line to cover the retreat of the 19th Indiana and the 24th Michigan of the Iron Brigade. It was here that they slugged it out with the 26th North Carolina in their front and elements of the 11th North Carolina to their left flank.

It may not be surprising to many that the 24th Michigan suffered the highest numerical loss of any Northern regiment at Gettysburg. Very few, however, know that the 151st Pennsylvania suffered the second highest. In their efforts to slow the driving Confederate forces on July 1st, the men of the 151st inflicted heavy casualties as well.

As a result of the first day's fighting and their subsequent participation in the third day's fight, the 26th North Carolina suffered the greatest total loss of any regiment, North or South, in the entire battle. Incidentally, the next highest numerical loss of a Southern regiment at Gettysburg was sustained by the 11th North Carolina, the unit positioned to the right of the 26th on July 1st. It should be noted that the advance of Pettigrew's Brigade ended at the edge of Herbst's woodlot. Although isolated squads followed the 151st as it fell back, the brigade as a whole did not move forward and was relieved by the arrival of fresh troops.

After a short lull, the 151st fell back to a breastwork in front of the Lutheran Theological Seminary. The position they occupied is today the site of the seminary tennis court and is not owned by the National Park Service. At this position, the remnants of the 151st faced off against the 14th South Carolina Infantry. As a result of this encounter, the 14th would suffer the highest percentage loss of any unit in General Dorsey Pender's Division at Gettysburg, and the second highest numerical loss of any Confederate regiment that assaulted the final Union defensive position along Seminary Ridge on the afternoon of July 1st. The 151st was pulled back only after the units on their left were driven in and their position made untenable.

In the following volume, the story of the 151st Pennsylvania at Gettysburg is brought to life. In what I believe to be one of the best books to be written on the battle in some time, Michael Dreese has spent many long hours pulling together unpublished material that has been scattered for years. In the process he has painted a graphic picture of the men who fought in this unit and how the Battle of Gettysburg affected their lives.

Today it is hard to imagine the scene that occurred in the fields west of town on the afternoon of July 1, 1863. What made these men stand and fight the way they did? The men of the 151st Pennsylvania are deserving of our respect and of our continuing devotion to their monument and their memory.

Timothy H. Smith
Gettysburg, Pennsylvania

INTRODUCTION

"Our poor boys fell around me like ripe apples in a storm. God bless them! They were and are heroes, every one." William Oren Blodget, an officer in the 151st Pennsylvania, penned these moving lines to his wife on the morning of July 2, 1863, from Gettysburg, Pennsylvania. On the previous afternoon, his regiment had participated in the bloody opening round of fighting in what would come to be recognized as the decisive battle in the eastern theater of the Civil War. The 38-year-old farmer and father of three had watched in horror as his friends and neighbors from Northwestern Pennsylvania were shot down all around him during a desperate rearguard action against overwhelming numbers of enemy troops. Blodget led 52 men of Company F into the fight and came out with only 13. "This is indeed the saddest moment of my life," he wrote. Indeed, the enduring bonds of love and devotion forged from hardship and death can only be fully appreciated by veterans of armed conflict.

At Gettysburg, the 151st Pennsylvania suffered 337 casualties from an engaged strength of 467 officers and men, which ranked as the second highest total regimental loss within the entire Union army during the battle. The vast majority of these losses were incurred in less than an hour on July 1st. The 151st also ranked at or near the top in its number of killed, wounded, and mortally wounded.

By nature, however, statistics are cold and impersonal. In stark contrast, Blodget's lament over the fate of his "poor boys" strikes an emotional chord, and the imagery of men falling "like ripe apples in a storm" is quite vivid. During my research of this regiment, I became increasingly familiar with the personal details of the men who served in its ranks, and throughout my manuscript preparation, I often felt a degree of the personal sorrow experienced by Lieutenant Blodget.

In fact, I have always maintained that the human element of warfare is far more compelling than dry dissertations on battlefield tactics. Therefore, throughout my narrative I have interwoven biographical sketches and anecdotes. In order to fully understand the cataclysmic events that took place in the summer of 1863, I thought it essential to examine what the citizen soldiers of the 151st were doing before the war, the factors that motivated them to enlist in the Union army, and the lasting impact that military service had upon the lives of the survivors.

Like Ripe Apples in a Storm has both a literal meaning and a less obvious emblematic interpretation. The 151st Pennsylvania was nearing the end of its enlistment term when the two opposing armies marched north toward destiny. The regiment had seen little combat thus far, but its soldiery was well-trained and disciplined. Many of its members were family men, operating farms and businesses or performing skilled trades or professions, when duty to country called them away from their peacetime pursuits. Nearly all were entering into the most productive phase of their lives. As a unit and as individuals, these soldiers were no longer green. They were "ripe apples" at Gettysburg.

Although the 151st played an important role in the opening day of the fighting at Gettysburg and then assisted in the repulse of Pickett's Charge two days later, surprisingly little has been published on this regiment, and it has been largely neglected in modern campaign histories. Following the publication of *An Imperishable Fame*, which focused primarily on Lieutenant Colonel George McFarland, I began to accumulate numerous primary accounts, copies of photographs, and correspondence relating to the regiment from a number of descendants. This influx of fresh source material prompted me to intensify my own research efforts. Although my original intention was to write a detailed article for a Civil War periodical, the abundance of new information and the increasing scope of my project soon outgrew this limited medium.

In the following study, I provide a detailed day-by-day analysis of the 151st's participation in the Gettysburg campaign, including the trying march north from Falmouth, Virginia, its role in the fighting of July 1st and 3rd, and the pursuit of Robert E. Lee's army after the battle. The aftermath of the campaign is covered as well, with one chapter devoted to hospital scenes and another dealing with the prisoner-of-war experiences of three officers. The epilogue traces the post-war lives of a representative sample of men and also includes a section on veterans' reunions and the dedication of the regimental monument at Gettysburg. The appendices to this volume include an essay on the origins and history of the "Schoolteachers' Regiment" nickname and a revised list of casualties compiled by Lieutenant Colonel McFarland in 1889.

Despite this in-depth coverage, it was not my intent to study the 151st in a vacuum. Rather, I considered it vitally important to discuss how the regiment fit into the context of overall military strategy throughout the campaign. Battlefield tactics and topography are discussed in detail to help the reader understand the specific battle actions in which the 151st participated. An examination of the role played by associated military units, particularly the other three regiments comprising Colonel Chapman Biddle's brigade, has been added to present a more panoramic view of the battle.

I hope that by taking a balanced and detailed approach to this study of the 151st Pennsylvania, I have created a work that will appeal to the novice and serious student alike, and that it will fill a void in the literature pertaining to this fascinating campaign.

Michael A. Dreese
Kreamer, Pennsylvania
January 2000

Chapter 1

COUNTDOWN TO GLORY

"The Government must be maintained and the Union preserved at all hazards."

Shortly before 3 P.M. on July 1, 1863, Lieutenant Colonel George Fisher McFarland, 151st Pennsylvania Volunteers, received orders to move forward with his 467 officers and men to plug a critical gap in the Union defensive line one mile west of Gettysburg. The Keystoners, with less than a month remaining in their enlistment term, advanced from behind a temporary breastwork fronting the Lutheran Theological Seminary, crossed an open swale, and crested the gentle eastern slope of McPherson's Ridge. As the troops neared an open grove known as Herbst's Woods, they ran headlong into the 26th North Carolina, the largest regiment in the Army of Northern Virginia. Closing to within twenty paces, the two lines exchanged devastating musketry volleys. The casualties mounted at an alarming rate as both units struggled to hold their ground in the midst of the deadly inferno.[1] This epic struggle was one of the bloodiest engagements of the three-day battle.

Commanded by 21-year-old Colonel Henry King Burgwyn, Jr., the 26th North Carolina was a seasoned unit by the time it marched to Gettysburg. The regiment fought its maiden battle at New Bern in March 1862 and then joined Robert E. Lee's forces during the Seven Days' Battles near Richmond. Following a tour of duty in southeastern Virginia and eastern North Carolina, the 26th rejoined the Army of Northern Virginia just prior to the invasion of Pennsylvania. The Tarheels arrived in splendid uniforms accompanied by a Moravian brass band, which had a repertoire of over 200 tunes. The regiment's dapper appearance provided a stark contrast to the tattered veterans of Lee's army. Nevertheless, no one questioned their fighting ability after Gettysburg. The North Carolinians entered the first day's fight with over 800 men and lost about 550. On July 3rd, the 26th assailed the Union lines near the angle during the Pickett-Pettigrew Charge and suffered an additional 100 plus casualties. No unit, North or South, lost more men in a single battle throughout the entire Civil War![2]

Just as the 26th North Carolina's unrivaled sacrifice had forever linked it with the tragic history of the Army of Northern Virginia, the bloody clash earned the 151st Pennsylvania a respected place in the annals of the Army of the Potomac. On the Union side, the unit's 337 casualties at Gettysburg were exceeded only by those of the 24th Michigan. The vast majority of these losses took place in less than thirty minutes during the regiment's desperate stand on McPherson's Ridge. A fierce encounter with Colonel Abner Perrin's South Carolinians on Seminary Ridge and the subsequent retreat to Cemetery Hill thinned additional men from the ranks.[3] Reduced to the size of a large company by the fighting on July 1st, the 151st still played a role in repulsing Pickett's Virginians on the final day of the battle.

Popular tradition holds that the 151st received its nickname, "The Schoolteachers' Regiment," for the large number of teachers in its ranks. Although it is true that at least 60 teachers served in the regiment, a far greater number of the recruits listed farming, lumbering, or a skilled trade as their principal occupations.[4] Indeed, the fundamental facts behind this sobriquet have been embellished considerably with the passage of time. An early 1900s newspaper article, for instance, made the ridiculous claim that the regiment "had been almost entirely recruited of young men not yet out of their teens, and Company D was composed wholly of the scholars and instructors of a country academy."[5] With all of its implicit exaggerations and half-truths, the colorful nickname further heightened the romantic appeal of the vignette.

Major General Abner Doubleday, who commanded the First Corps on July 1, profusely praised the 151st Pennsylvania when he wrote:

Union Mills, Virginia, the lonely outpost where the 151st Pennsylvania spent the early part of its service. Courtesy of the Library of Congress.

At Gettysburg, they won, under the brave McFarland, an imperishable fame. They defended the left front of the First Corps against vastly superior numbers; covered its retreat against the overwhelming masses of the enemy at the Seminary, west of the town, and enabled me by their determined resistance, to withdraw the corps in comparative safety ... I can never forget the services rendered me by this regiment, directed by the gallantry and genius of McFarland. I believe they saved the First Corps, and were among the chief instruments to save the Army of the Potomac, and the country from unimaginable disaster.[6]

At the commencement of the Gettysburg campaign in mid–June, it seemed improbable that the 151st Pennsylvania would earn any military laurels. In fact, a cloud of uncertainty hung over the regiment. First, a great deal of confusion existed over the expiration of the unit's nine-month enlistment term. A number of officers and enlisted men felt their obligation to the government should end on June 20, 1863, while the War Department had set August 25th as the official date of muster out.[7] Another matter of concern was the general health of the regiment. But for the 151st Pennsylvania, perhaps the biggest question mark of all was its lack of combat experience.

The unit had spent the early part of its service performing guard duty along Bull Run near Union Mills, Virginia. Here, the men battled homesickness and the bitter winter weather much more than the enemy. On January 6, 1863, Sergeant Simon Arnold wrote his brother, "We have very stormy weather now. Yesterday it snowed all day and today the rain pours down in torrents. Our company just returned from picket duty and a very hard time we had. I wasn't compelled to go, but went just for the sport. I don't think I will go out again in a hurry."[8]

The desolate surroundings further weakened the spirits of the men. Sergeant Robert E. Miller, a teacher and one-time law student from Warren, wrote his father the following description of his environs:

> The whole country as far as we went and as far as the eye could reach in either direction presented one wide field of desolation, there being not a vestige of civilization left.... There were houses of brick, stone, and wood, but none of them was inhabited, the windows and doors all being torn out, and the northern blast as it howled through the deserted halls seemed to be chanting a solemn requiem for the departed glory of the Old Dominion.[9]

In February 1863, the regiment joined the Army of the Potomac, which was stationed near Fredericksburg, as part of an exchange for the battle-depleted units of the Pennsylvania Reserves in the First Corps. It was assigned to the First Brigade of the Third Division. This division was composed entirely of Pennsylvania troops and was led by General Abner Doubleday, a veteran officer and West Point graduate.[10]

The Army of the Potomac was reeling from a costly defeat on the bloody slopes above Fredericksburg the previous December and had suffered further humiliation during the infamous Mud March in late January. These setbacks prompted President Lincoln to switch commanders once again. Major General Joseph Hooker, the army's brash new commander, immediately took steps to revitalize his dejected forces. He also made extensive preparations for a campaign aimed at forcing the Confederates out of their strong defensive position and into open ground, where his superior numbers could best be utilized. Like several of his predecessors, however, Hooker was bested by Robert E. Lee, the wily chief of the Army of Northern Virginia. At Chancellorsville, Lee won perhaps his most brilliant victory.

As a large portion of the Union army maneuvered above and around the Confederate entrenchments at Fredericksburg in late April, the First Corps remained behind as part of a diversionary force. The soldiers of the 151st received their first taste of combat during a severe artillery bombardment at Fitzhugh's Crossing, just below the city, on April 30th.

The raw troops were "very much confused and startled ... at the shells coming so unexpectedly and rapidly." After a shot burst directly over the colors, the men dashed for the protection of a nearby hillside "without order or regularity."[11] An officer in a nearby regiment thought that the 151st "was stampeded and scattered in most unmilitary confusion."[12] Sergeant George Heilig of Company H later confessed that during the two hours of shelling, "my back crawled rather hard." The former schoolteacher and storekeeper probably thought often of his wife and three children at home in Strausstown as he hugged the earth.[13]

Most of the missiles passed harmlessly overhead, but the regiment did not escape the ordeal entirely unscathed. Several men were injured by frantic horses which bolted away during the initial confusion. Captain William Boltz was struck by one of these runaways and knocked into a ditch. The impact of the blow fractured two of the captain's ribs and ruptured his abdomen. Boltz was treated by a surgeon on the field, and he reluctantly reported to the hospital the following morning. A soldier from the 90th Pennsylvania, on a visit to Company B, wasn't so lucky. The unfortunate visitor was struck by a projectile which passed directly through his body. Near the same time, the mortally wounded Captain George Bush of the 13th Massachusetts was carried through the lines on a stretcher. The captain had been struck by the same shell which had instantly killed a lieutenant and a corporal of his unit. Darkness brought an abrupt end to the artillery duel, and for the 151st, a welcome relief from the recently discovered horrors of war.[14]

Two days later, the First Corps completed a forced march of over 20 miles to reinforce Hooker's defensive perimeter in the tangled wilderness surrounding the Chancellorsville crossroads. An officer on Doubleday's staff vividly described the surreal conditions confronting the weary troops:

> There is one scene indelibly impressed on my mind, and that is the march of our Div. into the Battle of Chancellorsville at midnight ... the brilliant moonlight ... the blazing pines in the thick woods around us, the wounded and dying straggling to the rear or writhing by the roadside, the solemn steady tramp of the men as they marched into their first fight, the horrid din of battle just in front, and the swelling strains of "marching along," now drowned by the roar of artillery, now echoed back in a moment of strange stillness from the depths of the towering pines....[15]

The First Corps took position on the extreme right flank of the Union army and played a very minor role in the bloody contest. However, the 151st suffered its first casualties during several sharp skirmishes with Louisiana troops on May 3rd and 4th.[16] During the initial encounter with the enemy in a thicket of oak saplings and scrub pine, the men were "frightened and confused ... hence the line fell back irregularly." Fortunately, Lieutenant Colonel McFarland received some timely assistance from an officer in the nearby 12th Massachusetts, and order was soon restored. As minié balls went "Whiz, Phiz, and Whit" in every direction for the next several hours, the 151st advanced to its assigned position and held it resolutely. The green soldiers gained a degree of confidence when several of the enemy were brought down by their accurate fire. McFarland summed up the experience in his diary, "This affair was of some consequence as it was my first infantry fight. It was sudden and unexpected, and under disadvantageous circumstances very embarrassing."[17]

Colonel Harrison Allen placed the regiment's erratic performance in the best possible light when he concluded his official report with the following: "The men in my command behaved under fire and during the whole march with coolness and bravery."[18] Despite the colonel's lack of forthrightness, the lessons garnered at Chancellorsville would be invaluable in the near future. The men had "seen the elephant" and nearly all survived the experience.

Lieutenant Robert Kellogg, Company B, was cited for his brave conduct at the battle of Chancellorsville by Brigadier General Thomas Rowley. Courtesy of Robert Kellogg Crane.

The conduct of Lieutenant Robert Kellogg of Company B during the battle proved to be a notable bright spot. On the morning of May 3rd, Kellogg led a body of thirty sharpshooters a mile and a half in advance of the main line and deployed them at close intervals to support the picket line. In the confusing terrain, he was surprised and captured by a squad of Confederates, who disarmed him and began escorting him to the rear. A sudden volley from the Union lines hastened the movements of the Southerners and temporarily distracted them from their prize. At this opportune moment, Kellogg slipped away from his captors and was rescued by his men. The young lieutenant's actions elicited the praise of brigade commander Thomas Rowley, for his small detachment was credited with capturing over fifty prisoners and killing or wounding fifteen of the enemy with the loss of just one man.[19]

The unfortunate soul was Private Albert R. Greggs of Company C, who had the distinction of being the first man from the regiment to die in combat. During the course of the battle six others were wounded while nine were listed as missing. The wounding of Lieutenant William D. Lusk, Company C, was listed as accidental. Private William Manning of Company I would survive a gunshot wound in the knee, only to die nearly two months later on the bloody fields of Gettysburg.[20]

When the Union army retreated across the Rappahannock River early on May 6, the men of the 151st openly questioned the reason for the withdrawal. A large number felt the army should have maintained its strong position behind a series of recently constructed earthworks. The soldiers became extremely low spirited as they slogged through the rain and mud back to their former camp. During the retrograde movement, a whiskey ration was issued several times. McFarland was proud that in his old company less than half the men accepted the elixir.[21]

Over the next month the men rested from the rigors of the campaign and tried to determine how Robert E. Lee had whipped another one of their generals. Lieutenant William Blodget lamented, "The Southern army is disciplined — as machines — and are certainly more efficient than ours." Sergeant Robert Miller put a different spin on the situation as he maintained, "[T]he army is better able to whip the rebels now than it was before the late battle ... we have gained in everything except the morale effect of the repulse, and if it be true that they have lost [General Stonewall] Jackson, they have lost that which they cannot easily replace."[22]

Captain William Boltz did not participate in the regiment's maiden battle, but his introduction to infantry combat was just as harsh. A flood of wounded men filled the hospitals near Falmouth in the aftermath of the Sixth Corps' bloody fighting on Mayre's Heights and at Salem Church. Boltz declared, "I have seen the wounded with my own eyes. No one needs to tell me how it is. I have seen more than I would like and I will pray God about not seeing such sights again." The captain suffered a deep personal loss when he learned that a dear friend had been shot through the head on May 3rd during the desperate assault on Mayre's Heights. William poured out his emotions in a letter to his wife, "A few days before I was with him in his tent. I had eaten with him at midday ... Our people didn't keep the field, so had to leave dead and wounded behind in the hands of the enemy. You can easily picture to yourself how his wife and parents have much to hear that her man or son is dead and not to know whether his body is buried or not, or what from him is saved."[23]

Over the next several weeks many conjectures were raised about the regiment's uncertain future. Sergeant Miller noted, "The boys are having a great time talking about when we will be mustered out...." On May 17th, Boltz wrote, "I think that we won't need to be in any more battles until our time is up. I still don't know when our time expires, but I think not until the beginning of August." Four days later he added, "How long we'll stay here I don't know. I don't think ... that we might so quickly be in a battle again, except the Rebels could have passed us by. I don't think they will soon be attacked by our people. I also don't think that we will conquer them here ... I can tell you that this time it will cost many people." Unfortunately, Boltz's prediction was right on the mark.[24]

The controversy over the regiment's enlistment term dated back to its formation at Camp Curtin in Harrisburg, Pennsylvania, the previous fall. The 151st was organized in response to President Lincoln's calls for 600,000 additional state troops and militia in July and August of 1862. A militia law enacted by Congress at this time specified that all able-bodied men between the ages of eighteen and forty-five would be eligible for militia service. In order to maximize the manpower of the Northern states, new nine-month regiments were being raised in addition to the standard three-year organizations. Each state was assigned a specified quota of troops, which was then divided into county quotas, and then subdivided into borough and township quotas. Many local governmental units offered bounty payments of cash to those who enlisted, as volunteer enlistments reduced the local draft quotas.[25]

After several postponed deadlines, a draft was finally put into effect in Pennsylvania on October 16th

Corporal William C. Hittle, Company D, was one of the 54 soldiers from the 151st Pennsylvania who died of disease during military service. Courtesy of Pennsylvania State Archives.

to complete the organization of several regiments, including the 151st. However, many of the regiment's original recruits had enlisted with their respective companies a month earlier, but had not been sworn into federal service. Accordingly, these men felt their term had started back in September. In an attempt to clear up the misunderstanding, Adjutant Samuel Allen wrote the Adjutant General of Pennsylvania in early April 1863. Allen inquired as to whether the nine-month period had officially commenced during the initial enrollment phase or at the average date from which the various companies were mustered into the United States service. The War Department, however, selected November 25th as the start of the term since it represented the latest date of mustering for any man in the regiment! By this calculation, the nine-month term expired on August 25th, two months later than the date formulated by the members of the 151st.

Lieutenant William O. Blodget of Company F voiced the opinions of many of his comrades when he wrote, "If the Gov't. needs men and must have them, let them say so and detain us manfully upon the necessities of the case, not sneakingly swindle us in regard to time." One of Blodget's men, Corporal Nathan Cooper, also thought there was "foul play" involved, but he conceded that "the Government is not to blame and that is what we are fighting for." Ultimately, a compromise was reached and July 27 was fixed as the expiration date of the regiment's service.[26]

Any damaging effects on morale as a result of this debate were further heightened by the serious outbreaks of smallpox, typhoid fever, and dysentery which plagued the 151st following the Chancellorsville campaign. McFarland wrote that during the seven-day campaign it had rained during five and "being in the presence of the enemy we were permitted to make coffee only twice, thus having to eat wet and moldy hard tack and drink from the water puddles and mud holes plenty all about us…. This was hard on everyone, and about 165 men of my regiment became unfit for duty within a few days of our return…." The more severe cases were transported to permanent care facilities near Washington, such as the St. Paul's Church Hospital in Alexandria and the Georgetown Female Seminary Hospital.

Near the end of May, Sergeant Alexander Seiders, a semi-literate 23-year-old factory worker from Reading, wrote to his wife, Elmira, "We hav a grate many sick…. The dockter has excuseed 2 hundred forty some. They hav all got the Diarear." Seiders himself was just recovering from a severe bout of diarrhea and had lost 58 pounds as a result. After taking two days worth of medicine prescribed by the regimental surgeon, the sergeant switched to a concoction of teas prepared by a fellow soldier. The brew was dubbed "chicken guts tea" and Seiders reported that it soon cured him![27]

Corporal Nathan Cooper took a novel approach in recuperating from illness. While he watched many of his comrades feign sickness to avoid duty, Nathan performed double duty when he didn't feel well as he felt the extra exertion cured him. "A great many [of] the boys are unfit for duty," he admitted, "but many of them never was fit. They had better stayes at home with the[ir] mother. We have some from our town that ant no more fitt for a soldier than I am for a preacher. They coudent carry what belongs to them 10 miles if it would save them from Pergatory." Still, even the healthiest of specimens were susceptible to the numerous contagious diseases spreading through the camps. For example, Captain John Mitchell of Company F was prostrated by illness even though one of his men considered him "as well built as eny man I ever saw." The same soldier also claimed that the hulking six foot-four inch officer could "swar the wickidest of eny man I ever saw and I have herd men swair some."[28]

By the beginning of June 1863, over one hundred enlisted men were convalescent but not strong enough for severe duty or marching. Also, only twelve of the regiment's thirty line officers reported that they were physically fit for duty and three of these officers rarely performed their duties on a daily basis. The field and staff were also afflicted. Major John Young had been absent since April with a case of typhoid while Colonel Harrison Allen and Quartermaster Francis Parvin departed for Washington in early June on sick leave. Allen was diagnosed with typho malarial fever and granted a thirty-day leave of absence beginning on June 8th. And, amazingly, at one point both the regimental surgeon and assistant surgeon fell ill!

Thus, it is little wonder that Lieutenant Colonel McFarland, now the senior officer, felt "a little lonesome and weak handed" as a new round of campaigning approached. In light of his heavy responsibilities, McFarland was thankful for his own good health. He was fortunate, indeed, to have the assistance of Adjutant Samuel T. Allen and Sergeant Major Simon J. Arnold.[29]

Samuel Allen, the younger brother of Colonel Allen, was raised on a farm in Pine Grove Township, Warren County, Pennsylvania. His attendance at private academies in Southern New York bolstered a natural intelligence, and the young man developed a wide range of skills. Before his 25th birthday, Samuel had taught school, mastered the art of surveying, and entered the Warren law office of Lacy and Dinsmore as a student. When the 151st was organized, Governor Andrew Curtin appointed Allen as the adjutant, a position well-suited for his background.[30]

One of 13 children, 24-year-old Simon Arnold worked as a clerk for a bank president in Reading before he became first sergeant of Company K. He was a handsome young man with a sharp wit, a gracious manner, and warm blue eyes. In late April 1863, Arnold ascended to the rank of sergeant major by order of Colonel Allen. Lieutenant Colonel McFarland praised him as a young man with remarkable energy and character who "served faithfully and efficiently at all times."[31] Both Arnold and Allen would be in the thick of the fighting at Gettysburg.

By the time the 151st departed from its old camp near Falmouth, Virginia, on June 11th, the number of men on the sick list decreased. Still, its ranks had been reduced to about 500 men from an original strength of over 900. McFarland was much more concerned with his officers, "not in the nature of their disease, but in their loss of spirit and pluck. Some are shamefully dispirited and are constantly liable to the charge of cowardice, homesickness, or something of that nature." One enlisted man wrote home, "if this regt. should go in now I am afraid they wouldent make a very good show."[32]

Despite all of this adversity, "the material of the regiment was ... excellent, many of the men being experienced marksman, and most of them well formed and hardy." The command was well instructed and drilled. Some had seen prior military service in the three-months regiments of 1861 or in pre-war volunteer militia units. The men ranged from the well-educated and articulate to those who were barely literate. Its members came largely from small towns and rural districts throughout the Keystone State. Companies A and C from Susquehanna County and B from Pike represented the Pocono northeast. Company F was recruited in Warren County, located in the lumber rich northwestern region of the state. Central Pennsylvania contributed Company D from Juniata County (with a contingent of men from neighboring Snyder and Perry counties). Four full companies, E, G, H, and K, along with a portion of Company I, hailed from Berks County in the agriculture belt of southeastern Pennsylvania. The remainder of Company I was raised in adjacent Schuylkill County.[33]

These men enlisted for a variety of reasons. For Private Franklin Weaber of Company K, army life may have seemed an attractive alternative to the monotony of life in rural Berks County. Weaber marveled at the sheer size of the army, and he enjoyed the

Sergeant Major Simon J. Arnold. Courtesy of Mary H. Arnold Collection, USAMHI.

daily sampling of music played by the various regimental bands and solo performers. His grand adventure would come to a shattering conclusion. Private Franklin Wendling of the same company had a more practical reason for enlisting. Wendling, who had just turned seventeen in March, was the next to the oldest of nine children. His parents scratched out a living from a small farm near Kutztown. Franklin's pay of thirteen dollars a month was a welcome supplement to the family's meager income.[34]

Patriotism was still a motivating factor despite the number of bloody battles which took place in the eastern theater during the spring and summer of 1862. In December, Sergeant Abe Freet, a former student at the McAlisterville Academy in Juniata County, had written his ailing father: "[I]f you get sick have me know it and likely in such a case, I could get a furlow, but if you all keep well I don't want to come home until my time is up, and if I have not luck to get back, you know I died in the cause of my country and to protect those that protected me."[35]

The leadership echelon of the companies were in a depleted state by the summer of 1863. Half of

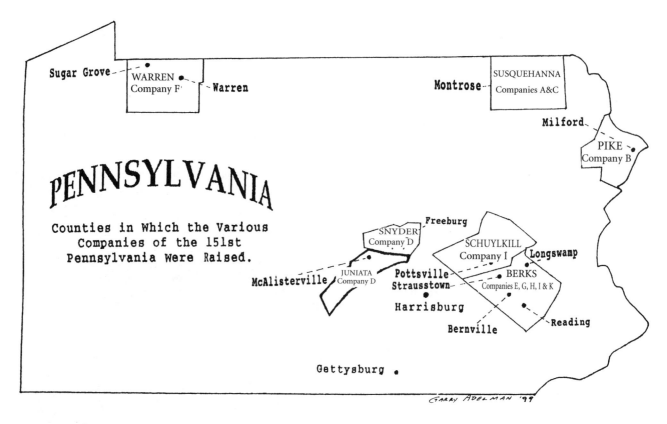

Pennsylvania: Counties in which the various companies of the 151st Pennsylvania were raised. Map by Garry Adelman.

them did not enjoy the full complement of three line officers, while three units fielded only one commander.[36] The men in charge of the ten companies were a diversified lot indeed. Generally, these officers were older men who had held respected positions in their communities prior to their enlistment. The line officers of a company were customarily elected by the enlisted men. Thus, the individuals who raised the majority of the recruits invariably secured the top positions. Of course, this system did not always ensure that the most qualified people received command posts.

Captain George L. Stone of Company A, a 38-year-old freelance carpenter, was a typical citizen soldier. Raised on a farm near Montrose in Susquehanna County, he received a common school education. George joined the Freemasons in 1848 and eventually earned the order of high priesthood. A lifelong Democrat prior to the disintegration of the Missouri Compromise, Stone opposed the extension of slavery more for practical reasons than for moral concerns. As a laboring man he felt convinced that free and slave labor could not coexist. At the outbreak of the war, Stone weighed matters carefully. Initially, he thought it might be best to cut the cords that had

bound the two sections of the country together for so many years. By the summer of 1862, Stone reached a far different conclusion:

> If the South is permitted thus to tear itself loose from the sacred compact it had entered into, how soon may not another follow in her footsteps, and then another, and so on until this glorious Republic is broken to discordant and belligerent atoms? This settled the matter and my mind was soon made up that the government must be maintained and the Union preserved at all hazards.[37]

By Stone's side was Second Lieutenant Amos Tucker, who could boast of prior military experience. Tucker served as a private in the 9th Illinois, a three months regiment, and as a lieutenant in the 47th Illinois before poor health forced his resignation. He originally joined Company A as a private, but was soon promoted to sergeant major, where his familiarity with the manual of arms came in handy. Following the death of Lieutenant Urias Hollenbach in late April, Tucker ascended to his current rank.[38] Hollenbach was a well-educated young lawyer with considerable talent.[39] His promise would never be fulfilled.

Perhaps the regiment's most distinguished officers resided in Company B. Captain Lafayette Westbrook was an influential member of the Pennsylvania Legislature prior to his commission. In his most recent term, he chaired the Committee on Railroads, a vital post at the time as many railroads in the state were being incorporated. Westbrook was highly regarded by his superior officers. Lieutenant Colonel McFarland praised him as "a prompt, faithful, efficient officer, [who was] always with his command, sick or well," while Major John Young regarded him as one of the best officers in the regiment. The 37-year-old captain was a well conditioned and robust man when he entered the service. His excellent physical condition was largely due to the six years he had spent as the county land surveyor traversing the rugged woodlands of Pike County.[40]

First Lieutenant John H. Vincent attended Lafayette College for two years and graduated from Williams College in Williamstown, Massachusetts, in 1849. Upon graduation, he spent several years tutoring and teaching school in the Deep South. Returning north, he studied law under former governor James Pollock in Milton, Pennsylvania. In May 1854, he was admitted to the bar in Northampton County. Vincent was appointed district attorney of Pike County in 1861, and he won the election for this post for a three-year term in the fall of 1862.[41]

Westbrook and Vincent could count on the assistance of Second Lieutenant Robert M. Kellogg, the hero of Chancellorsville. Kellogg, the son of a minister, was a native of Brooklyn, New York. When the war erupted, Robert resided in Milford, where he taught school and worked as a clerk in the prothonotary office of Pike County.[42]

The command structure of Company C was in shambles due to the absence of Captain George W. Crandall and both lieutenants. Prostrated shortly after the battle of Chancellorsville, Crandall would die on August 24, 1863, a few weeks after his men returned home.[43] Consequently, Second Lieutenant Charles P. Potts of Company I received command of the Susquehanna Countians.[44]

At 22, Walter L. Owens was the youngest captain in the 151st. Lieutenant Colonel McFarland, the original commander of Company D, recalled that Owens had shown such fitness for command that, at his suggestion, Walter was promoted over both lieutenants in his stead. Owens had been a student or teacher under McFarland during the four years before the war. George felt that his friend would make a good

officer in spite of his age and promised him all the assistance possible. At Gettysburg, the youthful captain inherited greater responsibility.[45]

Second Lieutenant Benjamin F. Oliver, a blacksmith who resided in East Salem, and First Lieutenant George S. Mills, a tailor from Oakland Mills, backed up Owens. Oliver's second son was born on April 26, 1863, just four days before his father experienced being under fire for the first time. As a youngster, Mills enlisted in the 1st Pennsylvania Volunteers during the Mexican War, but the conflict ended before he saw any active duty. This war would be an entirely different matter.[46]

First Lieutenant Aaron S. Seaman, a bright young teacher and theology student, guided Company E. He had seen prior service in the 14th Pennsylvania, a three-months regiment. Between enlistments Seaman established himself in the mercantile business. His brother, William, served as a corporal in the company. Tragedy awaited both men at Gettysburg.[47]

Another young teacher, Second Lieutenant Thomas L. Moyer, marched north with Company E. He was new to his post having just replaced Lieutenant Caleb Parvin. Parvin's story is valorous even though he never faced the enemy. A devout Quaker, Caleb joined the Union army out of his devotion for the cause of liberty. Soldiering, however, proved too severe for his delicate health, and he spent considerable time in the hospital. The surgeons who examined him urged his resignation from active service. Parvin disregarded the advice and rejoined his comrades in late February. One month later, a recurring heart disease forced him to leave the regiment. On April 7, 1863, while en route home, he died aboard a transport ship opposite Mount Vernon. Lieutenant Colonel McFarland wrote warmly of the 23-year-old teacher, "His was a life of purity, worthy to be held up as a model for imitation by all young men."[48]

The sole officer remaining in Company F was First Lieutenant William O. Blodget. Born November 6, 1824, in Chautauqua County, New York, near the Pennsylvania border, Blodget led the rugged backwoodsmen from the northern tier. After teaching school and farming for a number of years, William opened a mercantile business in Sugar Grove, Pennsylvania, and tended the family homestead. He and his wife had five children, but by the time of his enlistment only three were living. In 1855, his two-year-old daughter, Belle, died from the burns she received after her clothing caught fire in a freak accident. Her pain and suffering led William to question his belief in a supreme being. Two of his ancestors had fought in the American Revolution. His grandfather, Solomon Blodget, was shot through both legs at the battle of Brandywine and remained wounded on the field until he crawled back to camp the next day.[49] The letters Blodget penned to his family are full of wit and penetrating insight on military, political, and social issues. The following passage is particularly poignant:

> Revolutions like the present do not subside at once. This is not a simple rebellion it is a *revolution* involving *great* changes in political and social circles, as great perhaps as the world ever saw…. The social diseases it is destined to cure are of long standing and cannot be cured at once, nor by trifling remedies…. I am not sanguine that the world is to be *better* for as one evil is destroyed, another grows up. Slavery is doomed. What will come in its place, I know not. It may be years before it will all be gone, but *go* it must. The decree is as irrevocable as the laws of the Medes and Persians. In its place may come some other system equally odious — to be in turn swept away.[50]

Like Blodget, First Lieutenant Jonathan Witman of Company G led his men with no support.

Captain William L. Gray, Company I. Courtesy of Pennsylvania State Archives.

The former tinsmith, canal boatsman, and constable from Bernville would have a close brush with death before his service ended.[51]

Company H enjoyed a full complement of officers. Captain Boltz returned to his unit after being off duty nearly a month following his equestrian adventure. By June 1, Boltz reported, "Since I am again real healthy I have the time to do more as I like. My lieutenant Yost is sick and my lieutenant Reber is with the engineers and thus I am completely alone with my company, and so many of the other officers are sick in the regiment that I still must do much of the work of the others." Although he had never attended a day of school in his life, Boltz was quick and intelligent. Despite his lack of education, he could read and write in both English and German. His living was derived from a thriving mercantile business in Strausstown, where he and his wife, Levina, raised eight children. Boltz's abstention from alcohol and tobacco no doubt endeared him to the temperate McFarland.[52]

The adventurous James L. Reber had yearned for soldiering ever since the firing on Fort Sumter. Family considerations prevented his departure from Bernville until the early fall of 1862, when he was commissioned first lieutenant of H Company. While the regiment was stationed at Union Mills, General Alexander Hays placed Reber under arrest and seized his sword for permitting a soldier on guard duty to return to camp without proper authorization. Fortunately for Reber, McFarland intervened and persuaded Hays to return the eager lieutenant's sword. Second Lieutenant Albert Yost, a 24-year-old farmer, rounded out the company's slate of officers.[53]

The oldest officer in the regiment was 40-year-old Captain William L. Gray of Company I. Standing nearly six feet tall and weighing over 200 pounds, he was a large man by Civil War standards. Lieutenant Colonel McFarland wrote glowingly of him, "Always prompt to obey orders and efficient in executing them, a gentleman in his manners, and genial and big-hearted as a comrade, he was justly a favorite with me … and his company was one of the very best for every kind of duty."[54]

Gray's early life had been difficult. His father died in a freak farming accident near Sunbury, leaving behind a wife and eight small children. Due to financial constraints, young William was sent to live with a nearby family. At the age of 13, he set off on his own and traveled the Susquehanna and Schuylkill Canal for several years. Following this adventure, he learned the tailoring trade in Northumberland. Here,

William married and commenced raising a family. He soon left the tailoring business and obtained steady employment preparing lumber for the bridges spanning the Susquehanna River at Lock Haven, Williamsport, Danville, and Northumberland. After the untimely death of his first wife in 1847, Gray remarried and moved to Cressona, where he entered into the mercantile business. His oldest son also served in the Union army. Events at Gettysburg triggered a long odyssey for Captain Gray and yet another personal tragedy would befall him before the conflict ended.

Henry Merkle, another Cressona resident, served as first lieutenant of the company. The 38-year-old blacksmith supervised a shop for the Minehill Railroad and was an officer in a pre-war militia organization prior to his enlistment.[55]

As mentioned previously, Lieutenant Charles P. Potts commanded Company C during the campaign. At the outbreak of the war, Potts was a member of the Washington Artillery, a militia company based in Pottsville. When President Lincoln asked for 75,000 three-months militia to suppress the Southern rebellion, this unit was one of the five Pennsylvania companies that answered the call. Collectively known as the "First Defenders," these Pennsylvanians were the first troops to reach the beleaguered capital. On April 18th, an overjoyed Lincoln personally shook each man's hand. During Lee's invasion of Maryland in 1862, Potts enlisted in the emergency militia. The following year he joined Company I under his old friend, William Gray, and soon secured the position of second lieutenant. "Playing 'home guard' was all right," Potts later recalled, "but going to war was another matter ... for after being out a few months, the patriotism was pretty well sweated out of us." The lieutenant's patriotism faced a severe test before he returned home to his clothing store in Pottsville.[56]

The final company in the regiment was led by James W. Weida of Long Swamp. Before being elected as the captain of Company K, Weida worked as a stonemason, a literary agent, and also as an instructor for classes in instrumental music. He left his wife and one-year-old son to enlist in the Union army.[57] His survival at Gettysburg was miraculous.

Weida's first lieutenant, Jacob Hessler, operated a venetian blind manufacturing enterprise before the war. A member of the Ringgold Light Artillery of Reading, Hessler was another of the famed First Defenders. After this unit disbanded, Hessler and a fellow officer made strenuous efforts to raise another

Lieutenant Charles P. Potts, Company I. Courtesy of The First Defenders *(Pottsville, Pennsylvania: First Defenders' Association, 1910).*

company of light artillery. Failing in this effort, they raised part of an infantry company, which was consolidated into Company K at Harrisburg. In the absence of Francis Parvin, Hessler filled in as acting quartermaster during the Gettysburg campaign.[58] The unit's second lieutenant, 20-year-old Charles A. Trexler, had lived his entire life on the family farm near Mertztown, Berks County, before he entered the military. The young man would never return to his peaceful childhood home.[59]

As was typical in this largely volunteer army, not all of the enlisted men expressed confidence in their officers. An "observer" wrote the *Pottsville Miners' Journal* on April 18, 1863,

> I am sorry to say that the Captain of Company I is little thought of by his men, and, as regards his military capacity, he is not much in advance of any of his men. I do not wish to injure any person's reputation, but these are my candid sentiments. I, for one, came into the

Lieutenant Colonel George F. McFarland. Courtesy of Roger Hunt Collection, US-AMHI.

service with the welfare of our country at heart. But I am sorry to see in the army so much tyranny as is shown by some of the officers; and I am of the opinion that if not more than one half the salary was paid to officers, and a little more added to the pay of the private soldiers, we would have just as good officers and a great many more soldiers.

Another private wrote, "...our under officers ... are subject about every six weeks to fits of peevishness, pettishness, and a mental derangement leading to silly exhibitions of authority, with a steady current of disagreeableness permeating the whole system...."[60]

George Fisher McFarland, the man who would lead the regiment during this critical campaign, was an unlikely candidate for military office. Nevertheless, he would be the glue that held the organization together during the trying times ahead. McFarland had been an educator since the tender age of sixteen, and when the Civil War erupted, he was the principal and proprietor of the McAlisterville Academy in Juniata County. A devout Methodist with strong, loving ties to his family and his community, George was a reluctant warrior. His physical appearance contributed little to his military bearing. Carrying 145 pounds on a 5'6" frame gave him a short, stocky appearance. His elongated face, exaggerated by a high forehead, was accented by an angular nose and a neatly trimmed beard. The warm, sparkling eyes exuded energy and bespoke of an underlying geniality. In early September 1862, however, the 28-year-old husband and father of two "determined to go to war if a good company is raised." It was an agonizing decision for the young principal but at this point in the conflict, he concluded, "The continuance of the blessings now enjoyed seemed to depend upon the integrity and perpetuity of the union of our fathers, and this was now in jeopardy and only to be rescued by force of arms."[61]

Several of McFarland's teachers and students at the academy formed the nucleus of Company D, and the remainder of the soldiery sprang from the surrounding townships. During the regimental organization at Harrisburg, Captain McFarland received an unexpected promotion to lieutenant colonel.[62] He immediately embarked on a rigorous program of study by assimilating military manuals, and he later received the welcome tutelage of veteran officers such as Alexander Hays, Thomas Rowley, and Abner Doubleday.

Just as importantly, McFarland quickly earned the respect and admiration of the men. He combined natural leadership skills with compassion and common sense. Regimental Surgeon Amos Blakeslee noted that his commander "was always at his post, never a day off duty, temperate, industrious, and ever inculcating good moral principles in his regiment, never failing to encourage them in patriotic fidelity."[63] He also stressed to his charges the importance of camp sanitation and personal hygiene, a rare quality for a volunteer officer.

When the 151st was issued new Enfield rifles in January 1863, George noted almost by accident that men who had been skilled marksmen with the old smoothbores "were uncertain of hitting a five foot target" with their new rifles. He, therefore, "took every occasion, in season and out of season to secure target practice." Soon, the men became familiar with the new weapons and were confident they could "hold their own with any enemy they might meet."[64]

The former schoolmaster was looking after all the details just as he had once done in the classroom. The men responded to his practical approach to command and appreciated his lack of pretense. But

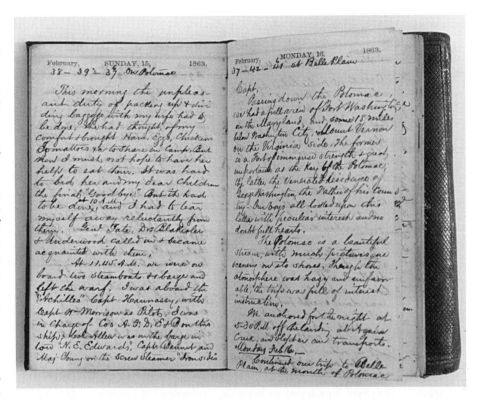

McFarland's 1863 diary. Courtesy of Sue Boardman.

McFarland was still an unknown quantity and not everyone expressed unbounded confidence in his abilities. Nathan Cooper was depressed to learn that Colonel Allen had gone home on a sick furlough for he described McFarland as "a perfect old grany [who] aint worth a shaw of tobaco." And while Private Peter Hayward considered George "a brave and efficient officer" he believed Allen was "the right man in the right place."[65]

General Doubleday, on the other hand, was elated at McFarland's elevation to sole command of the regiment as he felt there would be "less copperheadism in it than formerly" for Colonel Allen and Major Young were regarded by some as "copperheads of the most traitorous character."[66] (*Copperhead* was a derisive nickname applied to Peace Democrats in the North who were generally more conciliatory toward the South than were their Republican opponents.[67]) Like Doubleday, McFarland was a staunch Republican.

In fact, there appears to have been a strong Democratic element within the regiment. After Lincoln's Emancipation Proclamation went into effect on January 1, 1863, Private Peter Hayward of Company C declared, "From personal intercourse and conversation with most every man in our Company, I am satisfied there is not one left whom you can induce to say that they are supporters of abolitionism, or one who voluntarily will raise a gun for the purpose of carrying out the hellish programme of the R[adical] R[epublicans].... And that feeling exists not only in Company C, but the whole regiment...." Later, he asked, "And is there not another Washington to rise up — grasp the helm of state, pitch overboard the malign crew of desperadoes who are trying to wreck her on the shoals of abolition fanaticism, and pilot her into the harbor of the Union? A voice from the tomb of the illustrious dead seemed to answer, yes! Geo. B. McClellan must be your second deliverer." However, another soldier wrote of the proclamation, "I like this move, it seames they have to fall into Freemont's tracks after all."[68]

Although keenly aware of his growing responsibilities, McFarland was no doubt greatly relieved upon Allen's departure, for the two officers had never enjoyed a cooperative relationship. George complained of the colonel's "contrary and overbearing disposition" and felt that he was "arrogant in the extreme." Privately, in a letter to his wife, McFarland worried that Allen would "return to take charge of the regiment on the march homeward, to get the credit and honor of its reception, etc. while I do the work." George reasoned, however, "with sensible men the dodge is plainly visible and fully understood; with others it makes but little difference."[69] McFarland had favored another individual for the post of colonel, and friction between the two men developed at this early stage. Besides their implied political differences,

McFarland and Allen were equally strong willed and assertive men. As their respective military and post-war careers attest, both were intelligent and capable leaders.[70]

Despite General Doubleday's preference for McFarland, he must have had some reservations about the morale and combat readiness of the short-term Pennsylvanians in his division. Beset with political subdivisions, sickness, and an incoherent officer corps with little to show for its past service, the 151st entered into its final campaign with a decided handicap. However, one veteran soldier on a visit to the 151st concluded, "[I]t is a very good regiment and I think that they have learned very fast and ... will give a good account of themselves if they are called upon to defend their flag."[71]

During the afternoon of June 11, 1863, orders arrived from headquarters directing the command to pack up for a move requiring "great mobility."[72] The news created a bustle of activity in camp. Joseph Hooker was in the process of shifting his forces in reaction to Robert E. Lee's withdrawal from the Rappahannock and his subsequent shift to Culpeper and the upper reaches of the Shenandoah Valley. Lee's second invasion of the North was already underway. In the decisive battle that loomed ahead, Lieutenant Colonel McFarland would need all of the military lessons derived from his short career as well as a full measure of strong leadership, quick analysis, and sound judgment. The lives of his men and perhaps the fate of the Union hung in the balance.

Chapter 2

THE MARCH NORTH: JUNE 12–JUNE 30, 1863

"There are too many brutes or fools under shoulder straps."

At 3 A.M. on the morning of June 12th, the men of the 151st were awakened. After partaking of breakfast and packing up the last of the gear, the regiment moved out at 5:30. Although uncertain as to their destination, very few soldiers objected to the departure from Falmouth, described by one officer as "a wretched straggling old place, very dirty and now deserted almost entirely." An enlisted man observed that "the iron heel of war has passed with its scathing blighting footstep and a more God forsaken looking country than this it is impossible to imagine." Roughly 300 enlisted men and eleven officers from the 151st were still out on picket duty. About half of these men and three of the officers returned to camp before the regiment departed. The balance remained behind and served as the wagon guard for the corps trains, but rejoined their comrades on the 14th near Warrenton Junction.[1]

Considerable sickness still prevailed in the regiment. In fact, seven men had died of disease within the past week.[2] One of the victims was 44-year-old Corporal Lyman Beebe of Company C, who succumbed to dysentery. Before his death, Beebe requested that his body be sent home to Susquehanna County. His last request could not be granted, however, as the nearest embalmer was in Washington and the weather was extremely warm. Instead, his remains were buried on the open, windswept plain behind the hospital tents.[3] Captain Owens and Lieutenant Oliver of Company D hitched rides on an ambulance since they were not well enough to march with the column.[4]

The First Corps abandoned the Rappahannock line by taking a rather circuitous route to avoid being detected by the Confederate rearguard across the river. The troops marched around the rear of Hooker's headquarters, located north of White Oak Church, to take advantage of the cover afforded by a

series of low hills. After reaching Stoneman's Switch on the Richmond, Fredericksburg, and Potomac Railroad, the column changed direction to the northwest and struck the Falmouth and Warrenton Pike four miles above Falmouth.[5]

By this time the men were already footsore and weary due to their heavy loads, the oppressive heat, and the clouds of choking dust being churned up by thousands of men and animals (the Third Division was last in the line of march). Near Hartwood Church, a deserter from Wadsworth's First Division was shot and buried within sight of the road. The execution served as a grim reminder of the gravity of the campaign. The column tramped along the pike for another three miles before halting for the evening near Grove Church. McFarland felt the 24-mile march was about twice the distance unconditioned men should travel on the first day with full knapsacks and haversacks. He described the ordeal in a letter to his wife:

> They march till they are pale as death, then red as raw beefsteak ... and finally till every nerve and muscle in them trembles like a leaf. Then after a ten minutes halt, they repeat it; and when endurance longer is impossible, an hours halt, to make coffee out of water as thick as cream, scooped up out of mud puddles, they feel refreshed and go at it again! When they halt for the night, who can wonder that men fall down and sleep from sheer exhaustion just where they fall.[6]

The next day a march of 16 miles brought the men to Bealeton Station, which consisted of a few deserted houses along the Orange and Alexandria Railroad. En route, the column passed Gold Mine (one house) and Morrisville (two chimneys). McFarland considered both to be fair "specimens of Virginia towns." Water was scarce during the entire march, and the men suffered considerably from thirst and

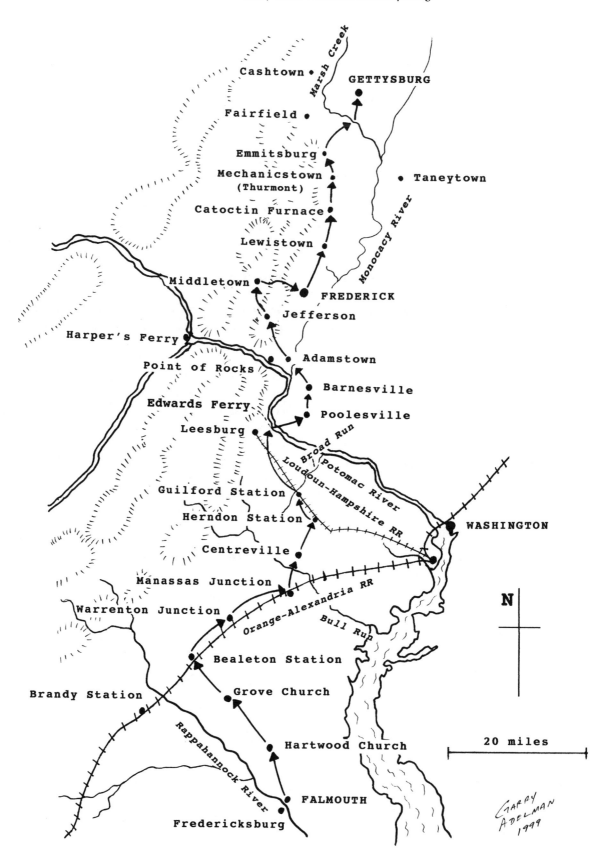

Route of the 151st Pennsylvania from Falmouth to Gettysburg, June 12 to June 30, 1863. Map by Garry Adelman.

dust. The 151st camped along the edge of a woods one mile south of the station. All were very weary and sore and "some earnest sleeping was done." A brief rain shower arrived in the evening but it was "by no means sufficient to lay the dust or cool the heated atmosphere." McFarland began to suffer from a severe case of diarrhea, but he resolutely stuck to his duties as he was keenly aware of the importance of his leadership.[7]

Abandoned camps of the Army of the Potomac near Falmouth, Virginia. Courtesy MOLLUS Collection, USAMHI.

On the 14th, the command rose early but remained idle during the cool morning hours. Robert Miller of Company F took advantage of the free time to write a quick letter home. He informed his brother, "We have had a very hard march the last two days but I have stood the march first rate and was one of the twenty of our co[mpany] that came in with the regt. the first night.... Last night we brought forty-eight men in with our company so that you can see that we are gaining on it some."[8]

Finally, at 10 A.M., the First Corps started along the railroad through open country for Manassas Junction. The troops broke into numerous columns to hasten the advance. From a distance, the sight might have resembled thin blue serpents slithering along a carpet of brown grass. The pace of the march increased with the intensity of the heat. McFarland wryly noted that this practice was "a strange but very uniform course adopted by the army." Another officer in the division remembered, "The heat of the sun was withering. Not a breath of air stirred the leaves; the dust rose like a white cloud, powdering the hair and clothes of the troops and almost stifling them.... Stagnant pools, on whose borders lay decomposing horses or mules ... were gladly resorted to by the men in passing." Falling behind was out of the question as John S. Mosby's Partisan Rangers scoured the countryside in search of stragglers. The severed telegraph lines near the railroad warned of this danger, and the troops advanced with loaded muskets. The men marched steadily along without stopping for dinner. After a tortuous trek of over thirty miles, the troops staggered into the junction at 2:30 A.M.[9]

A justifiably short march was completed the following morning. The column hiked across the open plains of Manassas, crossed Bull Run at Blackburn's Ford, and continued on to Centreville. Of course, the scenery was very familiar to the 151st as they had performed guard duty here from December 1862 to February 1863.

In this vicinity, the First Corps spent a day and a half to recuperate from the rigors of the previous three days and to collect stragglers. Sergeant Robert Miller of Company F proudly noted "I have kept up with the company all the time and have been with them every time they have stacked arms or been ordered to fall in." Robert had every reason to boast, for he had only recently returned to active duty following a long bout with typhoid fever and dysentery. Conversely, Lieutenant John Vincent had reached the end of his endurance. Weakened by diarrhea and racked with a high fever, Vincent was sent to Washington on sick leave. For him, the Gettysburg campaign had ended.[10]

Since the departure from Falmouth, the First Corps had clipped off over 70 miles in the midst of a severe heat wave to screen Washington, D.C., from Lee's advancing host. Colonel Charles Wainwright, the First Corps artillery chief, felt that Lee would follow one of two distinct courses of action in the near future. He would either cross his entire army over the Potomac River above Harpers Ferry or attempt to draw the Union forces north and then strike for Washington. In the first scenario, which was the correct one, he predicted "some pretty tall marching" would be required.[11]

Centreville, Virginia. Courtesy MOLLUS Collection, USAMHI.

After this brief respite, the corps pushed northward once again and reached Herndon Station on the Loudoun and Hampshire Railroad late on June 17th. Along the way, the troops passed through the old Chantilly battlefield. The march was a very fatiguing one. A delay in getting underway during the cool morning hours proved costly as the weather grew intensely hot as the day wore on. The sides of the road were lined with thousands of men who had dropped out from exhaustion. Indeed, many had fainted entirely away. Captain George Stone, who had suffered from sickness ever since the Chancellorsville campaign, was almost entirely disabled by diarrhea. Though he was suffering from the same ailment, McFarland loaned Stone his horse so that he could keep pace with his company. Fortunately, only a short march up the railroad to Guilford Station was required the next morning. Upon their arrival, the men were instructed to pitch tents and "rest contented for some days."[12]

The first phase of the campaign was over. Both armies had evacuated the last of their forces from the Fredericksburg vicinity. After gobbling up a large Union garrison at Winchester, the Army of Northern Virginia occupied the entire length of the Shenandoah Valley, and detachments of its cavalry were already raiding into southern Pennsylvania. Meanwhile, the Army of the Potomac was strung out along the major railways just east of the Bull Run Mountains facing west. Reports of Confederate activity in Maryland and Pennsylvania trickled in from a variety of sources, but Hooker chose to keep the army stationary for a week until he could decipher Lee's true objective.[13]

The soldiers of the 151st enjoyed their temporary camp as the country resembled Pennsylvania and reminded many of home. The newfound leisure time was utilized by the men for a variety of purposes. The first priority of many involved a welcome dip in the cool waters of nearby Broad Run to wash off a week's accumulation of sweat, dust, and grime. The bath also helped rid the men of a notorious pest, for it was difficult to find a soldier in the summertime who was not infested with lice. The enlisted men felt it was a great consolation "that he can have gray backs just as well as an officer."[14]

Letter writing was begun in earnest. Sergeant Alexander Seiders warned his wife that she might not recognize him since he had lost so much weight following his recent illness. He eagerly anticipated returning home to see his one-year-old daughter, Annie, and partaking of the simple pleasure of biting into a Pennsylvania peach. Better fare was certainly a major concern as most had subsisted entirely on hard tack and coffee during the movement. The beef herd that had been driven over a hundred miles in the intense heat failed to whet even the heartiest of appetites. In light of these extreme conditions, McFarland, who was normally opposed to foraging from innocent farmers, turned his head as the eager command descended upon a hapless flock of sheep and a few stray pigs in the vicinity. The colonel realized the necessity of bending the rules on occasion.[15]

The rank and file took full advantage of their commander's liberality as Sergeant Miller revealed in the following passage:

> We have very good times foraging here as we have been marching through a very fertile region.... Last evening [the 18th] we captured an animal that some of the boys called venison, but I thought the hair was very coarse and looked very much like bristle and this morning we have a leg of some animal which the boys also called venison, but if I were to judge from a little of the skin that was left on near the foot, I should say that it looked very much like wool. I do not think that the cows in this vicinity will give much milk this morning or that the hen roosts and gardens will be in as good condition this morning as they once was.[16]

A cold front passed through the region on the evening of the 18th, bringing with it heavy rains and a welcome relief from the heat. During a particularly heavy downpour the next night, orders arrived stating, "prepare to move at a moments notice!" The men dutifully obeyed, but before all the companies were notified, a second order came which countermanded the previous one. The disgruntled portion of the regiment that had responded to the initial set of instructions dragged wet blankets and gear back into their tents and turned in. Shortly afterward, a third order stating that the regiment should be ready to move at daylight was received. In response, the reveille was sounded near 3 A.M. and the tired soldiers hastily cooked breakfast and prepared for the anticipated move, which never took place! McFarland noted sarcastically that this was a simple outline of one night's "soldiering."[17]

The cold front also succored the Confederates marching down the Shenandoah Valley. While bivouacked on the lofty heights of the Blue Ridge near Chester Gap, Lieutenant Sidney Carter of the 14th South Carolina observed a thundercloud passing overhead so near that he felt he could reach up and touch it with a twenty-foot pole. On that very day, the former schoolteacher from Darlington was prostrated by the severe heat and finished the march in an ambulance. It marked the first time Carter had left the ranks during his nearly two years of military service. The storm pelted the Southerners with torrential rains and hail. Surgeon Spencer Glasgow Welch, of the 13th South Carolina, rated the night as "the worst I ever experienced." Welch managed to keep dry by sitting on a rock and draping himself with an oilcloth. But he was willing to endure anything for "the pleasure of getting into Pennsylvania and letting the Yankees feel what it is to be invaded."[18] These South Carolinians would meet face to face with the First Corps of the Army of the Potomac at Gettysburg.

Ever since the First Corps' arrival at Guilford Station, the ominous sound of cannonading intermingled with the thunder as the contending cavalry forces clashed in the Loudoun Valley. Meanwhile, in most of the infantry units, officers and men alike were chafed by the inactivity. The stress of being kept under arms, along with the agitation produced by conflicting orders, only exacerbated the tense situation. In an effort to relieve the boredom, McFarland led his men through a brisk, but purposely short, battalion drill. Death took no respite. On the 22nd, Private Alfred Staudt and his comrades in Company G completed the grim task of burying Private Lewis Diltzer, a victim of typhoid fever.[19]

During this time, McFarland faced an underlying rebellion within his command. As the service time of several companies expired according to the original enlistment papers, a number of men swore they would serve no longer. George took a firm hand in the matter and squelched the potential crisis. He expressed his own conflicting emotions in a letter to his wife: "My anxiety to see home and the dear ones there is growing with the flying moments. I resist the feeling all I can, for I know it can do no good, while it will make me more uncomfortable and more likely not to encourage the men as I should. Reason and feeling are in direct conflict ... But I will try to do my duty until regularly dismissed by the proper order."[20]

Corporal Nathan Cooper, a 29-year-old farmer from Warren County, also felt a strong sense of duty. Although he often apologized for his grammar, Nathan wrote insightful letters to his wife, in which he unabashedly conveyed his own firm convictions. Cooper asked, "What is the use of coming home as long as our home is in danger?" He concluded, "The war must be ended and then we will fly to our love[d] ones at home, never to part till parted by death." Earlier, Nathan declared that he would enlist for the duration of the war if he did not have a wife and child waiting at home. For now he intended to "go just as fur as this regt. goes as long as I am able to carry my gun and catrage box, [even] if I gett cut in a hundred pieces in doing soe." Privately, however, he confided his concern that "the boys won't stand fire as well as they would before the 20th."[21]

The matter of enlistment terms should have

become a mute point when the men read accounts of the growing invasion from newspapers and letters, which finally caught up with the fast moving army. Some of the accounts were greatly exaggerated. For instance, one report had the entire Confederate army within twenty miles of Harrisburg on June 17! In fact, the vanguard of Lee's infantry, the cavalry brigade of General Albert Jenkins, did not reach Chambersburg until the evening of the 15th. A week later, the first infantry units splashed across the Potomac.

Initially, McFarland felt that a Confederate raid into Pennsylvania would have a good effect, for he reasoned that few of the enemy would escape and the Southern sympathizers and draft resisters in the state would "have a chance to show their colors and probably to feel a little of the love the rebels have for them." Commenting on Pennsylvania's poor response to Governor Curtin's urgent calls for emergency militia troops, George declared, "If those who have property to save cannot find time to do it, let the rebels come and help them harvest. It will serve them right." But later he conceded "the innocent would suffer with the guilty, the brave with the cowardly."[22]

Others in the army echoed McFarland's sentiments. Lieutenant Blodget angrily declared, "Damn the Copperhead traitors ... I have yet to see the first man in the army that does not hate them and long for the time when he can go snake hunting at home." Sergeant Miller could hardly contain his rage as he observed the sneaky way the *Warren Ledger* had of "sneering at everything that our army did and praising the Rebels...." A private in Company I added, "It pains me to hear talk of Pennsylvanians resisting the draft ... when so many of her sons have already fallen, and many are still enduring hardships, in defence of their country." Lieutenant Colonel Henry S. Huidekoper of the 150th Pennsylvania wrote, "We are near the Potomac ... waiting for some definite movement of Lee's army. The raids into McConnellsville, Gettysburg and Chambersburg have been extremely pleasing to us, as we think it will aid the draft and arouse the people once more."[23]

General Hooker, however, was slow to recognize the scale of the enemy movement across the Potomac River, dismissing the numerous reports as the work of alarmists. The general's vacillation during this period allowed Lee to steal a two-day march on the Army of the Potomac. After realizing that Lee was invading in strength, Hooker readied his forces to move. Once again, a series of difficult marches was on the agenda. In order to achieve rapid movements of the army, Hooker wisely appointed General John Reynolds as commander of his advance wing, which consisted of his own First Corps together with the Third and Eleventh Corps. Reynolds was instructed to march rapidly through western Maryland and secure the South Mountain passes to screen the remainder of the army as it moved north toward Frederick.[24]

The much anticipated order to march reached the 151st Pennsylvania on the morning of June 25th. The command traveled northeast nine miles over broken country until it reached Edwards Ferry on the Potomac at noontime. The regiment crossed the river on the recently laid pontoon bridges and landed on the opposite shore.

The soldiers immediately noted the striking contrast between poverty-stricken Virginia and the prosperous Maryland countryside. "The march through Maryland, up toward Gettysburg, was over mountains and through a rich country in a high state of cultivation — a pleasant change from desolated and endless lowlands," wrote one veteran. More importantly, the boys in blue were greeted warmly by the cheerful and sympathizing residents, as opposed to the repulsive scowls they had grown accustomed to in the Old Dominion.[25]

As the long columns pushed north, it seemed every family along the route was busy baking delicacies for the soldiers. Five miles from the river, the troops passed through Poolesville, "a thrifty village of a few hundred inhabitants." On the right of the street, McFarland observed a sight dear to his heart, "a large common school house ... well filled with well dressed, laughing, lovely, innocent-looking girls." It was the only school George had seen for many months. Outside the village, the men received an additional morale booster when they spied the Stars and Stripes entwined around the pillar of an old portico in front of a farmhouse. Each passing regiment burst forth with hearty cheers at the sight. After a toilsome march of six more miles through rain and heavy roads, the 151st encamped for the evening near Barnesville.[26]

Following a wet, disagreeable night, the First Corps soldiers got off to an early start on the 26th. The long column traveled northwest through the lovely wheatfields of Frederick County, passed by Sugar Loaf Mountain, crossed the Monocacy River, pushed on through Adamstown, and climbed the narrow, steep, rock-strewn passage up the Catoctin

Mountain Range before halting near Jefferson. It was a common sight to see sore-footed and shoeless men marching barefooted over the stony mountain road. Rumors continued to circulate through the army concerning the Southern invasion. One stated that Harrisburg had been taken. Thus, the men trudged along, "contented that at least they were after the rebs."[27]

Just before crossing the Monocacy, McFarland enjoyed a first-rate meal of ham, wheat cake, butter, and coffee with cream at the home of William Yingling, "a fine old gentlemanly farmer." George delayed his departure long enough to wait for a large loaf of bread fresh from the oven. After tucking the prize under his coat cape, he galloped ahead furiously on his faithful stallion, Frank, to catch up with the regiment. Soon, he came upon knots of weary men who had fallen behind the main body. George was deeply affected by the sight as he had often observed that long marches taxed the human system to the utmost limits of endurance. As Jesus had done on the shores of Galilee, McFarland tore off chunks from the loaf and tossed them to the stragglers. Being only a mortal, he could not feed 5,000, but about 20 of his men greatly appreciated the act.[28]

One of the stragglers encountered by McFarland during his ride may have been Solomon Strause of Company H. During the long trip north, the 40-year-old private suffered with a badly swollen leg. At times Strause fell several hundred yards behind the column as he frequently sat down to rest his painful limb. Solomon continued to limp gamely along until he was picked up by a passing supply wagon.[29]

From atop the western slope of the Catoctins near Jefferson, Maryland, the troops enjoyed a splendid view. Harpers Ferry, though a dozen miles distant, was clearly visible. Spread out below them was the exquisite, bucolic landscape of Pleasant Valley. One officer judged that "as rural scenery, I have never come across its equal in this country."[30]

Late in the evening McFarland was detailed as the division field officer. He spent several hours in the rain posting pickets along the Point of Rocks and Adamstown roads. Picketing was a necessary safeguard to protect the army both in camp and during a march. McFarland was no stranger to this task as he had performed double duty in this capacity ever since Colonel Allen's departure. When the 151st moved forward the next morning at the head of the corps, the pickets were not called in through the error of an orderly. Consequently, McFarland had to remain behind

to withdraw the sentries, leaving the regiment in charge of Adjutant Allen. The men were considerably fatigued from the exertions of the prior two days, and the short seven mile march to Middletown was poorly executed. Perhaps the temptations offered by the large cherry trees lining the road contributed to the languid pace. Nonetheless, by midday, the First Corps controlled the gaps in the South Mountain range leading into Frederick.[31]

June 28th was an eventful day for the Army of the Potomac. In the early morning hours, General George G. Meade received orders instructing him to replace Joseph Hooker as the army's commander. Within a short time, the new commander formulated a course of action. He wired Washington that he planned to maneuver his army toward the Susquehanna River and seek an engagement with Lee at the earliest opportunity, while adhering to the administration's mandate of protecting Washington and Baltimore. In preparation for a general advance in the direction of the Pennsylvania border on the 29th, Meade concentrated the scattered elements of his army near Frederick.[32]

Accordingly, the First Corps recrossed the Catoctins and traveled east to the city. As the column passed over the mountain, the folks emerged in their best Sunday clothes to greet them. The outpouring of support "produced such an exhilarating effect upon the boys that cheer after cheer went up along the whole line." The jovial mood was short-lived in Company I as Corporal John F. Harrison died in Frederick shortly after the regiment's arrival. He was buried in Mount Olivet Cemetery.[33]

Before the 151st left Middletown, Lieutenant William Blodget, Company F, penned a letter to his sister in which he related his impressions of the campaign thus far:

> I expect hard fighting within a few days — do not see how it can be avoided. I have not until recently believed the move of the Rebs to Pennsylvania anything more than a raid on a large scale but it looks now like a repetition of last fall's move…. Our march from Fredericksburg has been a hard one. It certainly has not been well managed. There are too many brutes or fools under shoulder straps…. You probably know I am the only officer with the company, and I assure you 'tis tiresome business. Not from lack of patriotism. I think I am simply weary of striving with shirkers, grumblers, apes, knaves and idiots and kindred creatures, in every place and position from Private to Maj. General…. I am tired and want

Frederick, Maryland. Courtesy MOLLUS Collection, USAMHI.

to rest, that is all that ails my body, but there is something wrong about my head, growing out of the wretched management of affairs here. It is a lamentable fact that the good men are dying and being killed off while shirkers and intriguers are coming in to fill their places, either by seniority of rank or force of intrigue. Oh that Lincoln possessed Napoleon's capacity to judge men's capacity and promptness of action.[34]

Blodget's disparaging remarks aside, George Meade was moving the Army of the Potomac with firm promptness. On the 29th, the entire army streamed north via a number of routes. The First Corps made a very efficient march, reaching Emmitsburg a few hours before dark. One veteran termed the march a "veritable triumphal progress." He recalled, "In passing through the towns and villages, whose streets were lined with welcoming people, the colors were unfurled, the bands and drum-corps

struck up, and, quickly taking the step, with muskets at a shoulder, the regiments treated the delighted citizens to an exhibition scarcely less stately and impressive than a grand review."[35]

The trip was full of memorable sights and incidents as the soldiers received a warm welcome from the strongly Union inhabitants. At the little unpretending village of Lewistown, the people gave everything they had to the soldiers "with assurances of their sympathy and wishes for their success." A little girl at one home expressed her willingness to give her dinner to a soldier if he could break ranks to get it. McFarland noted that "such kindness and sympathy are worth a great deal to an army, especially when wearied and exhausted by long marches." After passing Catoctin Furnace, a Revolutionary War period iron furnace and forge, the soldiers moved briskly through the narrow streets of Mechanicstown (present day Thurmont). Here, the boys of the 151st let out three hearty cheers for a little girl donning an apron made out of the American flag. The people of Emmitsburg handed cakes and bread to the soldiers as they passed by. The regiment received the praise of brigade commander Thomas Rowley for the fine manner in which it arrived at the night's bivouac a mile beyond Emmitsburg. After making coffee, the men fell asleep on the wet earth, "perchance to dream of home and its loved ones longingly awaiting their return."[36]

Before turning in for the night, McFarland commenced writing a letter to his dear wife, Addie, which he closed hastily on the morning of June 30:

> This evening finds us only two miles from the southern boundary of the old Keystone State! I expected ere long to cross that boundary with my regiment, but on the home road, and not following up the rebels. Who would have thought it! But it is nevertheless true that we are approaching the State of our birth, not to enjoy peace and comfort there, but to drive out an invading foe. But they will pay for their temerity. They will not long pollute the soil of Pennsylvania with impunity....[37]

McFarland could not have known that before the close of the next day, his command would meet the "invading foe" near a little crossroads community named Gettysburg.

Near the end of June, the main body of the Confederate army was located at Chambersburg, with two strong arms of it stretched out toward the Susquehanna near Harrisburg and York. The fall of the state capitol in Harrisburg seemed imminent as militia troops had thus far offered little resistance to Lee's veterans.[38]

Rumors concerning the magnitude of the invasion and tales of Southern barbarities triggered widespread panic throughout much of Pennsylvania. A troubled Addie McFarland informed her husband that "Rebles" had reached Perryville, a small town in Juniata County located 35 miles northwest of Harrisburg. She observed panicked farmers from the lower counties driving droves of horses through McAlisterville and on farther for safekeeping. At Northumberland, nearly 50 miles upriver from the capitol, concerned residents prepared to fire the bridge that Captain William Gray had helped to construct over the Susquehanna.[39]

The Southerners were amazed with the "beautiful and magnificent country" comprising the Cumberland Valley. Surgeon Spencer Welch of the 13th South Carolina declared he had "never yet seen any country in such a high state of cultivation. Such wheat I never dreamed of, and so much of it!" Another South Carolinian, Lieutenant James Fitz James Caldwell, 1st South Carolina, also marveled at the rich bounty of the land, "In every direction yellow fields of grain extended themselves; on every farm were droves of the largest, fattest cattle; gardens thronged with inviting vegetables; orchards gave promise of a bounteous fruit-yield; ...full dairies, flocks of sheep, and poultry were almost monotonously frequent."[40]

Despite all of the temptations around them, the invaders displayed considerable restraint during the occupation. In fact, Lee's General Order No. 72 forbade the destruction of private property and outlined detailed procedures for acquiring supplies from private citizens and local authorities. For the most part these instructions were strictly observed. Lieutenant Caldwell proudly noted that "only such articles of food were captured as were of solid importance ... nothing was wantonly destroyed ... no man or woman was insulted. Many of them bade us help ourselves to ... whatever we wanted to eat, provided we spared more valuable property." Of course, there were exceptions to this rule. Near the little town of Fayetteville, a few soldiers from Pettigrew's North Carolina Brigade robbed a farmer of his beehives. Colonel Harry King Burgwyn and Lieutenant Colonel John R. Lane of the 26th North Carolina sought out the owner and paid him out of their own pockets. On the whole, the Confederates left the civilian population unmolested and contented themselves with living off the fat of the land.[41]

On the evening of June 28th, however, a startled Robert E. Lee learned of the proximity of the Union army through a spy. He immediately directed his scattered forces to concentrate in the Gettysburg and Cashtown vicinity in preparation for a major engagement. The rapid marches completed by the Army of the Potomac through Maryland had paid dividends for the Union cause. As a surgeon in the First Corps pronounced, "We had been endeavoring to make him [Lee] draw in his horns, as it were, from the direction of Harrisburg, and compel him to meet us somewhere in battle where our army lay, drawn out from east to west, masking toward the north, the capitol and Baltimore."[42]

By the evening of June 30th, nearly half of Lee's army was positioned east of the South Mountain range. The divisions of Robert Rodes and Jubal Early of Richard Ewell's Second Corps rested just northeast of Gettysburg, while Henry Heth's Division and Dorsey Pender's Division of A. P. Hill's Third Corps bivouacked near Cashtown, less than ten miles west of the town. These forces could easily converge on Gettysburg and wreak havoc on any portion of the Union army that arrived there. The remainder of Lee's infantry was spread out from Cashtown back through Chambersburg.[43]

Riding a string of victories over their northern counterparts and being in the midst of a highly successful invasion of enemy territory, morale in the Army of Northern Virginia soared to new heights. Lieutenant Caldwell asserted, "I have little doubt that we had now the finest army ever marshaled on this side of the Atlantic, and one scarcely inferior to any Europe has known." Surgeon Welch thought that in the battle which loomed ahead the army would "fight better than they have ever done, if such a thing could be possible." He confidently asked, "How can they be whipped?" Colonel Abner Perrin, who commanded a brigade in Pender's "Light Division," doubted whether "any army ever marched into an

Captain James Ashworth, 121st Pennsylvania. Courtesy of History of the 121st Regiment Pennsylvania Volunteers.

enemies country with greater confidence in its ability ... than the army of Gen. Lee." With the advantage of hindsight he admitted, "We had too much confidence. Had we been more cautious and circumspect, the result might have been different."[44]

Meanwhile, most of the Union army traversed only short distances on June 30th, giving the men a well-deserved breather from the hard marches performed on the previous day. General Reynolds, one of Meade's most trusted and aggressive subordinates, led the left wing of the army, which was nearest to the point of danger. John Buford's cavalry division pushed ahead to screen the infantry and to scout for the enemy. The 12,000 men of the First Corps, supported by Oliver Howard's Eleventh Corps and Daniel Sickles' Third Corps, functioned as the strong left flank of the infantry advance.[45]

Before the 151st Pennsylvania filed into line on the heights north of Emmitsburg early on the morning of June 30th, the regiment had already logged over 170 miles in less than three weeks. Of course, one idle week was spent during the layover at Broad Run. The hard road north had been trying for all, but for a few it had been nothing short of an ordeal. Captain Lafayette Westbrook had marched the entire distance with a lame right foot and with rheumatism in his left side, shoulder, and neck. When Lieutenant Vincent left his company at Centreville, he was certain that his commander could not march much farther. McFarland felt that Westbrook's condition entitled him to ride in an ambulance, but the rugged captain remained with his men.[46]

A few days prior to the departure from Falmouth, Private William Michael, Company C, was treated by Surgeon Amos C. Blakeslee for diarrhea and rheumatism. Predictably, Michael's condition worsened considerably as the campaign progressed. The 19-year-old farmer from South Gibson reported to Blakeslee's quarters near Emmitsburg on the morning before the battle. The surgeon offered William a pass to the ambulance, but the young private refused, choosing instead to tough it out with his comrades.[47]

Sergeant Robert Miller also suffered from severe diarrhea near the end of the campaign, but unlike Private Michael, he was unable to persevere. He later described his ordeal in a letter to his parents: "I kept up with the regiment till we crossed the Potomac ... it then began to rain and I stopped in a barn where there was some hay. It kept raining until about 3 P.M.

of Friday.... I got about a mile this side of Poolesville and staid at another barn where I got some warm supper by paying three shillings for it. On Sunday night I got to this place [Frederick, Maryland] some twenty-five miles from the river...." At Frederick, Robert found his brother James and his unit, the 111th Pennsylvania, which belonged to the Twelfth Corps. James took his ailing brother to the regimental surgeon who admitted him in the general hospital in the city. Robert would probably have given anything to be with his unit on the morning of June 30th as it prepared to march into Pennsylvania.[48]

A few hours after leaving Emmitsburg, the First Corps strode north over the Mason-Dixon line. The 151st crossed into their home state at about 2 P.M. The column crossed Middle Creek and halted for the day at a point about five miles south of Gettysburg. Although many of the Pennsylvanians in the corps rejoiced at being back on their native soil, not everyone was impressed with the conduct of the citizenry. Artillery chief Wainwright, an aristocratic New Yorker, felt the locals were "much more greedy than the Marylanders" and their "reputation for meanness" was fully deserved.[49]

Reynolds established his headquarters at Moritz Tavern, where he continued to interpret intelligence information sent by the vigilant Buford concerning the mounting enemy threat near Gettysburg. In response, Reynolds took steps to block the main roads leading from Fairfield and Gettysburg. Brigadier General James Wadsworth's First Division with Captain James Hall's 2nd Maine Battery proceeded a short distance up the Emmitsburg Road, the main route to Gettysburg. Brigadier General John C. Robinson's Second Division and most of the corps artillery remained behind in reserve. Meanwhile, the Third Division together with James Cooper's Battery B, 1st Pennsylvania Artillery, was positioned on the left flank to watch for an enemy incursion via Fairfield.[50]

The picket line of the First Brigade was centered at the intersection of the Bullfrog and Millerstown Roads near the residence of William Ross White. From this location a soldier could gaze west across endless expanses of rolling farmland to the lofty heights of South Mountain. Looking a short distance northeast the protruding peaks of the Round Tops were clearly visible. The bearing of the line was derived from a map in Mr. White's parlor and run by compass.

According to the historian of the 121st Pennsylvania, White had secreted his horses in the nearby woods in hopes of saving them from Confederate foragers.

When he instead was approached by Union officers, "His astonishment was indescribable, for he evidently had no idea of Union soldiers being so near at hand." In sharp contrast to this account, White claimed that he guided the Third Division westward to his property via the "Gettysburg and Nunemaker Mill Road" as the remainder of the First Corps continued to march up the Emmitsburg Road. White's statement appeared in a damage claim filed by his neighbor, Jacob B. Brown, in 1882. Brown testified that his 100-acre farm, which was located about a mile west of the Emmitsburg Road, was utilized by General Doubleday as his headquarters on June 30th.

The 151st anchored the right of the brigade line at the George Spangler farm. Since it was the last day of the month, the men were mustered for pay and the officers completed their monthly returns. Otherwise, it was a quiet day.[51]

Here, Lieutenant Colonel McFarland met Captain James Ashworth of the 121st Pennsylvania. Suffering from a pulmonary disorder, Ashworth was on his way home when he learned of the army's movement. The ailing captain decided it would be "better to die in the line of duty & defending our flag than to survive its disgrace, for I felt that the crisis had come." He rejoined his regiment at Centreville and accompanied it north to Pennsylvania.[52] This type of devotion did not bode well for Robert E. Lee and the Army of Northern Virginia.

On the eve of battle, the Third Division underwent changes in both its composition and command structure. Late in the afternoon, the 20th New York State Militia (80th New York) joined the First Brigade. Also known as the Ulster Guard, this veteran unit had experienced severe fighting at Second Bull Run, Chantilly, South Mountain, Antietam, and Fredericksburg. From January through mid–June 1863, the regiment served in the Army Provost Guard.[53]

Not all of the New Yorkers were pleased with their new affiliation. Captain John D. S. Cook of Company I later recalled:

> He [General John Reynolds] assigned us to duty with the Pennsylvania brigade.... They were enlisted for nine months, their term was nearly out and they had never been under fire. We very naturally were not pleased with the assignment, as we were by no means sure that we could depend on them for support in action.... Our apprehensions were not well founded. With one regiment, the 151st Pennsylvania, we ... had close relations in a trying

Officers of the Third Division, First Army Corps. Courtesy of Mrs. J. Roy Lauver.

time, and I can testify for them that they behaved as gallantly as veterans.[54]

Captain Cook's information on the brigade was partly erroneous. The two other Pennsylvania units comprising the First Brigade, the 121st and 142nd, were in fact three-year regiments. Both had performed admirably and suffered heavy losses at the battle of Fredericksburg.

The command shake-up within the Third Division took place as a result of Reynolds' elevation to wing commander. General Abner Doubleday moved up to take charge of the First Corps. Brigade commander Thomas Rowley filled in for Doubleday as leader of the Third Division. Colonel Chapman Biddle of the 121st Pennsylvania ascended to command of the First Brigade, leaving his cousin, Lieutenant Colonel Alexander Biddle, in charge of the regiment.[55] This reorganization would have far-reaching consequences during the coming battle as these officers assumed greater responsibilities.

Chapman Biddle, McFarland's immediate superior, was descended from a prominent Philadelphia family. His ancestors were Quakers, who had fled to William Penn's new colony to escape religious persecution. Biddle's grandfather fought under General Washington, and he played a prominent role in the adoption of the U.S. Constitution by his home state. His father was a lawyer, banker, and a War of 1812 veteran. Chapman followed in his father's footsteps and was admitted to the bar in 1848. When the war broke out, he raised the 121st Pennsylvania and was appointed its colonel. Like his ancestors before him, Chapman Biddle was destined to play an important role in the shaping of the young nation.[56]

After a rainy, uneventful day, the soldiers of the 151st Pennsylvania were drawn up in line of battle and the men slept on their arms throughout the night. The scribe of Company H entered this simple notation in his morning report for July 1st: "All went off quiet."[57] The men were oblivious to the great demands of courage and patriotism which would soon be required of them.

Chapter 3

JULY 1, 1863

"I know not how men could have fought more desperately..."

At 4 A.M. on July 1st, General John F. Reynolds was stirred from a short night's sleep by one of his aides with an important dispatch. The orders originated from army headquarters at Taneytown, Maryland, and directed that the First Corps, followed by Howard's Eleventh Corps, should march to Gettysburg to support Buford's cavalry, which was picketing the roads north and west of town. The Third Corps was ordered to occupy Howard's former position at Emmitsburg. The remaining four infantry corps were placed in position to react to developing circumstances.[1]

Meade's directive partly fulfilled a prediction made by General Doubleday at the outset of the campaign. Following a careful study of regional maps, the general told his staff "Gettysburg would be the field of a second Antietam if Lee crossed into Maryland."[2] In fact, as a meeting engagement between the two armies drew near, neither commander could overlook the importance of Gettysburg's road network. No less than ten roads radiated from the center of the town like spokes on a wheel. In addition, the terminus of the Hanover, Hanover Junction, and Gettysburg Railroad was located near Carlisle Street. Thus, the small community of 2,400 inhabitants was "a strategic point of no ordinary importance" and its possession "invaluable to Lee, shortening and strengthening his line to Williamsport [Maryland], and serving as a base of maneuvers for future operations."[3]

The Army of the Potomac's left wing commander did not anticipate an encounter on this particular day, however, and no sense of urgency attended his movements. Shortly after daybreak, Reynolds ordered Wadsworth's First Division to move out from its convenient jump-off point north of Marsh Creek. He then summoned Doubleday to his headquarters to apprise him of the general military situation. After this briefing, Reynolds galloped forward to join his lead division, entrusting Doubleday with the task of bringing up the remainder of the corps.[4]

Robinson's division and most of the corps artillery were to follow in Wadsworth's wake directly up the Emmitsburg Road. The Third Division formed the extreme left flank of the advance. Biddle's brigade and Colonel Roy Stone's Second Brigade, consisting of the 149th, 150th Pennsylvania (the 2nd Bucktail Brigade), and 143rd Pennsylvania, marched to Gettysburg by diversified routes over country byways. By traveling in this manner, the division provided flank support for the corps and also minimized any potential congestion problems on the Emmitsburg Road. The First Brigade with Cooper's Battery B, 1st Pennsylvania Artillery took the advance.[5]

Owing to the intervals between the division camps and the necessity of calling in the outposts, a considerable gap opened between the First Division and the rest of the corps. Therefore, the First Corps would arrive in Gettysburg in piecemeal fashion. Doubleday dashed forward to join the advance after the remaining columns were underway. Within a short time, he would face the greatest crisis of his military career.[6]

After spending their first night on Pennsylvania soil in seven months, the soldiers of the 151st Pennsylvania awoke to a drizzly, damp morning. Even at this early hour the weather was warm and sultry. Shortly before 8 o'clock, orders came to be "in line ready to march in ten minutes." The men hastily finished breakfast, gathered up their wet blankets, donned knapsacks and traps, and with stiff limbs, fell into line. As soon as the march commenced at Ross White's crossroads, the sun broke through the clouds. Most of the men were in good spirits as they looked forward to another short march and a lazy afternoon in the rich Pennsylvania countryside. A company of sharpshooters attached to brigade headquarters led the way, followed in order by the 121st Pennsylvania with skirmishers thrown out on both flanks, the 142nd Pennsylvania, the 151st Pennsylvania, the 20th New York Militia, and Cooper's Battery last.[7]

Riding at the head of the Third Division, Thomas Algeo Rowley was destined to become one of the most controversial figures involved in the fighting of July 1st. The Pittsburgh native and Mexican War veteran raised a regiment of volunteers under Lincoln's first call for troops. As colonel of the 102nd Pennsylvania, he was wounded in the head at Seven Pines during McClellan's Peninsula Campaign. By the end of November 1862, he had ascended to the rank of brigadier general. His association with the Third Division began in March 1863, when he was transferred from the Sixth Corps. Rowley's patriotism and bravery were unquestioned, but he also had a propensity for tipping the bottle before going into action. His erratic behavior at Gettysburg may have been attributable to an inebriated condition.[8]

A short distance from camp, the 151st passed the Francis Cunningham farm. Here, Emily Cunningham positioned herself at the head of the lawn with two brimming buckets of milk and a handful of tin cups. George McFarland was among the lucky recipients of the cold refreshment. This kind act made a lasting impression on the colonel, for he returned years later to express his gratitude. Before his departure, McFarland asked for directions and inquired about taking guidance from a man sitting on a horse nearby. Emily replied, "Don't trust him, he is a Copper Head!"[9] As the soldiers marched northeast along the Millerstown Road (also known as the Nunemakers Mill Road), they passed flourishing "orchards, meadows, fields of grain, substantial fences, comfortable farm houses and above all the mighty barns, which are the glory of the Pennsylvania farmer...."[10]

After trudging nearly three miles on the Millerstown Road, the column turned sharply to the right and crossed over the wooden Sachs Bridge, which spans the sluggish waters of Marsh Creek. By this time the weather had turned uncomfortably humid, and the men "perspired as they had rarely perspired before."[11]

All along the route, civilians lined the road to watch the long blue column with burnished steel slowly wind its way through the peaceful rural countryside. It certainly wasn't every day that hundreds of armed men marched past their doors. Curious barefooted children stared at the passing soldiers from atop post and rail fences or from large wooden porches.

Within the 151st Pennsylvania, the youngsters spotted clean-cut boys, not much older than themselves, marching beside middle-aged men with weathered faces and grizzled beards. More frequently, the onlookers spied young men in their mid–20s who stood about 5-feet, 8-inches tall and weighed approximately 140 pounds. Most of these soldiers were descendants of original German and Scots-Irish settlers.

Some of the men were recent immigrants. Company E's Michael Link arrived in the New World with his parents in 1856 at the tender age of 17. He settled in the Reading area and took up the blacksmith trade. Although he enlisted as a musician, Link served regularly as a private soldier and routinely carried a musket. Private Charles Ammarell, Company K, was born at Weimar, Saxony, Germany, July 17, 1845. On July 10, 1859, he immigrated to the United States and eventually settled in Bern Township, Berks County, where he obtained employment as a farm hand. Although he had been an American for only three years, Charles was now fighting to defend and preserve his adopted country.[12]

Near the front of the column, the regiment's unstained state color was held aloft by the plucky Sergeant Adam Heilman, formerly a clerk in the Old White Store in Reading. When Adam enlisted in Company K, his wife, Susan, was five months pregnant with their second child. The march to Gettysburg was a homecoming of sorts for Sergeant Major Simon Arnold, for as a youngster he resided in the borough until the family moved east to neighboring York County.[13]

Meanwhile, the Adams County farmwives worked feverishly throughout the warm July morning, turning out fresh loaves of bread "in pans as large as milk pans" served with crocks of sweet fresh butter. The distribution system was very efficient — "with one broad sweep of a huge knife they spread the butter over the face of the mighty loaf. A swift stroke detached a thick slice which was quickly seized by a soldier who hurried on to rejoin his comrades and was at once succeeded by another."[14]

The march continued north along the Black Horse Tavern Road for about one mile, when the brigade turned right and marched up the left bank of Willoughby Run, a small tributary of Marsh Creek.[15] The peaceful vistas of ripening wheatfields, verdant meadows, and mature woodlots of ash, hickory, and oak must have lulled many into daydreams of home

A modern view of the Francis Cunningham farm where Emily Cunningham refreshed members of the 151st with buckets of cold milk. Years later, Lt. Colonel McFarland returned here during a visit to Gettysburg to thank Emily for her kindness. Author's collection.

and loved ones. Suddenly, the deep booming of artillery and the sharp crackle of musketry became clearly discernible. A surge of adrenaline shook the men from their dreamlike trances and back to reality.

When the column neared the Fairfield or Hagerstown Road, Lieutenant Jacob F. Slagle, an aide to General Doubleday, spurred up with orders for the Third Division to hurry its march toward Gettysburg.[16] The leisurely pace of the route step gave way to the brisk movement of the double quick. The click and clash of metallic sounds mingled with the deeper tone of the tread of the fast-moving regiments and the shouts of orders barked out by officers as the troops rushed onward.

Sometime around 11 A.M., the First Brigade reached the broad Hagerstown Road about two miles west of Gettysburg. The fatigued troops were formed in line of battle facing north in "a beautiful grove of large trees with a carpet of springy sod." At this point

McFarland noted, "the shells began to fly" and the "enemy whom we had hunted for several days, were found, and we all felt that a decisive struggle was about to take place."[17]

In fact, the opening phase of the first day's bloody fighting was already over when the brigades of Biddle and Stone arrived on the field by their respective routes. Just after daylight, Buford's cavalrymen encountered two brigades of General Henry Heth's infantry division approaching Gettysburg from the west along the Chambersburg Pike. The dismounted troopers were being hard pressed when Reynolds arrived on the scene.

The sharp commander quickly evaluated the situation. On his way through Gettysburg he noted the dominating hills south of town, and a short time later, he observed a series of low, parallel ridges to the west, where Buford's men were fighting a well-executed delaying action. The hard-hitting Pennsylvanian

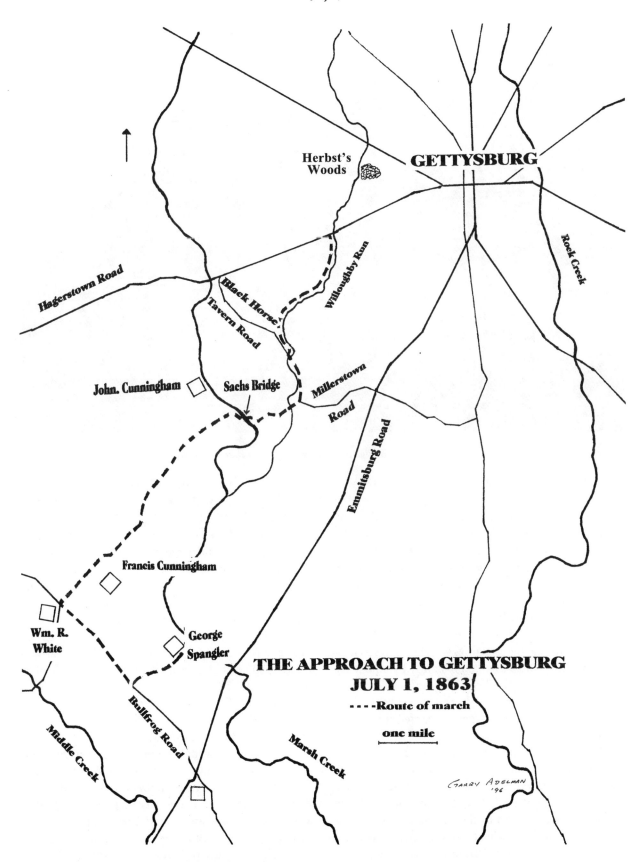

GETTYSBURG

Herbst's
Woods

Rock Creek

Willoughby Run

Hagerstown Road

Black Horse

Tavern Road

John. Cunningham

Sachs Bridge

Millerstown
Road

Emmitsburg Road

Francis Cunningham

Wm. R.
White

George
Spangler

THE APPROACH TO GETTYSBURG
JULY 1, 1863
- - - -**Route of march**

one mile

Bullfrog Road

Middle Creek

Marsh Creek

GARRY ADELMAN
'96

The approach to Gettysburg: July 1, 1863. Map by Garry Adelman.

The historic Sachs Bridge over Marsh Creek. Author's collection.

immediately committed his nearby First Division into the fray. His aides dashed off with orders for Doubleday and Howard to rush forward with reinforcements. Using the discretion given him by Meade, Reynolds chose to stay and fight at Gettysburg.[18]

Soon, savage fighting erupted as Wadsworth's division relieved Bufords's weary troopers along McPherson's Ridge. Eventually, the Southerners were repulsed and a considerable number were captured. But the cost of the initial Union success at Gettysburg was steep. Among the casualties was the beloved General Reynolds, who was killed instantly by an enemy volley while leading the "Iron Brigade" into battle.

The news of Reynolds' death spread like wildfire throughout the ranks and "many a tear fell at the sight of his stretcher."[19] His actions on July 1st were certainly not out of character for as Major Harry T. Lee, an aide-de-camp on Doubleday's staff, recalled, "It was always a fault of his to be right at the front when there was any fighting." Major Lee hypothesized that Reynolds rode forward to the advanced position on McPherson's Ridge "owing to his eagerness to occupy and hold the ridge beyond the one on which he fell."[20]

Indeed, the most important topographical feature

on the first day's battlefield was the system of low ridges or swells which rippled from the towering heights of South Mountain 10 miles to the west of Gettysburg. These ridges ran generally in a north to south direction and were divided by broad, gently sloping valleys or plains.

Located nearly a mile to the west of McPherson's Ridge and over two miles from the center of Gettysburg, Herr Ridge served as the launching point for Confederate assaults initiated by Heth's and later Pender's Division of A. P. Hill's Corps. The relatively high, open crest also formed a natural artillery platform. Whether Reynolds ever intended to push his forces out this far from town is purely speculative, but the Confederates certainly used the position advantageously throughout the day.

McPherson's Ridge would continue to function as the primary Union defensive position to resist a Southern entrance into Gettysburg. Actually, this ridge is composed of two distinct crests, a higher western crest, on which the McPherson farm was located, and a slightly lower eastern crest about 400 yards closer to town. There was a slight ripple or swale between these elevations. When clarification is important, the smaller crest will be referred to as East McPherson's Ridge.

A large, triangular-shaped grove of mature hardwoods known as Herbst's Woods covered the ridge about halfway between the Chambersburg Pike and the Hagerstown Road. These two roadways cut through the ridge from the northwest and southwest, respectively, and were about three-quarters of a mile apart at this point. Willoughby Run, the small stream which the First Brigade followed during its approach march, flowed past the western base of McPherson's Ridge and meandered its way southward.[21]

Herbst's Woods, General Doubleday observed, "possessed all the advantages of a redoubt, strengthening the center of our line, and enfilading the enemy's columns should they advance in the open spaces on either side."[22] Thus, this position guarded the two principal roads available to Confederate troops approaching from the west.

The eagle-eyed Colonel Wainwright was considerably less enthusiastic about the defensibility of McPherson's Ridge, for he wrote, "I did not like this advanced position at all, its right flank being exposed to a high ridge to the north, and approached by a number of ravines which afforded excellent cover to an attacking party."[23] One major obstacle standing in the way of an enemy advance from the north was a deep unfinished railroad cut, which paralleled the Chambersburg Pike approximately 200 yards to the north.

The next ridge to the east and the one nearest the town was Seminary Ridge. At this point the two roads mentioned earlier converged to within a quarter of a mile of one another. The campus of the Lutheran Theological Seminary stood on the narrow strip of high ground between these roads three-quarters of a mile west of Gettysburg. It consisted of a large four-story brick building flanked on either side by a professor's dwelling. These structures would be utilized as field hospitals throughout the battle.[24]

The ridge was nearly covered with a belt of timber, including a fine grove near the Seminary. Unlike Herr and McPherson's Ridge, which tapered off near the Hagerstown Road, Seminary Ridge stretched a considerable distance to the south. The northern extension of the ridge, named Oak Ridge, terminated near a broken, sparsely wooded knoll known as Oak Hill. This elevation dominated the surrounding area and it would play a prominent role in the fighting ahead. The ground fell away sharply from the side of Seminary Ridge nearest the town, while on the western

side it sloped more gradually. A moist, open valley of roughly 500 yards divided Seminary Ridge and McPherson's Ridge.

After the untimely death of Reynolds, command of the field devolved upon Abner Doubleday. The 44-year-old New Yorker was described as quiet, courteous, meticulous in preparation, and steady in battle. Unlike the charismatic Reynolds, however, the portly and sometimes quarrelsome Doubleday did not inspire universal confidence in his troops or among his fellow officers. Colonel Wainwright confided to his journal, "I had no confidence in Doubleday, and felt that he would be a weak reed to lean upon...." General Meade, the army's new commander, also formed a low opinion of Doubleday while serving with him in the First Corps throughout much of 1862.[25]

Not everyone was so captious. McFarland idolized him as a military mentor. In his own sarcastic manner, Lieutenant Blodget endorsed Doubleday when he wrote, "He is deficient considerably in the requisites of a commander. He does not drink whiskey, or at least I never saw him drink, stays with his command—and seems anxious to do his duty and fight Rebels.... He also allows his wife to stay with him when he ought to keep a mistress." Blodget had ample opportunity to observe the commanding general while his company served several months as the headquarters guard.[26]

The situation inherited by Doubleday during the late morning hours of July 1 was grim and uncertain. Heth was reorganizing his shattered front line and making preparations to bring his two fresh brigades forward. Dorsey Pender's division, with nearly 6,700 effectives, was moving up to support Heth, and powerful elements of Richard Ewell's Corps were coming in from the north. The concentrated fire of the Confederate artillery steadily shelled the Union position from Herr Ridge. Upon taking command, Doubleday had just one division on hand, and even with the remainder of his corps, he still faced the possibility of being outnumbered by at least a two to one margin. One of his staff officers despaired, "We all knew we were fighting against time with no earthly hope of ultimately holding our position against Lee's advance."[27]

Despite having the entire burden of the impending battle suddenly thrust upon him, Doubleday kept his head and set about organizing Wadsworth's division for a defensive stand. He reasoned since General Reynolds "had formed his lines to resist the entrance of the enemy into Gettysburg, I naturally supposed that it was the intention to defend the place." The commander also believed that a retreat without hard fighting would demoralize the troops and injure the morale of the entire army. "Final success in this war," he wrote, "can only be attained by desperate fighting, and the infliction of heavy loss upon the enemy." Furthermore, he knew Howard's Eleventh Corps was moving up in support, while the Third and Twelfth Corps were within striking distance.[28] Meanwhile, during the lull in the fighting, Doubleday and his staff waited tensely for the remainder of the First Corps to arrive.

When Colonel Charles Wainwright arrived at the Seminary shortly after 11 A.M., he observed Solomon Meredith's Iron Brigade reforming in Herbst's Woods near the spot where Reynolds had fallen. The tough Midwesterners had just completed a rout of James Archer's Brigade, capturing the general along with a number of his troops. North of the Chambersburg Pike, Brigadier General Lysander Cutler reorganized his scattered command after its desperate morning encounter with Brigadier General Joseph Davis' Mississippians and North Carolinians. The First Corps artillery chief worried that "should the enemy be in force enough to drive right ahead, they would eat us up piecemeal...." In the event the enemy were not strongly posted, he hoped the arriving Third Division would strike them on the flank.[29] The last mentioned event nearly took place.

Following a short breather near the Hagerstown Road, Colonel Chapman Biddle advanced his men due north in line of battle. The 151st Pennsylvania and the 20th New York formed on the extreme left of the brigade. After proceeding several hundred yards into the woodlands, the brigade encountered sporadic musketry fire in its front, possibly from the 5th Alabama Battalion of Archer's Brigade. Had Biddle continued on this course, he would have slammed into the right of Heth's line stationed on Herr Ridge. Not being aware of the size of this enemy force, however, Biddle slid his brigade to the right in an attempt to locate the rest of the corps.[30]

The men moved through the woods by the right flank, splashed across Willoughby Run between the Hagerstown Road and the John Herbst farm, and arrived in the open valley between Seminary Ridge and McPherson's Ridge. During this movement, the First Brigade sustained its first casualty when a member of the 20th New York Militia was struck by a stray bullet from the forest. Captain Cook wrote, "The incident thrilled everyone with a sense of danger as great

perhaps as that felt during the battle itself." The men also observed elements of Buford's cavalry sparring with Confederate skirmishers near the Herbst farm buildings.[31] These events were a mere prelude of what was to come.

Doubleday ordered the First Brigade and Cooper's Battery to occupy a position on East McPherson's Ridge on the left and rear of the Iron Brigade. Knapsacks were unslung as the men prepared for action. In Company B of the 151st, Private Solomon Brink was assigned the duty of guarding these valuable items. The 151st formed up on the right of the line near the southeast corner of Herbst's Woods as a reserve force.[32]

After only a few minutes, the remainder of the brigade moved forward over the ridge and down into the ravine formed by Willoughby Run. The three regiments immediately came under the fire of Confederate skirmishers hidden in a grainfield on the opposite side of the stream. A short time later, Biddle pulled his men back to the safety afforded by the reverse slope of the ridge. It is not certain just who ordered this particular movement, but strong evidence suggests that Rowley may have been drunk while on duty, and he consequently exercised poor judgment in the handling of his division throughout the day.[33]

Rowley's task was made more difficult because his command had been divided. Roy Stone's Second Brigade, which had taken a slightly different route, probably reached the field just prior to Biddle's command and was sent to occupy the open space north of Herbst's Woods between Meredith and Cutler. Thus, the two brigades of Rowley's division were separated by an interval of roughly 200 yards with the Iron Brigade interposed between them.[34]

The last elements of the First Corps, Robinson's division and the remainder of the corps artillery brigade, reached the field shortly before noon. Doubleday immediately directed Robinson to "station his division in reserve at the seminary, and to throw up some slight intrenchments, to aid me in holding that position in case I should be driven back." These "slight intrenchments" were hastily constructed by the men of Gabriel Paul's brigade and consisted of a barricade of fence rails, stumps, and earth. The breastworks were located near the front of a small woodlot that extended west from the main Seminary building. The semicircular line of works originated 200 feet north of this structure and ended roughly 100 feet below it. Although "weak and imperfect," the entrenchments would be greatly appreciated by the

Union defenders later in the day. The position was strengthened by an existing stone fence which began some 200 yards below the Seminary, near Professor Schmucker's residence, and ran southward along the crest of the ridge.[35]

Doubleday's dispositions provided for a strong defense against a Confederate attack from the west. He planned to fight an aggressive delaying action until the remainder of the army arrived on the scene. If driven back from the McPherson's Ridge line, he could rally his forces at the prepared position near the Seminary before falling back through the town to Cemetery Hill. But the position was quite susceptible to an attack from the north by elements of Ewell's Corps. The ever vigilant Buford reported that these forces were fast approaching Gettysburg via the Carlisle and Harrisburg Roads. Doubleday was counting on the Eleventh Corps to deal with this threat.[36]

Major General Oliver Otis Howard arrived at Gettysburg in advance of his corps shortly after 11 A.M. By virtue of his seniority, Howard assumed command of the field. He established his headquarters on Cemetery Hill, near the Baltimore Pike, just southeast of the town. Like his predecessors, Howard appreciated the strong defensive potential of this commanding height and realized that its location controlled the road network being utilized by the Army of the Potomac.[37] Soon after his arrival, Howard mistakenly interpreted the realignment of Cutler's brigade as a full retreat by the entire First Corps, and he forwarded this false information to army headquarters.[38]

The first brigades of the 9,200-man strong Eleventh Corps arrived in Gettysburg at about 12:30. By this time Doubleday had informed Howard, by message, that he would endeavor to hold his ground against A. P. Hill's Corps, if the Eleventh Corps was positioned to prevent Ewell from attacking his vulnerable right flank. In response, Howard instructed his acting corps commander, Major General Carl Schurz, to march two divisions through Gettysburg and occupy Oak Ridge and Oak Hill for the purpose of extending and securing the right flank of the First Corps. Howard stationed his remaining division in reserve on Cemetery Hill as a rallying point for the Union forces should a retreat become necessary. He also hoped the position would serve as the nucleus of a strong concentration point for the remainder of the army upon its arrival.[39]

A sudden explosion of Confederate artillery fire from Oak Hill squelched any hopes of the proposed link-up between the First and Eleventh Corps. Lieutenant Colonel Thomas Carter's artillery battalion signaled the much-feared arrival of Robert Rodes' 8,000-man division. Rodes' forces arrived on the field at a most opportune time, a pattern that would be repeated throughout the day for the Army of Northern Virginia. Carter's guns immediately opened a destructive enfilading fire on the Union forces spread out below them.[40]

Positioned on the open crest of East McPherson's Ridge, Biddle's brigade was greatly exposed to the destructive missiles. Soon, shells landed all around the 151st Pennsylvania, plowing shallow furrows in the rich soil. Sergeant Heilig, who had been through this experience before, casually noted, "Their wind is always the worst."[41] Private Charles Ammarell of Company K, on the other hand, became "fighting mad" when his haversack, containing three days worth of rations, was knocked to pieces by an exploding shell.[42]

Ammarell was considerably more fortunate than another member of his company. Private Peter Drumheller was struck in the midsection by a cannon ball. His abdomen was tore open and both of his legs were severed at the upper joint. Private Henry Yergey was standing directly beside Drumheller at the time of this incident. As his comrade fell to the ground, Yergey heard him exclaim, "I am shot!"[43]

Biddle's troops were soon shifted to a more sheltered location near the Hagerstown Road perpendicular to its former position. The 151st took position behind a fence running along the south end of the Seminary grove, its line now facing north. The remainder of the brigade also faced north in two lines of battle. Eventually, a portion of the brigade was posted directly in the road where the troops were "partially covered by the fence and bank at the roadside." Cooper's Battery also changed front to the north and replied to Carter's artillery. Shells continued to fall about "right lively" as the Confederate gunners zeroed in on their targets.[44]

In response to Rodes' threat, Doubleday directed General Robinson to send one of his brigades north to Oak Ridge with hopes of forming a connection with the Eleventh Corps. General Henry Baxter's brigade was chosen for this mission. When the action heated up in this sector, Doubleday ordered Robinson to go in person, with Paul's brigade, to assist Baxter.[45] Thus, the First Corps commander's valuable reserve force had been spent at a much earlier stage in the battle than he originally anticipated.

After losing the race for Oak Hill, the two Eleventh Corps divisions deployed on the open plain north of town. This improvised line was formed at a right angle to the First Corps line on Oak Ridge. A gap of about 400 yards existed between the two corps. Schurz's men covered the open farmland from the Mummasburg Road east to the Harrisburg Road. The demise of the ill-fated Eleventh Corps soldiers would take place later in the afternoon when Jubal Early's Division arrived on the vulnerable right flank of Schurz's line.

During the early afternoon of July 1st, Abner Doubleday faced the worst case scenario he had feared when planning his defensive stand. His available forces totaled about 8,500 men in six brigades. Opposing him were 12 brigades of Confederates numbering close to 16,000 troops.[46] The First Corps line stretched irregularly from the Hagerstown Road north to the Mummasburg Road. It was thinly held at spots and no large reserve force remained in support. As long as the Confederate attacks came from one direction, Doubleday stood a chance of fending them off. If, on the other hand, the Southerners mounted a coordinated assault against the First Corps, it would be only a matter of time before the line gave way.

Shortly after 2 P.M., Rodes' infantry emerged from the cover of Oak Hill to strike Baxter's position. Meanwhile, on the western front, Heth's Division remained motionless. Observing the attack from his vantage point on Herr Ridge, Surgeon George Underwood of the 26th North Carolina waxed poetically, "Never was a grander sight beheld. The roar of artillery, the crack of musketry and the shouts of combatants, added grandeur and solemnity to the scene."[47] Although aesthetically pleasing to Underwood, Rodes' initial attack was disastrous from a Confederate point of view. The assaults were poorly coordinated, and consequently these attacks were repulsed with heavy losses to the Southerners. But the pressure exerted on the Union line in this sector was considerable and the attacks would continue without abatement.

At around 2:30 P.M., Heth's Division, with the endorsement of General Lee himself, moved off to renew its attack on the McPherson's Ridge line. Soon fighting would erupt along the entire length of the Union army's half circle defensive position, established west and north of Gettysburg. Heth's new attack was spearheaded by Pettigrew's strong brigade,

which was supported on its left by Brockenbrough's small Virginia brigade. Pender's veteran division followed within supporting distance.

Pettigrew formed up his 2,500 men in the following order from left to right: the 26th North Carolina, the 11th North Carolina, the 47th North Carolina, and the 52nd North Carolina. The Tarheels alone outnumbered Meredith's and Biddle's brigades.[48]

The order to advance greatly relieved Colonel Burgwyn of the 26th who was "quite impatient to engage the enemy." The sun was high in the heavens and Burgwyn was concerned with "losing precious time." The young colonel served as an inspiring symbol to his men as he rode along the lines in "his grandest style," mounted on his beautiful dappled gray charger. Having been exposed to stray artillery rounds and the harassing fire of enemy sharpshooters throughout much of the day, the men were also eager to commence the attack, although all seemed aware of the "desperateness of the charge we were to make."

The officers assumed their posts. Burgwyn positioned himself in the front center of the regiment, Lieutenant Colonel John R. Lane attended to the right of the line, and Major John T. Jones guided the left. The gallant Sergeant J. B. Mansfield stepped to the front with the regimental flag flanked by the eight color guards. Company F was positioned on the left of the colors, Company E was stationed on the right, with Companies A and G near the center. In Company G stood Sergeant William Preston Kirkman, a 23-year-old teacher from Chatham County. He was accompanied by his three younger brothers, who were also members of the same company.

In the ranks of the 26th were a large number of backwoodsmen from the mountainous central and western region of the state. General Pettigrew once complimented their fine marksmanship by exclaiming, "They shot as if they were shooting at squirrels."[49] In a short time they would face an equally determined band of artisans, teachers, and rural marksmen from the Keystone State.

Soon, the order "March!" rang out along the entire length of the line, and the 26th stepped off with parade ground precision. Lieutenant Colonel Lane proudly recalled the "grand scene" as the men marched forward "so bravely and so gracefully!"[50]

Heth's advance was plainly visible from the Union lines. Colonel Wainwright could not help admiring the Southerners as "they marched along quietly and with confidence." At the same time, he despaired that Pettigrew's Brigade "outflanked us at least [a] half mile on our left," leading him to predict that "there was not the shadow of a chance" of holding McPherson's Ridge.[51] Major Thomas Chamberlin of the 150th Pennsylvania viewed the deployment of Heth's and Pender's divisions from near the McPherson farm. He noted, "While the Union line was but a skeleton, with noticeable gaps between the several brigades as well as between the regiments, the enemy was formed in continuous double lines of battle, extending southward as far as the accidents of the ground permitted the eye to reach, with heavy supporting columns in the rear. It was a beautiful spectacle, but their preponderance in force was so obvious that the Union troops might have predicted their own defeat, if they had not counted on the timely arrival of re-enforcements."[52]

Abner Doubleday agreed with the grim conclusions reached by his junior officers. He dispatched at least two of his aides to Howard with requests for reinforcements or for permission to withdraw from his exposed position. Howard ordered Doubleday to stay put, but offered no direct support because "he did not have a man to spare." When Lieutenant Slagle found Howard near the Evergreen Cemetery, he observed Adolph Von Steinwehr's division in reserve nearby, leading him to falsely conclude that the Eleventh Corps "did not have a man engaged at that time." Of course, most of Howard's men were deployed north of town, and these troops played an important role in protecting the right flank of the First Corps throughout the afternoon. However, no troops from the other corps had yet arrived. The regimental commanders on McPherson's Ridge were ordered to hold the line at all hazards.[53]

When Pettigrew's Brigade stepped off from Herr Ridge, the 151st Pennsylvania advanced a short distance into the Seminary grove and wheeled into the breastworks which had been constructed by Paul's brigade subsequent to its departure for Oak Ridge.[54] McFarland's 467 officers and men now represented the only reserve force available for the First Corps.

The regiment's selection for this duty was due in part to several factors. Most obviously, the 151st was nearest to the Seminary building when Robinson's men departed. It was also one of the largest units in the corps, and thereby represented a respectable reserve force. The regiment had also been serving as a reserve for the First Brigade throughout the day, perhaps due to its lack of battle experience.

The remainder of the brigade changed front to

the left and returned to its former position on East McPherson's Ridge, on the left rear of Meredith's brigade. Biddle's brigade had the unfortunate task of defending the weakest portion of the First Corps line. The troops were located in an exposed position with no strong terrain feature on which to anchor the end of the

The blanket carried by Adjutant James B. Jordan of the 26th North Carolina. Jordan was wounded in the hip and captured at Gettysburg. Courtesy of J. Howard Wert Gettysburg Collection.

line. With only about 800 men in his three available regiments, Colonel Biddle did not have enough men to reach the Hagerstown Road. The left of the 121st Pennsylvania fell short of the road by about four hundred yards. As the Tarheels advanced toward the low ridge, Colonel Theodore Gates of the 20th New York State Militia noted "their line extended the front of two regiments beyond our left flank."[55]

Gates' New Yorkers were next in line. Two companies of this unit occupied the Emmanuel Harman farm on the western side of Willoughby Run. From this advanced outpost, the New Yorkers harassed Pettigrew's skirmishers and delayed the progress of the Confederate attack.[56]

Two sections from Captain Gilbert Reynolds' 1st New York Light Artillery, Battery L, occupied the space between the 20th New York and Biddle's rightmost regiment, the 142nd Pennsylvania. Captain Horatio Warren of the 142nd recalled the moment when Heth's troops "pushed out of the woods into the open field … with two long lines of infantry, outflanking us by nearly one-third of a mile." A small gap existed near the southeastern corner of Herbst's Woods between the right of the 142nd and the left of the 19th Indiana, the very location the 151st had occupied earlier in the day. From left to right, the 24th Michigan, 2nd Wisconsin, and 7th Wisconsin extended the line of the Iron Brigade through the western portion of the woodlot. The above forces would confront Heth's new assault on the McPherson's Ridge line.[57]

Huddled behind the earthen entrenchments

near the Seminary, the soldiers of the 151st Pennsylvania observed the redeployment of the remainder of the First Brigade. On nearly every countenance one could detect the almost unbearable anxiety. Faces turned pale and nerves trembled. The enemy artillery fire, which intensified with the impendent infantry assault, added to the growing tension. Exploding shells whistled through the air, emitting showers of destructive iron spray on the troops below. Solid shot ricocheted through the grove of hardwoods and large branches occasionally crashed to the ground.

There were several near misses. Sergeant William Miller, Company H, was sitting near a small hickory tree, with the barrel of his rifle leaning on the tree and the stock resting on his shoulder. A 12-pound ball fired from one of Carter's artillery pieces on Oak Ridge struck his musket near the top and doubled it together. Sergeant Heilig observed the incident from nearby and thought Miller had been decapitated by the projectile. The sergeant survived the close call but his arm was incapacitated. His part in the fighting was over.[58]

Sergeant Charles Atlee, 121st Pennsylvania. Courtesy of MOLLUS Collection, The Civil War Library and Museum, Philadelphia, Pennsylvania.

In the midst of the growing storm, George McFarland was "exceedingly calm ... and while awaiting the infantry attack quietly sat on the ground taking notes, while the shells were flying in all directions."[59] His inspirational example steeled the men for the ordeal soon to come.

Soon, the sharp, irregular crack of the skirmisher's rifles broke out in the distance. The positions of these advance warriors were clearly marked by small puffs of white smoke. A few moments later, the solid columns of the enemy emerged in plain sight. Pettigrew's men stepped proudly and steadily toward the low ridge line. McFarland's men stared straight ahead with firm, compressed lips and rigid muscles. The pale expressions were gone. Suddenly, just to the front, the erratic crackling of the skirmishers erupted into a tumultuous roar as the contending lines crashed together. The exultant, high-pitched rebel yell mixed with the deafening volleys of musketry to produce a truly infernal noise.

On the far left of the McPherson's Ridge line, the 121st Pennsylvania, under Lieutenant Colonel Alexander Biddle, locked up with the 52nd North Carolina. The effective strength of the 121st at Gettysburg had been reduced to 256 men and six line officers after supplying details for various non-combat functions.[60]

As soon as the Confederates came within a few yards of the top of the ridge, the Pennsylvanians arose from the breast-high wheat and "delivered their fire directly in their faces, staggering them and bringing them to a stand." The North Carolinians promptly returned the fire and soon men were "falling fast in the face of the leaden storm that howled around them." Eventually, the longer line of the 52nd lapped around the left of the 121st and delivered a "crushing fire."[61]

Lieutenant Colonel Biddle, who seemed to be everywhere at once, attempted to change front and meet the threat to his exposed flank, but the "ranks were broken and became massed together" during the difficult movement.[62] The officers valiantly attempted to rally the men. Captain and Acting Major James Ashworth stood firm in the midst of the fury near the regiment's crumbling flank. The gallant officer was hit successively below the breast, twice in the right arm, and also in the right knee. Ashworth was later taken to the home of Sallie Myers on West High Street. His mother traveled to Gettysburg and carefully nursed him back to health.[63]

Sergeant Charles Atlee of Company C was hit in

the chin but still kept his place in line. Shortly afterward, a second bullet struck him below the right knee and forced him to go to the rear. The sergeant took refuge in a nearby home, and several of the ladies there cleaned his wounds. When the Union forces fell back through the town, Atlee was left behind. Fortunately, a Confederate captain ordered him to a field hospital for further treatment. With the aid of a Rebel soldier and a young man of the house, Atlee cheerfully complied.[64]

Its organization shattered, the regiment's survivors bolted for the cover of the Seminary woods. The time made by the men in reaching their destination "was remarkable, probably the best on record." The dead and severely wounded, among them Captain Ashworth, covered the ground along the entire length of the former position. Sergeant William Hardy carried off the regimental colors, which was perforated with bullets and the staff shot into three pieces.[65]

The Union artillery reformed on Seminary Ridge soon after the approach of Pettigrew's men, leaving the 20th New York Militia and the 142nd Pennsylvania alone to face the 47th North Carolina. Both regiments fought tenaciously. The brass eagle atop the 20th's flag staff tumbled from its lofty perch after being peppered by a shower of Rebel bullets. Color Corporal Enos Vail fell to the ground desperately wounded while ramming home his fifth round. The collapse of the 121st Pennsylvania in turn made the 20th's position untenable as the victorious 52nd North Carolina changed front to the north and poured in an enfilading fire. The New Yorkers held on stubbornly until more than half of its members had fallen. Colonel Gates personally attended to the colors during the unit's fighting withdrawal to avoid any possible confusion.[66]

Private Edwin Gearhart of the 142nd recalled that the North Carolinians "kept steadily advancing until we could see their officers stepping in front swinging their swords. Suddenly a cloud of smoke arose from their line and almost instantly the balls began to whistle about us and the men next to my right fell." First Lieutenant Andrew Gregg Tucker, the acting adjutant of the regiment, presented a conspicuous mark for the enemy riflemen. During the first volley, Andrew was shot in the right forearm and his horse was severely disabled. Captain Charles Evans ordered the recent University at Lewisburg graduate to leave the field. Instead, the young adjutant remained with the regiment "cheering and urging

the men by going into the thickest of the fight himself."[67]

Tucker's good friend, First Lieutenant Jeremiah Hoffman, Company K, was incapacitated when a projectile cut through his pelvis and lodged near the spine. Tucker pushed Hoffman up onto his wounded mount and sent him off to the Seminary for medical assistance.[68] Nearby, Corporal Jacob Bankes of Company E miraculously escaped death when a ball struck the brass eagle over his breast.[69] Captain Horatio Warren recalled men being "mowed down by the terrible fire from front and flank, and then in sheer desperation we were ordered to charge...."[70]

Throughout the desperate fighting, Colonel Chapman Biddle rode defiantly back and forth along the brigade line. The modest, unassuming, and intellectual former lawyer was "suddenly transformed into an illustrious hero, the admiration of friend and foe" and "his devoted horse seemed to partake of the heroism of the rider as he dashed along the line between the two fires, daring the storm of death-dealing messengers that filled the atmosphere." Seeing the line of the 142nd wavering under the increasing pressure, Biddle darted into the ranks, seized the regimental standard, and led the 142nd forward in an ill-fated countercharge. The scattered troops "swarmed around him as bees cover their queen ... when all guns ... turned on the mass and seemingly shot the whole to pieces."

Captain Joseph Davis of the 47th spied a gallant Union officer with colors in hand frantically attempting to rally the disordered ranks. In the heat and the excitement of battle, Davis directed a nearby sharpshooter to shoot down the enemy officer. An instant later, both horse and rider toppled to the ground. For many years afterward, Davis lamented that he had ordered the death of the brave Federal officer. Biddle, however, somehow survived the ordeal of July 1st, although he received a nasty scalp wound during the later stages of the battle.[71]

The 142nd lost heavily during the desperate counterattack. One company lost all but 5 men from the 34 who entered the battle "on a patch of ground no larger than an ordinary town lot."[72] Private John T. Reid was one of only three men left in Company K after the day's fighting, and he had been slightly wounded in the right hand.[73] In Company B, three brothers, Samuel, Enos, and Adam Cramer, died as a result of the wounds they received on July 1.[74]

In a last-ditch effort to rally the survivors, Colonel Robert P. Cummins, the regiment's beloved down in the shallow valley between the ridges. He related his close call with death as follows:

although I could not see the balls that whistled close over me, I could see the timothy heads around me falling from their stem as if by magic, the stalks standing still and their heads falling off apparently of themselves. There was a charming object lesson in philosophy before me and if I could have forgotten the fact that I had a head as well as the timothy, I think I should have enjoyed it. [76]

J. Robinson Balsley and family after the war. Courtesy of David Richards Collection, USAMHI.

The ground along the southern end of McPherson's Ridge was left strewn with the dead and wounded of Biddle's three regiments. The fierce engagements of July 1st cost these defenders 560 casualties from an engaged strength of nearly 900 officers and men. [77]

While the right portion of Pettigrew's line was sweeping Biddle's men from the eastern crest of McPherson's Ridge, the 11th and 26th North Carolina, with the assistance of Brockenbrough's Virginians, slammed into the Iron Brigade's stronghold in Herbst's Woods. The line of the 19th Indiana extended from the edge of the timber skirting Willoughby Run on the left, across the level ground in the southwest corner of the grove, and then followed the rising ground north where it connected with the 24th Michigan.

Colonel Collett Leventhorpe's 11th North Carolina, over 600 strong, gradually worked its way around the 19th's unprotected left flank, which was left exposed by Biddle's collapse. The enfilading fire "almost annihilated the regiment," reported Colonel William Dudley. Eight color bearers fell in succession. Finally, Dudley himself seized the colors from the ground and was promptly shot through the right leg. The Hoosiers slowly retired to the eastern edge of Herbst's Woods. [78]

In response to the 19th's withdrawal, Colonel

commander, pointed to the colors with his sword and shouted "rally round the flag." A knot of men halted long enough to fire a round at the oncoming Confederates. Colonel Cummins fell with a mortal wound an instant later. Several men were shot down as they endeavored to carry his lifeless body off the field. [75]

J. Robinson Balsley, a teenaged shoemaker, attempted to retrieve the regimental flag, but he was immediately hit by two bullets. Trapped in the no man's land between the hostile lines, Balsley later received a third wound and other stray rounds sliced through his haversack and cartridge box. The brave youngster was eventually rescued and treated at a field hospital. Likewise, Private Gearhart was pinned

Henry A. Morrow of the 24th Michigan ordered the left of his line to swing back and face the mounting threat on his flank. But Morrow had more than enough to contend with on his front.[79]

Advancing on the left of the 11th North Carolina, Colonel Burgwyn's huge 26th North Carolina maintained its perfect alignment until it reached the briers and underbrush along Willoughby Run. Here, the troops crowded toward the center near a narrow opening. A murderous crossfire from Union artillery added to the confusion. Undaunted, the Tarheels regrouped and sweated up the steep western slope of McPherson's Ridge.

Waiting in the mature timber, the 24th Michigan opened on the Southerners at point blank range. The bullets flew "as thick as hail stones in a storm," wrote the historian of the 26th.[80] The attackers were not checked and "came on with rapid strides yelling like demons." One Michigander, Private Charles McConnel, Company B, distinctly remembered being "cool and collected after the nervous thrill of the first crash of battle." Looking about, he detected no signs of cowardice, indecision, or hysterical courage on the faces of his comrades, but rather "a calm determination to fight to the death in defense of Old Glory."[81]

The advance hesitated briefly, but the Tarheels were not to be denied. Captain W. W. McCreery rushed forward with a message from General Pettigrew to Colonel Burgwyn, "his regiment has covered itself with glory today." The inspired Southerners pressed the attack with renewed vigor, and the Midwesterners began to give way. The 24th fell back slowly through the woods, stubbornly contesting every inch of ground. True to McConnel's words, the regiment lost 363 men during the bloody fighting of July 1st, and no fewer than nine color-bearers were killed or wounded.[82]

The 26th North Carolina paid a dear price for several hundred feet of Pennsylvania real estate. One survivor sadly recalled, "We lost many of our brave boys and our dear noble colonel, who was shot down with the colors in his hand, leading the charge. Fourteen of our brave men fell with the colors in their hands. Although they knew it was almost certain death to pick it up, the flag was never allowed to remain down...." Lieutenant Colonel Lane was among those shot while carrying the colors. A ball struck him in the back of the neck and crashed through his jaw and mouth. Lane survived his ghastly wound and forty years later he met the man who shot him, Private Charles McConnell.[83]

The 7th and 2nd Wisconsin regiments retired shortly after the 24th Michigan. Observing the retrograde movement from near the Chambersburg Pike, Sergeant William Ramsey, 150th Pennsylvania, admired "the cool, orderly manner" in which Meredith's brigade fell back.[84]

By now the smoky discharge from hundreds of muskets "settled down over the combatants making it almost as dark as night." Just a few moments earlier, the sun had been clearly visible high in the heavens.[85] Suddenly, out of the smoky fog, a new Federal battle line emerged almost ghostlike in the southeastern corner of Herbst's Woods.

The left flank of the First Corps line was falling apart by 3 P.M. After General Doubleday observed the 52nd North Carolina sweeping around Biddle's line and the pullback of the 19th Indiana, he knew the time had come to commit his last reserve, the 151st Pennsylvania. General Rowley rode up to McFarland and ordered him to advance his regiment into the interval between Biddle's and Meredith's forces.[86]

The resolve of the Pennsylvanians must have been severely tested as they crossed the open ground between the ridges. Streams of wounded men flowed back from the front lines, shells burst overhead, while deafening peals of musketry and the unearthly shouts of the combatants filled the air. The unsettling noises reached a crescendo as the regiment neared East McPherson's Ridge, portraying a scene from hell itself. As the troops crested the low ridge and moved down the gentle slope toward Farmer Herbst's woods, a long line of butternut infantry popped into view. "Then was the first sight I had of the rebel Stars and Bars," wrote Private Randle D. Sayre of Company B, "There was a full regiment from 50 to 100 yards in front."[87]

Flushed by their recent success against the Iron Brigade troops, Pettigrew's men unleashed a volley against the approaching Pennsylvanians. Before the 151st halted in line of battle, men began to fall. Lieutenant Colonel McFarland watched his neighbor, Private David Fry, a 22-year-old carpenter, fall dead from a gunshot wound. Nevertheless, when the Keystoners reached their assigned position, they calmly dressed their line under fire. A little more than one half of the regiment's left wing was positioned in the open ground beyond the edge of the woods.[88]

McFarland reported, "Having previously cautioned the men against excitement and firing at random, and the enemy being partly concealed in the woods, on lower ground than we occupied, I did not

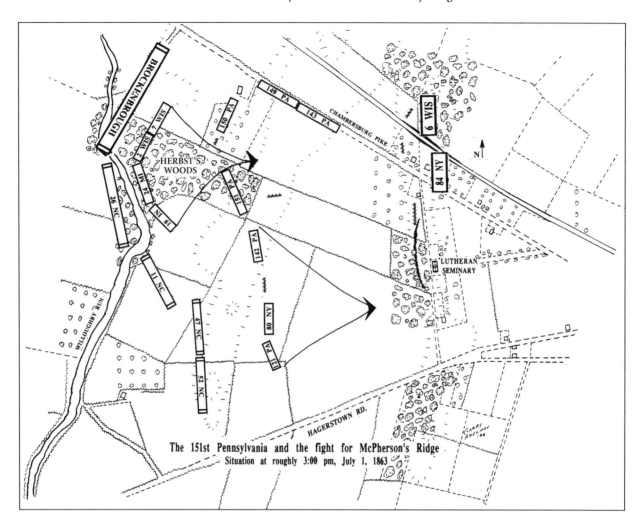

The 151st Pennsylvania and the fight for McPherson's Ridge. Map by Garry Adelman.

order them to fire a regular volley, but each man to fire as he saw an enemy on which to take a steady aim. This was strictly observed, and during the next hour's terrific fighting, many of the enemy were brought low." The extra target practice was now paying dividends. Expressions such as "there he goes" and "I brought my man" rang out along the line.[89]

"We were determined to whip them or die in the attempt," proclaimed Corporal Nathan Cooper of Company F. He continued, "It was a very hot day and I was in a hot place. My gun got so hot I could scarcely hold to it. The bullets was as thick as hale. I was very much deceived in myself for I was just as cool and composed as I ever was butchering hogs. The men were falling every second but I paid no attention to them. I could not help them."[90]

Major John T. Jones, who had taken command of the 26th following the death of Colonel Burgwyn and the severe wounding of Lieutenant Colonel Lane,

described the desperate fighting in his official report thus: "The fighting was terrible — our men advancing, the enemy stubbornly resisting, until the two lines were pouring volleys into each other at a distance not greater than 20 paces."[91]

The 151st stubbornly held its position, "but the fire of the enemy … was severe and destructive" and "officers and men fell thick and fast."[92] Company D was posted directly in front of the point of woods and suffered severely. A total of 12 men were killed or mortally wounded and 11 more were wounded out of the 33 engaged.[93] Included among the dead was Private Nathan Beisser, a 16-year-old who had lied about his age in order to enlist.[94] Another was Sergeant Abe Freet. Abe was killed instantly and thus fulfilled the pledge he had made seven months earlier to his father.[95] Neither body was ever identified and it is likely the remains are buried under unknown plots in the National Cemetery at Gettysburg.

Privates Benjamin Armstrong and John Amig were wounded simultaneously as they stood side by side. Armstrong was hit in the hand and the left breast, which damaged the upper portion of his lungs.[96] A bullet grazed the neck of Private Isaac Smith.[97] Corporal Michael Bratton also cheated death. A ball struck him on the left side of the face near the ear and exited on the opposite side just below the right ear. The wound caused total deafness in Bratton's right ear, affected the sight in his right eye, and fractured his jaw.[98] Michael was quite fortunate, however, for had the bullet entered a few inches higher, it would have undoubtedly taken his life.

The situation deteriorated rapidly for the 151st. Casting a glance toward the Hagerstown Road, Lieutenant Charles Potts realized "we could not hold our po-

Mathew Brady and assistant pointing to the location in Herbst's woods where General Reynolds was killed. The men are looking southeast from the swale near the Edward McPherson farm. The right flank of the 151st Pennsylvania's most advanced position on July 1st was located in the far right of this view. The cupola of the Lutheran Seminary is visible in the distance. Courtesy of MOLLUS Collection, USAMHI.

sition long, as the rebel reinforcements were being thrown on to our left flank, and our men gradually giving way. Occupying a position in the centre of the line, while the right and left were being driven back placed us in a very exposed position..."[99]

The extreme left of the regiment was held by Company B. As the balance of Biddle's line disintegrated soon after the arrival of the 151st, Private Sayre recalled, "Our regiment stood alone; no more men to the left of us, and just then our captain [Lafayette Westbrook] gave [the] command to deploy as skirmishers. That saved some of our lives, for we scattered."[100] Still, young Nelson Reaser's right knee was shattered by a bullet and 43-year-old Private Peter Cron was shot through the bowels.[101]

The left companies of the 151st tangled with the 11th North Carolina. The fighting here was also at extremely short range. The 11th's total casualties at Gettysburg were exceeded only by those of the 26th North Carolina within the Army of Northern Virginia. One company entered the battle of July 1 with three officers and 35 men and came out with one officer and four men! Colonel Leventhorpe was severely wounded and 20-year-old Major Egbert A. Ross was killed in action.[102]

Meanwhile, the right flank of the 151st's line was

also exposed to enemy fire. The officers of the Iron Brigade evidently regarded the full regiment of Pennsylvanians as a relief force, and, consequently, the brigade fell back to the hollow between the ridges and reformed before eventually retiring to Seminary Ridge. The realignment of Meredith's men was clearly visible from McFarland's vantage point and he recalled its officers "moving up and down the line acting with great coolness and bravery." M. C. Barnes of the 19th Indiana recalled, "...we fell back about halfway up the slope and made a new line, finally went back to the top of the hill, and a company came to our left, a Pennsylvania regiment I think (151st Pa. Vols.?), they gave the rebs, who were flanking us, a check ... then we fell back to the seminary...."[103]

"In battle all [of] our senses are quickened," wrote McFarland, "and moments seem to contain many times sixty seconds." For what must have seemed like an eternity, but was probably no more than fifteen to twenty minutes, the 151st stood alone as a human dam against the unrelenting wave of Confederate attackers. McFarland realized that while "we were holding the lines in our front in check handsomely, I could not close my eyes to the galling fire on both flanks, which was doing far more execution than that from the front ... the enemy's line on our

Major Egbert Ross, 11th North Carolina, was killed on July 1, 1863. Courtesy of Douglas Moore Collection, USAMHI.

left was slowly swinging around us, threatening to cut off our retreat."[104] The casualties in companies E, F, G, I, and K were proportionally higher than those of the remaining companies.[105]

Company F's William Blodget was extremely proud of his men as they held on tenaciously in the face of overwhelming odds. In a letter to his wife back in Sugar Grove, he poured out his emotions: "*Every man* stood right up to the work and fought like tigers — not a single exception. Our poor boys fell around me like ripe apples in a storm. God bless them! They were and *are* heroes every one.... Some were wounded and continued to fight till hit the second time."

Of the 52 men in the company who entered the fight, only 13 reported for duty afterward. Blodget knew of only four men from the 39 missing who came off the field unhurt. The lieutenant witnessed firsthand the deaths of several friends and comrades. Private Wilbur Kimball, also a Sugar Grove resident, was shot through the heart within three feet of him. Blodget spoke to Kimball, but there was no response, not even a groan. Sergeant Anil Frank fell with a severe

leg wound as he stood right by the lieutenant's side. A short distance away, a bullet crashed into the temple of 18-year-old Private Marcus Jaquay. William recalled that Sergeant James Lott, "the Judge," was "as cool as a cucumber" until he was struck through the right shoulder just below the joint, badly shattering the bone. Glancing to the rear, Blodget witnessed Private James Norris hobbling off the field. Considering the odds, he himself felt very fortunate to escape unscathed. "I am untouched, a fact I can hardly believe myself," wrote an amazed Blodget.[106]

First Lieutenant Aaron Seaman, commanding Company E, did not share Blodget's good fortune. He was killed instantly when a bullet struck him in the base of the skull. His younger brother, William, also fell dead on July 1st.[107] Command of the company devolved on Second Lieutenant Thomas Moyer, the stout young schoolteacher from Berks County. Moyer's men suffered heavily from the deadly enfilading fire. Private Lewis Rentschler was severely wounded in the left thigh near the hip, and an instant later, he received a second wound in the left wrist.[108]

Characteristically, Musician Michael Link was fighting in the ranks when a bullet smashed into his left eye, passed under the bridge of his nose, and emerged near the right eye. The blow knocked Link to the ground and he lost consciousness. Recovering a short time later, Michael made a horrifying discovery. One of his eyes had "run out" and the other was hanging down over his cheek. "The last thing I remember seeing," he said afterward, "was the rebel flag and I was shot just as I was leveling my gun to fire at the enemy." Isaac and John Hinkle, along with Albert Williams, carried Link back to a place of safety in an open field and placed a knapsack under his head. Despairingly, Michael asked Williams if he was badly wounded. Williams replied, "No," but as his comrades departed, Link overheard a remark that it was thought that he was "done for," and an expression of resignation spread over his face.[109]

Azariah and Nelson Body were heading toward the rear to receive treatment for their wounds when they noticed Lieutenant Moyer lying prostrate on the ground with a gaping chest wound. The two men immediately called him by name. The lieutenant was alive but only stared blankly ahead, seemingly unaware of their presence.[110]

Captain James Weida, Company K, valiantly held his men to the task until a round pierced his right side. The bullet broke a rib, injured his liver, and passed through the base of his right lung. Weida joined the ever-growing mass of wounded in the Seminary. His company's tally of 34 killed and wounded during the battle ranked second only to Company E's total of 36.[111]

Sergeant Alexander Seiders was among the victims. He would never again see his beloved wife or hold his dear little Annie.[112] Private Franklin Weaber, a former neighbor of Seiders, was shot in the left groin, the left shoulder, and through the thorax. Despite the severity of his wounds, the 24-year-old private clung tenaciously to life.[113] Young Franklin Wendling was shot through the groin and his prospects for recovery were bleak.[114]

First Lieutenant Jonathan Witman of Company G was one of the few line officers in the regiment who emerged from the battle unscathed, but he experienced a close call when a bullet zipped through the rim of his hat, barely missing his left eye.[115] Indeed, throughout the savage fighting, a few inches or seconds was often the difference between life and death.

Another illustrative example of good fortune was the experience of Private William S. Strause of Company H. The 20-year-old cabinet maker was in the act of firing his musket when a ball struck him square in the sternum. By luck, the projectile traveled across his chest wall instead of penetrating through the cavity. The ball came out next to his left nipple and then tore into his upper arm before coming out below the axilla. Miraculously, no bone or major vessel was damaged.[116]

Most, if not all, of the numerous Strauses serving in Companies G and H were at least distantly related to the same Pennsylvania German pioneer family. The five Strause boys of H Company were all first cousins and included two sets of brothers—all being grandsons of

Musician Michael Link was blinded for life as a result of the wounds he received on July 1, 1863. Courtesy of Dale E. Biever Collection, USAMHI.

Elmira Seiders, the young wife of Sergeant Alexander Seiders, Company K, killed in action on July 1, 1863. Courtesy of Sally Smith.

John Strauss, the founder of Strausstown in Berks County. When also including William W. Strause and Adam G. Strause of G Company, the latter a distant cousin, six out of these seven men would be wounded at Gettysburg, five of them on July 1st. One would later die of his wounds.[117] Solomon Strause, who had struggled during the long march to Gettysburg with a swollen leg, was struck by a musket ball in the upper left arm.[118]

Orderly Sergeant Heilig, who had recruited a number of the Strauses for military service, was also listed among the regiment's numerous wounded. The sergeant, who had grown somewhat disdainful of artillery fire, received a minié ball in the right shoulder from the gun of a Confederate infantryman.[119]

The sweating infantrymen on both sides toiled under the warm July sun as the battle raged on. The act of loading and firing a single-shot, muzzle-loading weapon required nine different steps. One of the steps involved pushing a cone-shaped lead bullet down the barrel with a ramrod. Each successive round became harder to load due to the buildup of soot inside the barrel. A skilled rifleman could fire three rounds per minute.[120]

One Confederate officer present on July 1st observed, "The day was a hot one, and the men had difficulty in ramming down their cartridges, so slick was the iron ram-rod in hands thoroughly wet with perspiration. All expedients were resorted to, but mainly jabbing the ram-rods against the ground and rocks."[121] Private Alfred Staudt of Company G was able to unleash five rounds from his .577 caliber Enfield before being hit in the left arm and left leg. Private Ammarell's bad luck continued when an enemy bullet shattered his gun stock. Gamely, Charles picked up the gun of a dead comrade and fought on.[122]

At around 3:30 P.M., McFarland began to realize the perilous situation his command was facing. He reported that "the Regiment held its ground and maintained the unequal contest until the forces both on my right and left had fallen back and gained considerable distance to the rear. Then finding that I was entirely unsupported, exposed to a rapidly increasing fire in front, and in danger of being surrounded, I ordered the regiment to fall back...." Like his fellow regimental commanders, McFarland acted on his own hook. "We held them till we was flanked on both sides [and] we were the last regt. that fell back," wrote Nathan Cooper.[123]

At this time, Private Sayre related an incident of much historical significance:

> Just as we were ordered to fall back there came up an old man wearing citizen's clothes. He said to me: "For God's sake, don't let them devils in the town tonight, and we will give you all you can eat and drink."
>
> My answer was: "Old man, we have to obey orders." I did not ask him his name, as I did not have the time ... I suppose it was John Burns.[124]

The historian of the 26th North Carolina described the final moments of the bloody encounter: "...a most formidable line yet remains, which seems determined to hold its position. Volleys of musketry are fast thinning out those left and only a skeleton line now remains. To add to the horrors of the scene, the battle smoke has settled down over the combatants making it almost as dark as night. With a cheer the men obey the command to advance, and rush on and upward to the summit of the hill, when the last line of the enemy gives way and sullenly retires...." Before falling back, Charles Ammarell took one last shot and had the satisfaction of seeing an enemy soldier fall, thus gaining a measure of revenge for his lost rations and shattered weapon.[125]

After nearly an hour of very hard fighting, Pettigrew's men were exhausted and did not actively pursue the retreating Federals across the open ground between the ridges. In fact, several of the regiments were completely out of ammunition. The tattered remnants of the 26th busied themselves in collecting ammunition from the enemy's dead.[126] Fortunately for the Southerners, help was on the way. Dorsey Pender's hard-fighting veterans, also known as the Light Division, were approaching McPherson's Ridge. These troops were among the best shock troops in Lee's army.

McFarland was justifiably proud of his regiment's performance in their first serious encounter with the enemy. "I know not how men could have fought more desperately, exhibited more coolness, or contested the field with more determined courage," he proclaimed.[127] The vast majority of the regiment's 337 casualties were incurred during this initial action. At great cost, the 151st had bought precious time for the withdrawal of Biddle's and Meredith's commands to the fallback position on Seminary Ridge.

The dead and seriously wounded of the 151st remained behind on the bloody slopes of McPherson's Ridge. Corporal John H. Schaffer and Wagoner William J. Wentz of Company H were among those who were unable to drag themselves to a field hospital. Both men expired on the field on July 3rd. Schaffer was buried on Edward McPherson's farm before being disinterred to Evergreen Cemetery in Gettysburg. Wentz was a mere 17 years old. Another youngster, Samuel Nailor, Jr. of Company D, was paralyzed with a severe hip wound. He, too, lay on the field until July 3rd. Nailor was taken to the Third Division Hospital for treatment, but he died on July 22nd. Solomon Brink of Company B was shot and killed while guarding his company's knapsacks. He had sacrificed his life while protecting the property of his comrades.[128]

When Major General Henry Heth rode through the position previously held by the 151st, he observed that the "dead marked his line of battle with the accuracy of a line at a dress parade."[129] An early 1900s Juniata County, Pennsylvania, newspaper article, "Valor of Pennsylvania Boys in the Civil War," contained the following dramatized account of this incident:

William S. Strause served in the 14th Pennsylvania Volunteers, a three-months regiment, prior to his enlistment in the 151st Pennsylvania. He narrowly escaped death at Gettysburg. Courtesy of Joe Smith, M.D.

...General Heth, of the Confederate Army, was riding with his staff across a part of the field. Suddenly he lifted his right hand. "Remove your hats, gentlemen," he said. "Let us salute this dress parade of the dead." There before them, in almost perfect order, where the tall grass had been trampled as smooth as a threshing floor and was deeply stained with blood, lay a long line of corpses in the Union blue. About almost all of them the Confederate officers saw the marks of extreme youth.... It was a scene over which a knightly heart might well have wept.[130]

Heth, a proud Virginian, also observed with great reverence the multitude of slain soldiers from the Old North State. "Pettigrew's brigade ... fought as well, and displayed as heroic courage as it was ever my fortune to witness on a battle-field. The number of its own gallant dead and wounded, as well as the large number of the enemy's dead and wounded left on the field over which it fought, attests better than any commendation of mine the gallant part it played on July 1."[131]

On July 9th, less than a week before his fatal wounding at Falling Waters, General J. Johnson Pettigrew wrote Governor Zebulon Vance:

> Knowing that you would be anxious to hear from your old regiment, the Twenty-sixth, I embrace an opportunity to write a hasty note. It covered itself with glory. It fell to the lot of the Twenty-sixth to charge one of the strongest positions possible. They drove three, and we have every reason to believe, five regiments out of the woods with a gallantry unsurpassed. Their loss has been heavy, very heavy....[132]

Captain J. J. Young, the regimental quartermaster of the 26th, wrote the Governor on the evening of July 4th to inform him of the regiment's frightening losses, "The heaviest conflict of the war has taken place in this vicinity.... We went in with over 800 men in the regiment. There came out of the first day's fight 216 all told, unhurt."

All of the field officers were hit. Colonel Burgwyn was shot through both lungs and died shortly afterward. As mentioned previously, Lieutenant Colonel Lane survived a serious wound to the neck, jaw, and mouth while Major Jones was struck by a shell fragment. Captain H. C. Albright was the only captain left in the regiment, and only four other line officers remained unhurt.[133]

The losses in Company F were unparalleled. This body of men from Caldwell County, commanded by Captain Romulus Tuttle, went into the first day's battle with three officers and 88 men. By the close of the day, 31 of its members were killed or mortally wounded and 60 were wounded! In this company were three sets of twin brothers. Five of the six lay dead on the field. Like the Strauses in the 151st Pennsylvania, the members of the Coffey family in Company F suffered terribly as five men with this surname were killed or mortally wounded while three others were wounded.[134]

The losses in the remaining companies were also appalling. In Company G, Sergeant William Kirkland, the former schoolteacher from Chatham County, was mortally wounded and died on July 2nd or 3rd. It is conceivable that he was shot down by a fellow teacher standing in the ranks of the 151st. His younger brother, George, was killed in action. The family's circle of tragedy was completed when the two remaining Kirkman boys died later as a direct result of the battle.[135]

It was nearly 4 o'clock in the afternoon of July 1st. The weary soldiers of the First Corps reformed on Seminary Ridge for a final, desperate stand. The regiments maintained roughly the same alignment in which they had fought earlier. For the next encounter, however, the hard-pressed infantrymen could count on the welcomed support of 21 artillery pieces, which were lined up nearly hub to hub from the Seminary north to the railroad cut.[136] The gradually sloping, open ground presented Wainwright's artillerists with "the fairest field and finest front for destruction on an advancing foe that could well be conceived."[137]

The line of the First Corps now stretched from the Hagerstown Road due north through the Seminary campus, across the Chambersburg Pike, and over Oak Ridge to the Mummasburg Road. Colonel William Gamble's dismounted troopers protected the left flank of the position from behind a stone wall in the Shultz Woods. The Eleventh Corps was still holding the ground north of town, but not for long.

Of the 28 First Corps regiments present on the battlefield, every one of them had already been engaged in the fight. A number of the units had been decimated and no fresh reserves were forthcoming.[138] General Doubleday despaired, "What was left of the First Corps after all this slaughter rallied on Seminary Ridge. Many of the men entered a semi-circular rail entrenchment which I had caused to be thrown up early in the day.... The enemy was now closing in on us from the south, west, and north, and still no orders came to retreat."[139]

The 151st Pennsylvania, along with Stone's Brigade just to the north, were the last Federal units to retire from McPherson's Ridge. Fighting in their first major engagement and on their native soil, these Pennsylvanians had literally "come to stay." The 26th North Carolina followed "closely but cautiously" until a well-directed salvo from the Union artillery on Seminary Ridge sent them scurrying back to the cover of Herbst's Woods. The remnants of the 151st regrouped behind the entrenchments in front of the Seminary, to the left of the 19th Indiana and to the right of the 142nd Pennsylvania.[140]

Shortly afterward, Captain Hollon Richardson of Meredith's staff rode up to McFarland with a regimental color and inquired, "Colonel, is this your flag?" McFarland continues the account:

> I remember distinctly the sensation that quickly passed through me at the thought of having lost my flag. Just then, however, a breeze wafting the flag revealed the inscription "142d' P. V." on its folds and relieved me.

"No," said I, "it is the flag of the 142d Penn. and belongs on my left, give it to a man there and let the men rally round it."

"I'll take it," said a member of the 142d. He did, and some of the regiment stood by it and fought under my orders.[141]

Apparently, the flag had been dropped to the ground during the 142nd's countercharge on McPherson's Ridge. A member of the 26th North Carolina eventually claimed the prize, but, owing to carelessness, he left it behind. Somehow, the colors, which had become a hot potato of sorts, ended up in Richardson's hands before being returned to the grateful owners.[142]

During the brief lull between the fighting, Captain William Gray of Company I also approached McFarland. His command cut to pieces, he asked gloomily, "Colonel, my men are nearly all killed and wounded, what shall I do?" "Fight with what is left," his friend responded simply. The captain would follow his commander's instructions to the letter and his men "covered themselves with glory."[143]

Meanwhile, as the First Corps prepared to give battle with what they had left, Confederate General A. P. Hill enjoyed the luxury of sending in fresh troops to carry the last Union stronghold west of the town. Throughout the morning and early afternoon, Pender's Division had followed within convenient supporting distance of Heth's men.[144]

Perhaps no body of men in the Southern army was better suited for this precarious mission than the Light Division. This unit was originally commanded by A. P. Hill, and it had served in Lee's army ever since the Seven Days' Battles near Richmond. This unit seemed to have a knack for heavy fighting and often played a critical role in the outcome of a battle. The division's march from Harpers Ferry, Virginia (now West Virginia), to Sharpsburg, Maryland, on September 17, 1862, is legendary. Hill's men arrived just in time to save the vulnerable Confederate flank below the town and then routed the Union attackers. At Gettysburg, the division was led by 29-year-old William Dorsey Pender, one of the rising stars in the Army of Northern Virginia's high command.[145]

Lieutenant James Fitz James Caldwell of the 1st South Carolina recalled that "The atmosphere had from the first a strong taint of battle to our experienced noses, and our suspicion was made conviction ... by the sound of artillery in front." As an engagement appeared imminent, Surgeon Welch of the 13th South Carolina "at once noticed in the countenance of all an expression of intense seriousness and solemnity which I have always perceived in the faces of men who are about to face death and the awful shock of battle."[146]

The frequent advances and long halts in the humid conditions greatly fatigued the troops, and the perspiration poured from their bodies. Rumors of both disaster and success spread through the ranks as wounded soldiers and prisoners flowed back from the front lines. The intensity of the artillery and musketry fire increased as Pender's men approached Herr Ridge.[147]

From the open heights, Welch and his comrades observed "the magnificent sight" of Heth's Division advancing in line of battle. As the veteran soldiers rested in the woods on the eastern face of the ridge, the fighting raged just to their front. "Many of the enemy's balls fell among us," wrote Caldwell, "but I recall no farther result than the startling of our nerves by their whistling past our ears and slapping the trees before us."[148]

Finally, at about 4 P.M., General Pender ordered his troops to advance "with instructions to pass General Heth's Division ... and charge the enemy's position" on Seminary Ridge. A line of battle was formed with three brigades. Colonel Abner Perrin's 1,600 South Carolinians would attack in the center directly toward the main Seminary building. General Alfred Scales' North Carolinians would advance on Perrin's left with the left of his line guiding along the Chambersburg Pike. Supporting Perrin on the right was another Tarheel brigade commanded by General James Lane. Pender held his remaining brigade in reserve.[149]

As Perrin's troops marched up the gentle slope of McPherson's Ridge, Caldwell found the field "thick with wounded hurrying to the rear, and the ground was grey with dead and disabled. There was a general cheer for South Carolina as we moved past them." "They had fought well," he continued, "but like most new soldiers, had been content to stand and fire instead of charging." Colonel Perrin pitied the "poor fellows" because they were so exhausted that they "could scarcely raise a cheer for us as we passed."[150]

Lieutenant Colonel Joseph Newton Brown of the 14th South Carolina described the panoramic view from the eastern crest of the ridge:

> In front and in view amid the grove of trees was the Seminary now changed from the halls of learning to a scene of bloodshed and carnage. Beyond was a beautiful town partly concealed from view by the shade trees surrounding the

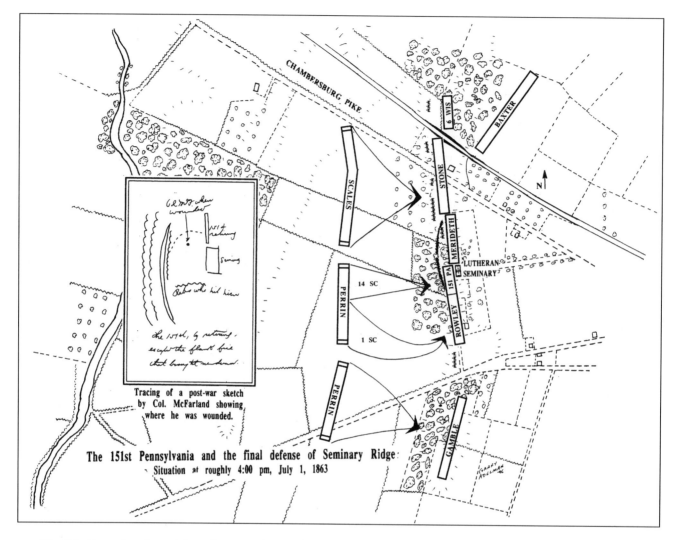

Tracing of a post-war sketch
by Col. McFarland showing
where he was wounded.

The 151st Pennsylvania and the final defense of Seminary Ridge:
Situation at roughly 4:00 pm, July 1, 1863

The 151st Pennsylvania and the 20th NYSM during the Pickett-Pettigrew-Trimble charge, July 3, 1863. Map by Garry Adelman.

Seminary ... Crests of ridges in successive ranges stretched southwardly with the richest valleys in between. Beyond and to the south of the town rising still higher was Cemetery Heights, so soon to become historic ground. It was but the glance of the eye for a moment and then grandeur was lost in the tumult of battle.[151]

Perrin availed himself of a small ravine in the open field to reform his line before the assault, where he instructed his regimental commanders "not to allow a gun to be fired at the enemy until they received orders to do so." The 14th was on the left, the 1st was next in line to the right, followed by the 12th, and the 13th on the extreme right of the brigade line. Perrin's men stepped off toward Seminary Ridge, now less than 500 yards distant, while preserving an alignment with Scales and Lane.[152]

"For a mile up and down the open fields in front, the splendid lines of the army of Northern Virginia swept down upon us," wrote Colonel Rufus R. Dawes of the 6th Wisconsin.[153] From his vantage point behind the lines, Surgeon Welch "could see from one end of the division to the other as it moved forward in line of battle. The scene was certainly grand, taking all the surroundings into consideration."[154]

The moment the Southerners popped into view, the vast array of Union artillery on Seminary Ridge "blazed with a solid sheet of flame, and the missiles of death that swept its western slopes no human beings could endure," observed Captain Robert K. Beecham of the 2nd Wisconsin. He continued, "After a few moments of the belching of the artillery, the blinding smoke shut out the sun and obstructed the view." When the smoke lifted, "Only the dead and dying remained on the bloody slopes of Seminary Ridge."[155]

Most of the "dead and dying" belonged to Scales' Brigade which advanced directly in the path of the deadly cannon. In a few moments the command was virtually destroyed. General Scales and every field officer in the brigade, except one, was wounded. The survivors of the brigade were pinned down several hundred yards from the Union line. Likewise, on the right flank, Lane was held in check by a small detachment of Gamble's cavalrymen.[156]

Therefore, when Perrin's men reached a dry creek bed between the ridges, they were entirely unsupported and thus exposed to a raking enfilade fire from both flanks without abatement in front. Lieutenant Caldwell recalled the desperate situation. "They had a perfectly clear, unobstructed fire upon us. Still we advanced, with regular steps and a well-dressed line. Shell and canister continued to rain upon us. A good many were killed and disabled, especially on the left of the brigade."[157]

As the South Carolinians approached a fence 200 yards from the grove, the brigade, in Perrin's words, received "the most destructive fire of musketry I have ever been exposed to." The line wavered under the murderous fire. Looking to his left front, he feared the 14th South Carolina was entirely destroyed. In Company K, 34 of the unit's 39 men fell from the first volley. Lieutenant Colonel Brown realized that the critical moment in the battle was now at hand. "To stop was destruction. To retreat was disaster. To go forward was orders." Instantly, Colonel Perrin dashed forward on horseback and "with his sword flashing in the evening sunshine and his voice above the din of battle, directed and led the charge."[158]

Lieutenant Caldwell vividly described the next few moments of the assault:

> Filled with admiration for such courage as defied the whole fire of the enemy, the brigade followed, with a shout that was itself half a victory. The Federal infantry opened on us a repetition of the fire that had already slaughtered a brigade.... Still there was no giving back on our part. The line passed on, many of the men throwing away their knapsacks and blankets to keep up. Struggling and panting, but cheering and closing up, they went, through the shell, through the Minie balls, heeding neither the dead who sank down by their sides, nor the fire from the front which killed them, until they threw themselves desperately on the line of Federals....[159]

The 14th South Carolina "pushed forward amid the minie balls sweeping the earth in front and flank. The dead, the wounded, the dying were falling at every step." Crouched behind the breastworks, directly in the path of the 14th, was George McFarland and the 151st Pennsylvania. Lieutenant Colonel Brown watched in horror as the line of breastworks in his front suddenly erupted into "a sheet of fire and smoke, sending its leaden missiles of death in the faces of men who had often, but never so terribly, met it before." From behind the earthworks, Nathan Cooper recalled "there was a gun blaze every minute by the side of my face."[160]

A Federal artillerist described the chaotic scene as follows:

> The whole line of battle from right to left was then one continuous blaze of fire. The space

Colonel Abner Perrin led the bold attack against the Union position on Seminary Ridge. Courtesy of MOLLUS Collection, USAMHI.

The 151st Pennsylvania's fierce encounter with the 14th South Carolina near the Lutheran Theological Seminary, from an engraving by Alfred R. Waud. Lt. Colonel McFarland is depicted on horseback near the splintered tree. Courtesy of Timothy H. Smith.

between the two ridges was completely filled with the thin blue smoke of the infantry, making it difficult to distinguish friend from foe, while the artillery from their higher position belched forth a tremendous fire of shot and shell, throwing their deadly missiles in rapid succession into the ranks of the enemy advancing on our direct front, covering themselves for the moment in dense clouds of white smoke.[161]

Peering through the thick smoke, Lieutenant James A. Gardner of Cooper's Battery watched as the combined fire of the infantry and artillery "staggered and checked Perrin and almost annihilated the left of his brigade." Even during the heat of battle, Gardner admired the bravery of a single color bearer who reached the rail barricade. This intrepid sole was the last surviving member of the 14th South Carolina's color guard. Apparently, Colonel Wainwright observed the same individual as he recalled "that a big fellow had planted the colours of his regiment on a pile of rails within fifty yards of the muzzles of Cooper's guns...."[162]

Hoisting the colors was an equally hazardous duty within the 151st Pennsylvania. Corporal Davis Meredith of Company D was struck in the right thigh at 4 o'clock as he gripped the standard in the face of

Perrin's assault. Apparently, Meredith volunteered for this precarious duty in place of Sergeant Adam Heilman. Earlier in the day, Heilman narrowly escaped death when he was hit in the right breast and forearm while yet another round passed through his kepi.[163]

Still, the advantage of position clearly rested with the Union defenders. The perilous situation confronting the attackers was clearly described by Lieutenant Colonel Brown:

The enemy in front of the Seminary were closely massed and strongly supported at the building as well as from the rear and on its flanks. The lines from this point curved slightly back on either side near to the crest of the ridge, and this made the Seminary the salient or point of attack, and to break the line and take the breastworks, here the Brigade threw itself against it with all its fury. Here the opposing forces grappled with each other, one determined to hold its position, and the other determined to take it. The close quarters at which they were now engaged made the losses on both sides heavy.[164]

McFarland distinctly remembered a tree in his front that "had been cut off— or rather splintered and shivered from the roots up at least ten feet just as the lightening splinters tough young trees. Limbs lay scattered all about, cut off by shot and shells." During the fierce exchange of musketry, McFarland's horse was shot from under him and his sword hilt hit, but he remained unhurt. Nathan Cooper, who had written disparagingly of his commander at the beginning of the campaign, felt he did a "first rate" job leading the regiment and proclaimed that "he was as brave as a lion." [165]

Colonel Perrin now realized that the Federal position could not be carried by a frontal assault. While the 14th gallantly stood its ground, he "directed the First Regiment, under Major McCreary, to oblique to the right, to avoid a breast-work of rails behind, where I discovered the enemy was posted, and then to change front to the left, and attack in his flank. This was done most effectually, under the lead of this gallant officer. The enemy were here completely routed." Meanwhile, Perrin ordered the 12th and 13th to change direction to the right and to charge Gamble's troopers posted behind the low stone wall to the south of the Seminary. "Too much credit cannot be awarded to Colonel Perrin and the splendid brigade under his command for the manner and spirit with which this attack was conducted," proclaimed Major Joseph Engelhard, Assistant Adjutant General of Pender's Division.[166]

Sergeant John A. Leach wrote that the right of the 1st South

The state colors of the 151st Pennsylvania. At least five different members of the regiment carried the flag during the fighting of July 1, 1863. Two of these colorbearers, Sergeant Adam Heilman of Company K, and Corporal Davis Meredith of Company D were severely wounded. Courtesy of Pennsylvania Capitol Preservation Committee.

Carolina had to contend with a post and board fence, "which was very difficult to knock down and was driving our regt. in to a solid mass." Consequently, the 1st was "not in good order" when it penetrated the grove, but the men soon commenced to fire effectively at the exposed Union troops.[167] Once again, the 121st Pennsylvania was the first regiment in line to be victimized.

The fighting was brief, but desperate. Colonel Biddle received a nasty scalp wound, but he soon returned to command the brigade. Colonel Gates' charger was shot five times and the colonel himself received a slight wound in the left shoulder. After a brief consultation, the two officers determined "[i]t was impossible to hold the position longer without sacrificing the brigade."

Gates reported that the 121st and 20th Militia "moved off in tolerable order, passing the Seminary and taking the railroad into Gettysburg." The historian of the 121st probably described the movement more accurately when he wrote, "[We] were compelled to 'get up and get' in the most approved fashion, hastening on, without semblance of order, through and beyond the town of Gettysburg, and halting on Cemetery Ridge."[168]

The next unit in line, the 142nd Pennsylvania, fought until "nearly surrounded by the superior number that swarmed from every direction." Captain Horatio Warren recalled:

Our men at this point used their muskets until, by fast firing, they became so hot they were compelled to drop them, when they would take the one nearest them on the ground, rendered useless because the owner of it was dead; and I will add here, there was no scarcity of muskets, as the dead and wounded were largely in the majority of our regiment. Here we were compelled to leave the lifeless bodies of many of our loved comrades. Notably conspicuous among that number was our brave, loyal and much beloved Col. R. P. Cummins and Acting Adjutant Tucker, for, as the enemy seemed to outnumber us four to one, it was apparent that unless we retreated down the hill and through the town we must all be captured. This we did in as orderly a manner as the circumstances would permit....[169]

After his initial wounding on McPherson's Ridge, Tucker was struck in the middle of the back during the retreat. He was then helped toward the Seminary, and when within fifty paces of this structure, another ball passed through his lower back and bowels. Finally, the brave young officer reached the shelter offered by the building.[170]

Shortly afterward, Private Adam Custer and three other captured men of Company D carried their husky colonel into the first floor of the Seminary by order of a Confederate officer. The dying Cummins remained defiant to the very end as he exhorted his listeners, "For God's sake men rally, we can whip them yet." The remnants of the 142nd, under the command of Lieutenant Colonel Alfred McCalmont, retreated to Cemetery Hill.[171]

Meanwhile, from his position near the Seminary, George McFarland distinctly remembered "seeing men passing to our left in single file at double-quick...." He reported, "[The] first attempt to flank us [was] greeted with such an accurate oblique fire that it failed. But in a second attempt, made soon after he gained our left flank...."[172] In a few moments, the flank attack swept through Biddle's regiments on the left of the Union line as previously described. In the following passage, McFarland described the ensuing action and a command decision which would alter his life forever:

> The regiments on my left had been driven back and the rebels were pressing down on my left. Seeing this I was about to order the regt. back when I noticed the rebel line in my front (14th S.C.) staggering under our galling fire. "Give them another volley, boys" said I. This was done with a will and followed by a hearty cheer as the boys saw the effect of it on the breaking line in front at the edge of the woods.[173]

Unfortunately for the 151st, the real danger to their position was the onrushing 1st South Carolina, which was barreling toward them from the left. It was with considerable pride that McFarland wrote of his command during the final moments of the sanguinary struggle:

> Up to this time the officers and men under my command had fought with the determined courage of veterans.... Not a man had left the ranks, even to carry a wounded comrade to the rear. But the regiment lost terribly and now did not number one fourth what it did two hours earlier in the day. The enemy on the contrary had increased and was now rapidly forming on my left. All support had left both flanks and were already to the rear. Hence I ordered the shattered remnants of as brave a regiment as ever entered the field, to fall back, and accompanied it a few paces.[174]

McFarland was only partly accurate in reporting the military situation on Seminary Ridge at roughly 4:15 P.M. Of course, he was correct in reporting that there were no troops on his left, but had he been able to see through the thick screen of smoke enveloping the field, he would have observed the Iron Brigade still in position on his immediate right. This example is highly illustrative of the limited field of vision available to most front-line soldiers amid the smoke and confusion of a Civil War battle.

In fact, as Perrin's South Carolinians rolled up the First Corps line near the Seminary, Confederate forces under Robert Rodes finally wrested Robinson's division from Oak Ridge. Then, as both extremities of the line began to crumble, Colonel Wainwright ordered his artillerymen to clear out. The situation was exacerbated by the simultaneous retreat of the Eleventh Corps, which was being routed from its position north of the town. General Doubleday painfully recalled, "Our tired troops had been fighting desperately, some of them for six hours. They were thoroughly exhausted, and General Howard had no re-enforcements to give me. It became necessary to retreat." In desperation, the First Corps commander threw in his headquarters guard to buy a few extra moments for "the few remaining troops, the ambulances, artillery, &c., to retreat in comparative safety."[175]

Following in the wake of his retreating command, McFarland halted about twenty paces from the northwest corner of the main Seminary building. Here, he stooped down and peered southward under the thick cloud of smoke to observe the movements of the enemy. Suddenly, a group of pursuing Confederates, who had nearly reached the south end of the edifice, unleashed a volley at the fleeing Union troops. McFarland was struck in the left ankle and in the lower right leg at nearly the same instant, and he fell to the ground upon his left side toward the enemy.[176]

Both Lieutenant Colonel Brown and Captain Gray witnessed McFarland's wounding.[177] Private Sayre, who may have briefly conversed with John Burns earlier, claimed to have been only three feet from his commander when he issued the order to "Retreat, men. Fall back in good order." An instant later, McFarland fell. Sayre related, "I stopped to help him, but he said: 'Never mind me, but run.' As I always obeyed orders, I did run so fast the rebs could not catch me."[178]

However, McFarland reported that the only man near him at the time was Private Lyman Wilson of Company F. Wilson scooped up his severely wounded commander and hastily made for the north end of the Seminary. The 30-year-old private nearly paid the ultimate price for his brave act as a minié ball clipped off a button from McFarland's coat sleeve while the colonel's arm was draped around his neck. Miraculously, the pair safely reached the sanctuary of the large brick building.

Shortly afterward, the Confederates took possession of the field hospital, and 173 wounded officers and men of the 151st Pennsylvania were taken prisoner.[179] These men faced an ordeal which would test the limits of their courage and endurance.

The remainder of the 151st under Captain William Boltz, the acting major, passed the north end of the building and escaped the devastating flank fire which felled McFarland. Adjutant Allen reported taking the colors from the field after having four color bearers shot down.[180]

The Confederates were right on their heels. Lieutenant Colonel Brown reported that his regiment passed on both sides of the Seminary and that the Union troops "were broken, pressed back, at first rapidly and disorderly, with our men close on them, still pouring into their ranks a deadly fire." Lieutenant Caldwell noted with satisfaction that now "the rebel turn came to kill."[181]

The converging Confederate forces funneled the throngs of fleeing First Corps soldiers into a narrow strip of ground running roughly from the unfinished railroad cut to a few hundred yards south of the

Captain Horatio Warren, 142nd Pennsylvania. Courtesy of Pennsylvania State Archives.

Chambersburg Pike. Numerous contemporary accounts referred to the area from Seminary Ridge to the edge of town as the "gauntlet."[182] It was basically every man for himself.

The 151st suffered additional casualties during the rapid flight from the Seminary through the town to Cemetery Hill. The nature and circumstances of their wounds seem to indicate that both Captain George Stone of Company A and Private Henry Patterson of D company were wounded at this time. A ball entered the sole of Stone's left boot and exited near his big toe. Patterson's wound was more serious. He was shot near the middle of the back of the head. The bullet traveled along his scalp toward the forehead laying open a three-inch section down to the skull bone. Patterson was taken prisoner sometime the next day.[183]

Some were simply too exhausted to escape their pursuers or lingered just a bit too long before retiring. "There is no dout a good many of our men back that have lost us," wrote Corporal Cooper afterward. He noted with amazement, "I should of been taken.

I was so used up with the heat I couldent run." Captain Gray fought to the very end and was among the last to fall back. His company was cut to pieces and the brave captain was taken captive. He now faced a long twenty-month ordeal in Southern prisons, which would nearly claim his life.[184] Captain Boltz was also seized by the Confederates. Sergeant Heilig wrote his wife, "It is no wonder since we had come nine miles that morning and were sent around the battlefield about five hours, and thus Boltz had very sore feet. It wondered me that he stood it so long."[185]

Yet another captured officer from the 151st, Lieutenant Charles Potts, related his experiences to the Historical Society of Schuylkill County over fifty years after the battle:

> …Retreating for the second time, we made directly for the town, thinking we would be able to make another stand, but, to our great surprise, the rebel cavalry had cut off our retreat, and we were well bottled up.
>
> It had never occurred to me that I might be taken prisoner, and when I found I was helpless in their hands, my feelings can't be described.
>
> Meeting a few wounded men of my company, I took them into the [Christ] Lutheran Church, then used as a hospital, and, rather than have the humiliation of delivering my sword to a rebel, I hid it in the building.
>
> After supplying the boys with water, I went to the front just in time to see the Chaplain of the 90th Penna. [Reverend Horatio Howell] killed, while standing in the doorway of the church. In company, with two others, we picked him up, but he had been instantly killed, the ball entering his mouth and taking an upward course through the brain. The rebels were picking up loose Yankees and sending them to a prison camp north of the town under command of Colonel [W. H.] French of the 14th West Virginia.
>
> He extended us a welcome, taking our names, rank, and regiment, but offering us no further accommodations than the cold ground for a bed and an empty haversack for supper.[186]

The Christ Lutheran Church located on the south side of Chambersburg Street was among the first public buildings in the town to be appropriated for hospital use. Most of its patients were from the Second Division, but as Potts noted, a few members of the 151st received treatment at this facility.[187]

The slaying of Reverend Howell was the most famous instance of a chaplain being killed in battle during the war. There are conflicting accounts as to whether the shooting was an accident or a deliberate act. A tablet erected on the spot states that Howell was "cruelly shot."[188]

Potts, Gray, and Boltz were destined for a trip to Richmond and long confinements in Southern prison pens. Lieutenant James Reber was also taken captive. Although unwounded and apparently healthy, he remained in Gettysburg and mustered out with his company at the end of the month.[189]

The First Corps soldiers who survived the gauntlet entered Gettysburg from the west. They soon faced a confusing labyrinth of streets, alleys, and town lots as their exultant pursuers fired at them or shouted orders of surrender. Unlike the Eleventh Corps, which had passed through Gettysburg on their way to the field, these unfortunate fugitives were not familiar with the town nor the location of Cemetery Hill. All told about 2,000 of Doubleday's men were taken captive by the Confederates during the late afternoon of July 1st.[190]

Colonel Wainwright provided us with a picture of the retreat, along with a damning account of General Rowley's conduct, in this passage from his journal:

> The streets of the town were full of the troops of the two corps. There was very little order amongst them, save that the Eleventh took one side of the street and we the other; brigades and divisions were pretty well mixed up. Still the men were not panic stricken; most of them were talking and joking. As I pushed through the crowd as rapidly as possible, I came across General Rowley…. He was very talkative, claiming that he was in command of the corps. I tried to reason with him, showing that Wadsworth and several others ranked him; but soon finding that he was drunk, I rode on to the top of the Cemetery Hill, the existence of which I now learned for the first time. Whether Rowley would have handled his division any better had he been sober I have my doubts….[191]

The experiences of Captain Cook of the 20th Militia were typical. He recalled that the air was filled with shouts of "First Corps this way, Eleventh Corps this way." In the confusion, however, Cook found himself alone among a mass of Eleventh Corps soldiers. Observing what he thought was an alley that would lead him to the proper street, he darted into it. Much to his chagrin, Cook discovered the passage "was obstructed with fences which enclosed a pig pen and as I clambered over these and waded through and stirred up the odors of the mud in the stye I did not form a very favorable opinion of the sanitation of the town." The crash of cannon balls through some nearby buildings quickly erased the issue of cleanliness from the captain's mind and he hastened on. At one point, he witnessed a Union soldier in the street ahead of him "throw up his hands with a shriek, spin round and fall heavily to the ground." Finally, Cook made the steep ascent up Baltimore Street to Cemetery Hill. On the reverse slope of the hill, Cook found what was left of his regiment and of the 151st Pennsylvania.[192]

Lieutenant Slagle of Doubleday's staff followed the crowd to the cemetery. "When we got there it was a pitiable sight — the tired, worn remnants of our fine regiments who had gone so proudly to the field in the morning were collecting together, and when all was told what a miserable remnant!"[193]

The flag of the 151st was hoisted in rear of the cemetery and there "collected the shattered fragments" of the regiment which then numbered 92, but during the night and the next morning, the number increased to 113 together with 8 remaining officers.[194] A member of Company K recalled that his unit went into the fight with over fifty men and came out with nine privates and one corporal and "that was just about the way the rest of the companies came out."[195]

At least four companies were without a captain or a lieutenant. Both companies H and I, for instance, entered the battle with a full complement of line officers, but had none remaining by the end of the day. In addition to the four captured officers taken from these units, lieutenants Albert Yost and Henry Merkle received wounds during the course of the fighting.[196] Yost's right forearm was punctured by a ball six inches above the wrist, for which he received treatment at the St. Francis Xavier Roman Catholic Church on West High Street. Merkle was struck in the right thigh just above the knee. He was treated by Assistant Surgeon Jonas Kauffman on July 4th at an unspecified location. Considering the location of their wounds, both officers were fortunate indeed to escape the surgeon's saw.[197]

Besides Lieutenant Colonel McFarland and a large number of line officers, the regiment also lost the services of Sergeant Major Arnold. McFarland wrote later that Arnold "distinguished himself at the battle ... where I commanded the regiment and had an opportunity to witness his actions. Here he was wounded in the leg and with myself fell into the hands of the enemy [at the Seminary]."[198]

Lieutenant Jacob F. Slagle, 149th Pennsylvania, judge advocate of the Third Division, and aide on General Doubleday's staff. Courtesy of MOLLUS Collection, The Civil War Library and Museum, Philadelphia, Pennsylvania.

A considerable number of unwounded or slightly wounded men from the 151st might also have been trapped behind enemy lines. One particularly interesting case involved Corporal Leander Wilcox of Company F, who was slightly wounded and who became winded during the withdrawal as enemy soldiers closed in on him. He sought refuge in the open door of the back porch at present day 155 South Washington Street. The red brick house was occupied by Catherine Mary White Foster and her elderly parents during the battle. The Fosters observed much of the day's action from the western balcony of their home, despite repeated requests from Union officers, including General Reynolds, to retire to the cellar. This advice proved sound as an artillery shell demolished the roof and ceiling above the balcony only moments after the family descended to the front of the house.

The Fosters also witnessed the pell-mell retreat of Union artillery, cavalry, and infantry down Washington Street past their home. After enemy bullets grazed their clothing, the family finally moved off to the security offered by the basement. On the way down Catherine spied Wilcox crouched in the doorway. The corporal discreetly invited himself to the underground hideaway. Catherine peered out the cellar window and saw victorious enemy officers whom she described as "...hatless, with long hair standing on edge." She also remembered "furious yelling and firing, curdling one's blood as the situation flushed upon us."

In the brief interval, Wilcox hastily concealed his gun in a stovepipe, buried his knapsack under the ashes of a fireplace, and hid himself under a potato bin. As Catherine followed Leander's instructions to cover him with some nearby kindling, the outer door suddenly burst open. A rebel captain and two privates soon appeared from above and commenced to explore the cellar for hidden Yankee soldiers. When these men came dangerously close to her new friend, not yet fully concealed, Catherine reacted quickly and sprang between the parties. She distracted the searchers by displaying nervous anxiety for the welfare of her aged parents. The captain bought the act and compassionately ordered his men upstairs. Catherine immediately finished the task she had started earlier, and although Confederate soldiers searched the premises repeatedly over the next couple of days, Wilcox escaped detection.

Leander returned to his home in Titusville, Crawford County, at the end of July and was married the following year. He spent the remaining thirty years of his life in the community, where he apparently worked as a lawyer.[199]

Another soldier from the regiment may have been hidden from the Confederates for at least a brief time. Oral tradition states that Private William S. Strause avoided capture when his brother, Joel, a corporal in Company H, concealed him under a pile of leaves until he was retrieved at some point during or after the battle. The exact location and other details of this alleged incident are unknown. William's wounding in the chest and left arm was detailed earlier. It is known that Strause received treatment at a field hospital two miles from Gettysburg.[200]

Meanwhile, the once peaceful slopes of Seminary Ridge were covered with the wounded and dying of both sides. Lieutenant Colonel Brown never forgot the dreadful scene.

> The nature of the ground was such and the contest so brief that the wounded could not be moved, and were wounded twice, thrice and as many as four times, after being first stricken down. Large numbers died of their wounds.... It was the only battlefield in which all avenues of escape for our wounded were closed.... The ground was swept at every point by the deadly minnie balls ... not a foot of ground presented a place of safety. The Union troops fired low, and their balls swept close to the ground on the dishlike field in their front. The terrible strife was over in a few minutes—fifteen, say twenty at most. Men never fell faster in this brigade....

Nearly 600 men from Perrin's Brigade alone fell in this short span of time.

Brown's 14th South Carolina was the largest regiment in the brigade, and it lost over 200 who were killed and wounded of 428 carried into action. No prisoners were lost to the Federals. Of 28 officers who went into the fight, all were killed or wounded but seven. Captain James Boatwright's Company B entered the battle with 54 men; only 8 reported for duty afterward.[201]

Among the many casualties suffered by the 14th was Lieutenant Sidney Carter of Company A. The former teacher received a mortal chest wound during the fiery encounter and died on July 8th as a prisoner of war. Less than three

The Foster home at present day 155 South Washington Street. Corporal Leander Wilcox eluded his Confederate pursuers by hiding in a potato bin in the basement of this structure. Courtesy of the author.

weeks earlier, Sidney had been awestruck by nature's fury atop the Blue Ridge and had wished for good health throughout the remainder of the invasion "so I won't have to leave ranks for the Yankees to get me over there." A descendant described him as "a serious, methodical, careful man, honest, religious, and not given to excess of any sort." This description might easily be applied to any number of men in the ranks of the 151st. Carter left behind a young wife and three children.[202]

The defenders also suffered greatly and "the ground strewn with their dead and wounded well attested the accuracy of the deadly aim" of the veteran South Carolinians. Two decades later, the western sides of the trees in the Seminary grove were still "thickly covered with scars, from the ground to the height of a man...." Brown recalled that "[i]t was no time for a thousand hair-breadth escapes with nobody hurt. It was not the clipping off of clothing, but the bodies of men that were struck."[203]

The body of Anson Miller, a 40-year-old private serving in Captain Gray's Company I, was perforated four times by enemy bullets. He was left behind as his comrades retreated through the town. A short time later, a group of opportunistic Confederates robbed the helpless Miller of his clothing, blankets, food, and personal items. Fortunately, the severely wounded private was also a Freemason. Sectional strife could not sever the bonds of this ancient fraternal organization as the following extract proves:

> In his extremity and distress, he [Miller] used those words which a Master Mason hears and heeds, even amid the fury and din of battle. Immediately there stepped out from among the Rebel soldiers one who remembered his duty to a needed brother. He was a Tennessean — Menturn by name. He declared that he had never robbed a wounded foe, and that he would not permit it to be done by others.

Not only did the Confederate Mason secure the wounded Pennsylvanian's property, but he also returned a few hours later with food and water for his fraternal brother. Miller was eventually removed to the Seminary Hospital where he was treated by another Mason, Dr. Andrew J. Ward of the 2nd Wisconsin, the surgeon in charge. From Ward and several other Masonic brothers, Anson "received the tender care and nursing suited to his condition...."[204]

Another touching incident involved Lieutenant William Brunson of the 14th South Carolina. After being struck in both legs, Brunson fell onto a wounded Union captain who was lying prostrate on the blood-soaked ground. The lieutenant pulled himself off his new acquaintance and inquired about the severity of his wound. He then offered the Federal officer a drink of whiskey. The captain eagerly accepted the flask, but quickly returned it upon discovering that only one drink of the intoxicant remained. He insisted that his adversary should take the final drink. Both men recovered from their wounds.[205]

These brief vignettes help to restore one's faith in mankind. It is refreshing to discover that even in the midst of war and its resulting carnage, a number of individuals maintained their dignity and their compassion for their fellow man, no matter what the color of his uniform.

Shortly after these touching incidents took place, General Robert E. Lee himself rode forward to the crest of Seminary Ridge to survey the situation with General A. P. Hill, the commander of his Third Corps.[206] As one of the many Union soldiers taken prisoner near the close of the day, 17-year-old Charles Ammarell of the 151st got a close-up view of the famous Confederate chieftain. He later wrote of this unforgettable experience:

> We were lying in a young orchard ... when suddenly a troop of soldiers in their nut-brown uniforms and faces begrimed with dust and perspiration, came riding along posthaste, for the purpose of throwing a guard around us. Presently, a number of officers rode up. Among them was Gen. Lee. I was able to recognize Lee through having seen pictures and engravings of him. He dismounted and walked around leisurely, eyeing the prisoners. I shall never forget the expression of his face — stern and well-set. There was not a smile to relieve it. He wore a slouch hat and his iron-gray whiskers were closely trimmed. His uniform was very plain. There was no gold lace or fancy trimming. I said to one of the Confederate guards "that must be General Lee." "Yes," he replied, "that is our commander."[207]

There were good reasons for Robert E. Lee's dour appearance. Although the wily chief and his lieutenant witnessed the thrilling sight of thousands of Federals in full flight through the town up to Cemetery Hill, Lee also observed troops there which had not yet been engaged, and being a professional soldier and engineer, he quickly ascertained the great strength of this new position. Although four hours of daylight remained, the Confederates were simply too exhausted and disorganized to mount a coordinated assault against the last Union stronghold.[208]

Meanwhile, one mile to the southeast, the battered survivors of the First and Eleventh Corps expected a full scale attack at any moment. Their fears and apprehensions were allayed by the reassuring sight of Major General Winfield Scott Hancock, the commander of the Second Army Corps. One soldier never forgot "the inspiration of his commanding, controlling presence, nor the fresh courage he imparted...." When news of Reynolds' death reached his Taneytown headquarters, Meade had ordered Hancock to Gettysburg to temporarily direct affairs and to evaluate the military situation. He arrived just in time to meet the weary soldiers from the two commands as they reached Cemetery Hill.

Together with Howard, Wainwright, Buford, and General G. K. Warren, the army's chief engineer, Hancock prepared the survivors of the two corps for further action and awaited the timely arrival of reinforcements. At around 5:30 P.M., Hancock felt confident about the defensibility of the new position. By nightfall, General Henry Slocum, who was now the senior officer on the scene, had over 27,000 officers and men along with considerable artillery support to repulse any attack. The emergency passed.[209]

In his classic study of the battle, historian Edwin B. Coddington asserted that "The Army of the Potomac had again displayed its resiliency under extreme adversity. The men of the First and Eleventh Corps and Buford's cavalry, though defeated, were able to regroup and turn once more to face the foe. They had forced the enemy to pay such a heavy price for his victory that he hesitated until it was too late to renew the contest." Thus, although the Army of Northern Virginia won an undeniable tactical victory on the first day of fighting, the strategic advantage clearly rested with the Federals.[210]

The stubborn and skillful opposition of the First Corps throughout the day paid huge dividends for the Army of the Potomac and the Union cause. The Confederates of Heth's, Pender's, and Rodes' divisions who opposed the First Corps suffered substantial losses. Even more importantly, these stalwart soldiers, fighting under the direction of Reynolds and Doubleday, had helped buy the time necessary for Meade to secure an impregnable defensive position at Gettysburg.[211]

Even the Confederates acknowledged the brave conduct of their Northern counterparts. Lieutenant Colonel Brown wrote that "It was no ordinary soldier we had met. The prisoners captured were more intelligent than on other fields. They were mostly Pennsylvanians fighting for everything they held dear." While a prisoner in the Seminary, George McFarland recalled that a number of enemy soldiers confessed respect for the "determined courage" of his men. And no less an authority than General Edward Porter Alexander declared that "the fighting done by the Federal brigades was of the best type."[212]

However, as Lieutenant Blodget painfully realized, these accolades came with a steep price tag: "Our brigade went into the fight 1,300 strong and now has 360. The whole corps suffered almost in proportion. The slaughter of our regiment was almost madness."[213]

Blodget was not exaggerating. The losses of the First Corps in just one day of fighting far exceeded those of any other Union army corps engaged in the battle. Rowley's Division suffered the second highest numerical loss of any federal division. Biddle's Brigade had the second greatest percentage loss in the Union army. Among the nearly 350 Union regiments in the Army of the Potomac present at Gettysburg, the 151st ranked second in greatest total loss, ninth in percentage loss, fifth in number of men killed, and first in number of wounded.[214]

One First Corps veteran wrote the following to conclude his reminiscence of Gettysburg: "The first day's battle of Gettysburg has never been given proper appreciation by students of the war, or by the public generally.... It was cold-blooded, grim determination, give and take, until both commands were nearly annihilated. It was the most desperate fighting of the entire war."[215] Former Union soldier and historian, William F. Fox, added that "The First Corps fought ... with no other protection than the flannel blouses that covered their stout hearts" and further asserted that "to the stubborn resistance of the First Corps of the Army of the Potomac, on the first day of July, 1863, the ultimate defeat of Lee's invading army is in a very large measure to be attributed."[216]

Major Chamberlin of the 150th Pennsylvania agreed wholeheartedly. In his regimental history, he attributed much of the First Corps' accomplishments to the brave and skillful leadership of Abner Doubleday:

In many published accounts of the battle, scanty justice has been accorded to General Doubleday for the part he took in the engagement of the first day. Coming upon the field

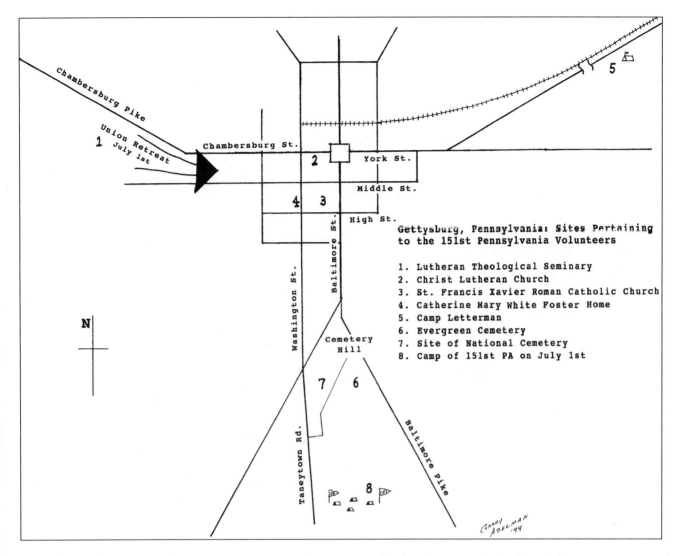

Chambersburg Pike

Union Retreat
July 1st

1

Chambersburg St.

York St.

Middle St.

2

4   3

High St.

Gettysburg, Pennsylvania: Sites Pertaining to the 151st Pennsylvania Volunteers

1. Lutheran Theological Seminary
2. Christ Lutheran Church
3. St. Francis Xavier Roman Catholic Church
4. Catherine Mary White Foster Home
5. Camp Letterman
6. Evergreen Cemetery
7. Site of National Cemetery
8. Camp of 151st PA on July 1st

Washington St.

Baltimore St.

Cemetery Hill

N

Taneytown Rd.

7   6

Baltimore Pike

8

5

GARRY ADELMAN '99

Gettysburg, Pennsylvania: Sites Pertaining to the 151st Pennsylvania Volunteers. Map by Garry Adelman.

without knowledge of what had already taken place, upon him, by the death of the lamented Reynolds, suddenly devolved the assignment and direction of the troops; and but for his prompt and able dispositions, and the magnificent stand made by every portion of his line, retarding the enemy's advance until the afternoon was nearly spent, Cemetery Ridge might not have been the scene of the Union defence on the following days, and Gettysburg might not have witnessed the victory which proved to be the turning-point of the war.[217]

Few survivors of the bitter fighting contemplated their role in history during the evening of July 1st. General Doubleday himself recorded this observation in his study of the battle "We lay on our arms that night among the tombs of the Cemetery, so suggestive of the shortness of life and the nothingness of fame; but the men were little disposed to moralizing on themes like these and were much too exhausted to think of anything but much needed rest."[218]

The "relics" of the 151st Pennsylvania and the 20th New York Militia bivouacked in a small field near the cemetery in reserve of the main line. The camp was located just east of the Taneytown Road. A short distance west of this road stood the small home of Lydia Leister, destined for fame as Meade's headquarters.[219] From this point until the end of the battle, the experiences and contributions of these two units would be nearly identical.

Captain Cook wrote the following account of the late afternoon and evening of July 1:

Except for an occasional cannon shot we were undisturbed for the rest of the day and no

Officers of the 20th New York State Militia. Captain John D. S. Cook is seated in the second chair from the left, Lt. Colonel Jacob B. Hardenburgh is seated fourth from the left, Lieutenant Edward Ross is standing second from the left, and Surgeon Robert Loughran is standing in the center of the group with the full beard. Courtesy of MOLLUS Collection, USAMHI.

dence saved us from this misfortune and by morning most of our army was in position and ready for the foe.[220]

Many officers and men in the two commands were grief-stricken over the loss of dear friends, family members, neighbors, and comrades. A private in the 20th recalled that Colonel Gates "inquired by name for many men whom we did not even dream that he knew and as the death of one and another was made known to him, tears ran down his cheeks."[221]

"This is indeed the saddest moment of my life," wrote William Blodget early on the morning of July 2nd after surveying his shattered command. After recounting the general military situation in a letter to his wife, his thoughts reverted to his beloved soldiers — "But O, my own boys — the tears will start this A.M."[222] Unknown to Blodget and his comrades, another test of courage and patriotism awaited them.

nightfall was ever more welcome than that which came to us, wearied, dispirited, mourning our lost comrades, and filled with apprehension lest the enemy so far successful, should attack and overwhelm us before our army could be got together to resist. Provi-

Chapter 4

July 2nd & 3rd, 1863

"Our regiment was in again in the very hottest of it."

Shortly before midnight on July 1st, a tall, thin, middle-aged gentleman spurred up to the Evergreen Cemetery gatehouse in company with a small entourage of officers. The central figure of the group did not present a striking appearance. He was thin-faced with a balding head, grizzled beard, bespectacled blue eyes, a hawkish nose, and a broad, high forehead. The new arrival more closely resembled a country schoolteacher than a military officer. It was George Gordon Meade, the commanding general of the Army of the Potomac.[1]

The general's route to Cemetery Hill led him directly past the sleeping soldiers of the 20th New York State Militia and the 151st Pennsylvania. The weary men of these commands were much too exhausted to notice or to be concerned about this distinguished visitor.

Earlier, Meade had wired Washington of his decision to concentrate the army and fight at Gettysburg. Understandably, the commander was relieved to learn that his assembled generals believed the position to be a strong one.[2]

In the pre-dawn darkness, Meade set off with a trio of officers to get a first-hand look at the surrounding terrain. The group rode south along Cemetery Ridge, a low swell of mostly open land which rose on average only twenty-five feet above its surroundings. A two-mile ride brought the officers to within sight of Little Round Top, a dominating 170-foot eminence, which would become the key to the southern portion of the Federal position. The western slope of this height was cleared of timber before the battle. Just to the south was Big Round Top, the highest point in the entire area. This small mountain was heavily wooded with steep slopes making it almost inaccessible for artillery.

If the party had chosen to ride to the summit of Little Round Top, they might have gazed northwestward across a large expanse of rural countryside dotted with farmhouses, large barns, ripening grainfields, orchards, and fencelines, occasionally broken by small patches of woods. In the distance, the Emmitsburg Road could be seen slanting through the area from the southwest. Instead, the riders retraced their steps and rode north to Cemetery Hill. This commanding height was bisected by the Taneytown Road from the south and the Baltimore Pike from the southeast. Meade last examined the right of the Union line on Culp's Hill, a rugged, wooded elevation located one-half mile southeast of Cemetery Hill.[3]

By noon of July 2 the entire Army of the Potomac, with the exception of General John Sedgwick's massive Sixth Corps, had reached the field. The famous fishhook-shaped Union line was now forming. From left to right, the army was deployed as follows: Sickles' Third Corps, on the southern half of Cemetery Ridge with its left resting near Little Round Top; Hancock's Second Corps, extended the line north along Cemetery Ridge to Cemetery Hill; Howard's Eleventh Corps, curved around the high slope of Cemetery Hill with the Second and Third Divisions of the First Corps at the base of the hill in reserve; Wadsworth's First Division held the summit of Culp's Hill; and Slocum's Twelfth Corps extended the line southeast from here and formed the tip of the hook. George Sykes' Fifth Corps rested in reserve near Power's Hill just west of the Baltimore Pike.[4]

The remainder of Lee's army, minus George Pickett's Division, had also arrived. The Confederate battle lines conformed to the Federal position with Ewell's Corps on the left, Hill's Corps in the center, and James Longstreet's First Corps on the right. Lee set up his headquarters at the Widow Mary Thompson's small stone house on Seminary Ridge, which was located a short distance north of the Lutheran Seminary. This ridge would be the staging area for

Confederate attacks throughout the remainder of the battle.

The opposing lines were located roughly one mile apart. The concave shape of Lee's line placed him at a great disadvantage as compared to Meade's convex formation. The Northern commander could easily shift his troops to threatened sectors in a minimal amount of time. Conversely, Lee's reinforcements and couriers were forced to travel on the circumference of a large arc.[5] At one point during the morning of July 2nd, Meade considered launching an offensive of his own from Culp's Hill, but then decided to assume a defensive posture instead.[6]

Covered with morning dew and still numbed by the shock of battle, the remnants of the 151st Pennsylvania awoke to a peaceful scene. The first shimmering rays of sunlight rose above the peak of Culp's Hill behind them and illuminated smoldering campfires, moisture laden trees and shrubs, and herds of fat cattle grazing nearby on the Catherine Guinn farm. The familiar whistle of songbirds pierced the calm morning air.[7] These tranquil sights and sounds were a welcome relief from the hellish scenes of the previous day.

As the soldiers attended to their usual morning duties, they noticed a stranger in their midst, for during the night Meade had assigned command of the First Corps to Major General John Newton, a division commander from the Sixth Corps, in place of Doubleday. The 40-year-old West Pointer was described as a "well-sized, shapely, muscular, well dressed man, with brown hair, with a very ruddy, clean-shaved, full face, blue eyes, [and] blunt, round features...." Newton, an experienced officer, was not regarded as either daring or brilliant. He performed creditably on the Peninsula and at South Mountain during the Antietam campaign. His most distinguished moment came at the Battle of Chancellorsville when his division successfully stormed Mayre's Heights.

Doubleday was justifiably rankled by Meade's hasty decision, but he dutifully obeyed the order and resumed command of the Third Division. The First Corps soldiers, who had witnessed Doubleday's courageous leadership and skillful dispositions on July 1st, were also angered by the change. Almost universally they thought Doubleday had earned the right to command the corps. Captain Cook, for example, always thought that Meade had acted "rather ungraciously" by replacing Doubleday. [8]

The fact that his division was substantially enlarged by fresh troops on the morning of the 2nd probably did little to appease the offended general. These reinforcements consisted of the nearly 2,000 men of Brigadier General George J. Stannard's Vermont Brigade. The Vermonters, fresh from the defenses of Washington, were derisively dubbed the "Paper Collar Brigade" by the hardened veterans of the Army of the Potomac because of their fresh, dapper appearance. Like the 151st, these were nine-month troops nearing the end of their enlistment period.[9]

It is likely that some of the Vermont officers inquired about the missing lieutenant colonel of the 151st. McFarland had spent a pleasant evening with a number of these men near Fairfax Station, Virginia, back in early February while en route to Washington, D.C.[10] The Vermonters must have been aghast by the thinned ranks of the regiments surrounding them. In fact, the Vermont brigade, now officially the Third Brigade of the Third Division, mustered over twice as many men as the First and Second Brigades combined.[11]

Captain Walter Owens took command of the 151st following McFarland's wounding. The former schoolteacher was assisted by Captain Westbrook, the Pike County politician.[12] In reality, the regiment now only comprised enough men to form a large company. The survivors spent a lazy day lounging about in camp. Most were quiet and reserved. Some, like Lieutenant Blodget, penned letters home in an attempt to articulate the momentous events of the previous day.

One of the writers was Corporal Nathan Cooper, who composed a letter to his dear wife, Mary. Nathan listed seven men from the town of Sugar Grove who had been either killed or wounded. After relating specific incidents of the previous day's fighting, he wrote:

> [T]he Army of the Potomac is all here now ... the rebs are pretty shy today. I think we can hold them flat now. I hope to God there wont one of them get out of Pa. I think our men must of been deceived in the strength of the rebs or they would of waited till the other corps came. It was awful to put us in the way they did. I don't see how eny of us escaped.... Mary, you have been praying ever since I left that I might be shielded from danger on the battlefield. Your prayers have surely been answered. I didn't receive a scratch. It don't seem possible for a man to be in such a shower of bullets so long and not get hit. I felt as if I had been protected by some kind hand and my life

spared for some purpose. We lost our knapsacks and everything. We haven't a thing, only
what we have on. Tents, ponchoes and all is
gone. The other soldiers that came up gave us
some paper or we couldn't of written.[13]

July 2nd developed into a typical summer day in
Southern Pennsylvania. Afternoon temperatures in
the shade climbed into the 80s and only a faint breeze
stirred.[14] Fresh rounds of ammunition were distributed to the troops, a sure indication that the fighting
would be renewed.[15] After a spirited skirmish between the opposing sharpshooters within the town
limits, an uncharacteristic silence settled over the
field. Occasionally, a stray shell exploded overhead
and broke the stillness. A bullet from a spherical case
shot struck between Captain John Cook and another
member of his company. "It was a close call," wrote
Cook, "but we hardly minded it. We had become
hardened."[16]

While the Third Division rested quietly near
Cemetery Hill, events were transpiring elsewhere
which would alter the course of the battle. Major
General Daniel Sickles was dissatisfied with his assigned position on the southern extremity of Cemetery Ridge. In the early afternoon, the impetuous
politician acted on his own and advanced his line
nearly half a mile west to take advantage of higher
open ground near Joseph Sherfy's peach orchard. His
rash movement isolated his corps from the remainder of the army and jeopardized the security of the
entire line.

At about 4 P.M., soon after Sickles took up his
new position, the Confederates attacked. The assault
was spearheaded by Longstreet's fresh corps against
the Federal left flank. The attack was to precede en
echelon northward to include Hill's Corps, which
would assault the Union center. Meanwhile, Lee ordered Ewell to make a demonstration against the
Union right with the discretion of launching a full-
scale attack if a favorable opportunity presented itself.[17]

The infantry attack was preceded by an intense
cannonade at both ends of the Union line. The gunners of Ewell's Corps blazed away at the Federal position on Cemetery Hill from Benner's Hill 4,000 feet
to the northeast. The artillerists of the First and
Eleventh Corps responded, and a heavy duel raged for
several hours. A number of veteran soldiers remembered it as one of the most severe artillery exchanges
they ever witnessed. Doubleday's division was shifted

a short distance south to a more sheltered location.
Lieutenant Slagle recalled, "It was terrible, but the
majority of the shots were too high." Eventually, the
Union artillerymen prevailed and the wrecked Southern batteries withdrew.[18]

The Union officers on Cemetery Hill watched
tensely for signs of an infantry assault. But for now,
the serious action was occurring to the south as
Longstreet's veterans slammed into the Union left.
Meade sent the entire Fifth Corps and a division from
the Second Corps to reinforce Sickles' hard pressed
line. The Union chief enjoyed this luxury because the
Sixth Corps had reached the field following a grueling 32-mile forced march from Manchester, Maryland.[19]

After furious fighting, the Confederates broke
through and the advanced Union line collapsed. The
jubilant Southerners pursued the retiring Federals to
the base of Little Round Top, where Union reinforcements checked their advance. Although the attacks by Hill's brigades farther north were ill-timed
and poorly coordinated, a brigade of Georgians under
Ambrose Wright gained a temporary lodgment on
the crest of Cemetery Ridge before being driven back
with heavy losses.[20]

Meade and Hancock seemed to be everywhere
at once, plugging gaps and sending fresh troops to
threatened sectors with an uncanny timeliness. At
roughly 5 P.M. as the Confederate attacks spread to the
center of the Union line, Meade ordered Newton to
rush forward Doubleday's and Robinson's divisions
from the reverse slope of Cemetery Hill to the threatened Second Corps front on Cemetery Ridge. Newton met Meade near the ridge crest and offered him
a drink from his flask. Suddenly, a shell exploded
nearby, covering both men with dirt.[21]

Rowley's brigade crossed the Taneytown Road
and began marching parallel to the narrow rutted
highway. The line of march led directly past Meade's
headquarters, which stood just west of the road. As
the column neared the Peter Frey farm after traveling south about one half mile, a stream of fugitive
troops passed through the ranks. Somehow in the ensuing confusion, the 151st and 20th Militia became
separated from the remainder of the brigade. The two
regiments marched by a right file and halted on the
crest of Cemetery Ridge. The battle-scarred infantrymen were probably greatly relieved when the Rebels
were seen retiring across the open fields below toward Seminary Ridge. The regiments were in the act
of turning back to search for Rowley when Brigadier

General John Gibbon halted the two small units and ordered them to remain on the front line in support of his division's left flank. Neither Owens nor Gates was about to question the ice cold Gibbon and they promptly obeyed.[22]

Receiving no further orders and finding himself the senior officer present, Colonel Gates assumed command of the two regiments, which he grandiloquently termed a "demi-brigade." The 151st filed into line on the immediate left of the 20th. The right of the New Yorkers eventually linked up with the left of Harrow's brigade.[23] The colonel immediately surveyed his new surroundings:

> [We] were halted on the last and lowest of the ridges running nearly north and south between the Taneytown and Emmitsburg roads. Some 300 yards on our right was a bluff, on which were standing a few trees and a battery. The trees on the westerly face of the bluff had been felled to clear a range for the guns. A rail fence stood at the foot of the bluff and extended along the ridge southerly. A little in advance and to our left was a small grove. The ground in front descended gradually to a little valley, wet and marshy, and then by a corresponding

ascent reached the Emmitsburg road and the position occupied by the enemy [on Seminary Ridge].[24]

On the "bluff" mentioned by Gates stood a nondescript clump of small scrub oaks. The nearby saplings and undergrowth were cut down to clear a field of fire for the artillery. This rough, rock-strewn area was dubbed "the slashing." As the rural soldiers gazed westward across a largely treeless expanse of green pastures and ripening yellow wheatfields, their eyes were surely drawn to the great barns, farmhouses, and outbuildings lining the Emmitsburg Road. The names of the proprietors — Klingle, Rogers, Codori, and Bliss — might just as easily have been Strause, Trexler, Nailor, and Himmelberger. The Nicholas Codori farm stood almost directly to the west about 400 yards distant. Stout post-and-rail fences lined both sides of the road, which slanted diagonally through the countryside, drawing nearer as it approached the town limits.[25]

The open pastureland occupied by the two regiments provided little in the way of cover. Furthermore, the rockiness of the ground and the lack of digging tools made entrenching virtually impossible. A number of the Second Corps units posted farther north benefited from the rudiments of a breastwork in the form of a low stone wall that jogged along the ridge crest and jutted outward at a sharp angle near the copse of trees.

Being an experienced officer, Gates improvised. He ordered his men to convert the rail fence in their immediate front into a barricade by augmenting it with "such other material as could be procured." This material may have consisted of loose dirt and stones and discarded knapsacks filled with gravel.[26] Napoleonic valor was tossed aside in favor of survival.

The only other First Corps troops present on the front lines were Stannard's Vermonters. The New Englanders extended the infantry line from the 151st Pennsylvania's left south to near the small grove of trees. The remainder of Doubleday's division was massed on slightly higher ground to the rear in support.[27]

As Gates' men busily strengthened their new position, elements of Ewell's Corps assailed the Union right in the gathering darkness. In his efforts to stabilize the left of his line, Meade had stripped all but one brigade of the Twelfth Corps from Culp's Hill.

Colonel Theodore Gates, 20th N.Y.S.M. (80th New York). Courtesy of Seward Osborne Collection, USAMHI.

The position was a naturally strong one, though, and it had been greatly enhanced by the men of George Green's brigade. The line held, although the Southerners gained a foothold in the abandoned Union trenches near the base of the hill. Although initially successful, an effort to storm Cemetery Hill from the east also failed. Once again Hancock rose to the occasion and rushed fresh troops to the scene just in time.

Finally, at around 10:30, the firing died away after more than six hours of desperate fighting. The Federal line had been dented but not broken. The full moon cast a pale, eerie glow over the grisly fields and rocky slopes, upon which lay scattered over 15,000 wounded in blue and gray. The unearthly moans and plaintive cries for help by these poor souls added a hellish audio to the horrid visual scenes of the depressing landscape.[28]

Lieutenant Slagle was invited by other members of Doubleday's staff to join them on a walk over the field. Slagle declined because he had "no taste for such sights." When the fighting subsided, a detail was assembled from the 151st to assist in carrying in the wounded. The work continued until nearly midnight. The balance of the night was spent in "sweet repose."[29]

While weary surgeons worked tirelessly under the light of overhanging lanterns in the aftermath of one of the bloodiest days of the war, the high commands of both armies were already contemplating strategy for the next day. Although he had already wired Washington announcing his intention of keeping the army in its present position, Meade called for a meeting at headquarters with his eleven chief generals. The officers met in the cramped bedroom of the Leister house for an informal exchange of ideas and a discussion of the fighting condition of the army. Meade's subordinates recommended that the army stay and fight it out, but thought it prudent to remain on the defensive. Ironically, the first course of action approved was for an offensive maneuver — the Twelfth Corps would launch an early morning assault to retake the lost entrenchments at the base of Culp's Hill.[30]

Likewise, Robert E. Lee, after two days of hard fighting and several near successes, was determined to stay at Gettysburg and resume the battle immediately. His initial strategy for July 3rd called for a double envelopment of the strong Federal position. Reinforced by Pickett's fresh division, Longstreet would renew his assault against the Union left. Simultaneously, Ewell was ordered to follow up his late evening gains on Culp's Hill. The stage was set for another bloody showdown.[31]

A full hour before daylight, the sleeping Union soldiers on Cemetery Ridge were shaken by the roar of cannon and the crack of exploding shells coming from their right rear. The racket was caused by a 26-gun Federal artillery barrage on the Confederate positions on the southern slope of Culp's Hill. The cannonade was followed by the longest period of sustained infantry combat of the entire battle.

The Confederates launched their attack before the planned Union offensive could get underway. Corporal James Miller, the aforementioned brother of Robert Miller of the 151st, participated in this furious fighting. He later wrote, "[W]e fought behind breastworks and the rebels had to come out in sight and we butchered them like sheep." The Southerners finally gave up their efforts to seize the rugged hill. The other extremity of the Union line remained quiet, however, as Longstreet failed to carry out his assault largely due to a misunderstanding between himself and Lee.[32]

Now the Southern commander was forced to alter his plans in light of these new developments. Lee shifted the target area of the assault to the Union right-center, where Wright's Georgians had temporarily pierced the Union lines the previous evening. The focal point of the attack was the Clump of Trees located near an angle in the stone wall not far from where the 151st and the 20th Militia were positioned. As Captain Cook expressed it, "Our little half brigade … was in the very front rank of the troops who held the Cemetery Ridge, and was wet with the spray of the topmost wave of the 'high tide of the Rebellion.'"[33]

The new plan called for a concentrated bombardment of the Federal position by roughly 140 artillery pieces. Afterward, nearly 12,000 men would move across a mile of open ground in an effort to smash through the center of the Union line. Pickett's Division would assault on the right or southern end of the line, while Heth's old division, now commanded by Pettigrew, advanced to the left of the Virginians. Thus, for the second time in three days, the 26th North Carolina was selected to carry a formidable enemy position. On this day, however, they would not encounter their old adversaries from the Keystone State. Two brigades of Pender's Division, led by Major General Isaac R. Trimble, would follow in Pettigrew's wake. On the opposite end of the mile-long line, two brigades from Anderson's Division of A. P. Hill's Corps were assigned the task of supporting Pickett's right.[34]

By late morning a strange quiet had settled over the field. As high noon approached, the heat, humidity, and relaxing stillness lulled many to sleep. The firing from Culp's Hill had ended, and the incessant skirmishing waged between the advance elements of the two armies had also subsided. A few energetic soldiers improved their scanty breastworks while other enterprising individuals collected and loaded extra muskets which could be readily found lying throughout the area. But the majority lounged about lazily and speculated over what was coming next. Nathan Cooper added some lines to the letter he had started a day earlier. He noted that the dead from the previous day were still "lying on the ground as thick as sheaves of wheat." He concluded with a conjecture, "I think before night the battle will be desided."[35]

The peaceful interlude was shattered shortly after one o'clock when the vast array of Confederate artillery thundered as one. Suddenly, the air vibrated with the scream of the shells and the discords of their explosions.[36]

Captain Cook wrote:

> a continuous storm of missiles of every kind poured in upon and over our heads.... We hugged the ground behind the low pile of rails which partly concealed us and awaited our destiny with such composure as we could muster. Again and again a shot struck one of these rails and knocked it around to kill or cripple men lying behind it. Again and again pieces of exploded shells would hit some one in the line with disabling or fatal effect. There was no getting away.[37]

Colonel Gates reported, "[T]he position occupied by my command was swept by a tempest of shot and shell ... and surpassed, in rapidity of firing and in the number of guns employed, anything I had before witnessed during the war."[38]

Occasionally, an ammunition chest was struck and immediately exploded with a bright flash followed by a billowy column of black smoke. Fortunately, for the men in the 151st and the other front line infantrymen, most of the shells passed harmlessly overhead. Captain Owens recalled, "[T]he shells flew thick and fast over and around us, though doing no harm except that of slightly wounding Lt. Blodget of Co. 'F' and Lt. Oliver of Co. 'D' both lying close to *me*, one on either side."[39]

Oliver suffered a severe bruise to his right arm and shoulder.[40] According to Blodget, however, this incident did not take place during the cannonade, but at a latter point in the struggle.

Blodget later wrote that compared to the infernal noise of the booming artillery, a severe post-battle thunderstorm "was but the cooing of a dove." Nonetheless, he made another telling observation: "Men generally tell that it requires more nerve to stand shelling coolly than musketry—but I was in the whole of that of Friday—the concentrated force of near 100 guns—so said—and would rather stand it a *month* than the musketry fire we were under on Wednesday for a *half hour*."[41]

Thus, the ultimate effect of the cannonade was largely psychological in nature rather than physically destructive. Of course, there were exceptions. Captain Cook recalled a peculiar incident in which a soldier in the supporting line was killed by "the wind of a cannon ball" which struck the ground near his head and tossed him violently into the air. No evidence of a wound was discovered on this poor lad. "He was thrown over and never moved a muscle—was stone dead," marveled another observer.

As most Union soldiers tightly hugged the ground or squeezed behind any resemblance of shelter, a few high-ranking officers exposed themselves to considerable danger for the sake of inspiring the men and hoping to offset the unnerving effects of the bombardment. General Gibbon, for example, was observed deliberately pacing up and down in front of the line "apparently indifferent to the rain of shot and shell that hurtled around him."[42]

Doubleday displayed considerable coolness throughout the ordeal. While munching a sandwich at the outset of the bombardment, a shell struck nearby and coated his bread with gravel. Unshaken by the blast, the former artillerist wryly exclaimed, "That sandwich will need no pepper!" The general ordered his brigade commanders to shelter the men as much as possible and when the fire slackened have them ready to spring to their feet and meet the enemy with the bayonet if possible.[43]

Meanwhile, Doubleday remained conspicuous to his command. At one point he and his staff toured the lines on horseback. Afterward, the officers remained mounted and observed the action from a nearby orchard. It was a hot location. General Rowley came up later and was struck on the arm and another fragment hit his horse.[44]

After about fifteen minutes, the furious intensity

of the cannonade settled down into a more deliberate and steady pace. The Union response to the Confederate aggression was measured. While General Henry Hunt, the chief of artillery, encouraged his battery commanders to fire at specific targets, he cautioned them against firing wildly and wasting ammunition. Hancock, in charge of the entire Union center, was more concerned about the morale of his infantrymen, and hence he ordered the gunners in his sector to fire more rapidly.

At nearly 3 P.M., the Union fire slackened and a number of batteries along Cemetery Ridge pulled back. The high command decided that a gradual cease fire would deceive the enemy into launching its much anticipated infantry assault by the perceived success of the bombardment. Thus, the Federal artillerists could preserve precious ammunition and replace damaged guns from its pool of reserve batteries.

In actuality, the cannonade achieved little real results for the Southerners. A large number of horses, caissons, and limbers were struck, but the troops were not panicked. In fact, some of the veterans smoked and relaxed during the monotonous exchange of heavy metal. For those lying in the open sun, however, the heat was oppressive. At 2 P.M. the mercury hit 87 degrees, the maximum temperature recorded in Gettysburg for the month.

Just as importantly, the Federal artillery was in excellent condition to wreak havoc upon Lee's infantrymen. The ruse worked. The Confederate guns fell silent. The stage was set for the climactic event of the three-day battle.[45]

From their residence in the southwestern section of the town, the Jacobs family enjoyed a unique perspective of both the cannonade and Pickett's Charge. Michael Jacobs was a professor of mathematics and philosophy at Pennsylvania College. His 18-year-old son, Henry, described the unforgettable sights and sounds of this historic occasion:

Such a symphony had never been heard before.... Above the tumult, one gun on Cemetery Hill was heard like an instrument carrying the air, while the rest accompanied it. The earth shook very violently when it sounded.... The shells were flying not only directly over us, but a badly aimed shot would occasionally fall in the town. A house near us was struck.... The Union guns began to slacken. We feared they were being silenced. But no. They had a respite only to be cooled. They are at it once more. The monster gun again leads the chorus.

All the rest join in. Slowly, more slowly, more slowly still! The intervals between the discharges of the great gun are becoming longer; the chorus is fading out like the pianissimo finale of some strain with its overwhelming Wagnerian din.

This silence again is portentous. There is too much art in it to have been forced. My father cannot be induced to remain with us. He felt by intuition what was coming. He has the glass with him in the garret. There he saw the line of Pickett forming on Seminary Ridge in magnificent array. He watched it as it moved steadily forward.[46]

After the bombardment ceased and the smoke lifted, the Union soldiers on Cemetery Ridge peered out across the open fields and took in the pageantry of the spectacle. "Every eye could see his legions, an overwhelming, resistless tide of an ocean of armed men sweeping upon us!," wrote Lieutenant Frank Haskell, an aide to General Gibbon. In like manner, Captain Cook recalled, "No one who saw them could help admiring the steadiness with which they came on, like the shadow of a cloud seen from a distance as it sweeps across a sunny field."[47]

Pickett's brigades advanced in the following order: James Kemper's on the right, Richard Garnett's on the left, and Lewis Armistead's following in support. At the same time Pettigrew's men stepped off just to the north. Almost immediately, the Federal artillery opened on them with solid shot and shell. As Pickett's troops neared the Emmitsburg Road, the Union guns at the lower end of Cemetery Ridge hammered away at the columns while a battery positioned on Little Round Top poured in an enfilading fire. Shot and shell cut huge swaths in the lines, but the Southerners closed up and pressed forward.[48]

The assault was also delayed by the stout post and rail fences which lined both sides of the road. As the Yankee skirmishers scrambled back toward the main line, the Union gunners blasted the attackers with canister rounds, tin cans packed with a multitude of deadly iron balls. The tense infantrymen gripped their muskets tightly in anticipation of the order to fire.[49]

As Doubleday watched the Virginians stream around the house, barn, and outbuildings of the Codori farm, he thought the main brunt of the attack would slam directly into his front. As the enemy forces approached the moist valley between the Emmitsburg Road and Cemetery Ridge, Gates ordered his men to their feet, and they instantly "opened a warm fire" upon the attackers. Almost immediately, the first line changed direction by obliquing forty-five degrees to the left and moved toward the Angle and the Clump of Trees. Gates watched as the second line followed and eventually closed its left upon the right of the first line. Then, the entire mass of the enemy "made a rush for a hill covered with some brush and trees to our right," wrote Lieutenant Colonel Jacob Hardenburgh of the 20th. The Union line seemed to come alive as thousands of muskets blazed forth nearly at once. Still, the Confederates kept coming.[50]

The two lines observed by Gates must have been the brigades of Garnett and Kemper. Pickett's supports from Anderson's Division were delayed, and instead of bearing to the left, they moved straight ahead toward the lower portion of the ridge. Stannard and Hancock immediately seized upon this golden opportunity. Under orders from these generals, the 13th and 16th Vermont pivoted ninety degrees to the right and fired a succession of devastating volleys into Pickett's exposed flank.[51]

Despite being exposed to heavy canister and musketry fire, the rebels pushed relentlessly toward their objective. Armistead's troops joined those of Garnett and Kemper. Thus, the Confederates had succeeded in concentrating a deep mass of troops directly opposite the exposed Union line near the outer angle of the wall.

Pettigrew's men to the north fought valiantly also, but owing to the topography and the proximity of the road to Cemetery Ridge there, they were exposed to an even heavier and more accurate fire than the Virginians. The well-positioned infantrymen of Alexander Hay's division mowed down the attackers as they approached the wall. The survivors reeled back in masses toward their starting point.[52]

The next crisis took place near the Clump of Trees where the sheer weight of the attacking column lunged forward and gained a toehold along the wall. Just north of the trees near the angle, General Armistead mounted the rocks and shouted, "Boys, Give them the cold steel!" A disorganized body of 150 odd men followed him. Other pockets of Confederates breached the line farther south. Some of these men clung to the cover offered by the rocks and fallen timber in the slashing and poured in a heavy fire.[53] The crisis had come for the defenders. In the words of Lieutenant Haskell, "The fate of Gettysburg hung upon a spider's single thread!"[54]

Fortunately for the North, a number of men

reacted swiftly to the danger and webs of reinforcements rushed to the threatened sector. The beleaguered artillerymen had fought gallantly by their pieces until the Confederates overwhelmed them. The conflict was now in the hands of the infantry. A number of nearby Second Corps troops reached the area first. In the wild rush which ensued, units became intermingled and lost all semblance of organization.[55]

Following in the wake of the Second Corps reinforcements was Gates' demi-brigade. According to Gates, Major Walter A. Van Rensselaer pointed out the fact that no infantry were present to defend "the little natural mound" of trees east of the stone wall. As this point appeared to be the enemy's objective, Gates immediately ordered his two regiments "to move by the right flank between the approaching rebels and this mound." Captain Owens hinted that the 20th and the 151st impulsively followed Harrow's brigade northward as these troops vacated their works instead of following any specified order.[56]

As they scrambled up the gentle slope, the Pennsylvanians and New Yorkers loaded and fired into the mass of Virginians off to their left. At the time none of them could have realized that they would soon participate in the climax of the great battle on an otherwise nondescript parcel of Adams County farmland, which future generations revered as the High Water Mark of the Rebellion.[57]

Unknowingly, Lieutenant Blodget foreshadowed his role in this climactic event when he wrote his sister the previous winter, "Men little know the part they are playing and to play in the great drama before them. When I used to read, in my boyhood, the history of remarkable events and times of the past, I used to wish I had lived *then* to participate in them, but I doubt now, if there ever was a time of greater events or changes than the present."[58]

Gates' men passed through the now silent guns of Rorty's battery to the southern edge of the Clump of Trees. Lieutenant Colonel Hardenburgh recalled that the two small regiments were positioned on the brow of the hill, "a little obliquely to the general line, some distance in advance of the other troops...." The fighting was building to a climax, but the outcome was uncertain. "The contest for the possession of this hillside and fence was especially obstinate, and for a considerable time the chances of success appeared to favor first one side and then the other," wrote Gates. "Each seemed to appreciate the fact that the possession of the heights was all-important, and each fought with the utmost desperation."[59]

Captain Cook vividly recalled that "the fire of the advancing line, the rush of the enemy to break through and the eager efforts of our men to stop them made a scene of indescribable excitement." Hardenburgh remembered the "perfect confusion" which gripped the great mass of troops congregated around the Clump of Trees. "As the Rebs advanced, they kept swaying back and I tried to get them to move up and hold their ground, but it was no use," he wrote.[60]

Due to their exposed position on the edge of the mound, Gates' men immediately drew the attention of pockets of Confederate riflemen hidden behind the low stone wall and concealed among the slashing. This "murderous fire" caused the men to waver and, at times, Captain Owens feared that "our line would be compelled to give way."[61] The Pennsylvanians and New Yorkers promptly returned the fire. "I fired fifty rounds on the gray figures & I never leveled a gun more deliberately on a squirrel than I did on them," wrote Nathan Cooper.[62] The number of shots claimed by Nathan seems high, but he probably included the rounds he fired earlier.

Although the volume of fire in no way

Top: *Looking north toward the clump of trees from the original position of Gates' command. The monument marking the location of the 20th New York State Militia on July 2nd and 3rd is visible in the right foreground.* Bottom: *A close-up of the clump of trees, which became famous as the High Water Mark of the Rebellion.*

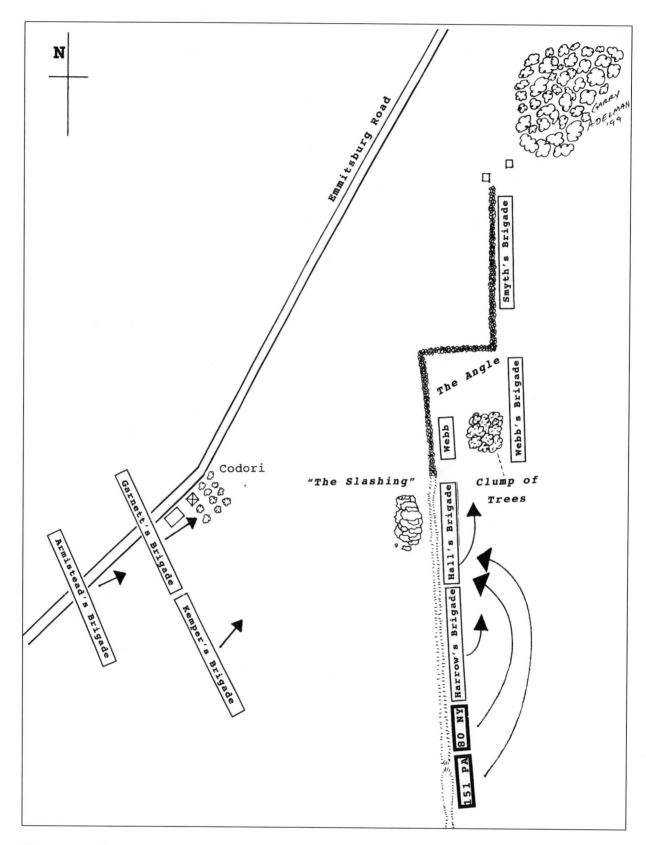

The 151st Pennsylvania and the 20th N.Y.S.M. during the Pickett-Pettigrew-Trimble Charge, July 3, 1863. Map by Garry Adelman.

compared to that of two days earlier, the 151st suffered a number of casualties. One estimate placed the figure at 17 killed and wounded, mostly the latter.[63] Once again the sickening thud of lead striking flesh mingled with the crackle of musketry and the shouts of the combatants.

Company H's John T. Strause, a mere 16-year-old, was struck just below the right knee in nearly the same location as his older brother, William T., had been hit on July 1. Fortunately for John, the missile passed below and outside of the patella without doing any major structural damage. Another fortunate individual was Private Valentine Painter of Company G. The husky iron worker was struck in the forehead by a projectile, but he quickly recovered. By the end of the month, he was back home in Robesonia with his wife and four young children.[64]

Fate did not protect another young soldier in the 151st, however. Charles Trexler, the beloved lieutenant of Company K, was killed during the sharp encounter. He died less than one hundred miles from the family farm in rural Mertztown.[65]

For those involved in this spirited engagement, time seemed to stand still just as it had on July 1. "Our regiment was in again in the very hottest of it," wrote Lieutenant Blodget. Once again minutes seemed "to contain many times sixty seconds." "In this manner we fought about 20 or 25 minutes," reported Owens. But he added the cautionary note, "perhaps not so long."[66]

What happened next was remembered differently by Owens and Gates. Sensing that the troops could not remain long in this exposed position, Owens wrote that he screamed out that the enemy was running, and promptly ordered a charge. "The order was promptly obeyed and with a deafening shout and a gallant dash, the two regiments were in the breastworks, and the boasted chivalry threw down their arms...."[67]

In Gates' recollection it was he who had ordered the charge: "I ordered the 20th N.Y.S.M. [and] the 151st Penn., to advance to the fence, which they did, cheering and in gallant style, and poured a volley into the enemy at a very short range, who now, completely broke, and those who did not seek to escape by flight, threw down their arms."[68] Perhaps both commanders simultaneously issued the decisive order. At any rate the end result was exhilarating for the weary troops of Gates' command. They had now gained a measure of revenge for the rough handling the Confederates had given them during the first day's battle.

Private Valentine Painter, Company G, was wounded in action, July 3, 1863. Courtesy of Stewart P. Biehl.

In retrospect, Blodget thought it "was comparative fun to fight them on Friday [July 3] when we had some chance."[69]

During the close quarter fighting, Captain Cook thought it curious that "although all the men were armed with bayonets no one seemed to be using them. Those nearest clubbed their muskets and beat each other over the head, while those not so close kept loading and firing as fast as they could. A few minutes ended the fray."[70]

While Gates' small command cleared out the slashing, numerous Second Corps units engaged in a furious assault on the Confederate front. In addition, Stannard's Vermonters and elements of Hays' division hammered away at the flanks of the Virginians. Soon outnumbered Confederates on both sides of the wall threw down their arms.[71] "Death had been busy on all sides," wrote Doubleday, "and few indeed now remained of that magnificent column which had advanced so proudly."[72] From his garret in town,

Michael Jacobs noted the striking contrast between the advance and the retreat. He watched the Southerners return to Seminary Ridge "no longer in serried ranks, but as individuals, broken, creeping through the wrecked corn-field, a handful compared to those who had sallied forth."[73]

In his Official Report, Gates wrote that "Very few of those who fled reached their own lines. Many turned after having run several rods and surrendered themselves. We took a large number of prisoners...." The captives were conducted through the lines and escorted by an officer to the provost marshal of the army.[74]

Once again Captain Cook recalled a colorful incident which greatly enhances our understanding of the larger event:

> [T]hose near our line sank to the ground and gave up the attempt to get away. Our men shouted to them to come in and promised not to hurt them and at the word hundreds rose up and came into our lines dropping their arms and crouching to avoid the fire of their own artillery which was pouring upon our position.... A short distance in front was a clump of bushes among which appeared a white cloth. At first I thought it a rag caught in the brush but it soon appeared that some one was waving it as a signal. Our boys shouted "Come in Johnnie; come in, we won't hurt you" and from behind the bush nearly or quite a dozen men arose and came hurrying and dodging into our line.[75]

It seems amazing that men, who only a few moments before had swung clubbed muskets to brain their adversary or had fired into the chest of an opponent at point blank range, now acted compassionately to save their foes from friendly fire. It was another unique oddity in this strange war. As one Pennsylvania corporal observed, "A soldier has as many characters as a cat is said to have lives."[76]

The renewed Confederate artillery fire was unleashed to cover the withdrawal of the retreating troops and to deter the threat of any Union counterattacks before the Southerners could organize their defenses on Seminary Ridge. In spite of this deterrent, a line of Federal skirmishers was thrown out and more prisoners were brought through the lines. Farther south, the tardy advance of Wilcox's Brigade was torn apart by the combined efforts of the Federal artillery and yet another flank attack by the Vermonters.[77]

The charge had started and ended in the space of about one hour. Out of the roughly 12,000 Southerners who stepped off from Seminary Ridge as part of the main assault force, about half were killed, wounded, or captured. General Pickett lost nearly one half of his division and all three of his brigade commanders had fallen. Only one, James Kemper, would survive his wounding. The loss in field officers was appalling. Of the fifteen regimental commanders who advanced across the deadly fields, only one returned unscathed.[78]

In contrast, Union losses for the entire day, including the morning engagement on Culp's Hill and two cavalry actions, amounted to approximately 3,300 men. The casualties were highest in Alexander Webb's Philadelphia Brigade, which happened to be positioned at the epicenter of the assault. The Northern high command also suffered some severe blows. Hancock, Gibbon, and Stannard were all severely wounded near the close of the fighting.[79] Meade's forces were simply too disorganized to follow up their success with a counterattack.

Lieutenant Blodget was leaning on his elbow after the charge watching the scattered Rebels, when a projectile struck him in the hand scraping within two inches of his knee, covering him with dirt and debris. The lieutenant described his battlefield memento to his brother, "I have the honor of getting a rake across my knuckles knocking the skin off two of them and bruising my thumb so I will lose the nail."

Blodget was proud of his depleted unit and relieved by their survival. "My company however did not lose a man in this fight, though the 'Old Thirteen' left of the first day all fought like tigers.... It was certainly a miracle."[80]

A few minutes after Blodget received his wound, Adjutant Allen was struck less than five yards away. The missile struck Allen in the right leg above the ankle. The force of the blow broke the leg bone and Samuel was carried from the field.[81]

After the repulse, Doubleday sent out stretcher bearers to collect the scores of enemy wounded. He bitterly recalled that the rebels did not appreciate his act of humanity for they vigorously shelled the position. Adding injury to insult, one of the exploding missiles slightly wounded Doubleday and a member of his staff. The General's neck was grazed by a shell fragment, and he was later observed with a white bandage over the wound, which gave him "quite a clerical appearance."[82] But soon the firing died away and the Union soldiers on Cemetery Ridge began to examine the hellish scene around them.

"[T]he ground [was] covered so thick with the dead and dying of both parties that I could step almost from one body to another..." wrote Blodget.[83] Colonel Wainwright rode to the site the next day and he verified Blodget's observation.

Outside the wall the enemy really lay in heaps; far more so at least than dead often do on the battlefield, for historians draw largely on the imagination when they talk of heaps of slain, and rivers of blood. There was about an acre or so of ground here where you could not walk without stepping over the bodies, and I saw perhaps a dozen cases where they were *heaped* one on top of the other. A captain lay thus across the body of a lieutenant-colonel. Both, especially the latter, were very handsome men. A wounded reb told me the colonel's name, but I have forgotten it; he was from Norfolk.[84]

The Lydia Leister property after the battle. Note the dead horses lying in the yard and along the Taneytown Road. The 151st Pennsylvania camped in this area on the evening of July 3rd. Courtesy of the Library of Congress.

Captain Cook also noticed a group of prostrate Confederate officers less than twenty yards away. All were dead except one, and he soon gasped his last breath while stretched across the body of another dead officer. The recently deceased man was Colonel James Gregory Hodges, 14th Virginia. His sword and scabbard were shot to pieces, but the belt, which had the Virginia state motto etched onto the buckle, was still serviceable. Cook retained this article and occasionally wore it throughout the remainder of his service. After the war Cook communicated with the widow of Colonel Hodges. He quickly sent the relic to Mrs. Hodges and received a greatly prized letter from her in acknowledgment of its return. In addition to the large number of killed and wounded in his immediate front, Colonel Gates noted that two stands of colors were left upon the ground by the enemy.[85]

At dusk the 20th and 151st were relieved by a portion of the Second Corps and were withdrawn to a point along the Taneytown Road near Meade's headquarters. Gates was proud of his demi-brigade and pointed out the fact that the two regiments were either engaged with the enemy or occupied a position in the front line, from the beginning of the battle on the morning of July 1 until its close on the evening of the 3rd, with the exception of about six hours on the 2nd. Gates felt his men never received the credit they deserved for their role in the repulse of Pickett's Charge. "Both regiments behaved with great gallantry, and I believe I do them but simple justice when I attest that to their persistent efforts the Army of the Potomac owes very much of its success..." wrote Gates just a day after the great battle.[86]

The weary soldiers under Gates and Owens had little need for such accolades at this point. Now that the fighting had subsided, the adrenaline was no longer surging through their bodies. The men suddenly noticed the pangs of hunger which had gone unnoticed in the excitement of battle. Mentally and physically exhausted, the men collapsed on the ground at the new bivouac site.

The new environs were not conducive for rest and relaxation. Seventeen dead horses littered the ground near the Lydia Leister property. The elderly widow's wheat crop was trampled, her orchard was destroyed, and the fences surrounding the property were torn up and burned. Worse, several shells had crashed through the tiny one-story dwelling which Meade had used for his headquarters. A short distance to the south stood the Peter Frey farm, which was transformed into a temporary aid station and field hospital on July 2nd and 3rd. A surgeon who labored inside the stone farmhouse on July 3rd recalled,

"The outbuildings, fences and fruit trees were completely torn to pieces. The roof of the house was torn up and the stone wall broken in one place & the stones thrown upon the floor." It was a somber scene indeed.[87]

As so often occurred following a large battle, a severe thunderstorm rumbled through the area in the early evening. A blanketlike darkness shrouded the battlefield except for brief interludes when brilliant flashes of lightning illuminated a macabre scene of mangled corpses, butchered animals, wrecked caissons, discarded muskets, and scattered accouterments. It was almost surreal, like a ride through a cheap carnival fun house. The peals of thunder and accompanying torrents of rain, which washed the blood from the grass and rocks, seemed to issue forth from the angry gods above in reprisal for the senseless slaughter of the past three days. But as one observer noted, "It suffered greatly by comparison with that which filled our ears a few hours before."[88]

Minus tents and ponchos, the soldiers of the 151st were at the mercy of the harsh elements. Drenched on the outside from the rainfall, soaked from the inside with sweat, and with stomachs gnawed by hunger, the men huddled together on the wet earth hoping to obtain some much needed sleep. At this point they had no way of knowing that the greatest battle ever fought on the American continent was essentially over.

Chapter 5

THE FINAL DAYS: JULY 4—JULY 27, 1863

"I thought I was most used up."

In retrospect, July 4, 1863, was a major turning point in the American Civil War. The country celebrated the national anniversary with news of U. S. Grant's capture of Vicksburg, the last major Confederate bastion on the Mississippi River. In the evening, Robert E. Lee and the Army of Northern Virginia commenced the long retreat back to Virginia. His army would never again penetrate this far into Northern territory. Meanwhile, William S. Rosecrans and the Army of the Cumberland were clearing out East Tennessee and threatening the major rail junction at Chattanooga.

The resilient soldiers of the Army of the Potomac sensed they had finally won a meaningful victory; it was a novel experience. The bands, which had been silent for several days, broke the stillness of the battlefield with the patriotic strains of the "Star-spangled Banner" and "Hail Columbia" to commemorate the nation's birthday and the army's recent success.[1] General Doubleday issued a general order in which he thanked the Vermont brigade, the 20th New York State Militia, and the 151st Pennsylvania for their gallant service in the previous day's fighting.[2]

When skirmishers crept forward from the Union right, they made a propitious discovery. The Confederates had abandoned Culp's Hill and the town. Indeed, Lee had consolidated his lines under the cover of darkness in preparation for a general withdrawal. The new Confederate battle line extended two and a half miles along Oak and Seminary Ridges from the Mummasburg to the Emmitsburg Road. The Southerners dug in and quickly constructed an extensive series of breastworks and rifle pits.[3] A wounded Union officer in the Seminary recalled that "bedlam reigned in the neighborhood" for half an hour as fences, outbuildings, and boardwalks were torn apart to serve as construction material.[4]

Lee hoped that Meade would attack this fortified position and give him a final opportunity to retrieve his fortunes at Gettysburg. But the Union commander had no intention of risking everything he had gained on such an uncertain undertaking. Skirmishers still popped away at one another in the no man's land between the lines, but the serious fighting was over. In the late afternoon, Lee ordered his long line of wagons and ambulances to start for the mountain passes in advance of the artillery and infantry. With his ammunition and supplies running low, the Confederate commander could ill afford to play a waiting game with Meade.[5]

The morale of the Union troops was further bolstered when rations of fresh beef, hardtack, coffee, sugar, and salt were brought forward and distributed.[6] Unfortunately, the sights and smells on Cemetery Ridge were not conducive for feasting. Lieutenant Blodget described the horrid conditions to his brother. "You cannot conceive the horrors of such a battlefield ... the *stench* after the battle was like that of a vast slaughter house.... I saw this morning over 100 dead Rebels on ten square rods of ground — our men buried 500 in one grave — very many are not buried yet."[7]

As the day progressed, Union officers experienced considerable difficulty in restraining their men from wandering over the field to take in these ghastly sights. A number of soldiers also took leave of their duties for the more honorable purpose of visiting family and friends in nearby units. Corporal James Miller of the 111th Pennsylvania was among the latter. He strolled over to the camp of the 151st Pennsylvania from Culp's Hill to check in on the Warren County boys. Miller soon discovered that the regiment had been nearly annihilated and that Company F had only fifteen men fit for duty. He also met an old friend who had just arrived on the scene.[8]

After learning that a major battle was about to

Colonel Harrison Allen reached Gettysburg on July 4, 1863, and retained command of the regiment throughout the remainder of its service. Courtesy of Pennsylvania State Archives.

be fought on the soil of his native state, Colonel Harrison Allen rushed forward from his Warren home to reach the army. He must have been appalled by the shattered condition of his command. Allen no doubt inquired as to the condition of his younger brother, Samuel, who was lying wounded nearby.[9]

Although his presence was welcomed by some, especially among his old company, others might have questioned the colonel's sudden recovery from illness. Less than two weeks earlier, Lieutenant Theodore Chase, who was a patient in a Georgetown hospital, warned Allen that if he wished "to retain the credit his Regt. has got he had better get back as soon as possible."[10] Whatever his motives, Allen's leadership would be sorely needed if the regiment should meet the enemy in its final weeks of service.

One thing was certain. The two armies would not collide again at Gettysburg. Well past dark on the evening of July 4th, the main body of Lee's army headed west on the Hagerstown Road toward the protective shield of South Mountain. The Union pursuit was cautious. A reconnaissance in force was sent out early the next morning to develop the Confederate

position. Meade soon gave up on the idea of a direct pursuit because of the ease with which the various mountain passes could be blocked by a small rear guard detachment. Instead, he positioned his forces for a sideling movement to the Frederick area, which had the added advantage of covering Washington and of shortening his supply line. This initial advance would be followed by a westward movement over the mountains near Middletown to the Potomac River crossing near Williamsport, Maryland.[11] Once again the army would have to move swiftly to intercept Lee.

Lieutenant Blodget was sanguine on the prospects of destroying Lee's army. On the evening of July 5th, William wrote his brother, "Our whole army started in pursuit today — We hear of strong reinforcements from every quarter and we do not see how half of Lee's army can ever get back to Virginia. They were terribly whipped … and are now pursued by a force much stronger than that which whipped them and the rain of yesterday and last night must seriously interfere with their crossing the river."[12]

The First, Third, and Sixth Corps, all under the command of Major General John Sedgwick, took the more direct route of pursuit by marching southwest through Emmitsburg, Mechanicstown, and Lewistown, the identical route by which the First Corps had traveled to reach Gettysburg. But on this occasion, instead of marching at the vanguard of the column, the shattered remnants of this proud organization served as the rear guard. Thus, the corps stayed put near the battlefield throughout the fifth.[13] Near the close of the day, Doubleday's division shifted several hundred yards south to a slightly higher elevation after their old camps were saturated by the recent rainstorms.[14]

A number of officers and enlisted men took advantage of the idle time by surveying the ground of the first day's field. Colonel Wainwright was shocked to discover that very few of the dead had been buried. "The bodies presented a ghastly sight," he lamented, "being swollen almost to the bursting of their clothes, and the faces perfectly black." During his early morning visit, Wainwright observed burial parties gathering up the dead, but he reported that their work was performed very haphazardly "for twenty or more were put in a trench side by side, and covered with only a foot or two of earth."[15] Captain Horatio Warren and a party of men from the 142nd Pennsylvania discovered their slain comrades "lying where they fell, and their upturned faces black from the burning rays of the scorching sun." Warren and his companions experienced much difficulty in distinguishing one from the other.[16]

Private George S. Bisbee and two of his comrades from the 20th New York State Militia were able to identify the body of George Babcock by the black silk handkerchief he had worn around his neck. Bisbee, who was captured on July 1st, indicated that the dead were buried by the Confederates on the evening of the 2nd, and that on the 5th, he and another soldier marked Babcock's shallow grave with a board on which they carved his name, company, regiment, and state. In late September, Bisbee wrote to Babcock's father and described the exact location of the burial site.[17]

Many of the remains on this part of the field would never be identified. Two weeks after the battle, Simon Arnold composed a difficult letter to the widow of Sergeant Alexander Seiders in which he verified the news of her husband's death. Arnold sadly informed her that it would be a hard matter to recover his body as the Confederates had possession of this part of the field for three days and that they had buried nearly all of the dead while the battle was in progress.[18] Seiders' body may have been removed later and interred in the unknown section of the National Cemetery, or perhaps it still rests peacefully near the spot where he gasped his last breath.

Thus, there is conflicting evidence as to just who interred the bulk of the Union dead on the first day's field, as it appears from the evidence above, that both Union and Confederate burial details worked in this vicinity. It is clear, however, that the work was performed hastily by both sides and that identification was becoming rather difficult after the bodies were exposed to heat, humidity, and rain for nearly four days. In addition, the first heavy rain washed away the few inches of soil covering the bodies, and one observer reported that "swine were found reveling in the remains in a manner horrible to contemplate."[19]

The troops that combed the battlefield in search of wounded and dead comrades opportunistically gathered up much needed articles of clothing and equipment. Unfortunately, less scrupulous individuals also robbed the dead of money and valuables. Later, Nathan Cooper regretted that he and his comrades had not taken advantage of this occasion to replace their lost tents and blankets, but he wrote that they had not yet been conditioned to "picking dead men's pockets & robbing them of their blankets."[20]

Camp talk naturally centered on the recent fighting and, invariably, comparisons were drawn to other famous battles. "There is no doubt but this has been the most sanguinary battle of the war," declared Blodget. He continued, "All say that Fredericksburg or Antietam or Chancellorsville were not equal to it. General Doubleday said today our loss was not less than 25,000, but I do not believe it will exceed 15,000. We have captured 10,000 prisoners and the Rebs loss in killed and wounded must exceed ours."[21]

Doubleday's estimate of Union casualties was closer than Blodget's, for 23,000 is the generally accepted figure for the number of killed, wounded, captured, and missing for the three days' fighting. Conversely, there is considerable disagreement over Confederate losses and estimates range from as low as 20,448 to just over 28,000. There is no doubt, however, that Gettysburg was the bloodiest battle of the entire Civil War.[22]

On the evening of July 5th, marching orders were promulgated and rations and ammunition were distributed to the soldiers.[23] General Abner Doubleday, however, would not be accompanying his men during the pursuit of Lee. Following the battle, the prickly New Yorker demanded that Meade restore him to corps command. When refused reinstatement, Doubleday departed for Washington, where he would spend the remainder of the war performing administrative duties.[24] The next morning, the First Corps headed south far away from the bloody fields which had virtually destroyed it.

For the next four days, Colonel Allen and the 151st Pennsylvania marched rapidly with the First Corps before halting near Boonsborough, Maryland, a distance of over fifty miles. The weather was muggy and the heavy rains made many of the roads nearly impassable, further fatiguing the weary foot soldiers. The poor condition of the roads, together with traffic congestion on the railways, severely hampered supply operations. A large number of the men were shoeless.[25] Nathan Cooper marched barefooted for three days before drawing a new pair from the quartermaster near Middletown. "I thought I was most used up," he wrote, "my feet were very badly bruised & so swollen. I was most discouraged trying to keep up."[26]

It was the same old story. "A soldier's life is a succession of extremes," explained one veteran, "first a long period of inactivity, followed by a time when all his energies both mental and physical are taxed to the utmost." Major John Young reported for duty after a three-month absence as the 151st clambered over the South Mountain range near Frederick. Young

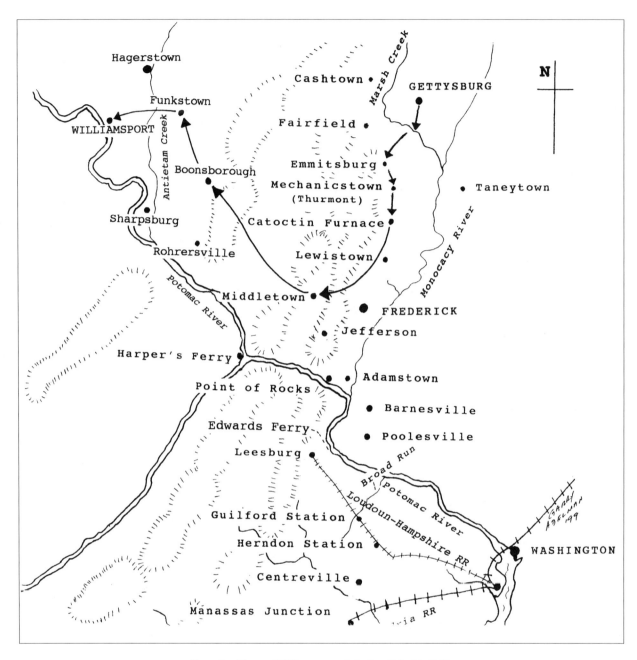

Pursuit of Lee to Williamsport: July 6 to July 14, 1863.

noticed that Captain Westbrook appeared quite lame and inquired about his sore right foot. The intrepid captain replied that it had been getting worse all the time, but vowed that he was determined "to go through with his company if he had to go on one foot." Meanwhile, Lieutenant George Mills was overcome with severe pain in his bowels. He was treated with three doses of morphine and then helped down off the mountain. Mills never returned to active duty and followed the regiment in an ambulance.[27]

By the evening of July 9th, the advance elements of Meade's army had established a five-mile line just west of South Mountain from Boonsborough south to Rohrersville. Although exhausted, the men hastily commenced piling up fence rails and scooping up earth to form a protection of breastworks. Wainwright thought this was a bad omen which did not speak well for the morale of the troops. After further consideration, the thoughtful colonel surmised that this behavior was not surprising considering the nature of the last three battles. "They see that victory has been with the defensive, and wish to be always in that position," he recorded.[28]

Finally, letters and papers from home reached the army and the soldiers received the joyous news that Vicksburg had fallen. At the same time, a congratulatory order was read from the commanding general in which he thanked the army for its heroic performance at Gettysburg. The good news and encouragement did much to bolster the spirits of the weary troops. Corporal Cooper, who was now acting as orderly sergeant, wrote his wife, "If we hadn't lost so many of our boys, we would be the best feeling set of fellows you ever saw. We would forget sore feet & how we had lain in the mud & rain without any shelter."[29]

But Cooper probably realized that the heavy rains were a mixed blessing as the Potomac River was now swollen to near flood level, thus preventing Lee's escape to Virginia. As the Federals rested near South Mountain, the Army of Northern Virginia was located between Hagerstown and Williamsport with its back to the swollen river. Lee prepared his men to receive an all-out attack. Indeed, by July 10th, a number of Union forces from various departments were cooperating with the Army of the Potomac, and together, they were closing in on the Confederates from practically all directions.[30]

For the next several days, Meade carefully maneuvered his army toward the Confederate position. Officers and men alike realized that if they bagged the Army of Northern Virginia, it would nearly end the rebellion. On the other hand, Wainwright pointed out that a severe repulse at the hands of Lee would gain back for the Southerners "all the prestige at home and abroad which they lost at Gettysburg and injure our morale greatly." The perceptive artillerist trusted that his chief would not risk such an outcome unless the chances of success were highly probable.[31]

A little past noon on the 12th, the First Corps marched northeast toward the left of the Confederate position near Hagerstown. The men advanced along a stone pike in the midst of a heavy shower, which according to one officer dumped on them "the most drenching rain I ever witnessed." At the small village of Funkstown, the column crossed a stone bridge which spanned the deep and sluggish waters of Antietam Creek. Upon reaching its western bank, the troops were exposed to a sharp skirmish fire from enemy riflemen deployed in their front. The men instinctively examined their weapons and then came the shouted order, "On the right by file into line!"[32]

As the Northerners passed through the stubble of a recently harvested wheatfield and approached the fortified position held by the Confederates, shells and bullets cut through the air all around them. Since they were not in a favorable position to return the fire, the Union soldiers earnestly commenced tearing down fences, and then with spades, picks, and bayonets, they hacked out an opposing line of earthworks. Soon, Nathan Cooper felt secure behind these defenses and he probably voiced the opinion of many of his comrades when he declared, "I would rather fight behind our breastworks than before the[i]rs."[33]

That very evening General Meade met with his corps commanders to discuss the strategic situation. The commanding general was eager for an offensive action, but since the Confederate position was so well screened, he lacked adequate knowledge of Lee's troop dispositions. Like Cooper, a few of Meade's lieutenants held on to the unlikely belief that if they remained on the defensive, Lee would attack them. Most agreed that the position was much too strong to be carried by a direct assault. Meade acquiesced to his underlings and refrained from ordering an attack until he could personally reconnoiter the enemy lines.[34]

The rank and file intuitively sensed that something was afoot. On the evening of July 12th, Nathan Cooper wrote his wife that "things look now as if we would have another round." Nathan assured her, "I never shall be where bullets fly thicker than I have been." But he closed with an ominous note, "[W]e have just recd. orders to be ready to move."[35]

Mrs. Cooper need not have worried. To the surprise of many in the ranks, the Army of the Potomac remained in position throughout the next day. "I fully expected that we should have a fight this morning...," wrote a puzzled, but partly relieved, Colonel Wainwright. In the late afternoon, a heavy downpour transformed the open fields into a muddy quagmire.[36] Mother Nature had proved to be a greater nemesis than the Army of Northern Virginia.

During the night, Meade issued orders for a reconnaissance in force by four of his infantry corps to be carried out on the morning of the 14th. The battered First Corps was to be held in reserve. When the Union forces moved forward at daybreak, however, they found nothing but empty trenches in their front.

The Potomac had finally subsided enough to be forded, and while Meade planned his much anticipated attack, the Confederates stealthily slipped toward the river under the cover of a pitch-black night. In the morning, Union cavalry clashed with Lee's rear guard near Falling Waters and took some 700 prisoners from Heth's and Pender's divisions. General Pettigrew fell with a mortal wound during the melee. By early afternoon, the last organized body of Confederate troops crossed over the pontoon bridge to the friendly soil of Virginia. The anchoring ropes were cut, the bridge swept downriver, and thus ended the Gettysburg Campaign.[37]

Almost immediately Meade came under fire from the Lincoln administration for allowing Lee's army to escape. "People at home of course will now pitch into Meade, as they did McClellan after Antietam...," wrote Wainwright. After examining the Confederate fortifications, the colonel wholeheartedly agreed with his superior's caution. "These were by far the strongest I have seen yet ... evidently laid out by engineers and built as if they meant to stand a month's siege."[38] It was a precursor of things to come.

The remainder of the 151st's service time was anticlimactic. As the rest of the Federal army headed south into Virginia once again, the Pennsylvanians were relieved from duty on the 19th. Two days later, they arrived back at Camp Curtin in Harrisburg. Here, they quietly waited out the remainder of their enlistment term until officially mustered out on the 27th.[39]

These were not the same men who had assembled at the capitol less than a year earlier, for they had just passed through the most eventful period of their lives. Unknowingly, all had played a supporting role in one of the greatest acts in the history of the nation. The Civil War experience of the 151st Pennsylvania reads like a Hollywood movie script. Chancellorville foreshadowed Gettysburg, where the regiment was forged by fire during the plot's central event. The pursuit of Lee's army, following the great battle, was the anticlimax of the saga.

For some the drama was not over; it merely shifted to a different stage. In early 1864, Private Charles Ammarell re-enlisted in Company E of the 46th Pennsylvania and marched with William T. Sherman through Georgia and the Carolinas. Privates Benjamin Naugle of Company D and George Briggs, Company F, had had enough of the endless trudging associated with the infantry. The former joined the 3rd Regiment of United States Cavalry, while the latter was enrolled into Company K of the 12th Pennsylvania Cavalry on March 1, 1864.[40]

The majority of the soldiers returned home to their old neighborhoods and the families they had left behind. They were the fortunate ones. Many of their comrades were lying in hospitals struggling for their very survival. Meanwhile, several of the officers who had gallantly lead them into battle were beginning a long period of captivity in Dixieland. For a number of these men, the physical and emotional scars would never be fully healed.

Chapter 6

HOSPITAL SCENES

"…We all awaited our fate with resignation."

The saddest, most pathetic sight in all the universe is a field of battle when the thunder of the cannon has ceased — when no longer, amid lurid belchings of battery and musketry, brigades and divisions are rushing to sweeping fires of death's high carnival….

When the splendor, the pomp and the circumstance of battle's magnificently stern array have gone, then the horrible and the ghastly only remain and remain in their most terrible forms.

Hideous is the sorrowful appearance of the bloated, distorted and blackened dead, so lately noble, stalwart men as they are packed together, side by side, some in blue and some gray. But yet more horrible is the agony of the wounded to whom speedy death often would be an unspeakable boon.[1]

Although over forty years had elapsed since the great battle, the vivid memories of its aftermath were still indelibly etched upon the mind of Professor J. Howard Wert when he penned these moving lines in 1907. A Maryland clergyman, who visited Gettysburg and its environs less than a week after the battle, was also moved by the sad scenes he witnessed:

On visiting Gettysburg, I found the Catholic, Presbyterian and two Lutheran churches, the Court House, the College, the Seminary, and the Odd Fellows' Hall, used as hospitals, and filled to overflowing: In the halls and rooms, vestibules and basements, on the steps and in the altars, were stalwart men in the bloom of health rendered helpless by the weapons of war. I conversed freely with many, and sought to direct them to the true fountain of happiness….

The ground was everywhere strewn with muskets, bayonets, balls, grapeshot, canteens, shoes, hats, &c. Dead horses were unburied, and wounded veterans were turned out to die. Houses are riddled, fences gone, and wheat and corn destroyed. The flight of the enemy was most precipitate, leaving their dead, wounded, and some sleeping in the town.[2]

Indeed, no early visitor to the battlefield with any amount of compassion could help being profoundly moved by the nightmarish scenes spread out before him. When Meade and Lee headed south, they left behind over 7,000 dead soldiers and more than 2,000 slaughtered animals. But the most paramount concern following the battle was the proper care of the 21,000 wounded men left behind, in and near Gettysburg.[3] The sheer volume of patients requiring surgical treatment, nursing, food, new clothing, and shelter quickly overwhelmed the medical departments of the opposing armies as well as the limited resources of the small crossroads town.

The 151st Pennsylvania's tally of 211 wounded was unsurpassed by any Union army regiment present at Gettysburg.[4] Their saga began on July 1st when the regiment first encountered the enemy on McPherson's Ridge. As has been related in a previous chapter, the 151st suffered a tremendous number of casualties during the late afternoon hours. Obviously, the regiment's medical resources were put to a severe test.

At Gettysburg, the medical staff of the 151st consisted of a surgeon and two assistants, who were aided by several orderlies and hospital stewards from the ranks. Dr. Amos Crammer Blakeslee was well-qualified to head this team. Born in 1825 at Springville, Susquehanna County, Pennsylvania, to parents of New England stock, he entered the sophomore class of Yale at the age of 17. Following his graduation, he attended the Yale Medical Institute. In 1848, Blakeslee was appointed resident physician of the Connecticut General State Hospital. Later, he operated a successful private practice in New Haven before the poor health of his wife and mother led him back to his native state. Amos was residing in

Wyoming County when he joined the 151st as an assistant surgeon in the fall of 1862. A promotion to surgeon was approved on March 2, 1863, upon the recommendation of George McFarland.[5]

Blakeslee's first assistant, Warren Joseph Underwood, graduated with honors from Jefferson Medical College in Philadelphia with the class of 1862. In September, the 22-year-old York County native accepted an assignment as assistant surgeon of the 19th Regiment of Pennsylvania Militia. After the militia was disbanded, Underwood worked briefly at a Chambersburg hospital before being transferred to the General Hospital at Camp Curtin in Harrisburg. Here, he joined the 151st in late November just prior to the regiment's departure for Washington.

When Surgeon Blakeslee fell ill in the spring of 1863, Underwood was left in charge of the sick and was said to have displayed great industry and skill until he himself was worn down by incessant labor. Furthermore, after an outbreak of smallpox during the winter, an enlisted man commented that Drs. Blakeslee and Underwood were "gentlemen of unquestioned attainments in their profession" and that "if scientific and medical skill is of any avail, deaths from like causes will be few here."[6]

Jonas Harrison Kauffman, the second assistant surgeon, was a newcomer to the regiment. The active and energetic young man joined the 151st on June 5, 1863, near the commencement of the Gettysburg Campaign. Kauffman's military service dated back to the beginning of the war when he enlisted as a private in the Tower Guards of Pottsville, a three-months regiment. Following this enlistment he completed his medical training in Philadelphia. After several assignments at hospitals in Maryland and Ohio, he was commissioned assistant surgeon of the 128th Pennsylvania in March 1863. Two weeks after this regiment was mustered out of service, Kauffman accepted a position with the 151st.[7]

Private George Shivery of Company D, a 23-year-old wagonmaker from McAlisterville, served as one of the regimental hospital stewards. He had replaced Private Peter Hayward on January 1, 1863. A steward assisted the surgeons by dressing wounds and administering food, medicine, or stimulants as needed. After the battle, George was assigned as a wardmaster in the Seminary.[8]

On July 1st, the initial field hospitals of the First Corps were positioned in the Lutheran Theological Seminary, which served primarily as a large aid station, and in churches, schools, warehouses, public buildings, and private dwellings inside the town limits. As the fighting escalated, Blakeslee and his staff worked desperately just behind the main lines attending to the large flow of stricken men. Generally, they performed only basic first-aid procedures to stabilize their patients before sending them farther back to the rear for treatment by the divisional operating staff.[9]

The more seriously wounded were set aside for transportation by ambulance. Private George Decker of Company B was detailed to serve in the ambulance corps at Gettysburg. Ambulance attendants and drivers were specially selected for their good moral character and had to be active, efficient, and devoted to their duties.[10]

Due to the 151st's proximity to the Seminary campus throughout the day, the main edifice naturally became the most important collection point for the regiment's wounded. By the 6th of July, McFarland reported that 173 wounded officers and men from his regiment alone had been collected inside the four-story brick building.[11] Other structures known to be occupied by the wounded of the 151st on July 1 included the Christ Lutheran Church, located on the south side of Chambersburg Street, and the St. Francis Xavier Roman Catholic Church, which was situated on West High Street.

By the evening of July 1st, all of these temporary hospitals fell into the hands of the victorious Confederates. Since the Seminary was the most prominent of these facilities, it will be dealt with first and in the most detail.

After his severe wounding, George McFarland was carried into the northwestern corner of the building's first floor by Private Wilson, where he recalled, "I lay on the floor in my blood...." Somehow George found the strength to scrawl a brief letter to his wife back in McAlisterville in which he assured her, "It will go all right with me."[12] He later penned this vivid account of conditions at the hospital:

> As soon as the rebels took possession of the hospital, they seized and carried off all the instruments, chloroform, and appliances and thus deprived Surgeon Blakeslee and his assistants ... the means of amputating shattered limbs or dressing painful wounds. And to make it still worse the rebel commanding officer ordered every sound or slightly wounded Union soldier out to be paroled, and though promising to return them as hospital nurses, he marched them off, leaving over

three hundred helpless wounded men without a single attendant! This unchristian and barbarous conduct probably cost some their lives and others months of unnecessary suffering. For three days we were left without food, drink, or attendance to listen with painful anxiety to the booming of cannon and the din of battle.

The hospital was on the rebel line of battle, and a heavy battery was posted under cover of the southern end of the building. The discharges of this battery were so heavy that they caused the building to tremble to its very foundation, and the window sash to rattle as though shaken by an earthquake. This sent many a pang not only through shattered limbs and aching heads, but through loyal hearts fully conscious of the fearful issues then trembling in the balance....

This battery ... soon drew a heavy fire from the Union batteries posted on the opposite heights. This fire was particularly accurate and ... put our hospital and its inmates into a very dangerous and critical position. A perfect shower of shot and shell was hurled upon us, and the building was frequently struck.... For a time there seemed to be no hope, and we all awaited our fate with resignation.[13]

Lieutenant Jeremiah Hoffman's first recollections of his hospital experience also concerned the lack of surgical instruments, but unlike McFarland, he wrote disparagingly of the Union surgeons, whom he claimed "found it much more safe to hide in the cellars and behind large trees than to stand and argue the point of international law as to the exemption of doctors ... from the fate of ordinary prisoners; and the hot cannonading made it especially unpleasant to stand about loose."

Indeed, the initial concern of both the wounded and unwounded Union prisoners inside the Seminary was the friendly fire which was being

directed toward the structure by Federal artillery positioned on Cemetery Hill. Late in the afternoon of July 1st, a number of enlisted men approached the wounded Lieutenant Hoffman, who was lying in the southeastern corner of the first floor, and inquired as to what signal could be made to identify the building as a hospital. Thinking quickly the young officer noticed "a generous petticoat of red flannel" lying nearby. A healthy soldier was persuaded into mounting the Seminary's prominent cupola to hang the largest piece he could tear from the garment. "Thus it happened during the fight and for some days after the undergarment of our hostess floated over the building," recalled an amused Hoffman.[14]

Jeremiah Hoffman, a 21-year-old graduate of Franklin and Marshall College, was a patient in the Seminary from July 1st to July 9th.[15] His rich and detailed reminiscences provides us with a rare glimpse inside a Civil War field hospital. His moving account covers the full range of human emotion from witty humor to intense sorrow.

Jeremiah recalled that worms generated rapidly in the warm weather and that they were especially plentiful on the lower floor. In the wounds of one unfortunate soldier these creatures "jumped as fast as you could snap your fingers."

An even more pathetic scene was witnessed by Hoffman during his second or third night in the

The Lutheran Theological Seminary in a view taken shortly after the battle. The camera angle is facing west. The rooms occupied by McFarland and Hoffman were located in the basement on the south side (left) of the structure. The garden was probably located near the southern corner of the building. Courtesy of Adams County Historical Society.

Lieutenant Jeremiah Hoffman, 142nd Pennsylvania, wrote a stirring memoir which detailed his stay at the Lutheran Seminary Hospital. Courtesy of the Archives and Special Collections Department, Franklin and Marshall College.

building. A patient on an upper floor was heard crying out desperately for water. When no one responded to his urgent pleas, the anguished soldier could be heard shuffling across the floor and then coming downstairs with a pronounced thump as he painfully rolled from step to step.

The remainder of the heartbreaking incident is related in Hoffman's words:

> His motions were slow, and his voice became each time more hollow and unearthly than before. By the time when he came to the bottom, he could utter only a whisper. We heard his voice grow less and less and finally we had our

former stillness. In the morning the man was found dead at the foot of the stairs. We had all lent him our voices, but not one … was able to go to his assistance, and the nurses, if there were any, were out of hearing.

Shortly afterward, Hoffman was affected in a more personal manner when Colonel Robert Cummins and Adjutant Andrew Tucker succumbed to their wounds. Jeremiah described Tucker's burial in his touching memoir:

> [T]hey brought his body downstairs in a blanket. They roughly lined his grave with fence palings and buried him beside the Col. I was then lying on the bunk, and by lifting my head could see into the garden…. They were holding the body over the grave when the head slipped over the edge of the blanket and the Lieutenant's beautiful, jet black hair dragged over the ground. The thought of his mother and sisters was called up, and surely it cannot be called unmanly that a few tears stole down my cheeks."[16]

Obviously, the lack of proper medical attention and the shortage of nurses in the facility significantly increased the mortality rate. Private Adam K. Siegfried of Company H, a teen-ager from Strausstown, died on July 3rd. He joined Private Aaron Sands, Company E, who had been buried on the Seminary grounds after being killed on the opening day of the battle. At 44, Sands was among the oldest members of the regiment to die at Gettysburg.[17] Following the battle, a visitor recorded viewing the graves of Cummins and Tucker on the south end of the edifice and that "Thos. D. Aften, Co. A, 151, Montrose, Pa." was lying by them. "Aften" was 26-year-old Corporal Thomas D. Allen. Considering the location of his temporary grave, it is likely that Thomas died during the Confederate occupation of the field. His remains were later removed to the National Cemetery (B-28 Pennsylvania plot).[18]

Immediately following the death of Cummins on the morning of July 2nd, McFarland was placed upon the bed formerly occupied by the colonel in the southwest corner of the building's first floor. Apparently, the makeshift hospital flag attached to the cupola did not deter the fire of the Union artillerists for it nearly cost George his life. During the furious cannonade that preceded Pickett's Charge, a solid shot crashed through a window, passed lengthwise over the recumbent officer, and lodged itself in a nearby partition, covering him with lime and stone fragments. Later, a relieved McFarland wrote that had he been sitting up, the stray round would surely have decapitated him. Lieutenant Hoffman recalled that George had changed position just prior to the dramatic incident and that afterward he was taken away in a fainting condition.[19]

It was just the beginning of an eventful day for the beleaguered officer, however. During the evening he was placed upon a bed, possibly on the second floor, and his right leg was amputated several inches below the knee. However, George steadfastly refused to consent to the removal of his shattered left ankle.[20]

McFarland's stubbornness had some merit. Early in the war, a general rule was established of amputating extremities if they were seriously damaged, especially if a bone was fractured. This practice may have caused the needless amputation of thousands of limbs that could have been saved. On the other hand, a large number of these operations were unavoidable due to the destructive power of the .58 caliber minié ball, the most common projectile used during the war. When one of these soft lead bullets struck a soldier, it often shattered bone and destroyed muscle, tissue, and arteries beyond repair. Amputation was frequently the only option.[21]

In a surgeon's certificate Blakeslee testified that, "In the consequence of the enemy taking all of my instruments, medicines, and assistants, I was unable to amputate his limb until the third day, at which time extravasation had taken place to such an extent that sloughing took place, and union by granulation was the consequence, making recovery long protracted."[22]

Blakeslee is vague on how he obtained the needed instruments to perform this operation. Fortunately, an article by J. Howard Wert, a respected author and early battlefield guide, sheds light on this mystery:

> I wish, however, to speak specially of another brave and thoughtful action of Miss Critzman's that was all her own. When fell the shades of evening and the conflict for the day had substantially ceased, she ascertained that the theological seminary and its adjacent grounds were crowded with wounded men lacking surgical attention.
>
> There is a scarcity of instruments, and the Confederate surgeons naturally were giving their care first to the wounds of their own army. She also learned that, while Dr. Robert Horner had one set of instruments in use in his volunteer labors of humanity at the College Church hospital [Christ Lutheran Church] … he also had an older set which he had concealed….

Lieutenant Andrew G. Tucker, 142nd Pennsylvania, died in the Seminary Hospital on July 5th after being mortally wounded during the first day's fighting. Courtesy of Alex Chamberlain Collection, USAMHI.

> With this brave woman, to see the line of duty open before her was to act. Obtaining the instruments and concealing them in her clothing, she made her way to the seminary, more than half a mile distant, amid the campfires and roaming soldiery of the enemy….
>
> She reached the seminary and there, finding one of the Union surgeons … committed to him the burden she bore. I am told that it was with these very instruments, carried to the seminary by Miss Lizzie Critzman, the amputation upon brave Colonel George F. McFarland, of Harrisburg, was performed.[23]

At the time of the battle, Elizabeth "Lizzie" Critzman was in her mid–40s and operated a student boarding house near Pennsylvania College, which was situated on a plain in the northern suburbs of the town.[24] McFarland's ties to Lizzie and her family would continue throughout his stay at the hospital.

Private Diedrich Dasenbuck of Company C was also among the fortunate few who received treatment during the Confederate occupation of the building. Dasenbuck had been wounded twice on July 1st. A battered conical ball plowed into his scalp an inch and a half behind the right ear and penetrated to the right cheek. A fragment of this same projectile struck the base of his neck and became lodged near the middle of his right clavicle. This hunk of lead was removed through a button-hole incision by Blakeslee on July 3rd. The larger foreign body may not have been detected at this time and remained inside. It was later determined that Diedrich's wounds were caused by a ball which had split upon some hard surface before striking him. The velocity of the projectile was nearly spent or diminished at the point of impact and thus made no exit wounds.[25]

On the Fourth of July, Hoffman recalled that the Confederates posted around the Seminary campus were frequently inside the building talking to the wounded and bringing them water and biscuits made from flour. Although some members of the 1st South Carolina could not reach an agreement with their Northern adversaries on the merits of secession, they gladly acknowledged that the Union position at Gettysburg was equal to the one the Confederates had held at Fredericksburg. Jeremiah disabused the fears of one Rebel who thought the Pennsylvania Dutch were "a terrible people, who would be apt to kill him upon sight." Hoffman reported that the "long, lank, ignorant North Carolina mountaineer" hid away in the basement when Lee's army retreated and then deserted into the countryside.[26]

But relations between the captors and the captives were not always this hospitable. In one instance, a Union prisoner detailed to gather up arms and material discovered a loaded weapon and shot one of his guards through the heart without being detected. On the other hand, a Yankee soldier was gunned down by a Confederate as he was assisting a wounded comrade toward the Seminary after the fighting, and following the Southern retreat, a Rebel prisoner shot and killed a wounded Union soldier.[27]

One of the first visitors to the Seminary Hospital following Lee's withdrawal was Ellen Orbison Harris, secretary of the Philadelphia Ladies Aid Society and their "worker among the soldiers." Mrs. Harris departed from Washington on the morning of July 3rd and arrived in Gettysburg the next day, where she observed "suffering of the most fearful character."[28] Her visit to the Seminary is documented through a letter she wrote to Addie McFarland following George's operation.

> Your husband is in Seminary hospital and has kind attentions.

> Gettysburg
> July 4th
> My dear Mrs. McFarland —
> Your brave husband has given a limit to his country — is doing well — was wounded on the 1st — you have my heartfelt sympathy; may the God of all consolation comfort you — your husband wrote his name on a slip of paper and gave it to me — so you may judge he is not very weak — is quite cheerful — am to[o] steeped in sorrow & death cannot rejoice over our victory — would be glad to write more — you have my heartfelt sympathy & prayers.
> Mrs. John Harris
> 1106 Pine St., Phila.[29]

In 1860 Ellen Harris was 48 years old and described as being "delicate, fragile, and feeble-looking." But author Frank Moore declared that:

> If there were any such vain decorations of human approbation as a crown, or a wreath, or a star for her, who in our late war has done the most, and labored the longest, who visited the greatest number of hospitals, prayed with the greatest number of suffering and dying soldiers, penetrated nearest to the front, and underwent the greatest amount of fatigue and exposure for the soldier, — that crown or that star would be rightfully given to Mrs. John Harris, of Philadelphia.[30]

By the next day, McFarland had recovered sufficiently to write Addie himself:

> At last the rebs have been driven back and we have some hopes of being able to send out a mail…. [T]he rebs were very ugly, taking away our hospital help and leaving some poor fellows there days on the field of battle. They also took for their own use the medicines and instruments we needed for our own use. But they made nothing by the operation and have been forced to withdraw…. You will find me in good spirits and condition. I am doing well. God has been merciful to me for your sakes.[31]

One of the "poor fellows" left on the field of battle was Michael Link. His ordeal was described in his obituary which appeared in the July 12, 1899, issue of the *Reading Eagle*:

> In that field with eyes shot out and under a blazing sun, Private Link laid for two days. His sufferings cannot even be imagined. He prayed for death to relieve his agony, but Link, though sightless and near to death's door, was destined to live. Rebels passed him, but they thought it was a corpse. Then on the third day some Boys

in Blue came along. They heard Link's moans. He was conveyed to the field hospital....[32]

Weakened from his wounds and from exposure, Link must have been in a delirious state when he was carried into the Seminary. Oral tradition states that Michael's damaged eye sockets were eaten away by maggots as he lay helplessly on the battlefield.

Captain James Weida was also struggling for survival. Surgeon Blakeslee probed his chest and removed what foreign material he could reach, but with a broken rib and an injured liver and right lung, Weida faced a long road to recovery. During the Civil War there was a 62 percent mortality rate associated with chest wounds. Private Aaron Smith testified that his captain "was very low and often complained to me of great pain in the region of his heart [and] also [of] pain in his arms and legs. He was short in his breath and could not speak above a whisper."

Smith was a patient in the hospital from July 1st to July 10th. Two of his comrades, Corporal Amos Fisher and Private Marcus Fegeley, who lost an arm, were also lying nearby.[33]

Conditions in the hospital did not improve immediately after Lee's retreat. On July 5th or 6th, the Ziegler family returned to their home in the main edifice of the Seminary. Emanuel and Mary Ziegler, the steward and matron of the building respectively, resided with their five children on the first floor. On July 1st, the family sought refuge in the cellar of the spacious building before departing for the home of a relative near Little Round Top during a lull in the fighting.[34] One can only imagine Mary's reaction when she spotted her undergarments floating high above the building as she passed up the Chambersburg Pike.

"It was a ghastly sight to see some of the men lying in puddles of blood on the bare floor," recalled a teen-aged Lydia Ziegler of the memorable homecoming. She added:

> Many a poor fellow died within the first ten days after the battle for want of care and nourishing food.... Nights and days were alike spent in trying to alleviate the suffering of the wounded and dying. How often did I receive the dying message of a father or husband to send to his loved ones whom he would never again meet on earth! So many pathetic scenes took place during those days.[35]

Young Lydia might have heard the last words of several men from the 151st. Strausstown's Henry Weber, who was only a few years older than Lydia,

died on July 6th, after being wounded on the 1st while acting as a brigade sharpshooter. He was temporarily interred in the Seminary woods before being removed to the Evergreen Cemetery of Gettysburg. Two days later, another Strausstown resident, 39-year-old George Livengood, succumbed to his wounds. That same day, Corporal Cyrus Lutz of Company K died after his left leg was amputated.[36]

Ten-year-old Hugh Ziegler viewed the strange surroundings with a boyish curiosity:

> We succeeded in getting back to our home, but it was in use as a hospital, all the space in the large building was filled up with wounded soldiers. The doctors in charge, learning it was our home, cleared two of the rooms and we moved in and got busy helping care for the wounded. My mother took charge of the kitchen and did the cooking, and hailed by the wounded and others connected with the hospital as "mother." There was one of the large rooms of the building used as a clinic, where many arms and legs were amputated and several times I was called on to carry one to the rear of the hospital and deposit with many others, that had been placed in a pile. There had been an accumulation of several days before they were taken away and buried: and the pile of arms and legs placed there like a pile of stove wood, would have filled a wagon bed.

Hugh probably spent much time roaming the building's many floors during those eventful days and he probably met a number of soldiers from both sides. George McFarland must have made a lasting impression upon the youngster, for nearly seventy years later, Hugh mentioned the wounded officer in his memoir. But after the elapse of so many decades, the details were a little fuzzy as he wrote of "seeing General McFarlane whose arm was amputated and he afterward died."[37]

Sarah Broadhead, who resided a short distance from the Seminary on West Chambersburg Street, visited the hospital early on the morning of July 5th at about the same time the Zieglers returned home. Overcome by the misery and human suffering, she confided to her diary, "It is heart-sickening to think of these noble fellows sacrificing everything for us ... and it out of our power to render any assistance of consequence. I turned away and cried."[38]

Sarah regained her courage and returned two days later with a supply of food, quilts, and pillows. She was partly relieved upon learning that a wagon filled with bread, butter, and hard tack had just arrived.

After assisting in the feeding of some of the more severely wounded patients, Sarah perceived that many of them had not yet had their wounds dressed. The volunteer nurse procured a basin of water and entered a room in which were quartered seven or eight bad cases. She stooped over one man and asked for his wound. He pointed to his leg which was badly infested with worms. "Such a horrible sight I had never seen and hope never to see again," Broadhead recalled.

A mortified Sarah demanded to speak to one of the surgeons, who candidly informed her that not enough men had been detailed to care for the wounded and that the few surgeons present were severely handicapped by the lack of available instruments. He regretted that many would die from sheer lack of timely attendance.

Broadhead returned to the hospital early on July 8th and found that several physicians and nurses had arrived from Washington the previous evening. The difficult task of extracting bullets and amputating shattered limbs was begun in earnest. It was probably at this time that Hugh Ziegler was detailed to carry the severed limbs outside. Upon descending to the basement of the building, Sarah made a horrifying discovery. "Men, wounded in three and four places, not able to help themselves the least bit, lay almost swimming in water." Broadhead and a contingent of nurses labored for hours to remove nearly one hundred men to the fourth story.[39]

Two days later, however, Sarah rejoiced when she observed considerable improvements taking place within the hospital. "Nearly all have been provided with beds and clothing, and a more comfortable look pervades the whole building," she wrote. In large measure, these improved conditions were made possible by the quick response and the efficiency of a number of relief agencies and civic organizations, such as the United States Sanitary and Christian Commissions, the Sisters of Charity, the Patriot Daughters of Lancaster, the Philadelphia Fire Department, and a number of ladies aid societies. Furthermore, by July 9th, rail service to Gettysburg had been restored and government supplies began arriving in abundance.[40]

On July 10, the *Union County Star and Lewisburg Chronicle* reported: "Several of our citizens have been to visit the battle field at Gettysburg. The little town is crowded, and odious with decaying bodies and the marks of battle. Our wounded at first lacked aid and supplies, but nurses and doctors were pouring in by the score, and supplies by the ton. Visitors are impressed to bury horses and aid generally."[41]

Sarah Broadhead also commented on the large numbers of strangers that were pouring into the village. "The town is as full as ever of strangers, and the old story of the inability of a village of twenty-five hundred inhabitants, overrun and eaten out by two large armies, to accommodate from ten to twelve thousand visitors, is repeated almost hourly."[42]

The Reverend E. W. Hutter, pastor of St. Matthew's Lutheran Church in Philadelphia, divided these visitors into three distinct classes. First were the thousands who came from nearly every Northern state to tenderly nurse their loved ones or to recover the body of a fallen hero. The second class consisted of the many altruistic individuals and groups who ventured forth to help alleviate the human suffering. The last class of visitor consisted of the morbid sightseers who flocked into the area merely to gawk at the hideous sights presented by the late battlefield. Reverend Hutter traveled to Gettysburg "through much tribulation" with seven other Philadelphians. The party was loaded with an immense quantity of clothing, refreshments, and edibles which had been donated by the congregation.[43]

Among the first class of visitors mentioned by the pastor was Addie McFarland. After she received word of her husband's severe wounding, Mrs. McFarland immediately made preparations to leave for Gettysburg. She also decided to take her two children, John Horace, age three, and one-year-old Emma, with her to the hospital. Upon reaching Harrisburg, Addie appealed to Governor Andrew Gregg Curtin for assistance, and through his courtesy, was provided with transportation aboard a construction train that was headed down river. Years later, Horace still had a clear recollection of crossing the Susquehanna River in a rowboat because the large covered bridge had been burned during the Confederate invasion. The last leg of the family's memorable journey was aboard the Gettysburg and Hanover Railroad. They arrived at their destination by July 10th or 11th.[44]

Although conditions at the Seminary had improved considerably by the time of Addie's arrival, there was still much to be done to help alleviate the human suffering that prevailed there. Perhaps sensing his wife's apprehension over his own condition, George reassured her, "I am sound of mind and of stomach and I do not intend to die." During her seven-week stay in Gettysburg, Mrs. McFarland stayed with the Critzmans. She visited the hospital daily and according to one observer, "She not only nursed her husband, but found time to contribute many acts of kind-

Lydia Ziegler never forgot the "ghastly sight" of men lying in puddles of blood on the bare floor after her family returned to their home inside the main Seminary edifice. Courtesy of Rev. R. Donald Clare.

Gettysburg is a very beautiful inland town and notwithstanding the bad reports about the inhabitants in some papers, they are the best and most patriotic people (especially the helpful ladies) that I ever became acquainted with. Many of them are giving their last things and doing without themselves in order to help. There is scarcely a house but you will find from one to five wounded men being taken care of by the ladies themselves.[46]

Despite the tender ministrations of family members and volunteer nurses, men continued to die. In late July, the Reverend Franklin Jacob Fogel Schantz, a former student at the Seminary, returned to his alma mater and later recorded his recollections of the memorable visit. On Saturday, July 25th, he wrote:

In the afternoon I took hospital stores to the Theological Seminary and visited the many sick and wounded in the building.... What different scenes from those of the two years I spent as a student in the building. Many of the soldiers who had lost an arm or a leg told me that they still felt sensations in the parts separated from their bodies.... I was by the bedside of dying men who departed this life away from their homes and friends, thus no mother, no father, no sister or brother, no wife or children near to hear the last word of their beloved.

The next day Reverend Schantz returned to the hospital.

I went to the Theological Seminary to hold service as I had been requested to do by the Surgeon in Chief with whom I had reason to be not well pleased. When I reached the Seminary, he had a party of men in his room, drinking and singing Negro melodies. I felt sad that this should occur ... in a Hospital where some of the sick and wounded were very low, some dying and one had died shortly before I reached the Seminary.... I stood near the stairway in the second hall of the building.... Very soon after ... the surgeon and his party came from the surgeon's room and passed me on a rush down the stairway and out of the building. I was glad the noise of the carousers had ceased. I preached to an audience which I could not see....[47]

ness to the hundreds of wounded and dying soldiers of both armies, which lay in the Seminary." The mother of Captain Weida traveled to Gettysburg as well, and with the assistance of a Miss Findlay from New York, she tenderly nursed her wounded son.[45]

At about the same time, Lieutenant Theodore Chase, in company with Orrin Allen, the younger brother of Harrison and Samuel, arrived in town "to look up the boys and take care of them." Chase and Captain Mitchell, both of Company F, were sent to Harrisburg from the Georgetown Female Seminary Hospital near the end of June. Chase was horrified by the condition of the battlefield. On July 16th, he wrote a friend: "The stench from the dead men and horses is becoming almost unendurable. Even in the village many of the horses have not been touched and many of the dead buried by the Rebels were not more than half covered and smell — well — *very bad*. I would not live here during the summer for half of the state."

Conversely, the young officer enjoyed his immediate surroundings. "We have a splendid boarding place at a widow womans, she is a splendid woman and has a *very nice young lady* helping her. Were it not for the bad stench in town, I don't know but I should spend the summer with the widow." Later, in the same letter, he extended his praise to include the general populace of Gettysburg:

Even if a patient initially survived his wounding and the stress of an operation or amputation, his ultimate recovery was not certain. Secondary hemorrhaging often occurred weeks after the battle and claimed many lives. Another leading postoperative ailment was tetanus or lockjaw, which developed as a direct result of the filthy and unsanitary conditions prevalent in Civil War field hospitals. Many amputees were also susceptible to gangrene. Unfortunately, surgeons in the mid–1800s knew nothing about bacteriology and antiseptics. They frequently probed wounds or severed limbs with dirty hands and unsterilized instruments. Thus, infections were rampant in large hospitals. These factors help explain the relatively high number of deaths in the Seminary from late July to early August.[48]

An illustrative example involves McFarland's roommate, First Lieutenant Henry Chancellor, Company B, 150th Pennsylvania. Like McFarland, Lieutenant Chancellor fell with a severe leg wound on July 1st. However, Henry's shattered left leg was not removed until the evening of July 5th. The stump healed rapidly during the remainder of the month, but in early August his condition suddenly took a turn for the worse. Tragically, Chancellor died on August 6th.

George and Addie had quickly become attached to the gracious young officer who was reared in an affluent household in the Germantown district of Philadelphia. Addie tenderly cared for Henry during her stay in Gettysburg. Henry's grief-stricken mother affectionately referred to Addie as "my darling lamented boy's valued friend."

George lamented:

> [T]here were none whose death affected me more deeply…. [I]t was my fortune to occupy the same room, partake of the same food, and endure similar sufferings and privations for several weeks after the battle. Though barely twenty-one years of age, of delicate build and "unused to the rougher sides of life," the patient, cheerful, hopeful manner in which he conducted himself would have done credit to the strongest and bravest veteran, and could not fail to elicit the admiration and win the sympathies of those around him.[49]

The soldier who died on July 26th just before Reverend Schantz held religious services in the building might well have been Private Reuben Beechert of Company E, 151st Pennsylvania. Earlier, Reuben's left arm was amputated at the shoulder. He died from pyemia, an infection of the bloodstream, which developed following the operation. During the Civil War, a little more than one-third of the men who suffered a major limb amputation could expect to survive. The closer the limb was removed to the torso, the lesser the chance of recovery. Another amputee, William S. Stamm of Company G, died a week later. Stamm's right leg was amputated at the thigh.[50]

The kind attentions received by Anson Miller from his Masonic brothers were not enough to save his life. The wounds inflicted to his left thigh and both knees were just too severe. Miller died on August 1st never to return to his home in Cressona. His remains were embalmed and shipped to relatives in Kinderbrook, New York, for interment. Anson was warmly remembered by his comrades at Pulaski Lodge #216 in Pottsville as "a mild, gentle, and honest man, a just friend and a true soldier." The patriotic Mason "died in the cause which his heart loved … the nation's life and honor."[51]

Many of the wounded had already been transported to general hospitals located in the major eastern cities or to Camp Letterman, the large government hospital established just east of Gettysburg along the York Pike. By July 25th, approximately 12,000 men had been sent away.[52] On July 9th, Michael Link and Diedrich Dasenbuck were transported to Philadelphia. By the 20th, Sergeant Major Arnold had recovered sufficiently from his leg wound to be transferred to the general hospital in nearby York, Pa. Near the beginning of August, Captain James Weida was convalescing at his home in Long Swamp.[53]

George McFarland's frail condition necessitated a longer stay in the field hospital. His shattered left leg was still "dreadfully painful" a month after his wounding. Several members of Company D returned to Gettysburg to check in on George after the 151st was mustered out of service at Harrisburg in late July. The family of George Shivery was greatly concerned when he did not appear at the Mifflin station of the Pennsylvania Railroad. Apparently, Shivery was more concerned over the welfare of his neighbor and former commander, for he immediately set off for the battlefield without informing anyone of his plans. George was accompanied by 19-year-old S. Brady Caveny, another McAlisterville native. Brady had once attended McFarland's academy and he readily left behind a clerking job in his father's store to serve under his former teacher.

The two "boys" provided George with a detailed account of the regiment's final days at Camp Curtin. McFarland recorded with a note of satisfaction, "From their account it would seem Col. Allen had a stormy time of it, getting partially paid for the arrogance and imposition the Regt. had to take from him."

Captain Owens also visited with McFarland and confirmed the account of Allen's treatment by the officers and men at Harrisburg. Owens stated that "he never saw a meeker, calmer man than the Col., though formerly arrogant in the extreme." He added that Major Young "recd. a little when he attempted to show off." George was gratified to learn from the Captain and from others that he was a favorite with the regiment and had not an enemy.[54]

During the middle of August, an order was issued directing all army surgeons to rejoin their regiments in the field. This news was despairing to McFarland as it meant losing Dr. Robert Loughran of the 20th New York State Militia. "He has been so faithful and so kind and I have such perfect confidence in him that I can scarcely let him go." Loughran had been the surgeon in charge of the Seminary hospital for seven weeks. Dr. Andrew J. Ward, Medical Director of the First Army Corps, also stopped in to see George before his departure. He "had been very kind to me," recalled George fondly.[55]

Dr. Charles Horner and Dr. Henry Huber, two local physicians contracted by the Government, attended to McFarland for the remainder of his stay in the hospital. Privates Nicholas Kizer and Benjamin Carr of the 149th Pennsylvania were detailed as his orderlies.[56]

But George's trademark patience and fortitude were wearing thin. He recorded in his diary for August 18th, "I am still confined as closely as ever, my stump about ⅔ healed over, and my left leg is still suppurating badly. The wound has become less, but when is it going to heal up? God only knows. It has been very painful for the past three weeks and is now."[57]

Slowly the building was cleared out. On September 1st, McFarland wrote to his wife who had left for home a day earlier with the children. "[T]hey are removing the wounded. Today the rebs go, tomorrow the 'one-armed' and the next day the 'one-legged' Union men. 60 or 70 were to go today but could not get off." Four days later he reported, "The work of clearing out the Hospital still continues though it goes slowly on account of so many being bad. Still nearly all are gone, not a half dozen left." Finally, on September 7th, George penned, "I am at last alone — so far as wounded are concerned — in this large building!" When McFarland departed for home on the 16th, a memorable chapter in the Seminary's history came to a close.[58]

Located about half a mile east of the Seminary, the Christ Lutheran Church on Chambersburg Street was also witness to many pathetic scenes during and after the great battle. This house of worship was commonly referred to as the "college church" because its ministers were often professors from Pennsylvania College, and the students regularly worshipped there. Reverend Henry L. Baugher, president of the College in 1863, was the pastor here at the time of the battle. The church was one of the first public buildings in Gettysburg to be used as a hospital.[59]

As will be recalled from an earlier chapter, Lieutenant Charles Potts assisted several wounded men of his company into the building during the Federal retreat on July 1st. Potts decided that "rather than have the humiliation of delivering my sword to a rebel, I hid it in the building." The lieutenant reached the front door just in time to witness the slaying of Reverend Horatio Howell, the chaplain of the 90th Pennsylvania, on the steps of the church. Charles was captured a short time later.[60] Although firsthand accounts of this hospital are quite numerous, there is very little specific documentation concerning members of the 151st.

The one exception is Frank Lyon of Company F. The 31-year-old private from Farmington Township, Warren County, was shot in the hip on July 1st. It is not known just how he reached the sanctuary. His wound must not have been crippling for one account states that "he walked some three miles two days after he was hit." Lyon died inside the church on July 19th. James Miller of the 111th Pennsylvania, who had resided near Frank before the war, was very surprised to learn of his death. He had heard from him two days after the battle and his recovery seemed likely.[61]

Frank left behind a young wife and a one-year-old son named Frank W. Months earlier, while stationed at Camp Curtin, Lyon had written a friend, "I shall submit patiently to whatever fate is in store for me...."[62] His fate was to die in defense of his country.

At least 150 men from the Second and Third Divisions were cared for at Christ Lutheran Church, mostly the former. The auditorium was on the second floor, and the wounded had to be carried up a long flight of stairs from the street. Beds were improvised by laying boards on top of the pews. About forty men were housed in the basement of the building.[63]

Conditions inside this hospital were initially very similar to those at the Seminary. However, Union surgeons inside the church hospital were permitted to ply their trade with little disturbance from the Confederates. A Massachusetts soldier recalled:

> An operating table was placed in an anteroom opening off the main hall and here our Surgeon worked with knife and saw without rest or sleep ... for 36 hours before the first round was

Surgeon Andrew J. Ward, 2nd Wisconsin, Medical Director of the First Army Corps. Courtesy of Marc J. Storch Collection, USAMHI.

made.... A Confederate guard was placed over the hospital, but otherwise we were left to ourselves. After the surgeons' work was done we had no care save such as the few less seriously wounded comrades could give.... The first night 23 dead were carried from our room."[64]

Mary McAllister, who lived a short distance from the church, recalled, "Every pew was full; some sitting, some lying, some leaning on others. They cut off arms and legs and threw them out of the windows." Charles McCurdy wrote that the surgeons were hard at work under very rude conditions and that afterward the church yard was "strewn with arms and legs that had been amputated."[65]

Fortunately, for the wounded sufferers lying in the church, a contingent from the Patriot Daughters of Lancaster arrived on the scene shortly after the battle and took charge of the nursing and cooking. Mrs. Martha Ehler recalled the trepidation she felt as she

walked across the street for the first time "to enter the scene of so much sorrow and anguish." Martha noted that with the exception of having their wounds dressed, most of the men were lying in the same condition as they were brought in from the battlefield. "Some were on a little straw, while most of them had nothing between them and the hard boards but their old thin, war-worn blankets; the more fortunate ones with their knapsacks under their heads. And when you think that they were, almost without exception, serious amputation cases, what must have been their sufferings!"[66]

The ladies worked quickly to remedy the dreadful situation. Soon the soldiers were provided with pillows, new shirts, sheets, and bed-sacks filled with straw. Freshly washed and dressed in clean clothing, the men could hardly express their gratitude. They were just as grateful for the home-cooked meals which were carefully prepared by the daughters. The daily bill of fare consisted of the following: breakfast, tea and toast with soft-boiled eggs; dinner, chicken or mutton soup, two vegetables, and sometimes a simple pudding; and for supper, tea, with stewed fruit, and buns.

Undoubtedly, the efforts of the Lancaster ladies saved lives and allowed the unfortunate soldiers with mortal wounds to die with dignity. Deaths were certainly not infrequent. On the Sunday following the battle, a religious service was conducted by Professor Baugher, and though it lasted but a short time, five men died.[67]

After four weeks, there were only seventy-eight soldiers left in the church, and the hospital closed after about six weeks of operation. The remainder of the wounded were transferred to the Seminary.[68] One of the surgeons that labored in the church was Dr. Robert Horner, who lived and practiced medicine diagonally across the street from the church. Like his brother, Charles, Robert's services were contracted by the government for about a three-month period following the battle.

John Radebaugh, the ten-year-old son of Mrs. Mary Horner from a previous marriage, spent most of his time in the hospital. His efforts at comforting the men were fondly remembered by Martha Ehler. "Every morning he came with some nice, cool drink, prepared by his own hands, or sugared berries, and if other duties claimed the attention of the attendants, he was always to be relied on, and would fan a very low patient for hours until relieved, and among my few pleasant reminiscences of the hospital is the bouquet of sweet flowers which he rarely forgot."[69]

Another "church hospital" inhabited by soldiers from the 151st was St. Francis Xavier Roman Catholic Church on West High Street. The Catholic church was located about two blocks due east from Christ Lutheran. Along with Chambersburg and Middle Streets, High Street became a major avenue of retreat for members of the First Army Corps on July 1st. Naturally, large numbers of wounded soldiers sought refuge in the Catholic Church as well as the United Presbyterian Church located across the street.

Lieutenant Colonel Henry S. Huidekoper of the 150th Pennsylvania reached St. Francis at about 5:30 P.M., with his right arm wrapped tightly with a cord above the elbow to prevent the loss of blood. Earlier, during the fighting near the McPherson farm, a minié ball had struck him at the joint and crushed the delicate bones in this region.

Huidekoper left behind the most detailed account of any soldier quartered in this hospital:

The Christ Lutheran Church on Chambersburg Street. Private Frank Lyon died here on July 19, 1863. Courtesy of Adams County Historical Society.

> On arrival at the church I found an operating table in the entry, with the double folding doors open for light ... and wounded men for hours had been making their way to the rear of the church. Awaiting my turn for examination and treatment, I went into an empty pew on the left-hand [west] side of the church.... About six o'clock an assistant to the general surgeons who were operating at the table came to me announcing it was my turn. I went to the table and got onto it with my head toward the west. I took some chloroform.... What I next remember was my saying, "You took off my arm, did you, Doctor? I thought you were only going to examine and dress it; well, when we next march through Maryland I will have to salute with my left hand."

After his operation, Henry was told to seek a place in the pulpit to lie down. Stepping carefully among the "hundreds of soldiers who were lying in the aisles," the colonel discovered that the pulpit was already filled to capacity. Spying the gallery at the other end of the church, he worked his way back past the operating table, ascended the stairs which led to the gallery, and found a "soft" board not far from the organ. "The night was a horrible one," he recalled, "All night long I heard from downstairs moans, groans, shrieks, and yells from the wounded and suffering soldiers."

Colonel Huidekoper remained in the gallery and recorded the following incidents which took place on the 2nd:

> General Ewell and several of his staff officers came up into the gallery for observation…. As the General had only one leg … he was unable to go up the ladder to the roof and sat down on the bench not three feet from me…. I had an opportunity to study his features and the gorgeous gold lace which adorned the sleeves and collar and front of his gray coat.
> About this time a Miss Myers and a younger girl came to me and asked whether or not I was badly wounded and wanted anything. In answer I threw back the blanket that covered me and said that I had nothing to eat since daylight the morning of the 1st and did want a bite. They went away but returned in ten minutes from their homes near-by and gave me a glass of home-made wine and one cracker, which Miss Myers had to carry hidden under her shawl lest she might encounter some hungry rebel.[70]

The Peter Myers family resided only six doors west of the Catholic church at present day 55 West High Street. On the evening of July 1st, Dr. James Fulton, assistant surgeon of the 143rd Pennsylvania, received permission to use the Myers' kitchen to prepare meals for the countless wounded. The house was soon transformed into a hospital auxiliary service as the family cooked, boiled linens and bandages, and performed other tasks to assist the surgeons and attendants in the two church hospitals nearby.[71]

The next morning Fulton returned to the Myers home and delivered an urgent plea to the daughters. "Girls, you must come up to the churches and help us. Our boys are suffering terribly from want of attention." Elizabeth Salome "Sally" Myers, a 21-year-old schoolteacher and the eldest daughter of Peter and Hannah Myers, responded to Fulton's urgent entreaty with understandable apprehension. Sally never forgot the numbing shock she felt when she entered the Catholic church. "Some of the wounded lay in the pews, and some lay on the floor with knapsacks under their heads, and there were very few persons to do anything for the poor fellows. Everywhere was blood, and on all sides we heard groans and cries and prayers."

After Sallie spoke to a dying man just inside the vestibule, it became too much for her overwrought nerves. She dashed out of the church, sat down on the front step and cried. But a short time later she composed herself and reentered the hospital. Somehow, Sallie Myers overcame her natural aversion to blood and suffering, and for the next four and a half months, she lovingly nursed the wounded on an almost daily basis, first in the churches and in her own home, and then later at Camp Letterman.[72]

On Sunday morning after the battle, twelve Sisters of Charity from the convent at Emmitsburg, Maryland, arrived in Gettysburg with bandages, sponges, refreshments, and clothing. Sister Camilla O'Keefe wrote of the horrible conditions the Sisters encountered inside St. Francis:

> The soldiers lay on the pew seats, under them and in every aisle. They were also in the sanctuary and in the gallery, so close together that there was scarcely room to move about. Many of them lay in their own blood and the water used for bathing their wounds, but no word of complaint escaped from their lips. Others were dying with lockjaw, making it very difficult to administer drinks and nourishment. Numbers of the men had their wounds dressed for the first time by the Sisters, surgeons at that juncture being few in number.[73]

The Sisters made excellent nurses and the doctors always preferred them to other civilian nurses. The soldiers were perhaps even more appreciative. Josiah Balsley of the 142nd Pennsylvania declared with great reverence:

> should I live to be a hundred years old I will always hold them in grateful remembrance for the kind and loving attention that they gave us while we were under their care and keeping. I never see one of them wearing their peculiar garb but my mind goes back to the time when wounded and sick and away from home and our own loved ones, they ministered to our every want as tenderly and cheerfully as our own mothers or wives or sisters could have done.[74]

The Catholic church contained some of the worst amputation cases. Among them was Nelson Reaser of Company B. Nelson's shattered right leg was amputated above the knee, probably on the same table where Colonel Huidekoper's arm was removed. The teenager from Pike County, who might never have been away from home prior to his enlistment, now faced extreme adversity in his strange surroundings with considerable dignity and courage.

When Nelson wrote his father on July 18th, it is apparent that he longed for a familiar face, but at the same time, he was quite optimistic about his prospects for recovery:

> I now set down to rite you a few more lines for to see if you will answer these. I thought it very strange in you for not answern my other. I suppose that you know where I am wounded. I will tell you anyhow. My right leg is amputated, but the doctor says it is a getting along the best of any of them. It is a shame for to see how some of the boys worie themselves to death. The doctor says he never saw a man keep up such good spirits as I do. I do my own riting. I am gaining very much. I can get out on a chair without any help, but I have wished for to see some of you so bad. I have not seen any botty that I knowed yet. I want to know if you can tell if Joe Brickley or any of the rest of the boys are wounded. If they are let me know. I have seen only two boys out of my company. It was George Decker and Levi Losey. Well I will bring my letter to a close for I am very week now. So no more at present.[75]

Five days later, Nelson passed away. His remains were later removed to the National Cemetery (A-39 Pennsylvania Plot).[76] One hopes that Nelson heard from his father or another family member before his untimely death.

Lieutenant Albert Yost and Private Solomon Strause of Company H were also patients at St. Francis. Yost stated in a pension claim that his wounded right forearm was treated by A. C. Blakeslee at the church.[77] Apparently, the tireless regimental surgeon was making his rounds among all the hospitals which contained men from his regiment.

Dr. Fulton, initially the surgeon in charge of both church hospitals on West High Street, was something of an enigma. George McFarland hailed him as "one of the most zealous and fearless of all surgeons on the field of battle" and added that he attended to the wounded with "the tenderness of a mother."[78]

By contrast, a visitor to the church on July 7th, observed: "The Dr. in attendance seemed to me a brute, he stepped about smoking and swearing, and

paying no attention whatever to the frequent appeals made to him, and for the sake of appearing to do something commenced sweeping out the house which anyone else could have done better."[79]

On this same date, William F. Norris, M.D., arrived from Washington, D.C., and was immediately assigned to the Catholic church. Norris noted that the hospital contained some 200 patients and was in a state of utter confusion. "Men with serious wounds lying about ... very little attention. There are no intelligent assistants or surgeons.... Even the food is insufficient."

On July 13th, Norris wrote that he personally tended to the cooking, the cleanliness of the wards, the hospital guards, the burial of the dead, and the distribution of medicine, sheets, and other essentials. "The Hospital is now getting into fair condition," he proclaimed, "We have arranged beds on top of the alternate pews."[80]

Unfortunately, it was a familiar story that was repeated in nearly all of the makeshift field hospitals at Gettysburg during and immediately after the battle. Despite the Herculean efforts of many individuals and groups, there were simply not enough supplies and manpower to provide adequately for the great influx of human misery. As a result, many, such as young Nelson Reaser, perhaps died needlessly.

The Catholic church hospital closed sometime between August 7th and August 15th. The remaining wounded were transferred to Camp Letterman. Other surgeons known to be in the church besides Fulton, Blakeslee, and Norris were Dr. Philip Quinan, 150th Pennsylvania; Dr. F. C. Reamer, 143rd Pennsylvania; and W. G. Hunter, 149th Pennsylvania. Dr. Quinan took charge of the hospital one week following the battle.[81]

With the retreat of the Union forces at the end of the first day's battle and the Confederate occupation of Gettysburg, a re-establishment of the First Corps hospitals was necessary. The main field hospitals of this corps were positioned along the Baltimore Pike southeast of the town. The Third Division took possession of the Jonathan Young farm, where 1,279 wounded men were cared for. The 124-acre Young farm was located on the east side of the pike, south of White Run and just north of the hamlet of Two Taverns. The Peter Conover farm, located across the pike one mile southwest of Young's, also housed wounded from the Third Division.[82]

Sergeant Heilig wrote, "We were three miles out

St. Francis Xavier Roman Catholic Church on West High Street. Private Nelson Reaser was among the many amputation cases treated here. Courtesy of Adams County Historical Society.

The vague references to barns or "barn hospitals" are understandable considering that farms were fairly generic in Adams County, and the soldiers often did not know the names of the owners. Solomon Strause, originally quartered at St. Francis, was also moved on the 4th to a "barn near the battlefield" where he remained until July 10th.[85]

After lying in an ambulance throughout the evening of July 3rd, Adjutant Samuel T. Allen stated that he was taken to a nearby barn on the following day. Two days later, he was moved to a private residence in town, quite possibly the boarding house so highly endorsed by Lieutenant Chase. John T. Strause, who had also been wounded on July 3rd, also specified being taken to a nearby barn, where he received no medical treatment "until he was taken with his company." The references made by Allen and Strause to a nearby barn may possibly indicate the Peter Frey farm, which was located just south of the Lydia Leister property. Frey's farm served as a temporary aid station and field hospital during the battle.[86]

Unfortunately, in many instances it is impossible to pinpoint the exact locations where certain soldiers were treated, given the sparse information available. A notable exception is Jacob Zimmerman of Company I. The 44-year-old private died and was buried on the Jonathan Young farm on July 14th. He was later moved to the National Cemetery and now rests forever in the E-14 Pennsylvania plot. Apparently, Peter Cron never made it to a hospital. Shot in the bowels and captured July 1st, he died on the pavement in the public square of Gettysburg on Independence Day.[87]

of the town laying in barns, all who could walk, and the others who were wounded in the legs were taken to churches and houses in the town."[83] Private Alfred Staudt of Company G recorded in his diary that on July 4, after the Confederates evacuated the town, he marched out to another hospital. Alfred had been wounded in the left arm and left leg. His entry for July 8th reads simply, "I am in the barn hospital."[84]

By mid to late August most of the corps and division field hospitals had been officially closed by the U.S. Government. As soon as railroad communication with Gettysburg was partially reopened, great trainloads of wounded were shipped away from the battlefield to large eastern cities which were better equipped to accommodate them.[88] The July 21st edition of the *Adams Sentinel and General Advertiser* reported: "Immense trains of cars loaded with the wounded have passed over our railroad, on their way to Baltimore. The wounded upon their arrival there are placed in the splendid hospitals in that city, or forwarded on to those at Philadelphia. The number conveyed over the road since the battle is estimated at many thousands...."[89]

The first evacuations began on July 7th, and by the end of the next day, 1,462 patients had already been removed. The tally of Union wounded forwarded from the Gettysburg area reached nearly 13,000 as the month of July came to a close.[90]

A squad from the 151st assembled at the depot on Carlisle Street on Thursday, July 9th, and at five o'clock in the evening, the men boarded the train for Baltimore. They traveled through the night in open cars, probably a blessing given the sultry weather conditions.[91]

Among the passengers were Sergeant George Heilig and Lieutenant Thomas Moyer. Apparently, Moyer was still suffering from combat shock, as both his appearance and conduct were somewhat peculiar according to Heilig's recollections. Thomas was timid, seemed anxious to reach home, and spoke very little. George had been acquainted with Moyer for about twenty years and had once instructed him at his school in Upper Bern Township, Berks County.[92] Therefore, he quickly noted the change in temperament.

After a short time the train clacked into Hanover Junction and then continued on to Baltimore, reaching the city by morning. "Through every place we went, the people gave us bread, cake, pie, water and everything that was needed," recalled Heilig fondly. "It followed therefore, that I and Joseph Meier were very sick for about 24 hours," he added.[93]

When the men detrained, they were treated to a bounteous meal in one of the city's large general hospitals. Perhaps not everyone partook in the feast. Lieutenant Moyer's behavior was still perplexing. As the group of soldiers walked toward the hospital, Moyer drifted away by himself and did not return for an hour or two.[94] The men reboarded a train in the afternoon and arrived in Philadelphia late in the evening.[95]

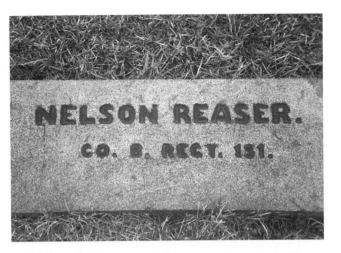

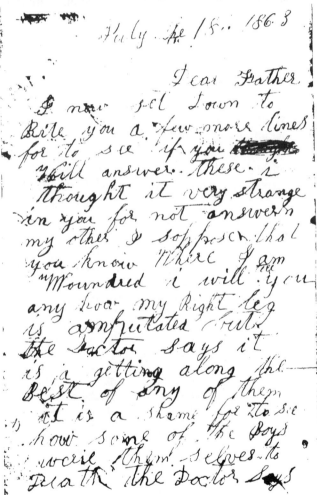

Top: *Private Nelson Reaser's grave in the Soldiers' National Cemetery, Gettysburg, Pennsylvania. Courtesy of the author.* Bottom: *The last letter of Nelson Reaser. Courtesy of the National Archives.*

Some members of the 151st remained in Baltimore during their convalescence. Quite possibly these were patients who could not endure further travel. A good example is Private Lewis Rentschler, Company E. It will be recalled from the battle narrative that Rentschler was struck twice on July 1st, first in the left leg twelve inches below the hip, and shortly afterward, in the left wrist. Lewis' brother, Henry, a medical student at the University of Pennsylvania, traveled to Gettysburg immediately following the battle and eventually located his brother lying wounded in a Baltimore hospital.

Dr. Henry found him "very low, emaciated, and prostrated with chronic diarrhea, and two bullet wounds." Henry remained with Lewis and cared for him until he regained sufficient strength to return home in early August.[96]

As a child, Aline Pinkard Rentschler, a granddaughter of Dr. Henry Rentschler, spent many hours listening to her father, uncles, and aunts recount old family stories. The most popular one concerned the exploits of Henry and Lewis during and after the memorable battle. We will follow Aline's colorful account from Henry's arrival in Gettysburg until the conclusion. The entire reminiscence is peppered with interesting anecdotes, some of which are barely plausible, while others are noticeably embellished. Obviously, Henry or one of his descendants livened up the story a bit for posterity.

> Dr. Henry continued on into Gettysburg just as the fighting was over, and found a town in complete disarray, everybody horrified at the scope and intensity of the battle and with much drinking going on to "forget" the thing. It was night and he slept on the floor of some unknown persons house....
>
> The next morning he went out to the wheatfield to look for his brother. He saw the dead lying all around and his brother was not among them. The wounded had all been taken to a hospital train which was bound for Baltimore. As he realized Lewis was not on the battlefield, he saw a piece of paper on the ground near him, picked it up and saw that it was a letter that he himself had written to Lewis, and knew then that his brother had been there. [Another version is that the letter was wedged in the base of a tree on the battlefield — and that Dr. Henry found his brother in a Lutheran church that was serving as a temporary hospital.]
>
> Dr. Henry found the hospital train and went through the cars searching, and found his brother lying there, "nearly gone." The train

went on and stopped at a small station (unknown) farther along. Dr. Henry spotted a nearby tavern, leaped out, plopped down a coin, asked for a glass of brandy ("quick"), ran back onto the train and kept his brother alive until the train reached its destination.

> It was also told that "Uncle Louie" was quite valiant on the battlefield. "Wracked with dysentery, his wound covered with maggots, he refused to quit. Too weak to load his gun, he begged his comrades to load it for him, and he kept on pulling the trigger."
>
> On the train to Baltimore ... was a young girl who was being somewhat bothered by some of the more mobile soldiers. Dr. Henry, seeing her plight, more or less protected her from them. When the train got to Baltimore, the young girl rushed over to her waiting parents and pointed to the nice young doctor who had come to her rescue. It happened that her father was one of the head doctors at the hospital in Baltimore and, grateful for young Dr. Henry's help, got him into the hospital as a physician, where he served and was able to care for his brother, Lewis.
>
> A sidelight of this was that one of the ensconced surgeons, was a rather jealous man, also a "drunkard," and did not care for the attention and new position given Dr. Henry. One evening while seated in a tavern, Dr. Henry glanced in the mirror over the bar, and saw the jealous doctor about to throw a knife at him. He was able to duck in time.[97]

In a footnote, Aline concedes that the story seems somewhat amazing, but that it was often repeated without variation, with the exception of the Lutheran church version. One thing is certain — the 151st was nowhere near the famous Wheatfield on July 2nd, 1863. Nonetheless, the essential elements of this uplifting story are preserved, and there can be no doubt that the loving care bestowed upon Lewis by his brother did much to ensure his survival.

In stark contrast to the saga of the Rentschler brothers, the plight of Benjamin Armstrong of Company D contains no humorous sidelights nor a happy ending. The 21-year-old private reached McKim's Hospital in Baltimore on July 10th with a damaged left lung and a shattered left wrist.

His detailed case history follows:

> He was placed on a full diet, with ale and ten drops of tincture of sesquichloride of iron thrice daily. The wound of the wrist becoming unhealthy in character, necessitated amputation of the forearm at the middle third. On August 31st, the patient was taken with pyaemic symptoms, and was ordered cin-

chona, with beef tea and milk-punch. On September 1st, the general condition was much worse, and the exhalations from the lungs and skin were very offensive. The stomach was irritable, and vomiting was not arrested by the administration of morphia in small doses, lime-water, etc. The patient continued to sink, and death occurred on September 6, 1863.[98]

Following Armstrong's death, Medical Cadet W. H. Bradley sent the perforated portion of the patient's lung with the above case history to the Army Medical Museum in Washington. Benjamin was buried in Loudon Park Cemetery far away from his home in Richfield, Pa.[99]

Private James Kaufman of Company G reached the Camden Street Hospital in the same city on July 11th and was later transferred to Harewood Hospital. Kaufman was suffering from a serious pelvis wound. A ball had entered his abdomen about one inch below the last rib on the left side and passed out the lower back. He was discharged on August 12th, his wound reported as being nearly healed. However, six weeks later, a Reading physician examined James and reported that both wounds were discharging freely. He also noted considerable swelling and irritation near the pelvic bone. The 21-year-old was determined to be three-quarters disabled.[100] It is impossible for us today to fully realize the pain and suffering experienced by disabled Civil War veterans long after the fighting ceased.

On July 14, 1863, Private James H. Morrison, Company B, age 26, died at Satterlee U.S. General Hospital in West Philadelphia. James never made it to the Gettysburg battlefield. Suffering with typhoid fever and severe diarrhea, he was admitted to a Washington, D.C., hospital on June 14th and then transferred to Philadelphia the next day. At the time of his death, Morrison's body was extremely emaciated and the skin marked with variolous scars.[101] He was one of the 195,657 soldiers who died in military hospitals in the North during the Civil War.[102]

Pennsylvania was one of four loyal states in which the fatalities from combat wounds exceeded those caused by disease within its soldiery, and additionally, the percentage of deaths from sickness relative to the total enlistments was lower in the Keystone State than in any other Northern state. These facts were largely attributable to the favorable geographical position of Philadelphia. From the very beginning of the war, the state employed transports to bring wounded Pennsylvania soldiers from tidewater Virginia and by rail from inland points to the fine military hospitals located in the city.[103]

A good example of Philadelphia's benevolence to the Union cause was the Union Refreshment Saloon. From its humble beginnings as a stove and a coffeepot in an old boathouse, this establishment grew to include dormitories, bathing facilities, and a medical center which served over 4,000,000 soldiers during the war.[104] To a Northern boy far from home, the city truly lived up to its nickname as the "City of Brotherly Love."

In 1862, the government built several large hospital complexes in Philadelphia to care for the sick and wounded from all of the Northern states. According to a report released in 1866 by the United States Sanitary Commission, 157,000 soldiers and sailors received care in the city, and at least twenty-five different facilities were in operation for varying periods from 1861 through 1865. The total capacity of these hospitals approached 14,000 beds.[105] It is easy to understand why Federal authorities shipped the wounded here from Gettysburg as soon as it was practical.

Oftentimes, a soldier's first introduction to the Philadelphia hospital system was the Citizen's Volunteer Hospital, which was located opposite the depot of the Philadelphia, Wilmington, and Baltimore Railroad on the northeast corner of Broad Street and Washington Avenue. It was specifically designed for the reception of the more serious cases arriving by train and was also utilized as a clearing house from which patients were gradually distributed to other area hospitals. Volunteer committees of concerned citizens regularly attended all incoming trains to provide quick help to the very ill and to fend off thieves and other miscreants seeking to prey on the soldiers.

This hospital was opened on September 5, 1862, and closed on August 11, 1865. Through May 10, 1864, 50,000 soldiers had passed through its doors.[106] It is likely that the group of wounded from the 151st spent the night of July 10th inside this building before being permanently assigned to other locations the next morning.

Alfred Staudt's diary entry for this date is typically terse, but nonetheless revealing: "We left Baltimore about three in the afternoon and reached Philadelphia at ten o'clock in the evening. There we laid in the hospital until morning." Sergeant Heilig wrote his wife, "We arrived at Philadelphia on Friday evening at 10 o'clock where we were overnight, and on Saturday morning to here."[107]

"Here" was ward 15 of the McClellan United States Army General Hospital. This hospital was the last government facility established in Philadelphia during the war. It was designed with an elliptic corridor from which eighteen wards radiated, the administrative offices being located in the center. Situated in the Nicetown district at the intersection of the Germantown Road and Cayuga Street, this hospital had a 400-bed capacity.[108]

Heilig listed the soldiers from Company H who were with him: William Miller, Franklin Boltz, Joseph Meier, John Fessler, William S. Strause, George Spangler, David Knoll, and William H. Scheaffer. Private Scheaffer had a "very terrible wound, found shot in the breast and out."

In contrast to the primitive field hospitals at Gettysburg, Heilig pronounced, "Living here is very good, all the best, and wounds well tended." Nevertheless, he felt his wounded shoulder could heal just as quickly at home, and he looked forward to being mustered out in about two weeks. However, this much anticipated event had lost some of its luster after the carnage at Gettysburg. "It wouldn't be [a] joy that we expected to have two weeks ago, since that's the time that near a hundred went to their eternal home, and a good two hundred were wounded."[109]

Heilig recalled that those riding in the car behind his were sent 2.5 miles farther to Mower U.S. General Hospital, which was situated on high ground near Chestnut Hill. A spur of the Reading Railroad led directly to the site. This vast compound covered 27 acres and contained beds for 4,000 patients! From a great, flatted, elliptical corridor, 47 wards, each 175 feet long, radiated outward like spokes on a wheel. The administration offices and medical department occupied a two-story building in the center of the complex which was bordered by kitchens, dining halls, power and heating plants, guard houses, and various other structures. Tramways extended through the corridors and along the center of each ward to facilitate the transportation of both food and patients. Water was supplied from a nearby reservoir. The staff included a steward, 47 ward masters, 141 nurses, and 2 firemen. A full band and drum corps furnished daily music.[110]

This extensive care and attention to detail could not save the life of Franklin Wendling. After lingering for over two weeks with a severe groin wound, the 17-year-old died on July 17th at Mower and was buried in the Odd Fellows Cemetery.[111] Young Franklin's death had serious consequences for the large Wendling farm family back in Kutztown.

Several other medical facilities in the city housed soldiers from the 151st. One of these sites was the Broad Street Hospital, which was formerly a station building on the Philadelphia and Reading Railroad. This hospital opened in February 1862, and branches were afterward established in the old market house on Broad Street and also on Cherry Street. The facility closed when the Mower hospital was completed in early 1863, but reopened for a short time after the battle of Gettysburg. Ladies from prominent families residing nearby took an active interest in the hospital. Interestingly, one of the staff surgeons was named Harrison Allen.[112]

Private David Scheimer of Company K died of pyemia (a blood infection caused by pus-forming bacteria) on July 26th inside this hospital. On July 3rd, his shattered right arm had been amputated above the elbow. He was buried in Glenwood Cemetery two days later. On this same day Charles Humbert died at Broad Street from the wounds he sustained on July 1st while acting as a brigade sharpshooter. Like Scheimer, Charles was a 21-year-old private in Company K and had resided in Reading before his enlistment.[113]

At Turners Lane Hospital near the junction of Twenty-second and Oxford, special studies were conducted concerning nerve diseases caused by combat wounds.[114] It was here that a large projectile was removed from the cheek of Private Diedrich Dasenbuck on July 17th. The ball was very much battered and included in its folds a tuft of hair. One month later, Diedrich had fully recovered from his unique wounds.[115] He was a lucky man indeed.

Corporal Davis Meredith, Company D, and Private Solomon Strause, Company H, received care at the Summit House General Hospital, a 522-bed facility located in West Philadelphia. Both men were released on July 21st and mustered out with their respective companies at Camp Curtin on July 27th.[116]

Others had to wait a bit longer. Alfred Staudt and another contingent of soldiers reached Harrisburg at eight o'clock on the evening of August 5th. The next morning the men were discharged, and in the early afternoon, they settled their accounts with the government and received their final pay. An hour later, they were homeward bound. Staudt noted that he received $127.63 in greenbacks and two wounds as compensation for his nine months of service.[117]

In addition to the large population centers of Baltimore and Philadelphia, wounded soldiers were also relocated to general hospitals in smaller cities and towns radiating in every direction from Gettysburg. To the west, a branch hospital was opened in Chambersburg. Others were removed north to Carlisle and Harrisburg, and by the 28th of July, 1,000 men had been sent eastward to York.[118]

From his correspondence with Mrs. Alexander Seiders described earlier, we know that Sergeant Major Arnold was quartered briefly in the latter city before being discharged by Dr. Henry Palmer, Surgeon, United States Volunteers. Private Ephraim Guyer of Company D was conveyed to York on August 23rd after being treated at an unspecified field hospital. Guyer was struck by a musket ball on July 1st, which fractured the humerus, passed along the clavicle, and lodged behind the sternum near a major artery. One day after his transfer, Ephraim died from an intermediary hemorrhage. He was buried nearby at the Prospect Hill Cemetery. Two days later, his personal effects consisting of his blanket, trousers, shoes, and pocketbook containing $7.07 were sent to his brother-in-law, A. Garver. Later, Ephraim's body was retrieved by his loved ones and placed in the Guyer family plot at the East Salem U. B. Cemetery in Juniata County.[119]

Some of the wounded were sent as far south as Annapolis, Maryland. Sergeant Robert Miller was relocated to ward six of St. Johns College Hospital in this city after poor health forced him to fall out during the northward march through Frederick. Writing to his brother on July 18th, he recorded, "Today I learned that there was one of the boys of our Regiment here in the Hospital wounded in the Gettysburg fight. I found him and learned that he belonged to Co. K of our regiment. He was wounded in the first days fight." The unidentified soldier told Miller that he had no specific information regarding Company F because their wounded were sent to a different field hospital. He added vaguely that his company and three others were quartered in "a large building."

Robert worried that his mother's frail health would be affected when she learned of the recent battle. He assured his brother that he was not dangerously sick and that he had been trying to get back to his regiment, but the doctors would not release him until he regained his full strength. "What makes me still more anxious than I otherwise would be is because I do not know exactly when the Regiment will be mustered out and of course I have a great anxiety to be with them when they are through," he explained.[120]

Indeed, even as Miller wrote these lines, Surgeon Blakeslee received an order to bring on to Harrisburg as many of the wounded as possible from the Gettysburg hospitals so that they might be mustered out with the troops gathered there already. Blakeslee mentioned that Captain Stone was among the number he accompanied to Camp Curtin in pursuance of the order.[121]

Franklin Weaber was transferred from Gettysburg on July 9th and entered Newton University Hospital in Baltimore two days later. He was eventually transported north to Harrisburg apparently to be mustered out with his company. On July 23rd, however, Franklin was admitted to the hospital at Camp Curtin, and four days later while many of his comrades were on their way home, he died. Thus, his army adventure ended just where it had begun.[122]

Not all of the wounded could be immediately transported from Gettysburg due to their fragile condition. Medical Inspector John M. Cuyler noted on July 25th that between 3,000 and 3,500 of these cases still remained near the late battlefield. The untransportable soldiers included those with deep penetrating wounds and patients who had suffered compound fractures of a limb. Therefore, it was determined that these patients would be temporarily quartered in a large general hospital "established at a suitable place near the town, where it was hoped they would receive all the comfort and attention they were so justly entitled."[123]

The "suitable place" ultimately selected for this purpose by Dr. Henry Janes, the surgeon in charge of all Gettysburg hospitals, was a portion of the George Wolf farm located one mile east of town and just south of the York Turnpike. The 80-acre site was named Camp Letterman in honor of Dr. Jonathan Letterman, the medical director of the Army of the Potomac.

This tract was particularly suitable for a hospital establishment because of its proximity to the railroad and the pike, which at this point ran parallel to one another. Food, clothing, and medical supplies flowed in from Washington via these transportation arteries. Following the required recovery period, soldiers could also be conveniently loaded upon railroad cars for transportation to other facilities.

The site also comprised several physical properties which made it highly desirable for its intended purpose. Historian J. Howard Wert wrote that "mature oaks provided shade and a natural spring flowed with cool, pure water." Located on an elevated knoll, the camp also benefited from good air circulation and water drainage.[124]

Final preparations were made at the site, and by July 16th the first tents were pitched in what would develop into a vast tent city. Three days later, volunteer nurse Sophronia Bucklin reported for duty at Camp Letterman. "The hospital tents were set in rows, five hundred of them, seeming like great fluttering pairs of white wings, brooding peacefully over those up between the rows, in order that they might dry quickly after summer rains," she recalled.[125]

A large cookhouse was built near the natural spring a short distance from the pike on the southern border of the camp. A relief lodge operated by the U.S. Sanitary Commission stood directly across the road adjacent to the railroad. Located on the camp's northern perimeter were the following: the headquarters of both the U.S. Sanitary and U.S. Christian Commissions, quarters for officers, surgeons, nurses, and attendants, an embalming tent, deadhouse, and a hospital graveyard.[126]

Next came the Herculean task of consolidating the scattered field hospitals and the delicate operation of transporting the severely wounded to the new general hospital. Dr. William Norris, who was introduced in the section pertaining to the Catholic Church hospital, recounted his efforts in complying with this order. In a letter to his father dated July 26, 1863, he wrote:

On Thursday afternoon [July 23], I received orders to break up the hospital and move all the men out to the General Hospital. This, however, would have been impossible to execute and it was finally countermanded. Our departure fixed for the next morning. At 4 o'clock A.M., our Hospital was astir and by 8:00 A.M., we were beginning to move. I sent those cases capable of transportation to Harrisburg, and most of our stumps by ambulance to the General Hospital, our com[pound] fract[ure]s of thigh and leg I had carried in stretchers and as the distance was a mile and a quarter, it was a considerable undertaking.... I succeeded in having everything moved out by 7:00 P.M.... Our patients bore the journey better than I had anticipated, those carried on stretchers did not appear to have suffered at all. The Hospital consists of hospital tents on the slope of a hill near Gettysburg and on the railroad; plenty of good water and woods on two sides of the encampment.

Dr. Norris noted that upon his arrival at Camp Letterman, he was placed in charge of the row of tents appropriated to the First Corps. This area consisted of 16 tents holding 192 beds, and was further subdivided into wards of 4 tents with a total of 48 beds each. An assistant surgeon was assigned to each ward.[127]

A very regimented routine was carried out by the nurses on a daily basis. Nurse Bucklin later described her duties:

The first round in the morning was to give the stimulants and to attend to the distribution of the extra diet.... [W]e were not called upon to dress the wounds, unless by specific request, wound dressers being assigned to each section of the ward.... Beef tea was passed three times a day, stimulants three times, and extra diet three times, making nine visits which each woman nurse made a day to each of the two hundred men under her charge. This was done besides washing the faces and combing the hair of those who were still unable to perform these services for themselves, preparing extra drinks ordered by the surgeons, and seeing that the bedding and clothing of every man was kept clean by the men nurses.[128]

After a month of operation, the Adams Sentinel lauded the hospital's efforts at caring for the hundreds of wounded gathered there. "Everything is being done to relieve and soothe the sufferers, that attention and kind human hands can do. Deaths do daily occur, but from the severity of many wounds, this cannot be prevented. All that skill and careful nursing can do, however, is being done."[129]

This careful attention could not save the life of 19-year-old William T. Strause of Company H, who suffered from wounds in the hand and knee joint. William died at Camp Letterman at 5 A.M. on August 1st, most likely from gangrene or tetanus. He was buried the next day in section 2, grave #13 of the hospital cemetery. On August 5th Sallie Myers wrote to William's father informing him of the death of his son. A month later, the elder William died at his home in Strausstown.[130]

On the very day that William succumbed to his wounds, Private Nelson McMicken's shattered right leg was finally amputated at the middle third of the thigh. It appears that this operation should have been performed much earlier. Nelson never recovered from the effects of the belated surgery. He died on August 12th and joined Strause in the temporary graveyard at Camp Letterman.[131]

Thus, Strause and McMicken were among the approximately three hundred patients from both sides who died at the hospital. Interestingly, one account noted that of the 180 soldiers quartered here who had bullet fractures of the thigh, 65 percent survived. As of November 15, only 60 patients remained, and the final soldier was scheduled to depart Camp Letterman on the 17th. The hospital officially closed on November 20th, the day following Lincoln's famous address at the National Cemetery.[132]

Not all those who made it home survived. On the opening day of the battle, Private William C. Carr was shot over the heart and also in the left leg and hand. He returned home

An amputation scene at Camp Letterman Hospital, August 1863. Private Nelson McMicken, Company A, had his right leg amputated at the middle third of the thigh on August 1st. He died 11 days later. Courtesy of MOLLUS Collection, USAMHI.

to his residence in Freehold, Warren County, where he died on September 28, 1863.[133] Unlike many of his comrades, William spent his final days in a familiar environment surrounded by friends and family.

More frequently, the family members of the slain descended upon the battlefield seeking to locate the bodies of their loved ones, in order to relocate them to regional plots and cemeteries. Thomas McClure, the chaplain of the 151st, became personally involved in one of these quests. The following notice appeared in an area newspaper on October 1, 1863: "Any person giving information of the grave of James M. Daniel, Twenty-seventh Pennsylvania volunteers, will confer a great favor on an affected family in Philadelphia. Address, Rev. Thomas F. McClure, Oakland Mills, Juniata County, Pa."[134]

Following his death at the Christ Lutheran Church, Frank Lyon's remains were transported all the way back to Warren County, where he was laid to rest in the Thompson Hill Cemetery. The body of Samuel Nailor, Jr., age 20, was removed to the family plot in East Salem, Pa., after his death on July 22nd.[135]

After learning of her son's wounding, Margery Tucker, the widowed mother of Lieutenant Andrew G. Tucker of the 142nd Pennsylvania, traveled to Get-

tysburg to help care for Union County soldiers in the Gettysburg hospitals. One can only imagine her shock and grief upon discovering her son's shallow grave and its improvised headboard upon which his name and regiment were carefully etched. Mrs. Tucker arrived back in Lewisburg a few days later with the remains of her only son.[136]

Meanwhile, plans were being made for the exhumation of the Union dead to a Soldier's Cemetery located adjacent to the Evergreen Cemetery on Cemetery Hill. Although the work was not completed until April 1864, the seventeen-acre plot was officially dedicated on November 19, 1863, when President Lincoln delivered his famous Gettysburg Address.

At least six men from the 151st were removed to the Soldier's National Cemetery: Thomas D. Allen, Nelson Reaser, William S. Stamm, Jacob Zimmerman, William T. Strause, and Nelson McMicken. With so many bodies to be relocated, mistakes were inevitable. For example, Private William T. Strause now lies under a granite headstone marked "William S. Strause," who in fact survived the battle. The stone marking the final resting place of Company A's Nelson McMicken was somehow translated into "N. McWitkin. Co. A. Regt. 15."[137]

The incorrectly engraved markers of Nelson McMicken (top) *and William T. Strause* (bottom) *in the Soldiers' National Cemetery, Gettysburg, Pennsylvania. Author's collection.*

As related earlier, both men died at Camp Letterman in August so that proper identification should not have been difficult. Rather, the errors may have been attributable to the fact that the temporary wooden headboards marking the graves were identified by pencil. A visitor to the cemetery in June 1864 noted that these markings were becoming obliterated by the elements. Thus, the stonecutters, who were still working during the summer of 1865, must have experienced considerable difficulty with the fading transient records.[138]

A short distance to the south in the Evergreen Cemetery rest the remains of Corporal John Schaffer and Private Henry M. Weber of the 151st. When Lincoln delivered his eloquent address on that chilly November afternoon, he stood within earshot of the graves of the eight men listed above. "It is rather for us to be here dedicated to the great task remaining before us — that from these honored dead we take increased devotion to that cause for which they here gave the last full measure of devotion — that we here highly resolve that these dead shall not have died in vain...."

Chapter 7

TWENTY MONTHS IN DIXIE

"We felt that our government had abandoned us."

During the course of the three-day battle, the Army of Northern Virginia captured over 5,000 Union soldiers.[1] At least two-thirds of this total were snagged from the First and Eleventh Corps on July 1st. The first reaction of these unfortunate souls was often that of extreme mortification and despair. "It had never occurred to me that I might be taken prisoner, and when I found I was helpless in their hands, my feelings can't be described," recalled Lieutenant Charles Potts, after he was picked up by a squad of rebels on Chambersburg Street.[2] The feelings of dejection expressed by Potts were well-founded, because by the summer of 1863, the prisoner exchange system adopted earlier in the war was in a state of flux.

When the Civil War erupted in 1861, the consensus on both sides was that the fighting would be of short duration. Very few envisioned the conflict grinding on for four long and bloody years. Consequently, neither side made any substantial preparations for the long term care and confinement of large numbers of prisoners of war. This neglect, exacerbated by other factors, ultimately lead to a logistical nightmare and the unnecessary suffering and deaths of thousands of soldiers from both sides.

During the first year of the war, the opposing armies adhered loosely to the old European tradition of parole and exchange. Under this system, captured soldiers were permitted to rejoin their units after a corresponding number of prisoners were taken and then exchanged by the other side. Any prisoner not exchanged within ten days of his capture was released upon signing a pledge that he would not take up arms against the enemy until notified he had been exchanged for an enemy captive. Remarkably, these soldiers often returned home while they served out their parole! The details of these informal transactions were usually left up to the discretion of the field commanders.[3]

Of course, not all prisoners of war were exchanged, and as the war continued longer than the few months nearly everyone had predicted, makeshift prisons were created in both the North and the South. These fortifications were an eclectic mix and consisted of existing jails and prisons, coastal fortifications, old buildings and warehouses, barracks and tents enclosed by high fences, and even barren stockades or barren ground. The Confederate States of America attempted to develop a centralized prison system in the capital of Richmond, but simply did not have adequate resources to feed, clothe, and shelter an ever-growing prison population.[4]

The Lincoln administration was reluctant to negotiate with President Jefferson Davis on a general exchange agreement because it feared that the Confederate government would be recognized as a legitimate, sovereign power by the European nations. Although several exchanges were carried out on an irregular basis, the stalemate continued. By June of 1862, roughly 20,000 Confederate soldiers languished in Northern prisons, while between 9,000 to 12,000 Union captives were being detained in Southern facilities.[5]

One Union officer remarked bitterly:

It may be ... one of the essentials of war, that places be provided for the confinement of prisoners, but they do not necessarily include every species of torment which the human mind is capable of conceiving. They should not naturally presuppose the absence of all humanity, and the annihilation of every condition of comfortable existence ... in almost every part of the South where the Confederate authorities have opened them.[6]

Sadly, the same could be said for Northern prisons.

Eventually, Washington officials yielded to intense media coverage and public pressure, and talks were initiated with the Confederacy. Secretary of War Edwin A. Stanton announced the appointment of the venerable General John A. Dix to represent the United States during the negotiations. His counterpart was General Daniel Harvey Hill, who was selected by Robert E. Lee, to look after Confederate interests in the matter.

The first discussions on a formal exchange were held on February 23, 1862. It was not until five months later, however, that an official agreement was announced. Known as the Dix-Hill Cartel, it stipulated that future exchanges would take place at two designated locations: City Point, Virginia, in the East and Vicksburg, Mississippi, in the West. In addition, a corresponding scale of equivalents was worked out. For example, a commanding general could be exchanged for sixty privates, one brigadier general for twenty, one colonel for fifteen, one captain for six, and so on.[7]

Invariably, difficulties arose almost immediately, and by the end of the year, a major impasse developed between the governments in regard to the exchange of black Union soldiers. Insisting that the African Americans were runaway slaves, the Southerners refused to exchange them for white soldiers. Furthermore, President Davis issued a decree which stated that any white officer captured while leading black soldiers in battle could be put to death under the laws of the Confederate States of America.

As a result, Secretary Stanton suspended the exchange of all commissioned officers on December 28, 1862. Then, on May 25, 1863, less than a month before the Gettysburg campaign commenced, all exchanges were terminated by Henry Halleck, Lincoln's General in Chief.[8]

Although the cartel had officially collapsed, Halleck later issued General Order No. 207, which contained a clause that paroles and exchanges were "not necessarily or absolutely forbidden." For his part, President Lincoln pointed out that "paroles for the convenience of the captor" should not be honored.[9]

Thus, any captured Union officer or enlisted man was now subject to a contradictory and confusing set of orders and protocol on the prisoner of war issue. Often, each man was forced to decide whether to accept parole and thereby risk legal censure or refuse all such offers and suffer the consequences in the notorious prison pens of the South.

Soon after their capture on July 1st, Union prisoners were escorted behind the lines under guard.

The initial collecting point was probably near the Samuel Cobean farm, along the Carlisle Road, which was located a little over a mile from the town square. After his capture, Captain Bernhard Domschcke, a captain in the 26th Wisconsin of the Eleventh Corps, was allowed one last look at the place where his regiment had fought only minutes before. He was then escorted by three Rebel soldiers to an open field next to a farmstead, where he joined "several thousand fellow wretches."[10]

This temporary prison camp was under the command of Colonel W. H. French of the 14th West Virginia, which belonged to Alfred Jenkins' cavalry brigade. Lieutenant Potts found French to be a "good hearted old Virginia gentleman." Captain Domschcke was less complimentary, calling the Rebel colonel "a half-humane man."[11] An incident soon occurred here which tested the humanity of the Southern commander.

Lieutenant Potts narrates the episode:

> I observed a boy, and asking him how he came there, he said he had been attending college, and with a number of others, had taken positions in the ranks, and had been in the fight all day. He was a son of Colonel Lamon of Pittsburgh.... I took him to Colonel French, and asked for his release. He said they found many boys with guns in their hands, and they should be treated as prisoners, but he finally released him.[12]

As darkness descended over the now quiet battlefield, Potts decided to have a bite to eat before retiring for the evening. To his dismay, he discovered only three and one-half pieces of hardtack in his haversack. On a partially full stomach, he reclined on a bed of clover near Captains Gray and Boltz. The next morning the three officers would face a decision that would affect their lives forever.

On the morning of July 2nd, officers and enlisted men were separated. An offer of parole was then made by the Confederates, but with the warning that these documents might not be accepted by the U.S. Government. Sergeant Joseph Arnold of the 26th Wisconsin received permission to discuss the matter with Captain Domschcke, who flatly informed him that the government would not recognize the paroles and that anyone accepting the offer must assume responsibility for the consequences. Arnold and three dozen of his comrades turned down the offer.[13] The three officers of the 151st agreed and also refused to accept parole. Afterward, with the benefit of hindsight, many regretted their decision.

Despite these warnings, over 1,500 officers and men decided to accept the parole offer. These soldiers needed only to answer as their names were called and afterward pledge "not to bear arms against the Confederate government until they were honorably released from the obligation they were about to assume."[14]

Lieutenant Edward Ross of the 20th New York Militia was among the 300 unwounded Union soldiers that were sent off from the Lutheran Seminary Hospital on July 2nd. Ross was taken to General A. P. Hill's headquarters and paroled by Major Wingate, the inspector general of the Army of Northern Virginia. In a letter to Colonel Gates dated Monday, July 6th, Ross related, "They left us until Friday night when we were started for here [Carlisle] with about 1,500 men and 16 officers, Capt. Hughes of the 2nd Wis[consin] regt. having charge. The men were sent to Harrisburg this morning by the provost marshall. I and the other officers start this afternoon."[15]

Meanwhile, the officers and men who declined the parole were marched southwest to a field behind Seminary Ridge in the proximity of Willoughby Run. One soldier pointed out that the field was off the main road a short distance near a low, one-story unpainted house where there was a spring. Potts remembered being quartered behind the Confederate artillery near General George E. Pickett's headquarters for the remainder of the battle. Another officer also recalled sleeping on the ground in front of the general's tent.[16]

The evening of July 2nd was spent in great anxiety as the prisoners were thwarted in their attempts to receive reliable information on the outcome of the day's fighting. When Rebel bands struck up joyous tunes and gray-clad soldiers chimed in with hurrahs, the Northern captives feared the worst.[17]

During their stay in this vicinity, the men viewed General Pickett up close. Captain Domschcke was not impressed by the future legend.

> The archetype of a Virginia slave baron strutted briskly, proud in bearing, head lifted in arrogance. On horseback he looked like the ruler of a continent. Obviously he took great pains with appearance — riding boots aglitter, near-shoulder-length hair tonsorially styled — but the color of the nose and upper cheeks betrayed that he pandered the inner man.[18]

Positioned just behind the Confederate battlelines, the Union prisoners must have been in a precarious position during the massive artillery bombardment which preceded the decisive infantry charge. Once again ignorance of the result doubled the suffering of the captives. The three officers of the 151st would have derived a great deal of pleasure had they known that the survivors of their regiment played an important role in the repulse of Pickett's Virginians.

Potts and Gray maintained that their squad received no food until the evening of July 3rd. The scanty ration consisted of a small quantity of flour which was mixed with water from the creek and baked on flat stones into a strange type of bread that Potts pronounced he had never seen before, "but would have been very glad to have had later on."[19]

Ironically, Potts and his comrades began their long trek south to imprisonment on Independence Day. The Southerners moved with great haste throughout the morning gathering up horses, wagons, and everything movable for the retrograde movement. Messengers galloped about wildly and troops were shuffled about.

Soon the captives were ordered to join the polyglot procession of supply wagons, artillery trains, and long columns of infantry. "As we marched along in the down pouring rain," recalled Potts, "We actually felt happy to think that after a three days hard fight, the rebels had been defeated and driven back to his own battlefield." But the knowledge of a Union victory was bittersweet for the men marching south. "Never had joy and grief so crowded at once into our souls," lamented Domschcke.[20]

Unknown to the Wisconsin captain and his unfortunate comrades, General Lee had sent a message to Meade at 6:35 A.M. that same morning by a flag of truce proposing an exchange of prisoners to be made at once for the comfort and convenience of the captives. Two hours later, Meade responded that he had no authority to make the exchange. He no doubt surmised that Lee's primary reason for making this offer was to avoid the drain upon his manpower and supplies that came with guarding and feeding 2,500 to 3,000 Union prisoners during the retreat.[21]

The miserable weather quickly sobered the men as they marched southwest along the Hagerstown Road. A terrific thunder and lightning storm exploded overhead. The rain fell in sheets and drenched the marchers. Large trees bent in submission to the violent winds. The torrential rain and muddy conditions weakened the soldiers and slowed the progress of the movement.

The enemy infantry and artillery commanded the right-of-way on the narrow roadway. Thus, the

Major General George E. Pickett. Courtesy of MOLLUS Collection, USAMHI.

Northern prisoners and their escort from Pickett's Division were forced to parallel the movement by trudging through wet fields and meadows, climbing over fences and hedges, and wading across creeks filled to capacity by the recent deluge. After six tortuous miles, the prisoners collapsed for the evening on the saturated ground.

When the column passed through Fairfield the next day, loyal women stood in the doorways and wept at the sight of so many boys in blue being herded south into captivity. As Lee's army and its captives ascended the South Mountain range, the various elements of the procession bunched together through the narrow defiles. The situation demanded caution. A careless slip could result in being crushed by the wheels of a heavy artillery piece or gashed by horses' hooves. A few of the prisoners opportunistically slipped away into the forest and escaped.

The column halted near Monterey where another offer of parole was extended to the Federals.

The Union prisoners defiantly refused to agree to something that so obviously benefited their captors.[22] At this time Potts remembered trying to appease his hunger by munching on green apples.[23]

Despite his aristocratic airs, George Pickett pitied his adversaries. Perhaps the slaughter of his division a few days earlier contributed to his sensitivities. In a letter to his sweetheart, the general confided, "Oh, the pity of it, guarding these prisoners through their own country, depleted and suffering mentally and physically as we are, and being forced to march forward with a speed beyond their own and our endurance."[24]

The arduous journey continued west through Waynesboro, Pennsylvania, where all of the houses were tightly closed, then southwest to Hagerstown, Maryland, and finally on to Williamsport near the Potomac River. The last named destination was reached on the afternoon of July 7th. The prisoners were hungry, tired, and weak following the 40-mile trek from Gettysburg. They had just marched thirty miles nonstop. The Northerners camped for the night on a grassy knoll near a wheatfield. A number of men plucked the kernels from the stalks for nourishment. It rained hard throughout the night.[25]

As mentioned in a previous chapter, the river proved to be a formidable obstacle in Lee's path, and he was forced to dig in and prepare for an attack until the water receded. The Union captives held on to the slim hope that their comrades would crush the fleeing enemy and liberate them before the crossing could be effected.

This optimism was dashed on July 9th, when the Confederates ferried the Federal prisoners across the swollen Potomac to the Virginia shore by means of an old flatboat. The crossing took nearly all day to complete. After a short rest period, the prisoners were ordered to form ranks for another march. The Northerners gazed across the river one last time, and with their eyes, longingly caressed the scenic Maryland mountains, which had come to symbolize freedom and hope.[26] It was a sight that many would never enjoy again.

At this point, Brigadier General John Imboden and his ragtag band of partisan cavalry replaced Pickett's infantrymen as the guard escort. The general was described as "a notorious character, who had small love for a yankee."[27]

A Virginia lawyer and legislator, Imboden organized the Staunton Artillery at the outbreak of hostilities. He was given a special appointment as brigadier general in early 1863. He then took command of a semi-independent brigade of mounted partisan troops. These armed riders were held in low esteem as combat troops, especially when compared to Jeb Stuart's veteran cavalrymen. They were unruly, undisciplined, and not bashful about robbing civilians of their horses and valuables. These attributes made them particularly well-suited for foraging, raiding, and guarding supply bases and wagon trains. Consequently, the command served in an auxiliary capacity during the Gettysburg campaign.[28]

Imboden's men had just recently piloted the Army of Northern Virginia's 17-mile ambulance train through enemy territory. With this assignment now complete, Lee selected them for the task of escorting the Northern prisoners up the Shenandoah Valley to the terminus of the Virginia Central Railroad at Staunton. It was a natural selection because these partisan troops were very familiar with the country.

On July 10th, the despised Yankees were pushed forward a dozen miles to Martinsburg, which several prisoners rated as the most patriotic town they had seen during the campaign. Nearly all of the citizens crowded in to assist the Federals, and several of them risked bodily injury to hand out food to the men.[29]

By July 12th, the men reached Winchester, which is located 22 miles southwest of Martinsburg. By contrast, the reception here was less cordial. The elderly gentlemen and aristocratic ladies of the town gathered on the verandahs and stood silently as the long blue column passed by.[30] The 16,000 residents of the Frederick County community had grown accustomed to the sight of soldiers. Winchester was the gateway to the Shenandoah Valley, one of the richest agricultural regions in the nation. The valley also served as a natural invasion route for both armies during various campaigns. Consequently, Winchester changed hands at least 72 times during the war.[31]

During the Gettysburg campaign, General Robert Milroy's Federal garrison was routed by Richard Ewell's Second Corps. The fortifications utilized by Milroy's men just northeast of Winchester could be seen as the column entered the town via the Martinsburg Pike. Several area hospitals were filled with the wounded from this battle.

The captives were then marched south along the Valley Pike, a macadam surfaced roadway constructed in the 1840s. The scenic Blue Ridge Mountains bordered the Shenandoah Valley on the east, and the Alleghenies rose up majestically to the west, framing the green pastures and ripening grainfields which flourished in the intervening valley floor. But the Northerners had little chance to enjoy these natural splendors.

Imboden's cavalry forced the prisoners to cover fifteen to twenty miles a day. Heavy rains fouled the roads and drenched the men. At one point the prisoners were forced to wade a swollen stream because the bridge had washed out. Building fires for warmth and cooking was nearly impossible. Often, the men arose in the morning soaked and chilled to begin yet another grueling march. According to Captain Gray, the daily ration consisted of only a pint of flour and a very small piece of meat.[32]

The journey led through Middletown, Strasburg, Toms Brook, Woodstock, Edinburg, Mount Jackson, New Market, Harrisonburg, Mount Crawford, and finally to Staunton, the last stop on the nearly 100-mile trek from Winchester. All of these towns and villages appeared either old-fashioned or weather-beaten to one Union officer. He noted viewing many empty houses and few commercial enterprises as the male populace consisted primarily of elderly men and boys. The females observed were "mostly shabby" and usually wore black.[33]

When the captives reached their destination on the evening of July 17th, they were placed under guard on a high hill overlooking the Staunton depot. In a little less than two weeks, the Northerners had traversed roughly 175 miles in miserable weather with poor food and little rest. Some of the men, such as Private Frank Elvidge of the 150th Pennsylvania, had marched barefoot over the rough turnpike road. Things were about to get worse, however.

During the next three weeks the Federal captives were shipped by train from Staunton to Richmond. Apparently, the officers were transported first. On the morning of the 18th, Boltz, Potts, and Gray were marched to the station and boarded the cars with a number of their comrades. Before their departure, one of Imboden's lieutenants searched the officers and confiscated the few blankets and coats still in their possession.[34]

The accommodations for the 136-mile journey were far from first-class. The train consisted of "dirt cars, with an old cattlebox of an engine to haul us." One enlisted man recalled riding in a rickety box car without a roof. He fully expected to be dumped out and left along the roadbed before the end of the trip. Nevertheless, the scenery was remarkable as the men enjoyed splendid views of the rugged mountains and peaceful valleys in the untamed Virginia countryside.[35] These pristine images would juxtapose sharply

Brigadier General John Imboden. Courtesy of MOLLUS Collection, USAMHI.

with the hellish scenes that would play out over the next twenty months.

Finally, on the evening of the 18th, the train rumbled into the Confederate capitol and stopped near a busy thoroughfare in the heart of the city. The prisoners formed a four-file column and moved off under a heavy guard. Hundreds of residents gathered on both sides of the dismal procession to catch a glimpse of the hated Yankees or perhaps to jeer and throw objects at the captives. Prisoner arrival times were often scheduled for daylight hours in the larger cities to create this submissive effect.

After a march of fifteen or twenty minutes, the Union officers were halted at the intersection of 19th and Cary Streets. In front of them stood a plain three-story brick building. A small wooden sign on the western corner read: "Libby & Son, Ship Chandlers & Grocers."[36]

Ironically, the building that became known sim-

ply as Libby Prison, and which eventually gained an infamous reputation second only to that of Andersonville, was first owned by a former Yankee from Maine. Luther Libby moved to Richmond in 1845 and entered into a partnership with a Richmonder in the ship chandling business. When a disagreement surfaced over business expansion, the partnership dissolved. In 1860, Libby and his son, George, constructed a brick warehouse near the James River. The new enterprise was just beginning to flourish when Confederate officials confiscated the building for government use in early 1862.

The Libby building soon became the headquarters for the Confederate States Military Prisons. All arriving POWs were processed here before being transported to other facilities in or outside the city. Only commissioned officers, however, were incarcerated at Libby. Most of the enlisted men were transported a short distance to Belle Isle, a small island in the James River that had previously been a favorite resort area for Richmond citizens. This site was in full view from Libby's southwest windows.

Libby's warehouse building was considered ideal for housing prisoners for several reasons. First, it was easily accessible by both railroad and water transportation. Too, the building's somewhat isolated location away from major residential areas made it attractive for security purposes. The fact that the warehouse had running water was another plus. The most important selection factor, however, might have been the building's spacious interior.

The warehouse measured about 135 feet across the front along Cary Street and extended 90 feet back to Canal Street. The interior was divided into three equal sections by heavy partitions which ran from the basement to the roof. Thus, each of the building's three stories were conveniently divided into three rooms, measuring 45 × 90 feet each. The upper six rooms were set aside for prisoners.[37]

An observer described one of these living spaces as "a room ... with bare brick walls, a rough plank floor, and narrow, dingy windows, to whose sash only a few broken panes were clinging. A row of tin washbasins, and a wooden trough which served as a bathing-tub, were at one end of it, and half a dozen cheap stools and hard bottomed chairs were littered about the floor, but it had no other furniture."[38]

The lower rooms were utilized for various purposes. The east room served primarily as a hospital, the middle functioned as a kitchen, while the west room was allocated for office space for prison officials.

Steep wooden stairs, without landings, connected the floors.[39]

The basement beneath the warehouse was divided into dungeons for the solitary confinement of unruly inmates. This area soon caused great trepidation among the prison populace. Captain Domschcke described the subterranean cells as "tiny dark holes infested by rats and other vermin."[40]

The exterior of the building forebode of the prison's interior spaces. Its unpainted walls were scorched to a rusty brown, and together with its weather-stained sunken doors and cobwebbed windows, filled here and there with a dusky pane, gave the whole building a most uninviting and desolate appearance. For added security, iron bars were installed over the windows, and the lower portion of the outer wall was whitewashed to make escaping prisoners more visible to the guards.[41]

When the Gettysburg captives arrived in front of Libby after their march through Richmond, a number of inmates appeared at the second and third floor windows. These officer prisoners had served under General Milroy at Winchester or under Colonel Abdel D. Streight of the 51st Indiana. Streight had surrendered a large portion of his command to Nathan Bedford Forrest on May 3, 1863, after a failed raid into Northern Alabama.[42]

The inmates tossed down a note of warning to their comrades on the street: "Hide your greenbacks!" The new arrivals responded to the warning by concealing their currency in caps, boots, and in coat linings. Others crushed the bills in their hands or placed them in their mouths to avoid detection.[43]

The warning proved to be timely and well-advised, for in a few minutes, the captives were led into the prison's administrative office and thoroughly searched and robbed of money and valuables. Even personal items such as photographs and souvenirs were seized.

One officer protested vehemently after a piece of shell was taken from him. The shell fragment had killed one of his men at Gettysburg and it had been saved as a memento. As a result of his defiance, the angry officer was struck in the face by a stern, well-built man with dark hair and flashing blue eyes.[44]

This introduction to Richard R. Turner, the head jailer at Libby, was a precursor of things to come. "Dick" Turner quickly developed an evil reputation among the prisoners. The 23-year-old former plantation overseer frequently displayed a propensity for physical violence in response to minor offenses. He once chained four inmates in the dungeon for refusing to clean his stable. On another occasion he lashed a black teamster 500 times. The whipping continued long after the victim had lost consciousness.[45]

Although not as openly hostile as his subordinate, Major Thomas Pratt Turner, the commandant at Libby, would eventually become deeply despised by his prisoners for the strict discipline imparted by his regime. Turner had attended the Virginia Military Institute for one year before he left to obtain a commission in the 1st Virginia Battalion. He was of thin build, quick, and energetic, with a deep voice. He always wore a full-dress Confederate uniform and was clean-shaven and well-groomed.[46]

Thomas and Richard Turner were apparently

Libby Prison, Richmond, Virginia. Note the barred windows, the whitewashed lower walls, and the guardhouses near the western side of the structure. The upper east room, which was occupied by the captured Gettysburg officers, is located on the far left of the view. Courtesy of MOLLUS Collection, USAMHI.

unrelated, but often confused in prisoner's memoirs. Captain Gray simply referred to them as "heartless men."[47] A Northern writer asserted, "The very name of Libby has become synonymous with that of terror; it carries tyranny and oppression in its simple sound." Undoubtedly, the harsh conduct of the Turners contributed a great deal to the prison's opprobrium.[48]

After the shakedown was completed, the officers were sent upstairs to the upper east room. "We selected a spot on the floor for our bed or sleeping place, as well as to occupy the same through the day as a sitting place, having neither bed, chair nor tables," related Potts.

The new arrivals were soon sought out by the other inmates for up-to-date information on military and national affairs. It delighted them to learn of Lee's defeat at Gettysburg. Potts was greatly surprised to discover an old acquaintance among the veteran prisoners, Lieutenant William Heffner of the 67th Pennsylvania, a former "First Defender" who was captured at Winchester in June.[49]

Initially, the Gettysburg officers occupied the upper east and upper middle rooms. Milroy's and Streight's officers had been assigned to the two rooms on the western side of the building. The upper rooms were preferred because of their higher ceilings and better lighting. A large number of captured Federal officers from Chickamauga arrived in Richmond in late September and were housed in the two middle rooms. The prison population would then swell to about 1,100 men. At first adequate space was not a major concern, however.[50]

The next morning the Gettysburg officers received their first prison meal. It consisted of wheat bread and soup made from bacon and rice "with about two inches of razor back oil floating on top, in company with numberless rice worms or weevils, to make it look inviting." Potts' appetite was not adversely affected by the disturbing sights for he was "hungry enough to eat swill." Captain Gray, on the other hand, was mortified. He begged his old friend not to show him the worms or speak of them, and then attempted to down his meal with closed eyes. Worse, the portions were minute and the only other ration issued throughout the remainder of the day was a second helping of bread at noon.[51]

The quality of the drinking water also elicited negative comments. Piped in directly from the canal adjacent to the James River, it was lukewarm in the summer and often laced with yellowish soil after a rain. The culinary situation improved somewhat when Thomas Turner ordered the installation of cookstoves in a portion of the upper middle room so that the prisoners could prepare their own meals.[52]

Turner also permitted the men to purchase additional food and other items through the prison commissary. This system was fraught with corruption, most commonly through the exchange rate used to convert Yankee greenbacks into Confederate currency. Several Union officers involved in these transactions were also suspected of unfair practices, and thereby profited at the expense of their fellow inmates. Nonetheless, an officer with purchasing power could do much to insure his personal well-being or perhaps his very survival by obtaining additional nourishment through Turner's commissary.

Another privilege afforded the officers was the opportunity to buy copies of the Richmond newspapers. Amusing at first for their obvious lack of objectivity, the Confederate organs soon became monotonous reading material.

In the early days, the officers themselves attended to the sanitation of their quarters. Later, a squad of Negroes scrubbed the floors, cleaned the stairways, carried wood, delivered rations to the prisoners, and performed other menial tasks. A number of these men had served as orderlies in the Union army before being captured by the Confederates.[53]

Despite these efforts at cleanliness, mice and vermin soon overran the building. Potts maintained that these creatures "would play hide and seek all over us, frequently running over our faces. We had to keep our mouths closed to prevent them [from] hunting for something to eat down our throats."[54]

After the prisoners settled in to their new quarters, they immersed themselves in a variety of activities to help fill the long hours. Captain Boltz wrote his wife on July 27: "[D]on't trouble yourself about me. I am perfect well and in good spirits and I hope these few lines will find you all in the same state of good health. I am with good companion[s]. We have religious services every day and I hope the Lord protects me to the end of this imprisonment...."[55]

For the less evangelical, a multitude of other pursuits were available. Potts recalled:

> We passed the time in playing cards, checkers, whist, or anything we could do to relieve the monotony of our confinement. Some of our ambitious comrades read law, others studied shorthand, and we had a large class in grammar. Some of the boys got a few musical instruments

out in the city, organized a good string band, and their music was very much enjoyed, even by the rebel officials, who frequently came in to hear them.[56]

Most of the intellectual and educational pastimes derived from the influence of Louis N. Bouldrye, chaplain of a New York regiment, and a man of diversified education and rather liberal religious views. Besides conducting daily worship services, the versatile chaplain instructed classes in stenography and French. Other officers taught Spanish and even German, despite the fact that many Americans harbored deep prejudices for those of German nationality.[57]

The prisoners formed a system of self-government by organizing the Prisoner's Club, and a number of foreign-born officers created the "Libbyan Society." A debating club called the Lyceum was formed, which took up all sorts of "bizarre topics," and "queer notions and ridiculous opinions came to light" almost daily. A minstrel society also appeared and its regular performances delighted audiences with songs, instrumental pieces, and more commonly, bawdy farces and skits.

One of the more interesting projects launched at Libby was the publication of a weekly newspaper, the *Libby Prison Chronicle*. A single handwritten copy was prepared and read to the prison population every Friday morning. This literary effort gave rise to "an extensive corps of able correspondents, local reporters, poets, punsters, and witty paragraphers."[58]

Of course, letter writing remained an almost universal activity. But these communications were often limited as to both length and content and were subject to strict censorship.[59] To adhere to this policy, German officers such as William Boltz penned their letters home in English by order of prison officials.

At the outset, when the rooms had not yet been filled to capacity, an effort was also made at physical fitness. Major George Van Buren of the 6th New York Cavalry recalled that Captain Gray frequently raced through the building and up and down flights of stairs. He declared that no one in the building could catch him. The other prisoners referred to the 41-year-old captain as "Pappy Gray." He was admired as "a fine, upright gentleman" and despite his age he entered prison life as "a particularly sound and healthy man."[60]

Despite all of these extracurricular activities, a prisoner's thoughts always seemed to revert to one common goal. "Each of us strove every which way to shorten the summer days, which seemed endless. Yet we could neither stifle boredom nor banish the thought of exchange," related Bernhard Domschcke. Lieutenant Colonel Frederick F. Cavada referred to the frequent rumors of exchange as "a frightful epidemic of that alarming malady known as 'Exchange on the Brain.'"[61]

As the summer days melted away into fall, the officers comforted themselves with the flimsy theory that the Lincoln administration had postponed a general exchange until the end of the autumn campaign season. By doing so, the U.S. government would avoid returning to the enemy a large number of well-cared-for prisoners, they reasoned.

Meanwhile, special exchanges still took place between the two governments. The first prisoner freed in this manner among the Gettysburg captives was Brigadier General Charles K. Graham. These special arrangements demoralized the general prison populace and naturally led to accusations of favoritism and sycophantic behavior.

By the end of autumn, the confined officers learned from Northern newspapers that prospects for exchange were bleak. The only hope for an early release now rested with a military success. But when Meade's Mine Run campaign ground to a halt by the beginning of December, the prisoners resigned themselves to spending the winter inside Libby. They pinned their new hopes on the spring campaign of 1864.[62]

As the hopes of the inmates faded, conditions at Libby steadily deteriorated. With the influx of prisoners from Chickamauga in early October, every room was filled to capacity. The new arrivals displaced a group of civilian prisoners caught at Gettysburg and other locations from the lower middle room.

The civilians were relocated to a space at ground level near the cellar. For some reason these captives were treated worse than their military counterparts. The officers communicated with these poor sufferers through a secret hole in the floor and passed down small pieces of food through the opening whenever possible.[63]

Meanwhile, rations diminished and the quality of the fare steadily declined. Bread changed from wheat to corn. The corn bread was "in the form and size of a paving brick, and nearly as hard, with the impression of the baker's hand upon each loaf." The meat issue was gradually replaced by medium-sized sweet potatoes and nearly rotten cabbage. Eventually, the daily ration consisted of only a few tablespoons of rice or beans, which were frequently worm-eaten.[64]

As stated previously, prisoners with money could improve their situation by purchasing milk and other delicacies from the commissary. As winter progressed, the exorbitant prices commanded for these supplementary foodstuffs put them out of reach of many. William Gray earned the required cash for these purchases by making and mending shirts, drawers, and pants for his fellow officers. "When I was a boy I learned the tailoring business," wrote Gray, "by that means I saved my health and many of my fellow prisoners," he maintained. By this stage, William could no longer digest the course corn bread and the other unrefined items that comprised the daily ration.

At Libby, Gray contracted catarrh and suffered from an infection of the sciatic nerve. These ailments may have developed from a period of confinement in the dreaded dungeon. The captain was arrested and placed here for slipping food to sick prisoners being confined below.[65]

Even a short stay in these underground hellholes could seriously affect one's health. Open tubs nearly filled with excrement were not removed for days, producing a most unhealthy atmosphere. No letters were permitted in or out of this area and scanty rations had to be eaten in the guard's presence.[66] The isolation and foul air exacted a great toll on the confined. It was the beginning of a long, downward spiral for Captain Gray.

In an effort to combat the growing food and clothing shortage, Commandant Turner issued a directive permitting packages to be sent to the prison from friends and relatives in the North. On October 10th, William Boltz wrote his wife with the following instructions: "I did write to you a few weeks ago about my box and ten dollars greenbacks. I want you to hurry about it, as I am in need of clothing. If you have not recd. my letter from Sep. 29th, then let me tell you in this one that there is no difficulty for a box to come through here. I want you to send me all the articles enquired for in my letters which I have written previous."[67]

Captain Domschcke recalled that these treasured parcels arrived promptly and in good condition at first, but that later on the boxes were often rifled and plundered by the enemy.[68] Whether a prisoner went hungry or not often depended on receiving provisions from the home front. Apparently, Levina Boltz's care package arrived safely, for by December 2,

William assured her that he had plenty to eat and drink and was getting along fine.

Later, on January 26, 1864, he made a new request. "I want you to send me another box with provisions, such as sugar, coffee, tea, flour, potatoes, butter … also a lot of candles & a ham if you can get one, and some newspapers…."[69]

In the late autumn of 1863, the U.S. Government dispatched a large shipment of uniforms for the prisoners at Libby and Belle Isle. Unfortunately, much of the apparel never reached the captives. According to the local newspapers, a number of citizens were observed wearing brand new blue coats. After an investigation was ordered, most of the outer wear disappeared. Reportedly, the stolen articles had been dyed black to avoid detection. Nevertheless, some of the soldiers benefited from the effort. Lieutenant Potts, for example, received a nice overcoat.[70]

Another relief effort was initiated by the United States Sanitary Commission. This benevolent agency dispatched large quantities of food and clothing to the various prisons. Once again, however, the shipments did not always reach the intended recipients. It was also alleged that prisoners who fraternized with their jailers received these items to the point of excess, while others received nothing.[71]

Any items of food or clothing that did somehow reach the men were greatly prized for winter was fast approaching. By November, the cold had already become painful as frosty blasts of air from the James roared through Libby's many openings. Lieutenant Potts recalled the first preventive measures. "We were very much in need of blankets, as the nights were getting cool, and our windows at each end of the room were open, excepting the iron bars. After a time the windows were closed up with muslin tacked on frames to fit in the windows, and with the addition of a stove, we managed to keep more comfortable."[72]

Unfortunately for the Union officers, the harsh weather intensified. "The cold at the end of 1863 and in January 1864 exceeded what we had expected, with some days as bitter as in Minnesota or Wisconsin," recalled one. The stoves placed in the rooms could not generate sufficient heat to warm the large spaces. This inadequacy proved to be a moot point as fuel was often in short supply. Wood rations typically consisted of only two to three armloads per room. On Christmas Day, the holiday meal was deferred to the following day because there was not enough wood for cooking purposes.[73]

Sleep was impossible at times due to the intense

cold, and the men often jogged in place in an effort to relieve their agony. A number of men froze to death anyway. When the officers attempted to sleep on the hard wood floors they "wormed and dovetailed together like fish in a basket."[74]

Efforts at sanitation seemed to cease as the prison population swelled beyond its intended capacity. The number of prisoners confined at Libby eventually climbed to over 4,000. There were never fewer than 1,200 on each floor, which averaged out to 400 in each room. The prison grew increasingly dirty. The floors were soon coated with several inches of accumulated filth, and the walls were covered with graffiti, mucus, and spittle.

Predictably, the overcrowded conditions combined with the lack of sufficient sleep, food, and heat led to an increase in illness. Epidemics of scurvy, chronic diarrhea, dysentery, and pneumonia spread throughout the compound. Two to three deaths per day were not uncommon.[75]

Conditions were even worse for the enlisted men held at Belle Isle a short distance away. By November, the isolated island held 6,300 POWs, over twice the intended number. Only about half of the prisoners had tents, the rest lived and slept out of doors. Many of the men had no pants, shirts, or shoes. They subsisted on half-rations and often had no fuel of any kind. Eventually, the hungry men resorted to eating mice, rats, and stray dogs for nourishment.

Tragically, this particular winter proved to be one of the most brutal on record in the South. Hundreds suffered with frozen feet, hands, and ears. Amputations were often necessary. According to the U.S. Sanitary Commission, as many as fourteen prisoners froze to death during a particularly cold night, and one prisoner claimed that as many as thirty perished from exposure on another occasion.[76]

Two members of the 151st Pennsylvania, Corporal Isaac Derr and Private Ezra Stupp of Company H, were incarcerated at Belle Isle from July 21st to September 23, 1863, when both men were released on parole. One can only speculate if these former neighbors from Jefferson Township could have survived the long ordeal faced by their fellow inmates.[77]

As 1864 rolled around, many of the prisoners began to suffer mental anguish in addition to physical discomforts from the great hardships associated with prison life. Bernhard Domschcke described the torment of captivity. "Steal an individual's freedom and you take his natural joy, you plunder a legitimate buoyancy of spirit, and you pile upon him a load to twist him emotionally and cripple him physically, if not to crush him."[78]

By late January, even the normally upbeat and hopeful letters Captain Boltz penned to his wife contained a hint of despondency. "The prospect for an speity exchange is rather dark from all I can lern," he informed her.[79]

Some of the officers inside Libby decided to take matters into their own hands and hatched an ingenious plan of escape. Utilizing makeshift tools, a selected group of prisoners cut through a chimney on the lower floor and gained access to a room in the east cellar. From here they took turns digging out a narrow tunnel leading to the yard of a warehouse across the street, a distance of some fifty to sixty yards. The men were nearly detected on several occasions.

The project was hampered by the large amount of material needed to be removed, the lack of proper tools, and the urgent need to conceal the plan from many of the inmates who colluded with the Rebels. Finally, on the evening of February 9th, after nearly two months of painstaking labor, the project was completed. Under the cover of darkness, 109 prisoners crawled through the tunnel and escaped into the streets of Richmond.

Dubbed the Hamilton-Rose tunnel for its chief architects, it was the scene of the most famous escape of its type during the war. Libby officials noted the absence of a large number of prisoners at roll call the next morning and the tunnel was discovered by evening. A total of 59 men made it back to Union lines, two men drowned in the James River, and 48 fugitives, including Colonel Thomas E. Rose, were recaptured. None of the 151st officers participated in the escape through the "Great Yankee Tunnel."[80]

Following this drama sterner measures were taken to prevent future breakouts. The sentries were ordered to fire at any prisoners seen near the windows. Sporadic shootings took place as a result of this directive. One Ohio officer received a fatal chest wound while sitting at a table at least ten feet from the window. Patrols often prowled the rooms at night, and personal property was frequently searched or ransacked.[81]

The harshest measure of all took place after a failed Federal cavalry raid on Richmond in early March. The primary object of this daring mission was to free the Union prisoners being held in the city. Confederate authorities learned of the plot in time to prepare emergency measures. Consequently, the raiders encountered heavy resistance and turned back. Alarmed by the audacity of the Yankees, Thomas and Dick Turner arranged for Libby Prison to be mined. More than two hundred pounds of black powder were placed under the center of the building. Dick Turner warned the inmates that any escape attempts would result in the prison being blown up.[82]

At the end of the month, the prisoners were astounded by the news that exchanges would be resumed immediately. Since they had been mislead so many times in the past, most of the officers refused to believe the reports. Then Thomas Turner appeared before them and read aloud a list of forty or fifty to be conveyed the next day to City Point for exchange.[83]

One of the names on the list was that of Captain William K. Boltz. William was paroled at City Point on March 21, 1864. He arrived at Camp Parole, Maryland, on the 25th and was then sent on to Harrisburg to be mustered out. By April, he was back home with his wife and children in Berks County. During his eight months of confinement, William never lost faith in God nor his promise to Levina that "we will see each other again in this world."[84]

Several times in the following weeks, groups of prisoners departed Libby for freedom. The remaining officers eagerly awaited their turn and even calculated when this much-anticipated event would take place. Their dreams of returning home were suddenly dashed at the end of April when a group of prisoners scheduled for exchange returned to Libby with frightful news that exchange had ended. It was a devastating blow for Potts, Gray, Van Buren, Heffner, Domschcke, and the other officers left behind.

Shortly afterward, on May 6th, Turner appeared and read the following order: "Be ready to be moved elsewhere tomorrow early." The prisoners were not told where they were going or the reasons why. A flurry of activity erupted in every room as the men assembled their belongings for the move.[85]

At about 2:00 A.M. the officers received an order to report to the kitchen downstairs. Names were called alphabetically and, one by one, the prisoners assembled in the street under a heavy guard. This slow process was not completed until dawn. Lieutenant Potts recorded his strange emotions on this occasion. "When I looked up at the old building, I could not account for my feelings, but when I came to think that I had been looking out of a third story window for nine months, I realized that the difference came from looking up, instead of looking down."[86]

After a slice of corn bread was issued to each prisoner, the column slowly moved off down Cary Street and over the James to Manchester, later known as South Richmond. Walking on solid ground seemed very odd after being confined indoors for nearly ten months. "The earth seemed to sway in the manner of the illusion experienced after a long sea voyage," related Domschcke.[87]

It was a beautiful spring morning: The sun shone bright and clear in a cloudless sky, the morning air was crisp and fresh, and the shiny new growth of spring flourished everywhere. The pleasant weather contrasted sharply with the somber moods of the Union prisoners brooding over a seemingly endless period of captivity. Unlike nature's promise of new life, they faced a very uncertain future.

The officers took one last look back at the capital of the Confederacy. Large and elegant private homes graced the city's upper region. Near the center of Richmond the capitol building towered above its surroundings. Large factories and warehouses crowded the shore of the river. Among the latter was Libby Prison.

Soon the men reached the station of the Danville and Richmond Railroad. A locomotive pulled up with a string of filthy cattle cars and the prisoners were packed in, fifty to sixty per car.[88] After all were aboard, the whistle was blasted and the locomotive rolled slowly forward with its human cargo. Worse horrors awaited the officers at the end of the journey.

A few of the men held on to the hope that they were being transported to City Point for exchange, but most realized they were moving farther south as the Army of the Potomac advanced toward Richmond. At 2 A.M. on May 8th, the train pulled into Danville, Virginia, after a journey of 143 miles through broken, rural country. As the passengers approached their destination, they gazed through the open side doors and noted the juxtaposition of resplendent Victorian and Edwardian mansions situated near small squat cabins.

The town of Danville was located in the extreme south-central part of the state just four miles from the North Carolina border. The small community had become a thriving center for the textile manufacturing and tobacco industries. Danville had grown into one of the largest tobacco auction centers in the nation. The swift-running Dan River flowed through the center of the town.

Not far from the station and overlooking the river, stood six three-story brick buildings originally used as tobacco and cotton warehouses. In late 1863, Confederate authorities transported 4,000 Federal prisoners to Danville to help relieve the overcrowded conditions in the Richmond facilities. The warehouses, each with about 7,200 square feet of interior space, were simply designated as Prisons No. 1 through No. 6. The first of these structures included an attached kitchen. Captain Domschcke and about 200 others were quartered in Building No. 1.

The prison complex was nearly vacant at the time. The former Libby residents learned from the remaining POWs that a deadly smallpox epidemic had broken out in the complex, and had spread rapidly through the town during the winter. They also heard about familiar deprivations — insufficient rations and little or no fuel for warmth. A number of men had escaped into the countryside by tunneling under the buildings.

During its peak occupation as many as 650 prisoners crowded together on each floor. After a horrific winter, the remaining prisoners were transported to a newly established site in southwestern Georgia known as Andersonville.

The new arrivals were permitted to walk down to the river, a few at a time, to obtain buckets of water. Their meals, prepared by several enlisted men, exceeded the quality of the Libby fare and consisted of salt pork, bean or rice soup, and a slice of corn bread.

Despite these culinary treats, the officers had no desire to remain here. In the warm weather the cramped, low-ceilinged rooms became stifling hot under the midday sun. The lower floors were off limits to prevent tunneling. The men soon discussed escape plans and a possible large-scale breakout. On May 12th, however, orders arrived stating that the inmates would depart in the morning. Much to the relief of the Northerners, Danville had been just a temporary layover.[89]

The men lined up at the station and boarded open platform cars for another adventure on the rails. It proved to be a miserable trip. During the first leg of the journey, the seating consisted of dirty, wet planks arranged crosswise on the cars. Later, the prisoners sweltered inside closed freight cars.

Over the next several days the officers traveled deep into the heart of the Confederacy. The train chugged through Greensboro and Charlotte, North Carolina, then passed over the South Carolina border to Columbia and Branchville, and finally, on May 16th, the locomotive reached Augusta, Georgia's second

oldest city, which was situated on the west bank of the Savannah River. Here, the prisoners were escorted down the city's wide streets past elegant homes and public buildings to the next transfer station. After a bumpy ride on the Augusta and Savannah Railroad to Millen, the men traveled to Macon on the Georgia Central Railroad, arriving on the morning of May 17th.

All were greatly relieved when the harrowing trip ended. At one point the prisoners were forced to disembark when the train encountered a 7-mile section of unserviceable track. Weighted down with baggage, the unconditioned prisoners struggled along a crude path obstructed by fallen trees, rocks, holes, and swampland. They also crossed an incomplete bridge of considerable height by walking across narrow boards laid tie to tie.

On another occasion the men bivouacked overnight in a forest. Having no shelter they were soaked by a heavy downpour. A skimpy ration of salt pork and two crackers was issued on alternating days.[90]

Upon arriving in Macon the prisoners marched out to the old county fairgrounds one quarter-mile southeast of the town. Above the compound's barred gate, a broad arch spanned from post to post with the inscription "Camp Oglethorpe," in honor of James Oglethorpe, the founder of the state.

The fifteen to twenty acre site was surrounded by a high board fence. Inside, about twenty feet from this enclosure, ran a smaller picket fence which marked the prison deadline. Guards paced back and forth on a catwalk attached to the outside of the wall. The sentries were under strict orders to shoot anyone who entered the area between them and the deadline.

Just inside the main entrance stood two large buildings; one of these structures served as a hospital and housed residing Confederate officers. Near the center of the complex, two hundred prisoners occupied a one-story frame building that once served as the floral hall for the fair. Some of the prisoners slept in the surrounding sheds and stalls.

As the prison population climbed to over 1,600 commissioned officers, new arrivals improvised makeshift shelters such as tents of blankets, simple barracks constructed of scrap lumber, and even burrows dug underneath the buildings. These arrangements offered little protection from the heat and rain.

A grove of pine trees near the northwest corner of the stockade offered a measure of shade, while a small stream running through the west end provided the camp's water supply. The water was of very poor quality and caused a number of illnesses. Every morning a detail ventured outside under guard to gather firewood.

Rations at Macon were distributed every fifth day and amounted to only seven pints of unsifted cornmeal, four ounces of salted pork, a half-pint of sorghum syrup, a small quantity of rice or beans, and two tablespoons of salt. The cornmeal was converted into a strange type of bread called "pone" or a simple concoction known as mush. In either case the petrified corn remained a tough, indigestible lump.

The hungry men often devoured the entire allowance in three or four days. The prisoners had very few cooking utensils at their disposal. The few available knives, forks, and spoons were shared by hundreds of men. Containers for holding rations were improvised from old stockings, legs cut from discarded pairs of pants, or from the lining of tattered coats.

The first commandant of the camp, Captain W. Kemp Tabb, was characterized as half barbarian and half fool. His successor, Captain George C. Gibbs, fared slightly better in prisoner accounts. He was considered more civil, calmer, and more reflective, but nonetheless, spiteful and malicious. Gibbs denied the prisoners permission to gather bark from white oak trees growing outside the compound for medicinal purposes and, under his regime, a New York officer standing well inside the deadline was shot and killed by a sentry. It was alleged that the shooter received a promotion to sergeant and a thirty-day leave.

A number of tunnels were constructed almost immediately, but most of them proved unsuccessful due to the sandy soil and the vigilance of the guards. Other security measures decreased the likelihood of escape. At night, the guards built fires between the deadline and the stockade fence for increased visibility. Outside the compound a group of cannon faced toward the interior of the complex, poised to blast away with deadly canister rounds during a potential uprising.

A large clearing near the main entrance of the camp served as an exercise and assembly area, but as daylight lengthened throughout the summer, most of the prisoners succumbed to idleness and slothful behavior. Unlike at Libby, the men soon resigned themselves to a hopeless situation in which escape or exchange seemed highly improbable. Living on meager rations and covered with only tatters of clothing, the inmates sank into a deep state of despair and bitterness.[91]

The daily monotony was frequently broken by cries of "fresh fish!" as recently captured prisoners arrived from various theaters of the war. Instantly, the older prisoners crowded around the new arrivals and plied them with all sorts of questions. By the end of June the news was encouraging. Under Grant's supervision George Meade and the Army of the Potomac had crossed the James River and laid siege to Petersburg. Meanwhile, Union forces under William T. Sherman drove deep into the mainland, threatening the city of Atlanta, a vital supply, manufacturing, and communications center.

For William Gray a personal tragedy accompanied this success. On June 18th, during an assault on the outer defenses of Petersburg, William's son, 19-year-old Arthur Lee Gray, was killed instantly when a bullet severed his jugular vein. After the expiration of his original three-year term, young Arthur had reenlisted in the 48th Pennsylvania Volunteers.[92]

As his son bled to death in front of the Cockade City, William struggled daily for his very survival. Lieutenant George L. Brown, Company I, 101st Pennsylvania, arrived at Macon on May 21st. Brown resided in Schuylkill County before the war, and he now lived in a burrow only twenty feet from his former neighbor. Upon his arrival Brown remembered Gray as being reasonably well considering his long imprisonment. But in the early part of June his friend began to suffer with a severe case of chronic diarrhea. This disease was compounded by rheumatism and swollen legs which he contracted from exposure and lack of exercise.

Eventually, William became so feeble that he had to be carried like a child to and from the sink by Potts and Heffner. The camp hospital offered little relief to the many sick prisoners and Gray nearly died from his ailments. "The poor water and food made him a complete wreck," lamented Potts.[93]

On July 4 the officers celebrated their second Independence Day in confinement. The festivities included speeches, hymns, and patriotic songs much to the chagrin of prison officials. These events shook off some of the indolence which prevailed in the camp.

For over two months some of the more devout inmates held daily religious services in the open area every evening. Typically, a prayer was read for President Lincoln, his cabinet, the U.S. Congress, and Generals Grant and Sherman.

Near the end of July, the prayers of many inmates were answered. With the approach of Federal cavalry under General George Stoneman, Confederate authorities ordered the evacuation of the Macon facility. By this point any change that broke the vicious monotony of life at Camp Oglethorpe was welcomed. Reflecting on his long captivity, Captain Domschcke regarded Macon as "the saddest place to be dumped by the cataclysms of war."[94]

During the evening of July 27th, 600 officers boarded cars for Charleston, South Carolina; the next day 600 more departed for Savannah, Georgia. Captain Gray and Lieutenant Potts were included in the first group. As the train chugged along the Charleston & Savannah Railroad through tidewater South Carolina, the two officers observed sights they had never beheld in Southeastern Pennsylvania.

The lowlands were covered by endless marshes and sluggish streams choked with grasses and reeds. An occasional alligator was spotted sunning himself near a swampy lair. Forests of gnarled oaks and scrubby pines dotted the high ground. Tresses of Spanish moss added a stately quality to the woodland canopy.

Arriving in Charleston on the 28th, the officers were marched across the Ashley River to yet another prison facility. For the next several weeks home would be the enclosed yard of the city jail. The Charleston City Jail consisted of a three-story stone building to which was attached a taller octagonal building. A workhouse occupied an adjoining lot.

The interior cells of the prison had been filled long ago and held mainly civilian criminals, prostitutes, captured Negro soldiers, and deserters from the Confederate army. Therefore, tents were erected in the nearly one-acre jail yard to accommodate the overflow. A high masonry wall formed the perimeter of the space and was connected to the main building and the workhouse. This sandy area was mostly devoid of vegetation except for an occasional patch of grass and a single fig tree growing in one corner. In the middle of the compound stood an old wooden water pump. Privies were located inside several small outbuildings. Ominously, gallows rose above the wall near the sinks.

It was a most inhospitable environment. The site was infested by vermin and swarms of mosquitoes, rations were scanty, the water supply was salty, and the yard permeated with foul vapors from the latrines. "All the offal and garbage of the prison is placed in the yard, and the stench is horrible," wrote inmate Captain Henry W. Gimber of the 150th Pennsylvania.[95] Charles Potts further described the ordeal:

> Our food here was of the poorest kind and quality, principally rice. If we had money, we could buy vegetables, but they never issued them to us. We spent three weeks in this jail yard, and our food and treatment were of the worst. But what could you expect from the meanest class of people of the most disloyal state in the Union, and a hotbed of rampant secessionists. After a time, they agreed to give us better quarters, if we would give our parole not to attempt to escape. We would agree to anything to better our condition, and we were then distributed between the Roper and Marine Hospitals.[96]

Compared to Libby Prison, Camp Oglethorpe, and the Charleston City Jail, the new accommodations seemed downright luxurious. The Roper Hospital, named for its benefactor, James Roper, was located near Calhoun and Courtenay streets on the west side of the city. It was a grand brick structure, rising four stories in the center and three in both wings. A broad, pillared verandah graced each story and overlooked a nicely arranged garden of flowers and shrubs, which was enclosed by a wrought iron fence. The bright interior contained six to eight spacious wards with immaculate floors and candelabra. The vast central ward on the first floor was even carpeted!

One officer described the exhilaration which accompanied the change in quarters.

> [We] passed through the gateway of "Roper" into the beautiful garden of the hospital. On our right is a palmetto, on our left an orange tree, while around us bloom flowers of every hue, whose very fragrance inspires us with new life. How great the change. Here we are comparatively free. Here all seem better contented. We are assigned quarters on the third floor *piazza*; the hard floor seeming a luxury, and the place itself a paradise.[97]

Although the rations could not be considered as princely as the surroundings, prisoners with money could purchase a variety of groceries from the numerous black vendors who peddled their wares on the sidewalk in front of the garden. Sweet potatoes, peanuts, peppers, cabbage, tomatoes, squash, apples, bread, and milk were just a few of the items offered. Potts remembered paying five Confederate dollars for four loaves of bread and that he and Heffner consumed the entire purchase in one meal.[98]

The officers spent their ample leisure walking in the garden and reading magazines and newspapers from the North. By early September, the military news was increasingly positive. Sherman's Westerners had captured Atlanta, while U.S. Grant was tightening his stranglehold on the Army of Northern Virginia at Petersburg. This war of attrition would ultimately lead to victory for the Union. The question remained: Did the Federal POWs have the strength and stamina to endure the resulting shortages of food, clothing, and adequate shelter?

As a direct result of Sherman's success, the 600 officers originally held at Savannah were relocated to Charleston. Like their predecessors, they suffered two weeks of hell in the jail yard before being assigned to the hospital facilities with their former companions. Although they had been treated well at Savannah, these prisoners too were awestruck by the extravagant new quarters.

Captain Domschcke was among the new arrivals:

> Had I been transported to another world? A clean floor — what luxury! Gaslight and carpet — such sybaritic splendor! And a roof, a tight cover overhead, protection against the tropical sun and the rain!

The captain's good fortune continued. Two of his former comrades met him with a cup of coffee and a fine cigar.[99]

Lieutenant Potts was intrigued by the culture and customs of the local black residents. During his short stay in Charleston, Charles developed a great deal of compassion for these people and was saddened by their plight. He penned the following observations:

> We noticed many odd customs among the people of the city. The bakers carry the bread on their heads in clothes baskets. Of course all these people were negroes, and setting their baskets on the ground, they cry out at the top of their voices, "Bread me! Bread me! See me quick! I 'spect you see me. I'se gwine now," and off they would go to the next corner. These people are all blacks and slaves, and do all the work, turning all earnings over to their aristocratic masters, who ride in chaises and live in luxury.
>
> The barber who came to shave us was the grandson of the Episcopal Bishop of the city, a fine looking, portly mulatto, who shaved the "Yanks," and took his earnings to his master. The Negroes seemed to take great interest in us, and would pass up and down in front of our building, giving us a friendly recognition. The young mulatto girls were remarkably fine

looking, with long black hair, hanging way below the waist, and, as they paraded about clothed in pure white, I could but wonder that these girls, born in a Christian land, were slaves, owned by a Christian people, and were kept on account of their fine appearance, and for immoral purposes, being owned by rich men, married and single.[100]

Perhaps the only negative aspect of prison life in Charleston during this period was the constant bombardment of the city by Union heavy artillery stationed on Morris Island. This attack on the civilian population outraged Confederate authorities. At the same time Federal officials maintained that Union prisoners were being held hostage in various parts of the city to prevent these attacks. They soon retaliated by placing 600 Confederate officer prisoners inside an open stockade on Morris Island within range of Confederate shore batteries. The artillery duel continued in spite of these harsh measures.[101]

Potts and his comrades had become hardened by a long string of adversities and the lively shelling seemed not to faze them.

> All day and night, while here, our guns on Morris Island were shelling the city, and it was an interesting sight to see these little shooting stars away up in the heaven sailing along, bent on destruction, to the rebel stronghold. Our men had no fear of these shells, as they burst high in the air, sending fragments flying all around us, but one man was injured, his arm was injured while eating his supper. But I saw a rebel guard throw down his gun and run for his life, when he heard the pieces whizzing in the branches of the tree.[102]

Lieutenant J. Quincy Carpenter, 150th Pennsylvania, described the frequent nighttime bombardments as a "beautiful exhibition of fireworks."[103]

From the verandahs of Roper Hospital, the prisoners viewed the effects of the shelling and the "Burnt District," a large section of the city that had burned during a devastating fire in December 1861. Captain Domschcke described the symbolic irony of the desolate scene:

> On nights of bright moon the view of the devastation was almost ghostly: a broad belt of rubble and ruins.... Elegant homes, where rich aristocracy used to live in the most exquisite luxury, had collapsed into piles of wreckage. The churches had once been meeting places for the elite; now only walls remained. Grass and debris choked the streets where slaveholding nobility had promenaded.[104]

The Union officers would have cheerfully endured the friendly fire for the opportunity to spend the remainder of their confinement in the relative luxury of the Charleston hospital suites. Their good fortune came to an abrupt end. During the end of September 1864, a deadly epidemic of yellow fever broke out in the city. On October 4th, the Union officers received the news that they would be relocated to a healthy region near Columbia northwest of Charleston.

Accordingly, the next morning the prisoners gathered up their accumulated household effects and marched down several streets under a scorching sun to the train station. When the train departed, an assembly of Negroes who had befriended the Northerners shouted a hearty farewell to their future liberators. In contrast, the white citizens asked the officers why they did not go home and leave the South alone. As if in response, the Union guns off the coast commenced shelling the city at a furious rate as the prisoners departed.[105]

The final phase of the long odyssey would in many ways be the most trying. After months of incarceration many of the men were reaching the end of their physical and mental endurance.

Following a twelve-hour ride on the South Carolina Railroad through a sparsely settled region, the men were eventually led to an abandoned plantation two miles west of Columbia near the Congaree River. The new site was situated upon a four-acre field partly covered with young scrub pines. A small brook running along the base of the field provided a potable water supply. No tents or buildings of any kind were provided.

Initially, the officers camped beneath the pine trees in the open air or burrowed deep into the ground. When the weather turned increasingly colder, the prisoners were provided with axes and shovels to construct shelters. Under heavy guard the men were escorted outside the camp limits to obtain firewood and building materials. A shortage of tools hindered these construction efforts. The few who had money left purchased axes from a local sutler for $45 to $50 each.

Huts were constructed by excavating about four feet of earth to the desired dimensions for a living space and then roofing it over with brush. Others created more elaborate log structures. Soon a little town of wooden houses emerged in the old field. However, these makeshift shelters proved gravely inadequate

during a prolonged rainy spell. Badly clothed and unable to maintain fires, the prisoners were soaked and chilled to the bone for extended periods.[106]

Meanwhile, the men subsisted on very meager rations. Due to shortages, no meat of any kind was issued. The food supply consisted of cornmeal, a little rice, and salt, but chiefly large quantities of sorghum molasses. For this reason, the site was named Camp Sorghum.[107]

The location had been selected with such haste that no barrier of any kind was erected to enclose the prisoners. Eventually, a thirty-foot clearing was cut through the brush around the perimeter of the camp. Along the inner edge of the clearing, stakes were pounded into the ground to serve as a deadline.[108]

The guards assigned to duty at Camp Sorghum came from both South Carolina and Georgia. For the most part, the Georgians were regarded as good-natured and agreeable, while the Carolinians gained a reputation for brutality. The companies were principally undisciplined militia troops who had been forced into military service through conscription. These reserves ranged from young boys to old men with grey hair. Domschcke characterized them as poor whites, ignorant and illiterate.[109]

Captain Gray placed the number of prisoners being confined at Camp Sorghum at 1,500. He stated that the inmates could only get outside of camp to attend to the causes of nature by being escorted one at a time under heavy guard. William recalled nearly starving to death here while being confined outdoors with very little shelter. So acute was his hunger that he confessed he could have eaten anything — even a piece of a dog or cat.[110]

These deprivations, together with the limited security, led to numerous escape attempts. By early December there had been 373 successful escapes. One officer believed that a significantly higher number of men might have slipped away if so many had not lacked footwear. In the cover of darkness the escapees simply sprinted between the sentries.

In desperation, bloodhounds were brought in to help track down the fugitives. The runaways faced the danger of being fired upon by the guards or mauled by pursuing dogs. Attesting to the savagery at Camp Sorghum, Captain Gray reported that quite a number of his comrades were shot down, some dead, others wounded and crippled for life. Apparently, not all of the victims had crossed the deadline, for Gray added, "I have seen them shot dead without any provocation." Captain William Gimber testified that a man who had merely reached over the line to get an axe was shot through the heart by a sentry.[111]

In response to the rash of escapes, Confederate officials decided to quarter the 1,200 or so remaining officers inside a temporary stockade on the grounds of the South Carolina State Hospital. Located on the north side of Columbia, this facility had served as the state's asylum for the mentally ill since 1822. Thus, the prisoners named their new home "Camp Asylum."[112]

The men arrived at the asylum in late December. A drunk near the entrance of the enclosure taunted the prisoners with a request for demonic intervention, "May all Yankees go to Hell!" The officers grimly shook off the superfluous wish. They had already been in Hell for a year and a half.[113]

The yard at the asylum embraced two acres surrounded by a ten-foot board fence. A small ditch marked the deadline. Water was piped from the outside into six wooden troughs, three of which were designated for washing and bathing. Although it was frequently covered with ice, a number of men bathed in the frigid water.

Two buildings near the gate housed the sick. Otherwise, adequate shelter was scarce. Many sought refuge under the buildings, others assembled tent-like shelters of blankets, and the remainder camped beneath the sky with no protection from the elements. Later, several makeshift wooden barracks were erected. This situation became life threatening as many lacked blankets or sufficient clothing to brave the winter weather. Some of the poor sufferers walked all night to keep warm and slept in the sun during the day.

"Our condition was becoming very bad," reported Potts, "having poor food and small quantity, and our clothing was nearly worn out. We felt that our Government had abandoned us. We were living exclusively on corn meal, and often thought we were nothing more than animals."[114]

The food situation had indeed reached a crisis. Most of the prisoners were destitute of cash and lacked possessions to pawn for money. If they did manage to obtain additional funds from the North, they were shortchanged by the Confederates on the exchange rate or charged exorbitant prices for foodstuffs by the camp sutler.

Once again the prisoners managed to cope with the adverse circumstances in a variety of ways. Mail call was received with great joy in camp even though letters from home were required to be sent unsealed. Surprisingly, mail was distributed more often at Columbia than at any other facility, with the possible exception of Libby. During periods of favorable weather a choir and glee club entertained the prison populace. It was here that the lyrics and music for "Sherman's March to the Sea" were composed.

The men learned of Sherman's progress through Georgia from sympathetic Negro workers, who kept the prisoners informed of outside rumors and smuggled newspapers into the compound. Important news items were then copied on slips of papers and posted at conspicuous locations throughout the camp.[115]

At this stage encouraging news was sorely needed by the inmates at Camp Asylum. Sadly, many of the inmates had already suffered permanent physical damage. A few, like their civilian neighbors, exhibited signs of mental degradation. Lieutenant Potts described the sad scenes he witnessed in the early portion of 1865:

> Some of our men had lost their minds, and it was a sorry sight to see these poor unfortunate men cooking sticks and stones, or bones that some more fortunate person has cast away. I have known these men to put bones in the fire and burn them, and then crush and boil them into a kind of a soup, and eat it. Some fine, intelligent men abandoned all hope, and made no effort to cheer up, or be hopeful for the future. They neglected to keep themselves clean, and would parade about the camp by the hour, caring for no one, and buried in deep thought. We burned yellow pine wood, and this oily smoke coated our skin so that we looked like a lot of hobos. It was indeed laughable to look about our camp and see what a change had taken place in the appearance of our officers. When captured, they were fine looking, well dressed, with costly uniforms, and lots of pride; now nearly naked, dirty, filthy and well supplied with those pests of all camps, gray backs, they looked like the worst set of tramps you ever saw. Our guards were old men, what is known in the South as poor white trash, and a more degraded set of bloodthirsty murderers, I never saw, many of our men being shot down without provocation.[116]

Fortunately, the end was near. Sherman's troops swept up the South Carolina coast in February, destroying everything in their path while meeting little resistance from the Confederates. As mentioned previously, young Charles Ammarell, now a member of the 46th Pennsylvania, was part of this force. When the Union juggernaut approached the state capitol at Columbia, the Federal officers were relocated yet again.

The prisoners were quickly shuttled to the station in the midst of a bone-chilling rain storm. After enduring a miserable ride in old and drafty cars, the weary travelers detrained at Charlotte, North Carolina, on the afternoon of February 15th and marched one mile to an open field. The weather continued to be raw and rainy. The wind grew colder and sharper as night approached.

The following day the prisoners were paroled for exchange and informed that preparations were being made to transport the entire group to Wilmington for release into the Union lines. The Confederates no longer had the resources to guard and feed the Union POWs.

The initial transfer to the state capitol at Raleigh was delayed by the shortage of railroad cars. The men continued to be confined out in the open by only a light guard. The food consisted of small quantities of pork and cornmeal. The only available drinking water came from a muddy pond nearby. A number of the men refused to believe that the Confederates intended to release them and they quietly slipped away.

The prisoners finally reached Raleigh on the 22nd. Here, they were provided with raw flour and given permission to make bread at the city bakeries. Before the men could partake of the meal, a trainload of prisoners who had been confined at Andersonville pulled into the station. The officers were shocked by the pitiful appearance of the enlisted men. Their emaciated bodies, blackened skin, and haggard faces told of the indescribable hells they had been forced to endure. Immediately, the officers distributed the bread among the poor sufferers, for they realized that the depths of their suffering far exceeded their own.

The following morning the officers reached Goldsboro, 40 miles southeast of Raleigh. Potts and his comrades obtained a few sweet potatoes from a black woman. It was the first food they had eaten in 24 hours.

Finally, on the morning of March 1, 1865, the POWs arrived within sight of the Union lines at the farthest Confederate outpost, approximately ten miles from Wilmington along the east branch of the Cape Fear River. The released officers were officially received by the black troops from Major General Godfrey Weitzel's Twenty-fifth Corps, Army of the James. The bands played patriotic tunes for the occasion. "The Negro troops looked fine. They were delighted to see us—pure, genuine delight," recalled Henry Gimber. "I was agreeably disappointed at the appearance and bearing of the colored troops, and all my prejudices vanished," he related.[117]

The old Stars and Stripes was a welcome sight that many had doubted they would ever behold again. Many cried with joy at the sight while others shouted until they were hoarse. After exactly twenty months of captivity, Captain Gray simply remarked that the long-awaited occasion was "a happy day for one and all the rest of my fellow prisoners." Captain Gimber was more exuberant. "Every prisoner I talked with pronounced the first day of March, 1865, the happiest day of his life," he proclaimed. The former captives were provided with the very best the commissary could furnish: meat, hardtack, and good coffee.[118]

The next morning, after marching through Wilmington, the men boarded the steamer *General Sedgwick*, which was bound for Annapolis, Maryland.

Captain William Gray after his long imprisonment. Courtesy of MOLLUS Collection, The Civil War Library and Museum, Philadelphia, Pennsylvania.

The boat steamed northward in the afternoon, crossing the bar at New Inlet and then passing Fort Fisher, which had defiantly guarded the port at Wilmington until finally surrendering to Union forces in January 1865. As the steamer passed Cape Hatteras during the night, it ran into a fierce storm with gale force winds. "We feared for the safety of our old wooden tub," wrote Potts. But the stormy voyage continued and many suffered from sea sickness. Fortunately, the Sanitary Commission provided the boat with plenty of good food and fresh milk.[119]

The steamer reached Annapolis on March 4th, and shortly afterward the former POWs stepped onto Northern soil. Potts never forgot the memorable occasion: "A motley crew we were, and here were wives and mothers looking for husbands, and sons, and what a meeting! Mothers who knew their sons not, and sons that had lost their reason, and could not tell who they were, or where they belonged. It was a sad sight to see these people looking for friends and relatives whom they could not recognize." William Gray had been reduced to a mere living skeleton having shed nearly ninety pounds from his nearly six-foot frame during his imprisonment.[120]

After their names were recorded and quarters obtained, the first priority of most was procuring a new wardrobe. The city's shopkeepers extended unlimited credit to the former prisoners. A merchant approached Charles Potts after he disembarked from the steamer and inquired if he needed some new clothing. Charles laughed at the obviously rhetorical question, for at the time, his entire wardrobe consisted of a torn blouse, ragged pants, a pair of badly worn shoes, and a cap fashioned from a coat tail. He had been without a shirt for six months. Potts entered the entrepreneur's shop and fitted himself out with a brand new wardrobe.[121]

Two days later a paymaster arrived from Washington and distributed two months of pay to the soldiers. The men paid their bills and reported to Washington for their final pay and discharges. On March 12, 1865, Potts and Gray left the capital for home.[122] Their new attire and freshly cleaned bodies could not hide the scars of twenty months in Dixie.

EPILOGUE

On March 14, 1862, just before launching the Peninsula Campaign, Major General George B. McClellan issued a stirring address to his well-trained and well-equipped army of over 100,000 soldiers. The address contained the Napoleonic flair and bombast so characteristic of "Little Mac." But the general concluded his communication by acknowledging the difficult task confronting his beloved army:

> God smiles upon us, victory attends us, yet I would not have you think that our aim is to be attained without a manly struggle. I will not disguise it from you: you have brave foes to encounter, foemen well worthy of the steel that you will use so well. I shall demand of you great, heroic exertions, rapid and long marches, desperate combats, privations, perhaps. We will share all these together; and when this sad war is over we will all return to our homes, and feel that we can ask no higher honor than the proud consciousness that we belonged to the Army of the Potomac.[1]

McClellan, however, could not have envisioned the staggering number of casualties his grand army would suffer before finally forcing the surrender of its old nemesis: Robert E. Lee and the Army of Northern Virginia. The general himself would not be present for this momentous event for Lincoln cashiered him in November 1862 when he failed to crush Lee after the bloody battle of Antietam.

The army he had meticulously prepared for success continued to fight — at Fredericksburg, Chancellorsville, Gettysburg, the Wilderness, Spotsylvania Court House, through the nine-month siege at Petersburg, and finally to Appomattox Court House. Each campaign was accompanied by lengthening casualty lists. Families and communities throughout the North struggled to cope with the never-ending losses. At the Battle of Gettysburg, for example, the little village of McAlisterville in Juniata County suffered the loss of five men killed and three wounded from Company D of the 151st Pennsylvania.[2]

The survivors of the American Iliad faced the difficult task of readjusting to civilian life. Some would cultivate full and productive lives after the guns fell silent, a few drifted aimlessly, while others simply could not overcome lingering physical and mental disabilities brought on by military service.

In the following pages, the post-war lives of select former members of the 151st will be examined to illustrate the lasting impact the Civil War had on their futures, and how these experiences affected family and community relationships. A brief study of veterans' reunions and the dedication of the 151st's regimental monument at Gettysburg is included at the end of this section.

Colonel Harrison Allen

The year of 1865 was an eventful one for Harrison Allen. On March 13th, he received a brevet to brigadier general for his distinguished service during the war. His election to the state legislature as the representative for Warren and Venango counties marked the beginning of a long and successful political career. On the personal side, Harrison married Anna Page Cobham, the widow of Colonel George A. Cobham, Jr.

Cobham, who was born in England, gave his life for his adopted country at the battle of Peach Tree Creek, Georgia, on July 20, 1864. He was rewarded with a posthumous brevet as a brigadier general of volunteers. It was a promotion that George deserved much earlier for he had commanded a brigade throughout much of his military service, including at Gettysburg, in the battles around Chattanooga, Tennessee, and during the early part of the Atlanta campaign. His first military assignment was a commission as lieutenant colonel of the 111th Pennsylvania. Company B of this regiment had been formed in Warren County.

George F. McFarland, circa 1880. Courtesy of Dr. Charles Lloyd Eater, Jr.

It is possible that Harrison first met his future bride when he spoke at a testimonial dinner held for her husband in the winter of 1863. Colonel Cobham was at home on a furlough and it may well have been the last time he looked into the eyes of his beloved. If indeed a spark was ignited between Harrison and Anna on this occasion, they discreetly observed a respectful mourning period before tying the knot. Allen became the guardian of his stepson, Frederick P. Cobham.

Anna Cobham was no stranger to romantic intrigue. At the age of eighteen, she was married to George Parmlee, Esquire. The union was dissolved a short time later, but no mention of the event was made in the write-up of Anna's marriage to George Cobham in the *Warren Mail* of February 17, 1858, nor in Parmlee's obituary of June 25, 1907. Therefore, Harrison may have been her third husband.

Following consecutive one-year terms as representative, Allen built upon his success in the political arena. He was elected to the state senate in 1870

and then to the position of auditor general. Harrison filled the latter post from 1872 to 1875. In the midst of this public service, the ambitious politician met the requirements for admission to the bar. Next came an appointment as United States marshal for North Dakota from President Chester Arthur.

In June of 1895, Allen sent a dispatch to his hometown newspaper from Fargo announcing that he had divorced his wife for desertion. The couple had one child together during their thirty years of matrimony. Anna died the following spring back in Warren.

Allen returned east in 1901 when he received an appointment to the post office department in Washington, D.C. It was here that he met and married Susanna Bowers, a native of Jamestown, N.Y. Harrison died of heart failure on September 23, 1904, at the age of 69. He was buried in Arlington Cemetery. Susanna continued to reside in the capitol until her death in 1926.

Thus, Harrison Allen transformed his military service into a successful civil service career and blazed a path for his younger siblings to follow.[3]

Adjutant Samuel T. Allen

Back in his native Warren, Allen recuperated from his leg wound and studied law. In February 1864, both Samuel and his younger brother, Orren, were admitted to the bar of Warren County. Another sibling, George W., achieved this honor in 1866 less than a month after his eldest brother's admission. Following in Harrison's footsteps, Orren and George were elected to seats in the State Legislature.

It appears Samuel may have lived in his older brother's shadow. He served as a clerk in the auditor general's office during Harrison's term and then worked in the same capacity in the treasury department at Washington, D.C. Returning to his hometown, he was thrice elected burgess of Warren borough. He also entered into a partnership with Orren in a drug store at the corner of Second and Liberty streets. At the end of a year he and his brother sold their interests.

Samuel married Martha Fenton on April 5, 1864. The couple had no children. Allen died in his home on January 10, 1885.[4]

Lieutenant Colonel George F. McFarland

After returning home to McAlisterville following his protracted stay at the Lutheran Seminary

Hospital, George was confined to his bed for 42 weeks. The students of the re-opened McAlisterville Academy gathered by his bedside for recitals. McFarland's war injuries crippled him for life and were a constant source of excruciating pain. His stump was slow to heal and over fifty pieces of splintered bone surfaced from his shattered left ankle. On one occasion, the diseased leg was lanced below the knee joint and "about two quarts of pus was discharged from the limb."

Despite his handicap, McFarland pressed forward. A long-time acquaintance testified: "He was a man of wonderful energy and will power, and worked to maintain his family, hobbling about on crutches and a wooden leg ... and pushed his business affairs against all obstacles, when many a well man would have been disheartened."

In November 1864, George converted his academy into one of the first Soldiers' Orphans' Schools in the state. Governor John W. Geary appointed McFarland to the position of "Superintendent of Soldiers' Orphans" in May 1867. In this capacity he was responsible for the inspection and administration of all 37 schools in the statewide system. During his four-year term, McFarland led the system through its peak enrollment period.

During this superintendency George moved his family to Harrisburg, where he entered into a partnership in a large nursery and greenhouse operation. He also edited and published a weekly newspaper.

Throughout his life McFarland played a prominent role in veterans' organizations and activities. He was an active member of the Grand Army of the Republic Post No. 58 in Harrisburg and secretary of the Society of the First Army Corps. Oftentimes, George wrote affidavits in support of pension claims filed by his former comrades.

When the 151st Pennsylvania formed a survivor's association, McFarland was elected as president and served as chairman of the monument committee. On July 1, 1888, George delivered the main oration at the dedication ceremony for the regimental monument at Gettysburg.

After the ceremony, George returned to Harrisburg to supervise his business affairs. But after years of stubbornly resisting the ill effects of his wounds, his health began to deteriorate. Addie McFarland recalled her husband growing weak and emaciated and being so thin that she could carry him herself. In August of 1891, the McFarlands journeyed to northwestern

Georgia with the hope that the warmer climate would help alleviate George's pain. In his weakened condition, George contracted bacterial pneumonia, and on the morning of December 18, he died peacefully at the age of 57. His body was prepared for burial and shipped north for interment in the Harrisburg Cemetery. He was survived by Addie, three children, and three grandchildren.

Perhaps George himself best summarized a lifetime of service to his fellow man in his final annual report as Superintendent of Soldiers' Orphans:

> I have labored faithfully, earnestly, painfully and as efficiently as my abilities and crippled condition enabled me.... In doing this I have had but one object in view — the best interests, educationally, industrially, socially and morally — present and future — of the destitute orphans of fallen comrades placed under my care.... If I have contributed toward their preparation for the duties of life and their fitness for eternity, I feel grateful to God for having been permitted to do so.[5]

Major John W. Young

Young suffered throughout the remainder of his life from the residual effects of the typhoid fever and malaria he contracted during his military service. John's first wife died of typhoid in 1882. Two years later, he married Lydia Gardner in Montrose. A son born in 1888 was named in honor of his father. Unfortunately, John's recurring health problems prevented him from earning a living. Ultimately, he received a monthly pension of $30 from the government. In the late 1880s, Helen Joslin stated that her father "has not been a well man" since his return from the army. Although he was a tall man, Young's weight diminished to just a little over one hundred pounds as he battled heart and kidney disease and a variety of bronchial ailments.

At 2 A.M. on October 12, 1893, John died from an overdose of morphine at his home in Minneapolis, Kansas. The drug had been prescribed by a doctor as a pain killer and sleep aid. Lydia moved back to Montrose after her husband's death, and in April of 1900, she enrolled 11-year-old John W. in the Soldiers' Orphans' Industrial School at Scotland, Pa. This institution was part of the educational system that George McFarland had supervised during its fledgling stage.[6]

The badge worn by Lt. Colonel George McFarland at one of the Gettysburg reunions. Courtesy of Sue Boardman.

Sergeant Major Simon J. Arnold

Arnold convalesced at his father's home in Reading following his discharge. The bullet which tore into his lower left leg severely damaged the tibia. For months the limb was stiff and entirely powerless, confining Simon to his bed. By February 1864 he had recovered enough to consider service in the Invalid Corps.

Instead, Simon traveled west and settled in St. Louis, arriving there between late 1865 and early 1866. His brother, Levi, a fellow veteran, accompanied him on the journey. Simon obtained employment as a bookkeeper for the Great Western Dispatch Company and then for the freight department of the Toledo, Wabash, & Western Railway. Afterward, he served fifteen years, and through four different administrations, as deputy

collector of revenue for the city of St. Louis. During this tenure, he worked in the famous domed courthouse where the landmark Dred Scott case was tried.

Known simply as "Sam" in the business community, Arnold earned a reputation for honesty, firmness, and integrity in his dealings. One associate characterized him as "a gentleman in whom full reliance and confidence may be placed." Perhaps it was these qualities that famed journalist Joseph Pulitzer sought when he selected Arnold as his agent during the sale of the St. Louis *Evening Dispatch* at an auction held in the courthouse in December 1878. Arnold delivered the high bid of $2,500 in behalf of Pulitzer.

Above all else, Sam was a family man. He married the love of his life, Miriam Levi, on February 19, 1871. Over a decade later, he was still smitten. When Miriam traveled to Memphis to visit friends, a disconsolate Samuel wrote, "I never knew how much I loved you until you were gone from me. When I get you home I will know how to appreciate you.... I think the Memphis folks are a little bit selfish in wanting to keep you there.... Your place is with your old man to keep each other warm. I am just like a boy waiting for the holy days to come...."

Arnold died before his 51st birthday from heart disease. He died on July 24, 1889, while sitting in a chair inside his home at 2954 Clark Avenue, leaving behind six children ranging in age from two to seventeen.

He was deservedly popular among his business associates and deeply beloved by friends and family. His daughter, Myra, was only four when he died. She lived to be 97, and throughout her years, she kept her father's memory alive by recounting every highlight of his life and passing around scrapbooks during family gatherings. Miriam died on Christmas Day in 1930.[7]

Surgeon Amos C. Blakeslee

Amos practiced medicine at Nicholson, Pa., until his death in 1882. He was survived by his wife, Jane, whom he had married in 1845, and a son named Merrick.[8]

Captain George L. Stone, Company A

Stone was diagnosed with partial paralysis of the left foot due to the gunshot wound he received at Gettysburg. The government awarded him an invalid pension of $12.50 a month.

Two of Stone's brothers also bore the scars of battle. Charles served as a corporal in his brother's company and was also wounded at Gettysburg on July 1st. After the war he took up farming in Nebraska. Stanley, a member of the cavalry corps of the Army of the Potomac, received a wound in the campaign as well. He was later captured during General Judson Kilpatrick's botched raid on Richmond in March 1864, and afterward languished in Confederate prisons. Stanley survived the ordeal and returned to Susquehanna County, where he worked as a farmer and carpenter. The Stone brothers had carried on a military tradition that had originated with their grandfather, Benajah, the captain of a company from Litchfield County, Connecticut, in the Revolutionary War.

After his return home to Montrose, George was commissioned postmaster, an office he held for over four years. Afterward, he settled in New Milford and served as justice of the peace. He died there on May 12, 1896. His widow, Sarah, died in 1910. The couple had two daughters.[9]

Second Lieutenant Amos Tucker, Company A

After his military service, Tucker married Annie Sebastian on June 8, 1864. The couple raised three children. Working as a conductor on the Erie Railroad, Amos' right leg was crushed during an accident near Port Jervis, N.Y., on August 12, 1873. The limb was immediately amputated as a result of the mishap. Later, the Tuckers moved to Cheney, Kansas. Amos died on January 18, 1908.[10]

Captain Lafayette Westbrook, Company B

Westbrook returned to civilian life with the same sense of responsibility and gritty determination that

Simon and Miriam Arnold, circa 1870. Courtesy of Mary Haney Arnold.

characterized his military career. Although he continued to suffer from rheumatism and lameness in his right foot, Lafayette resumed his business of land surveying. These labors usually took place in rugged country and required considerable walking. He resided in a remote area of Pike County, the nearest physician being nine miles away. Westbrook treated his rheumatism by following the advice of medical friends he met during his travels. In the first several years following the war, he visited Milford at least once every two months. During his stay, he roomed with fellow officer John Vincent and occasionally saw a local doctor. For the most part, however, he avoided physicians just as he had done in the army.

As Westbrook grew older, physical exertion became more difficult. He was not able to raise his left arm above his head and his crippled foot became more deformed. Ultimately, he applied for an invalid pension and was awarded $20 per month.

In 1864, he was drafted for military service, his prior nine months of service not excluding him from the process. Oddly, rather than providing medical proof of his disabilities, Lafayette opted to purchase a substitute for $600 to serve on his behalf. Drafted at the same time, his brother also exercised this option.

Brothers George and Isaac Decker, former privates in Company B, lived with and worked for Westbrook for nearly two decades after their discharge. After a hard day's labor, Isaac carried his employer upstairs and helped him bathe his ailing joints. When

Isaac died in a mill located on the property, his brother took over these duties.

Lafayette married Emma Hill in 1876. He died on January 22, 1908, at the age of 82. This brief sketch illustrates the close bonds which existed between veterans long after the war.[11]

First Lieutenant John H. Vincent, Company B

Following his discharge at Harrisburg, Vincent traveled upriver to Northumberland County in Central Pennsylvania to be with his family. Suffering with chronic diarrhea and piles, John was entirely helpless. After a six-week convalescent period, he returned to his home in Milford, Pike County, to resume his law practice. His illness continued, however, and Vincent grew increasingly weak. As a result, he lost nearly all of his clients and was unable to support himself.

John returned to Northumberland County in 1866, sick, poor, and broken down. The next year he wed Caroline Montgomery at McEwensville. The couple was blessed with three children, but John's poor health continued to plague him. He was attended by Dr. Joseph Priestly, the son of the renowned scientist and Unitarian theologian by the same name.

Vincent succumbed to dysentery and paralysis on August 19, 1909.[12]

Second Lieutenant Robert M. Kellogg, Company B

Kellogg survived the battle of Gettysburg and mustered out with the regiment in late July 1863. After returning home to Milford, Robert married his sweetheart, Martha Roys, and the couple commenced raising a family. The Kelloggs soon moved to Port Jervis, which was situated just across the border in New York, where Robert secured employment with the Erie Railroad. He eventually rose to the position of conductor. On March 12, 1870, Kellogg's right arm was caught and crushed between the bumpers of two cars near Jersey City, New Jersey. His arm was amputated at the shoulder, but he died four days later due to shock and loss of blood. The 29-year-old left behind his wife and three young daughters.

As noted earlier, Amos Tucker lost his leg in a similar accident three years later while working as a conductor on the same railroad. The mishap occurred near Kellogg's former home in Port Jervis.

In 1888, Martha Robertine Kellogg, the youngest daughter of Robert Kellogg, married Wilbur Fiske Crane. Wilbur was the brother of novelist Stephen Crane, the author of *The Red Badge of Courage: An Episode of the American Civil War*. Published in 1895, this work became a bestseller and is considered a classic of American literature. Crane based his historical novel on the 124th New York, which had recruited men from Port Jervis during its organization, and its participation in the Battle of Chancellorsville. Interestingly, it was during this same Battle that Lieutenant Robert Kellogg of the 151st was cited for bravery by his brigade commander.[13]

Private Randal D. Sayre, Company B

Randal married Catherine Dangler in 1866. The couple resided in Sussex County, New Jersey, for 23 years, but spent their final days in Pike County. Randal remained a colorful character. In January of 1916, he wrote the commissioner of pensions: "I write to you for a little information. I am sick, my pension is 75 cents a day. If I should not live till Feb. 4th, what course would the widow take to get what is coming to me. It would be a great help to her. On June 16th this year we have been married 50 years. I have been a F[ree] and A[ccepted] M[ason] 52 years."

Four months later, Sayre died of kidney disease. He was 76 years old.[14]

Private William Michael, Company C

William returned to his farm in South Gibson, Susquehanna County, after his enlistment expired. Because of his severe diarrhea and rheumatism, he was unable to walk the final fourteen miles home and had to be carried in a wagon. Surgeon Amos Blakeslee, now his family physician, periodically treated him for these ailments.

William fathered at least five children. His wife, Elizabeth, died sometime around 1893. At this time seven-year-old Ethel was placed in the Soldiers' Orphans' Industrial School at Scotland by application of William's brother, David, who may have been her guardian at the time. Thus, by the turn of the century, the children of two 151st Pennsylvania veterans from Susquehanna County were attending the same school in distant Franklin County. Ethel stated that she never knew her father because she and her sister had been brought up by others since they were quite young. By

1900, William was a widower living alone. He died five years later and was buried in the Welch Hill Cemetery in Clifford Township.[15]

Captain Walter Owens, Company D

Soon after returning home to Granville, Mifflin County, Pa., Walter married Mary Elizabeth Price. Over the next decade the union was blessed with four children. Owens suffered from chronic diarrhea, which he had contracted at Union Mills, and his left hand was mangled in a grain binder shortly after his discharge.

Owens experienced considerable difficulty in readjusting to civilian life. He drifted through a number of jobs in various parts of the state. In addition to operating a farm and general store in Granville, Walter held the following positions: farm laborer, schoolteacher, instructor in the Soldiers' Orphans' Schools at McAlisterville and Cassville, laborer, lumber yard supervisor, and postal clerk for the Pennsylvania Railroad at Altoona, and superintendent of public schools in Mifflin County and later at an Indian school in Philadelphia. Finally, in 1888, a quarter of a century after the Battle of Gettysburg, he returned to his farm in Granville.

Owens' weight ballooned up to 226 pounds on his five-foot, nine-inch frame. He died on April 12, 1912, at age 71.[16]

Corporal Davis Meredith, Company D

Meredith received $4 a month for the gunshot wound of his right thigh commencing in October 1866. Four years later, the amount increased to $12 due to disease of the heart and general debility. After the death of his first wife, Meredith married Ann Eliza Garman, the widow of Jacob Garman, a former member of the 16th Pennsylvania Cavalry.

Davis died at Thompsontown, Pa., on February 26, 1894, of pulmonary consumption. He was buried by veterans of the community.[17]

William Michael with his son and grandson, circa 1897. Courtesy of Eric Michael.

Private S. Brady Caveny, Company D

Brady was one of only four members of Company D who escaped unscathed on July 1 at Gettysburg. After visiting the wounded McFarland at the Seminary Hospital, Caveny returned to McAlisterville in early August, where he worked in his father's store and assisted him in the marble cutting business. He also served for a time as the town's postmaster. After being elected recorder of Juniata County in 1883, Brady moved to the county seat in Mifflintown. In 1888, he relocated to Harrisburg. After selling insurance for a brief time, Caveny was elected alderman of the Second Ward, a position he would hold for 38 years.

Brady fathered 13 children, but his wife, Mary, ran a formal, orderly home. Apparently, the Cavenys lived rather well, for they were affluent enough to hire a Negro maid named "Brownie" to perform housekeeping chores and to assist in the care of the children.

Caveny was a past commander of Post 58, Grand Army of the Republic, and a long-time member of several fraternal organizations such as the Knights of Pythias and the Free and Accepted Masons. A devout Republican, he also served as president of the Harrisburg Republican Club.

Brady died of heart failure in 1928 at his residence at 338 South 17th Street. He was 85 years old and had just been sworn in for another term as alderman. He was laid to rest in the nearby Paxtang Cemetery.

As a magistrate he was known as "a kindly, courteous gentleman of the old school." He believed in tempering justice with mercy and settled a number of cases out of court. His obituary recounted that, "Many an erring youth he started back toward the right road. Many a quarreling couple he saved from the divorce courts. Many a young man and woman went from his office man and wife who had they gone as they came would have had to pay for having transgressed the conventions. Thus he dealt with all men, and so men will remember him."[18]

Private Henry S. Patterson, Company D

The shoemaker from East Salem experienced excruciating pain as a result of his nasty scalp wound and frequently remarked to inquirers that his head "was not right yet." A family physician testified that, prior to his enlistment, Henry was quite intelligent, but his pain became so intense that "he would partially lose his mind" and that, from the time he came home until his death in 1874, he suffered from dementia. He was survived by his wife, Mary, and five children, one from a previous marriage.[19]

Second Lieutenant Thomas L. Moyer, Company E

Moyer recovered at home for two months following his severe chest wound. Later, he obtained employment on the Philadelphia and Reading Railroad as a mail agent, frequently traveling between Pottsville and Reading. Although he seemed to improve physically, Thomas displayed classic symptoms of what is known today as post-traumatic stress disorder.

According to his brother, Frederick, he first showed signs of insanity eighteen months after coming home. However, Captain Jacob Graeff, who was absent at Gettysburg due to sickness, visited his fellow officer soon after the battle and found him to be "quiet and very much changed in appearance." Near the same time, Nelson and Azariah Body recalled that unlike his former self, Moyer seemed "quick and indifferent," and that he would often wander aimlessly in the woods away from his home and family. Sergeant Heilig also noted a continual pattern of the strange behavior he had observed from the lieutenant just after the battle. "Moyer was then laboring under some aberration of the mind and was at times very violent. His conduct was that of an insane man."

In early 1867, while under the employment of the railroad, he was taken to the Pennsylvania Insane Asylum in Philadelphia, where he was examined by Dr. S. Preston Jones. The doctor stated that there was often a close relation between diseases of the chest and the brain. After being detained here for six months, Thomas was admitted to the Pennsylvania State Lunatic Asylum in Harrisburg, which interestingly enough, was located on an elevation near the former site of Camp Curtin. The superintendent of this facility, John Curwen, M.D., found Moyer in a state of considerable mental disorder and also testified that his wound had permanently impaired his nervous system, and together with the associated shock and suppuration, combined to produce mental aberration.

Thomas was declared permanently insane for pension purposes in 1878. He lived out his final years in the Harrisburg asylum until his death on March 8, 1908. His marriage to Mary Ann Hart in 1861 produced three children, none of whom would ever get to know their father. Similar to the case of Henry Patterson, the sad plight of Thomas Moyer serves to illustrate the lasting traumatic effects of the war, which all too often had devastating results.[20]

Musician Michael Link, Company E

Upon being discharged from a Philadelphia hospital, the former blacksmith returned to Reading. His unique wound was often the cause of intense head pain, and pus frequently discharged from the eye sockets. His wife, Margaret, whom he married in 1868, recalled in a deposition that a swelling as large as a chicken egg appeared several times where the right eye had been, and it had remained for a six to seven week period.

Undaunted by his disability, Link gained admission into an institution for the blind to obtain training and vocational skills. With his full pension of $72 per month, Michael built two three-story brick homes at 144 and 146 Penn Street. At this location he opened a shop where he cane-seated chairs. A splendid musician, Link entertained friends by playing the French horn, violin, accordion, and other instruments. He became known simply as "Blind Mike."

William Kunkleman, one of his best friends, warmly remembered that dominoes was one of Mike's favorite pastimes and that he seldom lost at competition. Kunkleman operated a shoemaker shop a few doors from Link and spent considerable time in his company. He recalled that his friend was an intelligent man who kept up to date on current topics, but seldom discussed the late war.

Nonetheless, he never missed Memorial Day celebrations and every year accompanied fellow members of McLean Post G.A.R. to local cemeteries, riding in a carriage with other disabled comrades. He was a general favorite among the other veterans for his jovial personality. One of the happiest days of the last year of Blind Mike's life was his attendance at the reunion of the 151st at Womelsdorf on Thanksgiving Day 1888.

The following year, on July 12th, Link died after an attack of paralysis, two months shy of his 50th birthday. His often repeated request that Albert Williams, John Hinkle, and Isaac Hinkle, who carried him off the field of battle, should act as pall bearers at his funeral, was carried out.

Margaret carried on the business after her husband's death. She lost her leg in an accident during the summer of 1899 and died on December 12, 1904.[21]

Private Lewis W. Rentschler, Company E

Lewis was treated at his home in Berks County by his brother and Dr. D. L. Schurner after a month's stay in Baltimore. A little more than a year after his wounding, Rentschler reenlisted in Company B, 195th Pennsylvania, but was discharged after less than four months of service. Bladder disease claimed his life on June 28, 1895.[22]

First Lieutenant William O. Blodget, Company F

"I am feeling very well, but very indolent, can sleep at least 13 hours of the 24.... When I first got home I considered myself a pretty much used up institution, a 'gone coon,' played out, but now I am recruiting considerably," wrote Blodget nearly a year after the battle. William, however, would not live long enough to witness the fulfillment of his prediction that the country would continue to experience growing pains. In fact, he never seemed to fully recover from the rigors of military service.

After his return, his wife, Esther, wrote, "Will has not been well for two weeks. You know about how it is — up, then down again. There is not much perceptible change ... I do not see much to encourage." William also seemed to resign himself to his fate. In a letter addressed to his older brother, Lorin, dated September 28, 1864, he stated, "I have sold my store and have got my affairs into pretty good shape generally — all but that affair of yours. I wish that might be settled that no trouble should be incurred by my heirs or executors." He ended the letter with the following line, "God grant old Abe may be our next president."

Fifteen months later, on January 1, 1866, Blodget died at the age of 41 of tuberculosis. His wife succumbed to the same disease just a day earlier. Esther Ann Blodget was 40 years old at the time of her death. Her father was Canadian-born, the son of Hazelton Spencer, an English Loyalist. Hazelton's father died fighting for the crown at the battle of Bennington, Vermont. Esther was said to be a crack shot with a rifle.

William's will was completed in the brief period between his wife's death and his own. The document called for his property to be divided equally among his three surviving children: Martha, age 14; Hugh, age 10; and Spencer, age 7. The following paragraph concluded his last testament: "I wish my family kept together at their present home and Mrs. Martha Ann Spencer to live with them. All income from said property to be used for their support and hers. Mrs. Spencer to have a home with them during her life, and be provided for from said property the same as my own family." Martha was William's mother-in-law. She died in 1885.

Lorin Blodget later assisted 15-year-old Spencer in obtaining an appointment to Annapolis. Ultimately, all three of William's children settled in the West.[23]

Sergeant Robert E. Miller, Company F

On Independence Day 1863, an anxious Robert Miller wrote to his son Robert E., "[Y]our mother is as well as we can expect from her, but she is very much troubled about you and James and more so as we have had information that there is another big battle expected, but if it comes my prayer is that you may be spared and that you may be successful."

In the days before CNN, news traveled slowly. When father, Robert, wrote these lines the issue had already been decided, and the Confederates were preparing to retreat. Both of the Miller boys survived the great battle. James' 111th Pennsylvania partici-pated in the desperate struggle for Culp's Hill and would soon be sent west to fight under Grant and Sherman. Younger brother, Robert, occupied a hos-pital bed in Annapolis while the battle raged in south-ern Pennsylvania. His desire to reach Harrisburg be-fore the 151st was mustered out of service would not be realized.

After his return to Warren County, 24-year-old Robert entered into a partnership with brother, Joseph, in a general store located in the small hamlet of Lander. His interest in education continued, and he served as director of schools in the Warren area for over a dozen years. Robert's intelligence and trust-worthiness earned him a three-year term as county treasurer, and later, the position of justice of the peace in Farmington Township. He married a local girl, Martha A. Ewers, on September 10, 1868, and four children were born as a result of the union.

Robert's concerns for his mother's health were well-founded. Jeanette Miller's frail condition was se-verely taxed by the considerable anxiety she experi-enced during the absence of her two sons. After Robert returned home safely in the late summer of 1863, she continued to worry about James as the 111th participated in the fighting at Chattanooga, Ten-nessee. James was wounded on October 29, 1863, at Wauhatchie, but he recovered in time to serve in the Atlanta campaign the following summer.

Jeanette's health continued to deteriorate, and she died in June of 1864. A month later, her eldest son was killed at Peach Tree Creek, Georgia, in the same battle which claimed the life of Colonel George A. Cobham, Jr. Interestingly, the elder Robert learned of his son's death via a letter dated August 2nd from Harrison Allen, who had himself learned of the tragedy through the correspondence of a local soldier serving with James.

Robert E. Miller died in Lander on July 1, 1892, during the 29th anniversary of the battle he had longed to participate in with his comrades. Martha died on September 22, 1928, in Jamestown, N.Y.[24]

Corporal Nathan J. Cooper, Company F

Cooper returned to his wife and child in Sugar Grove and resumed farming and lumbering on his small property, located at the intersection of the Turnpike and North roads. In this remote region of

the state it probably seemed as if the war had never happened. Nathan's first priority was a refreshing dip in a nearby stream. He asked his wife for a clean set of clothes and then burned his lice-infested wardrobe.

Mary Isabelle Cooper gave birth to four more children over the next seven years. Two years after Mary's death in 1888, Nathan wed 36-year-old Viola Gates Nichols, who was over twenty years younger than he was. Mary Cooper Baker was born to this union in 1891. She died in Westerville, Ohio, in 1991.

A double rupture and recurrent rheumatism netted Nathan a $25 monthly pension. He served as chaplain of the James P. Younic G.A.R. Post. Nathan died at the age of 84 in 1917. Viola joined him in death seven years later.[25]

Private Adam G. Strause, Company G

Following his discharge from the 151st, Strause served in Company F, 14th Veteran Reserve Corps from March 3, 1864, through November 14, 1865. For the remainder of his life Adam walked with a pro-nounced limp, due to the effects of a musket ball that struck him just above the right knee on July 1, 1863. Worse, the wound seriously hindered his ability to earn a living as a carpenter. Commencing March 26, 1864, he was paid the princely sum of $2.66 a month by the government for his ugly scar. In 1871, Adam applied to the pension bureau for an increase to "one half" or $4.00. The claim was rejected!

Adam and wife, Mary, went on to have six more children after the war. Their first child, Wilson Jacob, was only ten months old when his father enlisted in the Union army. The couple's youngest daughter was just over a year old when Mary died in February of 1882 at age 40. Adam died four months later at the age of 43.[26]

Private Alfred D. Staudt, Company G

Staudt fully recovered from the multiple gun-shot wounds he received at Gettysburg, although he did experience some stiffness in his left knee joint and a loss of strength in his injured wrist. He mar-ried Elmira Staudt, possibly a cousin, on Christmas Eve of 1867. The couple reared seven children on a sixty-acre farm near Bernville. Alfred was never a wealthy man as he relied upon the income generated from a small mill and a modest $12 monthly pension to sup-port his large family. When the Gettysburg veteran fell victim to a pulmonary hemorrhage in early 1907, he left little behind for the support of his spouse. He bequeathed no stocks, bonds, or notes and carried no life insurance. The G.A.R. presented Elmira with a cash donation of $75. She outlived her husband by twenty-one years.[27]

Captain William K. Boltz, Company H

After his release from Libby Prison, William settled in Pottsville, where he supported his large family by working as a slating contractor. Later, he operated a knitting mill. Boltz was quite successful in his business enterprises and accumulated considerable real estate in various parts of Pottsville. He was a pillar of Zion's Evangelical Church, in whose welfare he took great interest.

Over the years William filed numerous depositions concerning the rupture he suffered as a result of the horse-kicking incident at Fredericksburg. Somehow he gained possession of the company record book after the war and nonchalantly utilized it for a business ledger in the 1870s. In order to bolster his claim for a pension in 1884, he added the remark, "Captain Boltz was hurt and taken to hospital," to the entry for April 30, 1863, and submitted the book as evidence. An examining officer at the bureau wrote the following note on the same page: "This was possibly added since the alleged date. A companion of this sentence with Capt. Boltz's hand writing on file in his pension claim convinces me that this sentence marked is in his hand writing."

Nonetheless, Boltz later received a monthly pension of $10 until his death on May 3, 1906. He was 75 years old. Levina died three years earlier. William was survived by 8 children, 25 grandchildren, and seven great-grandchildren.[28]

Second Lieutenant Albert Yost, Company H

Albert's injured forearm became weak and deformed as he grew older. As a result he experienced considerable difficulty in lifting objects. When Yost filed for a pension in 1908 at the age of 69, he was earning $5 a week working as a clerk in a wholesale liquor store in Boyertown, Pa. His claim was approved for a $32 monthly allowance. Elizabeth Yost

died in 1886 after giving birth to four children. Albert died in 1920 at the age of 81.[29]

The Strause Clan, Company H

William Strause died a month after his son, William T., perished at Camp Letterman. Since William's wife had died earlier, his brother became legal guardian of several of the children, including John, the underage veteran who had been wounded on July 3rd.

Another personal tragedy befell cousin Solomon Strause, the eldest member of the group. While he was laid up in a field hospital with a shattered left arm, his father died. Therefore, it is doubtful Solomon ever saw his father again after leaving for active service.

Back in Strausstown, the 40-year-old farmer and

Albert Yost in 1908. His old Gettysburg wound is clearly visible on his right forearm. Courtesy of the National Archives.

carpenter struggled to support eleven children and Sarah, his wife of nineteen years. Due to his wounds and medical problems, however, Strause worked on a very limited basis, and he depended heavily on an invalid pension. He was hampered by chronic inflammation and pain in his wounded arm and continued to suffer from swollen veins in his legs as well.

When Solomon died on January 8, 1891, at the age of 67, he left behind a very small estate for Sarah's support. Percival Goodman and Daniel Badgeustos, former members of Company H, visited their comrade during his last illness, a few days before his death, and attended his funeral together with a number of other veterans. The two men also assisted Sarah in obtaining a widow's pension. This touching story demonstrates the strong bonds which existed among veterans years after the war. Indeed, the enduring slogan of the G.A.R., the powerful Union veteran's organization, was "We have drunk from the same canteen."

Brothers Joel and William S. Strause also came back to Strausstown after the completion of their military duties. Joel farmed land which had been in his family for many generations. He married Amelia Miller and fathered six children, two of whom died in childhood. One of their offspring, Cameron Eugene Strause, enjoyed great success in the insurance and real estate business.

William S. resumed his trade as a cabinet maker and carpenter. He experienced some loss of strength and atrophy in the left arm and shoulder, but it did not seem to have a major impact on his ability to work.

William married Amanda Alspach in 1866 after moving to Fleetwood, Pa. The couple had two children, both boys. William A. enlisted in the 6th Pennsylvania Volunteers during the Spanish-American War, but the conflict ended before his unit left the country. As a young man Howard lost both his legs in a trolley or train accident. The Strauses moved about frequently, from Fleetwood to Leesport, then to Reading, Philadelphia, and finally on to Bethlehem in the Lehigh Valley.

Robert Kunkle was born in his great-grandfather's home located at the corner of 9th Avenue and

From left to right: *Howard, Amanda, William S., and William A. Strause. Courtesy of Joe Smith, M.D.*

Broad streets on October 23, 1915. He recalled William S. as being a reserved gentleman with little inclination to play with a young child. On December 19, 1926, William S. took the trolley to his son William's home in Allentown for Sunday dinner. During the meal that afternoon, he suffered a stroke and lapsed into a coma. William never recovered consciousness, finally expiring after 10 P.M. that evening. He was 83 years old. Amanda had died six years earlier.

Sometime before his death, William bought two copies of Benson Lossing's *History of the Civil War* from a salesman. He had a color picture of himself in uniform painted inside the front cover of each volume and presented them to his children as family heirlooms. Indeed, it was this gift passed down through the generations that led Dr. Joe Smith to flesh out the story of his great-great-grandfather. The photo of William appears in this study.[30]

Sergeant George W. Heilig, Company H

George's right shoulder healed quickly following his discharge from the Philadelphia hospital. He continued his partnership in a Strausstown store for a total of six years, when he moved to Shartlesville and went into business for himself. After a year, Heilig became a bookkeeper for a Reading firm. In 1869, he was appointed assistant revenue assessor, which office he filled until 1886.

Of the six sons and three daughters George and Catherine raised to maturity, all moved west. In 1909, the couple moved into the home of their oldest daughter in Tacoma, Washington. The Heilig family became well known in theatrical circles throughout the Northwest. George died on November 1, 1918, at age 82. Catherine joined him on August 4, 1921. They are buried at Mountain View Cemetery in Tacoma, along with a number of their children. In 1994, John Hunt Walker, M.D., published his grandfather's Civil War letters in *Appointment at Gettysburg*.[31]

Captain William L. Gray, Company I

William never fully recovered from the ill effects of his long imprisonment. He suffered from rheumatism, varicose veins, and heart disease. The death of his son and his long ordeal in captivity also affected his mental health. As a result, the formerly robust officer was often bedridden and his business interests suffered.

"I found Captain Gray a mere wreak; he was very much emaciated … his feet and knees pained him very much," observed Frank Simon, a neighbor and Union army veteran. Charles Potts recalled that his old friend and tentmate was completely broken down after returning home to Cressona and that he had no use of his right arm.

Eventually, William gained back some of the weight he had lost due to his confinement. On his 65th birthday in 1887, he weighed 170 lbs., an increase of nearly 40 lbs. since his release from captivity. Frail health would still plague him for the remainder of his life. In 1883, George McFarland wrote to William W. Dudley, the commissioner of pensions, who had also lost a leg at Gettysburg: "I have no doubt that his twenty months in prison pens so affected his health that he would long since have been in his grave if not possessed of a strong constitution and excellent habits. And I feel equally certain he deserves a pension, and hope you can grant him one without delay. His present broken down condition and poverty plead strongly for prompt action."

The affidavits submitted by McFarland and other comrades netted Gray a $20 per month invalid pension. Except for several years in Kansas, he spent the remainder of his life in Schuylkill County.

On January 27, 1890, the *Pottsville Republican* reported: "Captain W. L. Gray, an old and highly respected citizen of our town, although he had borne the heat of many battles, was conquered by the hand of death on Friday evening [January 24]. His funeral will take place on Tuesday afternoon." Gray died of heart failure in his Cressona home. Wife Elizabeth died in 1906.[32]

Second Lieutenant Charles P. Potts, Company I

Pott's readjustment to civilian life was somewhat smoother than that of his friend William Gray. Charles operated his clothing store and fruit orchard as he had before his departure from Pottsville, which probably seemed like another lifetime. In addition, he served several terms on the city council. One neighbor considered him "a first-class citizen — sober, industrious, attentive to business, honorable in all his

William S. Strause.

dealings, and a man devoted to his family ... we have no better citizen in the town."

Charles' family consisted of his wife, Sallie, and eight children. Daughter Annie died in 1863 while her father was away in the military. Potts became a member of the "First Defenders' Association," and in 1913 he recounted his colorful war experiences for the Schuylkill County Historical Society.

The nervous debility and rheumatism which afflicted Potts in his later years were attributed to his twenty months in captivity. However, the resilient old soldier lived well into the next century. He was less than two months from his 87th birthday when he died on December 4, 1922.[33]

Captain James Weida, Company K

Miraculously, Weida recovered from his severe chest wound and fathered four additional children with his wife, Angeline, in Long Swamp, Pa. James lived another forty-four years after his near fatal wounding at Gettysburg. Intestinal cancer claimed his life on June 12, 1907.[34]

Sergeant Adam J. Heilman, Company K

The former color-bearer never recovered from the multiple gunshot wounds he received on July 1, 1863. A Philadelphia surgeon examined Heilman at his residence in Reading in early June of 1865. He noted profuse hemorrhaging from the lungs through the mouth, difficulty in breathing, coughing and expectoration, and extreme tenderness in the chest region. As a result, Adam could barely speak above a whisper. In addition, his right arm was entirely useless and he was scarcely able to walk. The surgeon concluded his report with a grim prognosis: "The disability … is permanent in character and must of necessity terminate fatally in a very few years...."

Remarkably, one year later, the gritty veteran proudly carried his old flag in a veterans' parade held in Philadelphia, which culminated in the return of the banners to the Commonwealth. Heilman battled his war injuries as tenaciously as he had once fought the enemy and lived beyond the expectations of his doctors. In fact, he fathered three more children from 1867 to 1872.

In order to support his wife and five children, Adam obtained employment as a watchman at the repair shop of the Reading Railroad. As a supplement, he received an invalid pension of $8 per month. This hardly seems just compensation for the horrible wounds he suffered while defending his country.

Heilman died at his residence on June 16, 1878. His death was attributed to the internal injuries he had sustained fifteen years earlier.[35]

Private Charles M. Ammarell, Company K

After participating in the Grand Review in Washington before the president and the commanding generals of the various Union armies, Ammarell mustered out of the 46th Pennsylvania on July 16, 1865. Willing and cheerful, brave and faithful, he became an ideal soldier, and won the respect and admiration of both officers and men. In over two years of combined military service, Charles never missed a day of duty due to illness.

These attributes served him well in civilian life. After farming for a number of years, Ammarell came to Reading in 1896. Two years later, he joined two other investors in the construction of the West Buttonwood Street Market House, serving as manager and superintendent of the enterprise. Afterward, he erected numerous dwelling and business blocks in the Reading area, including over 100 residential homes. Charles also became director of the Berks Coal Company. In the real estate, financial, and commercial circles of the city, he was recognized as "a man of great business capacity, sterling integrity, and staunch adherence to the principles of right."

Charles used his wealth to pursue his love of travel and adventure. In 1906, with his wife and another couple, he logged over 9,000 miles on a trip to Southern California. During the journey the foursome explored Yellowstone Park and parts of Canada. Charles also traveled to his native Germany with his brother, Robert, where he visited old scenes and reestablished old acquaintances. He also stayed in touch with his former comrades through his membership in McLean Post No. 16, G.A.R.

Charles and Amanda Ammarell celebrated their golden wedding anniversary on October 14, 1916. The couple had four children, three daughters and a son.

On Tuesday morning, February 20, 1923, while walking home from the market house, Charles slipped on the icy pavement, and in the fall sustained three fractured ribs. The veteran of Gettysburg, Atlanta, and the March to the Sea died of pneumonia less than two weeks later. He was 76 years old.[36]

The Family of Private Franklin Wendling, Company K

Young Franklin's death at Mower U.S. General Hospital in Philadelphia on July 17, had serious consequences for the large Wendling farm family in Kutztown. The father, David Wendling, began to drink heavily and became abusive to other family members. In the fall of 1864, he abandoned his wife and eight children, half of whom were less than ten years of age. He traveled west and drifted from town to town before he died almost twenty years later when he choked on a piece of meat in a restaurant. After her husband's departure, Sarah Wendling struggled to maintain the farm and to feed her family. She received $12 each month from the government through a mother's pension and frequently hired out the older children to neighboring farmers. The death of a soldier often had serious repercussions for family and community relations.[37]

A large number of veterans who had served in the 151st never returned to the now hallowed ground at Gettysburg. Perhaps the memories were too painful or time and financial constraints prevented even a brief visit. Others visited the battlefield frequently, possibly because of a need to stay in touch with an unforgettable chapter in their lives. These pilgrimages had to border on a religious experience for the former combatants. These men may have pondered why they had survived the carnage while friends and neighbors, perhaps even family members, had perished there.

George McFarland made a number of trips to Gettysburg after the war. His first visit took place in 1866 in company with Professor Samuel P. Bates, the recently appointed state historian, who would soon author the multi-volume *History of Pennsylvania Volunteers, 1861–65.* The visit was initiated through an invitation by John B. Bachelder of New York. Bachelder, a New Hampshire–born artist, was destined to become the most prominent historian of the famous battle. He had previously met McFarland in the Lutheran Seminary shortly after the fighting. A close personal and business relationship developed between the two men. Accompanying Bachelder was artist James Walker, who was commissioned to produce a series of historical paintings.

On June 28th, McFarland recorded an emotional moment in his diary: "Though things are very much changed and the debris of battle mainly removed, our positions and movements were readily traced by one acquainted with them by earlier knowledge. I stood upon the spot on which I was wounded with strange emotions."

The next day George entered the Seminary through the same door he had been carried into when wounded nearly three years earlier. Next, he examined the rooms he occupied during his long confinement there. His memorable visit culminated when he was carried into the building's landmark cupola

through the courtesy of Reverend Doctor Charles Hay. As the former commander gazed westward across the ground where he and so many of his men had been either killed or permanently maimed, he may have pondered whether this sacrifice had indeed not been in vain.

Later in the evening, a Congressional party arrived from Washington. Among the delegation was future president Rutherford B. Hayes of Ohio. Over the next few days, a number of tours were arranged for these dignitaries and the Gettysburg veterans who accompanied them. During a tour of the first day's field, General William Gamble, who was in charge of the cavalry brigade that opened the battle, confided to McFarland the interesting fact that he had personally warned General John Reynolds of the danger of riding to the front on the fateful morning of July 1.[38]

An Act of Congress approved June 9, 1880, provided for a detailed survey of the Gettysburg battlefield "to provide for the compilation and preservation of data, showing the various positions and movements of troops at that battle illustrated by diagrams." This bill, signed into law by President Hayes, provided the sum of $50,000 for John Bachelder to write a detailed history of the battle. Accordingly, two years later, Bachelder invited veterans from both armies to Gettysburg for the purpose of ascertaining troop movements and positions during the engagement.[39]

During June 14th and 15th at least two dozen officers, representing both North and South, gathered on the old battlefield for a careful study of the fighting which took place on July 1st. A large public meeting was held in the Adams County Courthouse to greet the former combatants. Robert G. McCreary, Esq., made a brief reception speech on behalf of the citizenry "bidding all the gentleman present a cordial welcome to the hospitality of the town." Afterward, a number of veterans delivered addresses to the assembly. Among the speakers was George McFarland.[40]

One of the invited guests from the Army of Northern Virginia was McFarland's old adversary, Lieutenant Colonel Joseph N. Brown of Anderson, South Carolina. During the inspection Brown marveled that the field presented precisely the view it did nineteen years earlier. "Time seemed to have made scarcely a change," he wrote, "The impressions on the mind had been so strong that the hills, valleys, parcels of woods, Seminary, slopes, houses, streets, fencing, then thrown down, and roads, were all of them fresh in the memory." Brown told McFarland that he had witnessed his wounding near the close of the fighting on Seminary Ridge.[41] Unfortunately, no other details of their conversation has been preserved. Although the country was still suffering from the four years of civil strife, the veterans of both armies were on the road to reconciliation.

As the 25th anniversary of the battle approached, the Commonwealth of Pennsylvania took an important step to memorialize the ground where so many Keystone State soldiers had fallen. The General Assembly passed the following act during the 1887 session: "That the sum of one hundred and twenty-one thousand five hundred dollars, or so much thereof as may be necessary, be and is hereby specifically appropriated out of any funds of the State Treasury for the purpose of perpetuating the participation in, and marking ... the position of each of the commands of Pennsylvania volunteers engaged in the battle of Gettysburg."

Another provision provided for a board of five commissioners

> whose duty it shall be to select and decide upon the design and material for monuments of granite or bronze to mark the position of each Pennsylvania command upon the battlefield of Gettysburg ... and they shall co-operate with five persons representing the survivors of the several regimental organizations or commands of this State engaged in the said battle, in the location of the said monuments and the selection thereof....

A sum of $1,500 was appropriated to each qualifying organization for the erection of a suitable memorial. On June 15, 1887, Governor James A. Beaver, a Civil War veteran, approved the legislation.[42]

Accordingly, the survivors of the 151st Pennsylvania formed a regimental organization at Reading in September 1887 by electing George McFarland president; Walter Owens, secretary; and Levi Gerhart, treasurer. The following committee was selected to work on the monument project: McFarland, who was elected as chairman, Owens as secretary, William Gray, George Heilig, and Azariah Body.

After considerable travel, many meetings, and the examination of numerous plans and proposals, the committee, with the consent of the Pennsylvania Board of Commissioners on Gettysburg Monuments, contracted with the firm of P. F. Eisenbrown of Reading for a monument to be completed and in place for a dedication to be held on July 1, 1888, the 25th anniversary of the day on which the regiment first engaged the enemy at Gettysburg.[43]

The five-member delegation from the 151st also worked under the auspices of the Gettysburg Battlefield Memorial Association (GBMA), which had been chartered in 1864 by the Pennsylvania Legislature "to hold and preserve the battle-grounds of Gettysburg ... and by such perpetuation, and such memorial structures as a generous and patriotic people may aid to erect, to commemorate the heroic deeds, the struggles, and the triumphs of their brave defenders." By the summer of 1867, this group of concerned citizens had purchased 140 acres of historic ground, including a small parcel in Herbst's Woods, and portions of Little Round Top and Culp's Hill. Throughout the 1880s, the GBMA developed rules, recommendations, and suggestions to insure the protection, permanence, and historical accuracy of the many memorials and monuments being placed on the battlefield.

The requirements included the following: all monuments must be constructed of granite or bronze; on the front of each monument must appear the number of the regiment or battery, state of origin, and the brigade, division, and corps to which the unit belonged in letters not less than four inches; and if the unit was actively engaged, effective strength and casualty figures were to be included on the monument. These numbers had to agree with the official records of the War Department. Another resolution required that the monument be positioned on the line of battle held by the brigade and that the right and left flanks of the regiment or battery be marked with stones not less than two feet high. It was recommended that upon one side of the monument should be noted the part of the state from which the regiment was recruited, dates of muster in and muster out, total strengths and losses during its service, and the battles in which it participated. In addition, the State of Pennsylvania required that the state seal be prominently displayed on all of its monuments.[44]

Today, on a battlefield filled with artistic and ornate memorials, the 151st's plain regimental monument on McPherson's Ridge is easy to overlook. Standing just over seventeen feet tall and composed of New Hampshire granite, the only extra ornamentation consists of polished circles on the capstone, symbols of the First Army Corps, and a sculpture of three bronze muskets in a recessed section on the western face. But this simplicity in design seems appropriate for the unassuming men who fought so valiantly on the afternoon of July 1, 1863. Indeed, the unembellished memorial contains a powerful message of self-sacrifice and bravery in the face of great adversity.

McFarland and his committee scrambled to have everything prepared in time for the ceremony. On June 13, less than three weeks from the planned dedication day, a second circular was sent out to survivors of the regiment. The announcement read in part:

> During the quarter of a century that has passed since the battle, many who endured the severe ordeal of that day have since answered to their last roll-call. Surely every remaining survivor should greet his comrades at this reunion. Come, fellow-soldiers, let us meet once more on this hallowed ground and dedicate our monument, to mark for those who come after us the spot sacred to us and our children as the place we bravely risked our lives that the nation might live, and "under God, have a new birth of freedom."

The circular also announced that Rile & Company had been contracted to photograph the survivors around the monument at the moment of dedication. The photograph rooms of this establishment, which were located on Chambersburg Street directly opposite the Eagle Hotel, served as the regimental headquarters during the gathering. Here, every visiting member was requested to sign his name, post office, company, and rank into a register book immediately upon his arrival. Arrangements were made to procure meals at the Eagle Hotel on the northeast corner of Chambersburg and Washington streets. A turn of the century ad boasted, "The Eagle Hotel has entertained all the notable persons that have come to Gettysburg since the battle in 1863 — Headquarters for veterans, commercial men, organizations."[45]

A serious glitch nearly developed when McFarland learned a few days later that the Board of Commissioners had reached a tentative agreement in conjunction with the governor to dedicate all of the state monuments on the same day in early October of 1888. George immediately consulted with Governor Beaver and then wrote to Samuel Harper, secretary of the commission, that his selection of an earlier date for dedication did not result "from any disposition to ignore the commission or deprive it of any rights or consideration," and that at this late stage, he could not postpone the event without being "subject to much censure."[46] Fortunately, the matter was quickly resolved and the original plans remained intact.

At 3 P.M. on July 1, 1888, precisely twenty-five years from the time when the 151st first encountered the 26th North Carolina on McPherson's Ridge, about 75 survivors of the regiment assembled at Gettysburg to dedicate the newly erected monument. The festivities began with a 13-gun salute from the 3rd U.S. Artillery and a prayer of invocation by Walter Owens. Mrs. Emma McFarland Wharton, who as an infant was on the field with her mother as she carefully tended to her wounded husband, unveiled the memorial amid the hearty "huzzas" of the gathered crowd.

Judge Wheelock Veazy, the former colonel of the 16th Vermont, was a special guest speaker at the ceremony. Pointing to the nearby commemorative monument for General John Reynolds, which had been erected two years earlier by the Commonwealth of Pennsylvania, Veazy pronounced the 151st "a worthy guard of honor to that heroic soldier." He added that if the general could speak one of his first acts would be "to compliment it for the undying fame it had won on this bloody field, and express his satisfaction that it stood guard over the spot where he paid the last penalty of a soldier's devotion to his country in the trying hours of that country's need." The Judge characterized the small band of veterans gathered around him as "good types of the volunteer soldier that spring to arms at the call of patriotic duty, as compared with those who make war as a chosen profession" and he wished them many years to enjoy their now fully acknowledged accomplishments on the field.

Other speakers included Colonel John Bachelder, Captain Owens, as well as Major Samuel Harper and General J. P. S. Gobin, representing the Board of Commissioners.[47] The main oration was then delivered by George McFarland, who recounted the highlights of the regiment's history and its great sacrifice at Gettysburg. "We meet on the very line on which we fought … to dedicate a monument … for the information and inspiration of future generations," he told his listeners. McFarland hoped that a nation dedicated to the principle that all men are free, "should live and grow, and spread throughout all the world its benign influence and encouraging experiences."

Looking out over the audience at his former comrades, George realized that the fires of youth had long since given way to crutches, canes, and long gray beards. Perhaps feeling that his own life was slowly slipping away, McFarland closed with the following thought:

> Dear comrades, many of us have met each other today for the first time since the battle, and may never see each other again. We can return to our homes, feeling satisfied with our record and grateful to the great State, whose sons we are, for this handsome monument to permanently mark the spot so sacred to us all. These thoughts will serve to soothe the evening of our lives. But as we fight the battle over with our friends let us not forget to impress upon all, especially the young, the great principles for which we fought and suffered.[48]

A little over a year later, however, the survivors of the 151st Pennsylvania were back at Gettysburg for "Pennsylvania Day," which was held on September 11 and 12, 1889. As mentioned earlier, this event had been contemplated since the previous fall. Veterans residing in the Commonwealth who had served in Pennsylvania regiments at Gettysburg were provided with round trip transportation to the battlefield. A number of survivors' associations, including those of the 121st and 142nd Pennsylvania, dedicated their monuments on September 11th. At an extravagant ceremony held in the National Cemetery the following afternoon, the monuments representing the eighty-six Pennsylvania commands present at Gettysburg were officially transferred to the Commonwealth and then to the GBMA. Brevet Lieutenant Colonel George Meade, the son of the commanding general and one of his staff officers, presided over the event.[49]

In comparing the photographs from the two reunions, it appears that more veterans from the 151st attended the latter event than did the dedication ceremony a year earlier. Perhaps the free transportation and the grandeur of Pennsylvania Day accounted for the difference.

One veteran present for the dedication ceremony was very proud of the monument and thought that its designers deserved a great deal of credit. "Everything is nicely proportioned and well built, and will stand for ages to mark the spot of that day's battle," he wrote.[50] However, the monument admired by this veteran is not the same as the one viewed by

visitors today. The alcove on the front of the shaft was originally adorned with a carved stack of arms, knapsack, cartridge box, and canteen in bold relief. Sometime around the turn of the century, this design was replaced with three bronze muskets.

Another less noticeable change involved the inscription of casualties near the base of the monument. In 1889, McFarland petitioned the Pennsylvania Board of Commissioners and the GBMA to replace these figures, which were based on the report he had submitted to the War Department in November 1863. A careful company-by-company accounting after the war had altered the categorization of wounded, mortally wounded, and killed. The total number of casualties remained unchanged. The revised figures were accepted by the Adjutant General's Office in Washington, and they were etched into the monument in place of the old ones.[51]

Yet another interesting aspect of the monument's early history was its proximity to a once famous resort hotel and a series of therapeutic mineral springs. Located due west of Willoughby Run on the site of what is now the Gettysburg Country Club, the Springs Hotel opened for business with much fanfare on June 28, 1869. The magnificent four-story structure, complete with "French roof" and cupola, could provide first-class accommodations for over 200 guests.

The major drawing point of the hotel was the healing waters of the mineral springs which were located a short distance away. Legend states that during

Veterans of the 151st Pennsylvania gathered around the monument on September 12, 1889, as part of the "Pennsylvania Day" activities at Gettysburg. George McFarland is standing with the aid of crutches to the right of the monument. Courtesy of J. Roy Lauver.

the first day's battle soldiers drank from the springs and bathed their wounds in the cool water. Later, these men alleged that the spring waters had miraculous healing powers. One early visitor to the resort agreed. In the August 13, 1869, issue of the (Gettysburg) *Star and Sentinel*, Colonel W. H. H. Davis, a reporter for the *Doylestown Democrat*, proclaimed: "The water contains lithia and from its effect, on invalids, it is found that cures have been astonishing. It is a remedy for rheumatism, affections of the liver, rheumatic gout, and kindred diseases. It is the only remedy in the world that will dissolve calculus or stone found in bladder. From the effect it produces it really seems to come close to the 'Fountain of Youth.'" The katalysine spring water became a booming business and sales amounted to about $70,000 in the first year alone! H. Yingling, the proprietor of the hotel in 1881, claimed in an advertising circular that the water "has produced some of the most wonderful cures on record in cases of Kidney Affections, Rheumatism, Dyspepsia, etc.... The Hot Baths of this spring are pronounced by experienced physicians and surgeons as fully equal, if not superior, to the Hot Springs of Arkansas."

During the early years of the hotel, a lake for fishing and boating was created by damming Willoughby Run near the crossing of Old Mill Road. Other social activities included lavish dining, dancing, billiards, bowling, and of course, battlefield tours.

In the fall of 1868, just before the opening of the hotel, investors in the enterprise purchased a right of way through the grounds of the Lutheran Seminary for a rail car drawn by horses. A route was then laid out from the town square directly to the hotel. Guests of the establishment traveled west from the square via Chambersburg Street. Immediately after passing West Street, the traveler entered the newly constructed Springs Avenue, which led over Seminary Ridge through the seminary grounds. After passing over the ridge, the avenue turned sharply to the north, skirting the edge of a wooded grove for a distance of about 500 feet, before veering westward. Another 1,500 feet carried visitors directly past the eventual site of the 151st Pennsylvania's monument. The journey continued through the southwestern portion of Herbst's Woods and then over Willoughby Run via a small trestle bridge. A large loop driveway passed through the resort complex.

Springs Avenue was heavily traveled during the heyday of the resort in the late nineteenth century, as guests came from all along the eastern seaboard to drink and bathe in the healing waters and to enjoy the luxurious surroundings. Among these visitors were Civil War generals, such as George Gordon Meade, prominent state and national political leaders, writers, artists, and industrialists. The Springs Hotel was a bustling, exciting

The campus of the Lutheran Theological Seminary in 1925. The Seminary grove and the remnants of Springs Avenue are visible in the upper portion of the view. All of the buildings shown in the photo are post-war structures with the exception of the original edifice in the center. Author's collection.

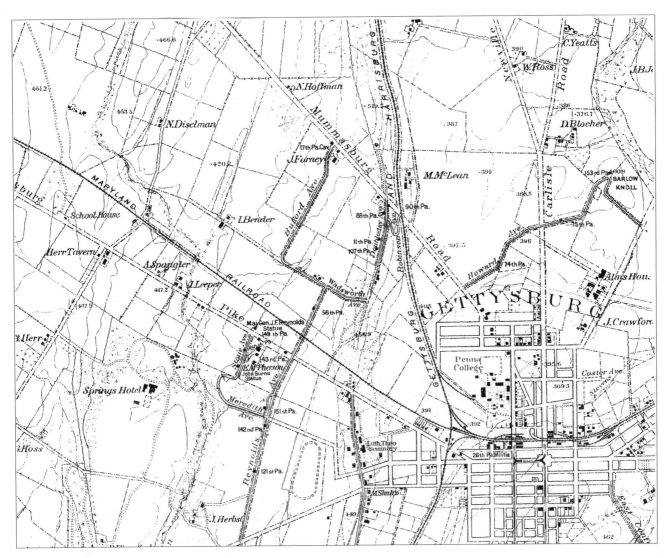

A section of a map of the Gettysburg National Military Park depicting the locations of monuments and avenues in the early twentieth century. From Nicholson, Pennsylvania at Gettysburg.

place indeed, and the monument of the 151st Pennsylvania was highly visible to anyone traveling to and from the resort.

In 1876, a Gettysburg newspaper reported on an ambitious expansion project for the Springs Hotel enterprise, including the statement that "The woods where the Battle of Gettysburg started and where Gen. Reynolds fell, is to be made into a park with another boulevard surrounding it and upon the edge a new hotel will be built." Fortunately, for future generations of Americans, these development plans never reached fruition and the historical integrity of Reynolds' Woods was not compromised.

The popularity of the Springs Hotel waned after the turn of the century and the last public use of the facility took place during the 50th anniversary of the

battle in 1913. Four years later, on December 13, 1917, a fire broke out in a flue between the second and third floors, and in a short time, the entire structure was consumed by flames. A deep cover of snow prevented any fire fighting equipment from reaching the blaze. Present day Springs Avenue terminates on the campus of the Lutheran Theological Seminary at its junction with West Confederate Avenue. A small portion of the original road between the Lutheran Seminary and McPherson's Ridge is visible today.[52]

When the United States Congress authorized and created the Gettysburg National Military Park in 1895, the holdings of the GBMA were transferred to the federal government, with the War Department having direct jurisdiction over the new park. Over the next forty years, this agency oversaw many improvements to the park lands, including the construction of twenty miles of semi-permanent avenues. Reynolds Avenue, completed in 1899, follows the battle line of the First Corps from the Hagerstown Road to north of the Chambersburg Pike, a distance of nearly one mile. Three minor sections, Wadsworth, Doubleday, and Robinson avenues, link Reynolds Avenue to Oak Ridge and the Mummasburg Road. At the same time, Reynolds Branch Avenue was constructed through the eastern edge of Reynolds Woods. This piked roadway stretched nearly 500 feet from the 151st's monument past the Reynolds commemorative marker to the north before joining Reynolds Avenue. Only a trace of this road is visible today.

These avenues were not entirely new, but rather a rehabilitation of the infrastructure originally developed by the GBMA. After assuming stewardship of the battlefield, the Gettysburg National Military Park Commission reported that these dirt roads were in bad condition and that the old bridge constructed over the historic railroad cut presented a safety hazard. The new avenues were constructed of a compressed base of stone 14 or 15 inches thick with a drainage system.

By the summer of 1903, Stone Avenue, which runs along the line held by Colonel Roy Stone's brigade from the Chambersburg Pike to the northwestern edge of Reynolds Woods, was completed. Most of Meredith Avenue was also finished by this time. This roadway follows the line of the Iron Brigade and connects Stone and Reynolds avenues. Construction of the final 800 feet of this avenue near its junction with Reynolds Avenue was blocked by a "land improvement company," which refused to grant right of way over, or convey title to, a small strip of land under acceptable terms. This company was most likely the same one that had planned a hotel for this area nearly three decades earlier. The United States secured title to the disputed tract through condemnation proceedings the following year, and the final span of the avenue was finished. The network of avenues surrounding the advanced position of the 151st Pennsylvania on July 1st was thus completed. In 1933, the War Department was replaced as chief steward by the newly formed National Park Service of the U.S. Department of the Interior, which continues to administer the park today.[53]

The modern battlefield visitor can easily reach the monument of the 151st Pennsylvania Volunteers by turning onto Chambersburg Street from Lincoln Square and by following the signs for U.S. Route 30 West. After traveling about one mile, a left turn is made at the signal light for Reynolds Avenue. The monument is located on the right after a distance of about one-quarter of a mile near the intersection of Reynolds and Meredith avenues.

Perhaps the modern visitor to the battlefield should take the advice of a First Corps veteran, who fought on this very ground and survived to write about his experiences in the new millennium:

> I will not tell here the horrible, sickening sights that met my eyes. I will not attempt to describe the demonous yell, the zip-zip of the minie balls, and the whizzing of shells on that, now historic field, of Gettysburg, and if you ever gaze upon the marble or granite monuments standing there ... let your imagination have free course and picture that which cannot be told. As for my part, I can never look upon a monument or statue commemorating these fearful days of war without seeing or hearing again ... the sights and sounds so indelibly impressed upon my memory.[54]

When one stands near the monument of the 151st Pennsylvania, one is positioned at what was once the center of the regiment's most advanced line of battle on July 1, 1863. The small concrete flank markers are easily visible from this location. With a little imagination, the visitor can picture the double lines of blue infantry feverishly loading and firing their muskets under a hot July sun. Gazing into the corner of the grove, perhaps fleeting glimpses can be seen of butternut riflemen as they dodge from tree to tree. It is quite possible that the remains of fallen patriots such as Abe Freet and Nathan Beisser still nourish the luxuriant grass growing around the base of the granite monument. And perhaps on a quiet day, if the wind is right, one can still hear the words of George Fisher McFarland echoing through time, "...let us not forget to impress upon all, especially the young, the great principles for which we fought and suffered."

What's in a Name?

The nickname "Schoolteachers' Regiment" has become synonymous with the 151st Pennsylvania Volunteers. In light of its popularity, a detailed analysis of the history of this moniker is in order. When and by whom was the phrase first used and how many teachers actually served in the ranks of the 151st? Unfortunately, no concise or entirely accurate answers are available for these questions.

Interestingly, in the numerous primary accounts I have examined during my research of the 151st, not a single member of the unit mentioned this nickname, nor did any of the early Gettysburg historians. Rather, the seeds of this colorful sobriquet can be traced to an obscure article penned by George McFarland in January 1863, which subsequently appeared in the March 1863 issue of the *Pennsylvania School Journal*. The article was aptly titled "Teachers in the Army."

McFarland, a lifelong educator, observed that "many, very many, of the teachers and friends of education in the old Keystone are found among her gallant sons in the army...." George took great pains to ascertain how many teachers were serving in the 151st. Following a detailed survey, he concluded that the regiment included 60 former educators. He listed the following individuals by name: Colonel Harrison Allen, himself, Adjutant Samuel Allen, Surgeon Amos Blakeslee, Assistant Surgeon Warren Underwood, and Chaplain Thomas McClure.

The fact that McFarland undertook such a time-consuming project indicates that he took a great deal of pride in his profession and its contribution to the Union war effort. He concluded his article with a prophecy: "...if this unequaled government, this glorious Union is saved, future generations will tell by whom it was done; if it falls, which let us hope it never may—the teachers of Pennsylvania at least will not be to blame."[1]

Following the war, George submitted another article to the same journal in which he assigned the Northern educator a very prominent role in the outcome of the war, particularly in the Battle of Gettysburg, which was beginning to be recognized as the turning point of the long conflict. In "The Victory at Gettysburg, the Work of the Teacher" (October 1866), McFarland asserted, "To the presence of the Teacher in the North during the last half century, and his patient though ill-requited labors in disciplining mind, cultivating intellect, supplanting the blind efforts of brute force by the more rational efforts of intelligent action, do we owe the discomfiture of the rebel hordes on the ensanguined fields of Gettysburg." He further maintained that the only superiority the Union army had over the Confederate forces was its "moral and intellectual power." Certainly, many in the South would have disagreed with this conclusion! George noted that it was his good fortune to lead sixty teachers into battle in the first day's fight.[2]

It is doubtful, however, that many outside of the teaching profession read either of these articles. During his dedicatory speech at the monument dedication in 1888, George made reference to his 1863 piece: "In an article I wrote for the *Pennsylvania School Journal* at that time, I enumerated one hundred and thirteen school teachers in its ranks."[3] Why this figure almost doubled from the total he had originally quoted in the article is unclear. Was this revision an intentional embellishment or a result of new information obtained from veterans of the unit in the quarter century following the battle? Unfortunately, we will probably never know the answer to this question.

McFarland's speech was published in *Pennsylvania at Gettysburg* in 1904. This publication was widely distributed throughout the state and was readily available to all subsequent historians of the battle. McFarland's revised figure of the number of teachers in the regiment would be accepted by Gettysburg scholars from this point forward.

Nearly twenty years before this speech, Professor Samuel P. Bates' landmark *History of Pennsylvania*

Volunteers was published. In the capsulized history of the 151st, which appeared in Volume 4, Bates planted the seed for a popular myth concerning the regiment: "Company D was largely composed of the instructors and students of McAlisterville Academy, of which Lieutenant Colonel McFarland was the principal...."[4]

A close examination of the academy attendance books and the company muster rolls shows this statement to be a great exaggeration. In fact, only eight men of Company D, including McFarland, who was its original captain, had ties to the McAlisterville Academy. Of the 92 men who joined this company, 30 listed their occupation as farmers, four as millers, and 19 more as laborers, probably farm hands. Therefore, well over half of the members of Company D were directly involved in agricultural trades. This statistic is not surprising as Juniata, Perry, and eastern Snyder counties remain heavily agricultural regions to this day. Furthermore, as the Civil War intensified, attendance at the academy declined sharply. By the end of August 1862, McFarland had only 41 pupils, some of them female. Therefore, the romantic image of nearly a hundred schoolboys and their instructors rushing from the halls of a small country academy to defend their country is simply absurd.[5]

Once again, McFarland may have contributed to this misconception. As mentioned previously, Samuel Bates accompanied George to Gettysburg in 1866, after the former was appointed as state historian. These men were well-acquainted with one another from their mutual employment in the Pennsylvania school department at Harrisburg. It is obvious that Bates relied heavily on his friend for his sketch of the 151st. At this time McFarland was working on a detailed history of the Third Division, First Army Corps, which unfortunately was never published.[6] A comparison of McFarland's manuscript and Bates' account of the 151st reveals many similarities and a number of verbatim passages. Although the statement concerning the formation of Company D did not appear in McFarland's version, it seems probable that he proofed Bates' work prior to its publication. Given McFarland's propensity to exalt the role of the North's superior education system in the ultimate Union victory, it seems unlikely that he would have opposed this statement.

The unique story of Company D, and the regiment's composition of over a hundred schoolteachers, appeared in some form in nearly every account which mentioned the 151st near the turn of the century. For example, in *Gettysburg Then and Now: The Field of American Valor*, Author John M. Vanderslice, a director of the Gettysburg Battlefield Memorial Association, wrote: "In it [the 151st Pennsylvania] were several companies recruited from academies, one company being exclusively composed of boys from the academy in Juniata County, of which Colonel McFarland ... was the principal, and in the regiment were over a hundred who had been schoolteachers."[7]

A nearly identical account was included in a booklet of human interest stories of the battle of Gettysburg compiled by Civil War veteran, St. Clair A. Mulholland. "The regiment was unique in many particulars: McFarland, a school principal, in command, with 100 school teachers marching and fighting in the ranks. The whole of Company D was composed of scholars and school boys from McFarland's academy ... on that day [July 1st] Pennsylvania's teachers and schoolboys left a rich legacy to others who come after them."[8]

The reader will note the subtle substitution of the phrases "exclusively composed of" and "the whole of" as opposed to Bates' "Company D was *largely* composed of the instructors and students of McAlisterville Academy...." Vanderslice even introduced the idea that several other companies were organized from academies.

Nevertheless, these accounts pale in comparison to an early 1900s Juniata County newspaper article, "Valor of Pennsylvania Boys in the Civil War," which pushed poetic license to the limit. The columnist made the ridiculous assertion that the 151st "had been almost entirely recruited of young men not yet out of their teens" and that "a very large percentage of them were fresh from their school desks."[9]

Still, no one had specifically referred to the 151st Pennsylvania as "The Schoolteachers' Regiment" in the fifty years that had elapsed since the battle. The first appearance of the nickname discovered by this author appeared in William C. Storrick's *Gettysburg: The Place, The Battles, The Outcome*, which was published in 1932. Ironically, this book was printed by Mount Pleasant Press of Harrisburg, which was owned by J. Horace McFarland, the eldest child of George McFarland.

Storrick was born near Gettysburg in 1856. Following a 34-year career as a public school teacher, William was employed by the National Park Commission as a caretaker. In 1917, he was designated "Superintendent of Guides" at the Gettysburg National Military Park. During his active guiding years, Storrick "encountered many great men—hundreds of officers and privates, both Union and Confederate, who fought the battle...." He was considered an "estimable and scholarly gentleman."[10]

In the section of his book devoted to "first day highlights," William included a brief vignette of the 151st Pennsylvania under the subtitle, "The School-Teachers' Regiment." He claimed that the regiment was known by this name for the preponderance of teachers and students in Company D, who had once been associated with McFarland's school in McAlisterville.[11] Perhaps Storrick, a longtime teacher, coined the phrase himself or perhaps it originated with another early battlefield guide.

As visitation to the park grew to nearly 150,000 sightseers per year by the late 1890s, an assortment of men were able to earn a living as "hack drivers" or tour guides. Most of these individuals worked out of local hotels, livery stables, and the railroad depot. Until the guide service was regulated in 1915, the knowledge and conduct of these entrepreneurs varied greatly.[12] Even the more reputable guides, such as Storrick, probably enhanced their accounts slightly for more visitor appeal. Colorful nicknames and human interest stories were obviously more appealing than official military designations and dry tactical descriptions of battlefield maneuvers.

Modern historians have continued to accept the accounts of their predecessors without reservation whenever they discuss the regiment. Some contemporary writers have added their own colorful interpretations. For example, George R. Stewart, the author of *Pickett's Charge*, wrote:

> The 151st was an interesting regiment, containing several companies that had been recruited from academies. More than a hundred schoolteachers had enlisted in it, and its commander had been a principal. To the honor of all egg-heads be it known that this schoolmaster colonel took 466 of his unblooded regiment into the first day's battle. He himself fell wounded, and the schoolboys fought so desperately that next morning they mustered only 121, under a captain.[13]

Indeed, the regiment's perceived ties to the teaching profession are deeply ingrained in its history. But exactly how many teachers served in the ranks of the Schoolteachers' Regiment? On the surface this appears to be a fairly simple question to answer. The company muster rolls for the 151st Pennsylvania are part of the microfilmed collection of the Pennsylvania State Archives in Harrisburg, Pa. The age, occupation, and residence for each soldier was recorded upon these rolls at the time of enlistment. Therefore, it seems logical that a researcher need only to tabulate the number of men who listed "teacher" as their occupation to ascertain the exact number of educators who served in the regiment. Unfortunately, some of the company rolls are nearly illegible, making a precise count impossible. Even a casual glance at these documents, however, reveals that considerably less than 60 recruits were listed as teachers. Why the disparity?

It must be remembered that teaching in the mid–1800s was often considered a transient position and no universal accreditation system was in place. Many students also did not attend classes on a regular basis. As a youngster, George McFarland recalled that he attended school for only five to six weeks a year during the winter months because his labor was needed on the family farm.[14] Of the six officers McFarland listed as teachers in his 1863 article, only one, himself, was earning a living at this profession when the regiment was organized.

Harrison and Samuel Allen are prime examples of the temporary nature of teaching during the antebellum era. For varying periods in their youths, both of these men assisted their father in farming and lumbering during the spring and summer months, attended academies in Southern New York for the fall term, and taught school in their native town of Warren over the winter. Both men were studying in local law offices when the war broke out. Likewise, Assistant Surgeon Warren J. Underwood instructed students in the common school system for one year before he commenced the study of medicine. George Heilig taught school in Berks County for five terms in the mid–1850s, during which time he earned $28 per month. Afterward, he entered the mercantile business.[15]

From this limited sampling it can be assumed that a number of men who served in the 151st taught school at some point prior to their military service, but relatively few earned a complete living in the profession. Given the nature of the education system in the United States before the Civil War, it is virtually impossible to ascertain just how many members of the unit worked in the teaching field.

Since it is nearly certain that few, if any, veterans of the 151st ever heard their beloved regiment called the "Schoolteachers' Regiment," should modern historians and students of the battle discard the nickname altogether? Besides, if the occupational sampling of Company D is representative of the entire regiment, and since nearly half of the companies were recruited from rural Berks County, would it not be more accurate to rename the 151st the "Farmers' Regiment?" Perhaps, but on the other hand, the origin and popular usage of this unit's unique nickname is as much a part of its history as its battle experiences. The important point to remember is that bravery and self-sacrifice are not confined to any one occupation. At Gettysburg, each member of the 151st Pennsylvania, whether he was a farmer, a blacksmith, a shoemaker, a merchant, a lawyer, a politician, or a teacher, faced death or serious injury with courage and dignity for the cause he believed in.

List of Casualties of the 151st Pennsylvania Volunteers in the Battle of Gettysburg, July 1–3, 1863[1]

Field and Staff

Wounded

Lieutenant Colonel George F. McFarland
Adjutant Samuel T. Allen
Sergeant Major Simon J. Arnold

Total: 3 wounded

Company A

Killed and Mortally Wounded

Corporal Thomas D. Allen
Corporal Hugh McCready
Private Henry W. Brown
Private Charles F. Fish
Private Nelson McMicken
Private Andrew Shoemaker
Private Seth Shove

Wounded

Captain George L. Stone
Sergeant William Perrigo
Sergeant Charles H. Stone
Private George Brotzman
Private Melville J. Buck
Private Wallace J. Foster
Private Ezra K. Kent
Private Franklin M. Kent
Private Isaac Melhuish
Private Orlando Parks
Private Benjamin Sherwood
Private Joel Sherwood
Private Silas Squires

Private Gardner Taylor
Private Daniel Tucker
Private William H. Ward

Total: 7 killed, 16 wounded, 8 missing = 31

Company B

Killed and Mortally Wounded

Sergeant Thomas W. Beardsley
Sergeant Henry Smith
Private Charles Blackmore
Private Solomon B. Brink
Private Samuel McCormick
Private James W. Morrison
Private Valentine Hipsman
Private George W. Parr
Private Nelson Reaser

Wounded

Corporal Charles Bates
Private Peter Cron
Private Robert A. Kayser
Private Rush K. Kellam
Private Levi Losey
Private Charles McCarter
Private John L. Pearson

Total: 9 killed, 7 wounded, 10 missing = 26

Company C

Killed and Mortally Wounded

Henry Tupper

WOUNDED

Private Franklin S. Barnes
Private Deidrich Dasenbuck
Private Theodore O. Gunn
Private John C. Lomis
Private William C. Trumbull
Private Andrew O. Tyler

TOTAL: 1 KILLED, 6 WOUNDED, 2 MISSING = 9

Company D

KILLED AND MORTALLY WOUNDED

Sergeant James M. Dunn
Sergeant Abe C. Freet
Corporal George H. McCahren
Private Benjamin Armstrong
Private Nathan H. Beisser
Private David Fry
Private Ephraim Guyer
Private John Haines
Private Davis H. Ingram
Private Samuel Leister
Private Samuel Nailor
Private John Wesley

WOUNDED

Second Lieutenant Benjamin F. Oliver
Sergeant Michael Gable
Corporal Michael C. Bratton
Corporal Davis Meredith
Private John Amich
Private William Boyer
Private Malchom Buchanan
Private Thomas B. Landis
Private William P. Noble
Private Henry S. Patterson
Private Isaac Smith

TOTAL: 12 KILLED, 11 WOUNDED, 6 MISSING = 29

Company E

KILLED AND MORTALLY WOUNDED

First Lieutenant Aaron S. Seaman
Corporal Henry M. Miller
Corporal William F. Seaman
Private Reuben Beechert
Private William H. Butler
Private Lewis Gambler

Private Solomon Huy
Private Beneville Harner
Private William H. Kutz
Private Allen Miller
Private Aaron Sands

WOUNDED

Second Lieutenant Thomas L. Moyer
Sergeant Azariah P. Body
Sergeant John R. Schwambach
Corporal James Dubson
Corporal Benjamin F. Egolf
Corporal William M. Heckman
Corporal Edmund Kauffman
Musician Michael Link
Private Amasa G. Adams
Private Cornelius Beechert
Private Nelson P. Body
Private Jonathan Dreibelbies
Private Charles Eisenhower
Private Adam Grimes
Private Henry Y. Holtenstein
Private Ephraim Ney
Private Benjamin F. Pearson
Private John H. Phillips
Private Lenhard Ran
Private Lewis H. Rentschler
Private Samuel Schlear
Private Percival Snyder
Private Andrew B. Wagner
Private Isaac Weaver
Private John A. Wentzel

TOTAL: 11 KILLED, 25 WOUNDED, 6 MISSING = 42

Company F

KILLED AND MORTALLY WOUNDED

Private James Cotton
Private James Green
Private Pardon Hazeltine
Private Marcus Jaquay
Private Wilbur Kimball
Private Frank Lyon
Private Robert Young

WOUNDED

First Lieutenant William O. Blodget
Sergeant Anil D. Frank
Sergeant James L. Lott

Corporal Raymond B. Jones
Corporal Samuel A. Tuttle
Corporal Sylvanus Walker
Corporal Leander W. Wilcox
Private John W. Allen
Private Jehiel Carr
Private William C. Carr
Private Perry F. Chandler
Private Andrew J. Gantz
Private William Gray
Private John Knupp
Private Alfred C. Lacy
Private Edwin Matteson
Private Frank McIntyre
Private John Myers
Private James E. Norris
Private Parson C. Phillips
Private Daniel Porter
Private George A. Schuyler
Private Hiram Sturdevant
Private Stephen Sweet
Private William Sweetland
Private Daniel West

TOTAL: 7 KILLED, 26 WOUNDED, 8 MISSING = 41

Company G

KILLED AND MORTALLY WOUNDED

Private Thomas B. Faber
Private Jacob Gehret
Private John E. Geiss
Private Jonathan Himmelberger
Private Adam L. Kleinginnea
Private William S. Stamm

WOUNDED

Sergeant John Yeager
Corporal Henry D. Bentz
Corporal Christian R. Koenig
Private Girard Berger
Private Jonathan Christ
Private Jared Dunkelberger
Private George D. Fahrenbaugh
Private Erasmus H. Gruber
Private Jared Heck
Private Levi Heck
Private John D. Heffner
Private Frederick Holden
Private Isaac Kalbach

Private James H. Kaufman
Private Henry S. Kintzle
Private Levi Kline
Private Jonathan Kreitz
Private Daniel Livers
Private John Rentz
Private Willowby Shearer
Private Alfred D. Staudt
Private Adam G. Strause
Private William W. Strause
Private Joel S. Stump

TOTAL: 6 KILLED, 24 WOUNDED, 10 MISSING = 40

Company H

KILLED AND MORTALLY WOUNDED

Corporal John Schaffer
Private John Bender
Private George Livengood
Private Adam Siegfried
Private William T. Strause
Private Henry M. Weber
Private William J. Wentz

WOUNDED

Second Lieutenant Albert Yost
Sergeant Franklin R. Boltz
Sergeant George W. Heilig
Sergeant William M. Miller
Corporal Jonathan G. Haag
Corporal Joseph Y. Moyer
Private John Fessler
Private Adam L. Gottshall
Private William Hollenbach
Private Jacob B. Klahr
Private David K. Knoll
Private John Lengel
Private Jacob Loeb
Private Andrew Miller
Private William H. Scheaffer
Private George K. Spangler
Private John T. Strause
Private Solomon Strause
Private William S. Strause
Private Jonathan S. Wenrich

CAPTURED

Captain William K. Boltz
First Lieutenant James L. Reber

Corporal Isaac K. Derr
Private Ezra Stupp

TOTAL: 7 KILLED, 20 WOUNDED, 4 MISSING = 31

Company I

KILLED AND MORTALLY WOUNDED

Corporal Jacob Haertter
Private William Borrell
Private Patrick Brennan
Private William Delph
Private Henry Felton
Private William Manning
Private John McClure
Private Anson C. Miller
Private Jacob Zimmerman

WOUNDED

First Lieutenant Henry H. Merkle
Sergeant Charles Bartolett
Sergeant Joseph Kantner
Sergeant J. Peter Koch
Corporal Elias Bartolett
Corporal Samuel B. Snell
Private Jonathan Auchenbach
Private Albert Bacon
Private Elias Delcamp
Private Daniel Fessler
Private Michael Fessler
Private Truman Halbert
Private William W. Jenks
Private Moses Keller
Private William Kendricks
Private William Moycr
Private Jeremiah Reed
Private Peter Schnerring
Private Jeremiah Starr
Private Daniel Yeik
Private George Zechman

CAPTURED

Captain William L. Gray
Second Lieutenant Charles P. Potts

TOTAL: 9 KILLED, 21 WOUNDED, 17 MISSING = 47

Company K

KILLED AND MORTALLY WOUNDED

Second Lieutenant Charles Trexler
Sergeant Alexander Seiders
Corporal Cyrus Leitz
Private Peter Drumheller
Private Jonathan Eagua
Private Franklin Geiger
Private Nicholas Guinther
Private Adam Keennor
Private David Scheimer
Private Charles Smeck
Private Franklin B. Weaber
Private Franklin P. Wendling

WOUNDED

Captain James W. Weida
Sergeant James B. Brown
Sergeant Adam Heilman
Sergeant John Y. Seiders
Corporal Amos Fisher
Corporal Franklin Rowe
Corporal George Weidner
Private Ephraim Bingaman
Private Lewis B. Bluck
Private John Borrell
Private Marcus Fegley
Private John Gross
Private James B. Hayman
Private John H. Herb
Private Charles Humbert
Private James B. Kerchner
Private Henry Kline
Private Mahlon Lease
Private Lewis Mechley
Private Hillorous Roth
Private Aaron Smith
Private John Weyandt

TOTAL: 12 KILLED, 22 WOUNDED, 4 MISSING = 38

TOTALS FOR REGIMENT = 81 KILLED, 181 WOUNDED, 75 MISSING OR CAPTURED = 337

NOTES

Chapter 1

1. John P. Nicholson, ed. *Pennsylvania at Gettysburg: Ceremonies at the Dedication of the Monuments Erected by the Commonwealth of Pennsylvania to Mark the Positions of the Pennsylvania Commands Engaged in the Battle*, 3 vols. (Harrisburg, Pa.: Wm. Stanley Ray, State Printer, 1914), Vol. 2, p. 769; George McFarland, undated account of battle of Gettysburg, George McFarland Papers, J. Horace McFarland Collection, Pennsylvania State Archives (Hereafter cited as PSA); *The War of the Rebellion: A Compilation of the Official Records of the Union and Confederate Armies*, 79 vols. in 128 parts (Washington, D.C.: Government Printing Office, 1880–1901), Series 1, Vol. 27, Part 2, p. 643. (Hereafter cited as *OR*.); John M. Vanderslice, *Gettysburg Then and Now: The Field of American Valor* (New York: G. W. Dillingham, 1897), p. 95.

2. George C. Underwood, *History of the Twenty-sixth Regiment of the North Carolina Troops in the Great War, 1861–'65* (Goldsboro, N.C.: Nash Brothers, 1901; reprint edition, Wendell, N.C.: Broadfoot's Bookmark, 1978), pp. 3, 24, 31, 39, 58; Weymouth T. Jordan, Jr., and Louis H. Manarin, eds., *North Carolina Troops, 1861–1865*, 12 vols. (Raleigh, N.C.: Division of Archives and History, 1971–1996), Vol. 7, pp. 455–460; Julius Leinbach, "Regiment Band of the Twenty-sixth North Carolina," *Civil War History*, Vol. 4, 1958, pp. 225–226, 234–236; John W. Busey and David Martin, *Regimental Strengths and Losses at Gettysburg* (Hightstown, N.J.: Longstreet House, 1994), pp. 236, 299; William F. Fox, *Regimental Losses in the American Civil War, 1861–1865* (Albany, N.Y.: Albany Publishing Company, 1889), pp. 555–556. Interestingly, the companies of this regiment were raised from the central and western counties, which had opposed secession prior to Lincoln's proclamation of April 15, 1861, calling for 75,000 militia. The 26th's original commander, Zebulon Vance, resigned on August 12, 1862, after being elected governor.

3. Busey and Martin, *Regimental Strengths and Losses at Gettysburg*, p. 264; Nicholson, *Pennsylvania at Gettysburg*, Vol. 2, p. 769. To his death, George McFarland maintained that his unit lost more men at Gettysburg than any other Union regiment. In a letter to Major Samuel Harper, McFarland pointed out, "...In Bates' History, Vol. 4, p. 680, this loss is 30 greater than now made, which is thus explained.... Many of the missing were not recorded, and I put down only those I can give the names of—thus reducing the missing to 71—and the whole loss to 337. In reality 367 is correct." The total loss of the 24th Michigan at Gettysburg was reported as 363 officers and men. George McFarland to Major Samuel Harper, March 30, 1889, 151st Pennsylvania Monument File, Gettysburg National Military Park Library. The reader is left to draw his or her own conclusion.

4. *Muster Rolls, 151st Pennsylvania Volunteers*, PSA. See Michael A. Dreese, *An Imperishable Fame: The Civil War Experience of George Fisher McFarland* (Mifflintown, Pa.: Juniata County Historical Society, 1997), p. 14, and Appendix I of the present publication for a full discussion of the regiment's nickname.

5. Undated newspaper clipping, "Valor of Pennsylvania Boys in the Civil War," copy in possession of author.

6. Samuel P. Bates, *History of the Pennsylvania Volunteers: 1861–1865*, 5 vols. (Harrisburg, Pa.: B. Singerly, 1869–1871), Vol. 4, pp. 680–681.

7. See Lieutenant William O. Blodget (Company F) to "Dear Brother," May 10, 1863, May 19, 1863, and June 7, 1863, Rosemary McCorkel Collection; Corporal Nathan J. Cooper (Company F) to "My Dear Mary," November 9, 1862, and April 25, 1863, Warren County Historical Society Collection, Warren, Pa.; Sergeant Alexander Seiders (Company K) to "Dear Wife," May 8, 1863, and June 8, 1863, Sally Smith Collection; Private John Criswell (Company D) to Governor A. G. Curtin, May 29, 1863, letter in *Muster Rolls of the 151st Pennsylvania Volunteers*, PSA; Sergeant George W. Heilig (Company H) to "Dear Wife," June 1, 1863, in John Hunt Walker, M.D., *Appointment at Gettysburg* (Seattle: ARS OBSCURA, 1994), p. 69; *OR*, Vol. 25, Part 2, p. 532. Dr. Walker is the grandson of Sergeant Heilig. Much to the benefit of historians, he has faithfully preserved and published the letters George wrote to his wife, Catherine. Passages from these letters will be quoted throughout this work.

8. Simon J. Arnold to "Dear Brother," January 6, 1863, Mary Haney Arnold Collection.

9. Robert E. Miller to "Dear Father," December 9, 1862, Schoff Civil War Collection, William L. Clements Library, University of Michigan.

10. Bates, *History of Pennsylvania Volunteers*, Vol. 4, pp. 677–678; *OR*, Vol. 25, Part 2, pp. 10, 12, 69–70.

11. Dreese, *An Imperishable Fame*, p. 97.

12. Thomas Chamberlin, *History of the One Hundred and Fiftieth Regiment Pennsylvania Volunteers, Second Regiment, Bucktail Brigade* (Philadelphia: F. McManus, Jr., 1905; reprint edition, Baltimore: Butternut and Blue, 1986), p. 85.

13. Walker, *Appointment at Gettysburg*, p. 57.

14. Dreese, *An Imperishable Fame*, p. 96; Pension Records of William K. Boltz, National Archives, Washington, D.C. (Hereafter cited as NA); George McFarland to "My Dear Wife," May 8, 1863, George McFarland Papers, PSA; *OR*, Vol. 25, Part 1, p. 173.

15. Major H. T. Lee to George McFarland, July 11, 1866, George McFarland Papers, PSA.

16. *OR*, Vol. 25, Part 1, p. 175.

17. Dreese, *An Imperishable Fame*, pp. 98–99.

18. *OR*, Vol. 25, Part 1, p. 295.

19. *Ibid.*, p. 291.

20. *Ibid.*, p. 175; Colonel Harrison Allen, "Report of killed, wounded, and missing of Regt. since April 28th 1863," May 9, 1863, Casualty Reports, NA. The other wounded were listed as follows: Michael Hissam, Company B, in hand; Benjamin Heffner, Company K, in leg; William S. Fisher, Company K, in shoulder; and Henry S. Lindecukle, Company K, in face.

21. Dreese, *An Imperishable Fame*, pp. 100–101.

22. William O. Blodget to "Dear Brother," May 19, 1863, Rosemary McCorkel Collection; Robert E. Miller to "Dear Parents," May 12, 1863, Schoff Civil War Collection, William L. Clements Library, University of Michigan.

23. William Boltz to "worthy woman," May 21, 1863, Pension Records of William K. Boltz, NA. The deceased friend mentioned by Captain Boltz was Second Lieutenant William D. Boltz, Company F, 93rd Pennsylvania, perhaps a distant relative.

24. Robert E. Miller to "Dear Parents," May 12, 1863, Schoff Civil War Collection, William L. Clements Library, University of Michigan; William Boltz to "worthy woman," May 17, and May 21, 1863, Pension Records of William K. Boltz, NA.

25. James M. McPherson, *Battle Cry of Freedom* (New York: Oxford University Press, 1988), pp. 491–493; Ted Alexander, *The 126th Pennsylvania* (Shippensburg, Pa.: Beidel, 1984), p. 3. Most of the bounty payments were not excessive. For example, Monroe Township in Juniata County divided $475 between ten members of Company D, 151st Pennsylvania. Dreese, *An Imperishable Fame*, p. 39.

26. William Blodget to "Dear Brother," May 10, 1863, and June 7, 1863, Rosemary McCorkel Collection; Adjutant Samuel Allen to the adjutant general of Pennsylvania, letter in *Muster Rolls of the 151st Pennsylvania Volunteers*, PSA; Nathan Cooper to "Mary," April 25, 1863, Warren County Historical Society Collection; Bates, *History of Pennsylvania Volunteers*, Vol. 4, p. 681. See also Robert E. Miller to "Dear Parents," November 2, 1862, Schoff Civil War Collection, William L. Clements Library, University of Michigan. Miller, a sergeant in Company F, wrote, "Last Thursday we were mustered into the service of the United States for nine months from the 20th of September which has gained for us over a months time and makes our time expire on the 20th of June 1863." The last man to be mustered into the 151st was Private Samuel Hower of Company I.

27. Affidavit of George McFarland in Pension Records of Walter L. Owens, NA; Alexander Seiders to "Dear Wife," May 31, 1863, Sally Smith Collection.

28. Nathan Cooper to "Dear Mary," December 27, 1862, and March 20, 1863, Warren County Historical Society Collection.

29. Dreese, *An Imperishable Fame*, pp. 115, 119; George McFarland to "My Dear Wife," June 7, 1863, George McFarland Papers, PSA; Pension Records of Harrison Allen, NA.

30. Samuel T. Allen to George F. McFarland, undated letter, George McFarland Papers, PSA.

31. Mrs. Mary Haney Arnold to Author, March 31, 1998, and April 8, 1998; George F. McFarland to Simon J. Arnold, February 24, 1864, Mary Haney Arnold Collection. This cited source was a letter of recommendation for a lieutenancy in the Invalid Corps following Arnold's wounding at Gettysburg. There is no indication that Arnold ever served in this organization.

32. *OR*, Vol. 25, Part 2, p. 532; George McFarland to "My Dear Wife," June 7, 1863, George McFarland Papers, PSA; Nathan Cooper to "My Dear Mary," June 7, 1863, Warren County Historical Society Collection. At Gettysburg, the 151st Pennsylvania fielded 21 officers and 446 enlisted men. Busey and Martin, *Regimental Strengths and Losses at Gettysburg*, p. 27.

33. Bates, *History of Pennsylvania Volunteers*, Vol. 4, p. 677; Nicholson, *Pennsylvania at Gettysburg*, Vol. 2, pp. 767–768.

34. Pension Records of Franklin Weaber, NA, including Franklin Weaber to "Dear Brother," February 27, 1863; Pension Records of Franklin Wendling, NA.

35. Abe Freet to "Dear Father," December 2, 1862, Pension Records of Abe Freet, NA.

36. Nicholson, *Pennsylvania at Gettysburg*, Vol. 2, second part, p. 159.

37. Biographical Sketch of George L. Stone, George McFarland Papers, PSA. The biographical material included in this section was collected by McFarland during his military service. He had hoped to write a detailed history of the Third Division, First Corps. Unfortunately for historians, the project was never completed.

38. Pension Records of Amos Tucker, NA; Biographical Sketch of Amos Tucker, George McFarland Papers, PSA; Bates, *History of Pennsylvania Volunteers*, Vol. 4, p. 681.

39. Dreese, *An Imperishable Fame*, p. 91.

40. Biographical Sketch of Lafayette Westbrook, George McFarland Papers, PSA; Pension Records of Lafayette Westbrook, NA.

41. Biographical Sketch of John H. Vincent, George McFarland Papers, PSA.

42. Biographical Sketch of Robert M. Kellogg, George McFarland Papers, PSA.

43. Rhamanthus M. Stocker, *Centennial History of Susquehanna County, Pennsylvania* (Baltimore: Regional Publishing Company for the Susquehanna County Historical Society and Free Library Association, 1974), p. 247.

44. Nicholson, *Pennsylvania at Gettysburg*, Vol. 2, second part, p. 159.

45. Biographical Sketch of Walter L. Owens, George McFarland Papers, PSA; Pension Records of Walter Owens, NA; Dreese, *An Imperishable Fame*, p. 42.

46. Biographical Sketches of Benjamin F. Oliver and George S. Mills, George McFarland Papers, PSA; Pension Records of Benjamin F. Oliver, NA.

47. Biographical Sketch of Aaron S. Seaman, George McFarland Papers, PSA; Bates, *History of Pennsylvania Volunteers*, Vol. 1, p. 136; John W. Busey, *These Honored Dead: The Union Casualties at Gettysburg* (Hightstown, N.J.: Longstreet House, 1996), p. 299.

48. Biographical Sketches of Thomas L. Moyer and Caleb Parvin, George McFarland Papers, PSA; Dreese, *An Imperishable Fame*, p. 87.

49. Biographical Sketch of William O. Blodget, George McFarland Papers, PSA; William Blodget to "Dear Brother," April 17, 1855, Rosemary McCorkel Collection; Rosemary McCorkel to Author, April 23, 1998. Mrs. McCorkel is the great-granddaughter of William Oren Blodget.

50. William O. Blodget to "Dear Sister," February 10, 1863, Rosemary McCorkel Collection.

51. Biographical Sketch of Jonathan Witman, George McFarland Papers, PSA.

52. Biographical Sketch of William K. Boltz, George McFarland Papers, PSA; Pension Records of William K. Boltz, NA.

53. Biographical Sketches of James L. Reber and Albert Yost, George McFarland Papers, PSA; Dreese, *An Imperishable Fame*, p. 61.

54. Pension Records of William L. Gray, NA, including letter from George McFarland "To whom it may concern," September 14, 1886.

55. Biographical Sketches of William L. Gray and Henry Merkle, George McFarland Papers, PSA.

56. Charles P. Potts, "A First Defender in Rebel Prison Pens," *Publications of the Historical Society of Schuylkill County*, Vol. 4 (1914), pp. 341–342; Heber S. Thompson, *The First Defenders* (First Defenders' Association, 1910), pp. vii, 12–15; Richard A. Sauers, *Advance the Colors!*, 2 vols. (Lebanon, Pa.: Sowers, 1987–1991), Vol. 1, p. 8; Biographical Sketch of Charles P. Potts, George McFarland Papers; J. Horace McFarland Collection, PSA.

57. Biographical Sketch of James W. Weida, George McFarland Papers, PSA; Pension Records of James W. Weida, NA.

58. Biographical Sketch of Jacob Hessler, George McFarland Papers, PSA; Richard A. Sauers, *Advance the Colors!*, Vol. 1, p. 8.

59. Biographical Sketch of Charles A. Trexler, George McFarland Papers, PSA.

60. Private Peter Hayward to Lieutenant Gardner, April 23, 1863, printed in *Montrose Democrat*, May 12, 1863.

61. Dreese, *An Imperishable Fame*, pp. 5–7, 38.

62. McFarland received his commission as lieutenant colonel from Governor Andrew G. Curtin on November 18, 1862. Dreese, *An Imperishable Fame*, p. 41.

63. Affidavit of Amos C. Blakeslee, Surgeon, 151st Pennsylvania, September 16, 1880, Pension Records of George F. McFarland, NA.

64. Nicholson, *Pennsylvania at Gettysburg*, Vol. 2, p. 768.

65. Nathan Cooper to "My Dear Wife," June 11, 1863, Warren County Historical Society Collection; Letter of Private Peter Hayward, *Montrose Democrat*, January 6, 1863; Peter Hayward to Lieutenant Jonathan Gardner, April 23, 1863, printed in *Montrose Democrat*, May 12, 1863.

66. George McFarland to "Dear Wife," June 11, 1863, George McFarland Papers, PSA.

Major John W. Young was a native of Scotland who served eight years in the British army. His service took him to Ireland and Scotland as well as the West Indies, where he was stationed on the islands of Grenada and Trinidad. Originally the captain of Company C, Young was promoted to major during the regiment's organization at Camp Curtin in Harrisburg. One private in the company felt Young's appointment to this rank was "a high tribute to his military qualifications, his patriotism, and his untiring energies." *Montrose Democrat*, January 6, 1863.

Colonel Harrison Allen, a native of Warren, Pennsylvania, acquired a taste for the military early in his life. Before the Civil War, he served as an officer in the Pennsylvania militia. After the firing on Fort Sumter, Allen was appointed commander of Camp Wright near Pittsburgh. On June 29, 1861, he was elected major of the 10th Pennsylvania Reserves. His tenure was brief, however, as poor health forced his resignation in early 1862. By the fall, Allen regained his health and recruited a body of men which became Company F of the 151st Pennsylvania. At Harrisburg, he secured the position of colonel. Biographical Sketch of Harrison Allen, George McFarland Papers, PSA.

67. Patricia Faust, ed., *Historical Times Illustrated Encyclopedia of the Civil War* (New York: Harper & Row, 1986), p. 564.

68. Letters of Private Peter Hayward, *Montrose Democrat*, January 27, 1863, and March 10, 1863; Nathan Cooper to "My Dear Wife," January 3, 1863, Warren County Historical Society Collection.

69. Dreese, *An Imperishable Fame*, pp. 78, 144; George McFarland to "Dear Wife," June 11, 1863, George McFarland Papers, PSA.

70. Dreese, *An Imperishable Fame*, p. 41.

71. James T. Miller to "Dear Father," December 28, 1862, Schoff Civil War Collection, William L. Clements Library, University of Michigan. Miller served in the 111th Pennsylvania. His brother, Robert, was a sergeant in Company F of the 151st Pennsylvania.

72. Dreese, *An Imperishable Fame*, p. 116.

Chapter 2

1. Dreese, *An Imperishable Fame*, p. 119; Allan Nevins, ed., *A Diary of Battle: The Personal Journals of Colonel Charles S. Wainwright, 1861–1865* (New York: Harcourt, Brace, & World, 1962), p. 131; James T. Miller to "Dear Parents," May 15, 1863, Schoff Civil War Collection, William L. Clements Library, University of Michigan.

2. Bates, *History of Pennsylvania Volunteers*, Vol. 4, pp. 683–697.

3. Letter dated June 7, 1863, in Lyman Beebe Letters, United States Army Military History Institute, Carlisle Barracks, Pa. (Hereafter cited as USAMHI); Dreese, *An Imperishable Fame*, p. 115. During the Civil War 57,265 men died of diarrhea and dysentery. Bell Irvin Wiley, *The Life of Billy Yank* (Baton Rouge: Louisiana State University Press, 1952), p. 124.

4. George McFarland to "My Dear Wife," June 13, 1863, George McFarland Papers, PSA.

5. *Ibid.*

6. *Ibid.*; Chamberlin, *History of the One Hundred and Fiftieth Regiment Pennsylvania Volunteers*, p. 108; Nevins, *A Diary of Battle*, p. 217. The unfortunate deserter was John P. Woods of the 19th Indiana Infantry. Woods deserted his unit no less than four times between August 20, 1862, and April 28, 1863. The young Ohio farmer paid the ultimate price for his last offense. Robert I. Alotta, *Civil War Justice: Union Army Executions Under Lincoln* (Shippensburg, Pa.: White Mane, 1989), p. 68.

7. George McFarland to "Dear Wife," June 16, 1863, George McFarland Papers, PSA.

8. Robert E. Miller to "Dear Brother," June 14, 1863, Schoff Civil War Collection, William L. Clements Library, University of Michigan.

9. George McFarland to "Dear Wife," June 16, 1863, George McFarland Papers, PSA; Nevins, *A Diary of Battle*, p. 219; Chamberlin, *History of the One Hundred and Fiftieth Regiment Pennsylvania Volunteers*, p. 109; Morning Report Book, Company H, 151st Pennsylvania Volunteers, Record Group 94, NA. This item is the only surviving ledger book from the entire regiment. Daily entries and tabulations were made by Orderly Sergeant George Heilig. His comments were typically terse and usually included such items as daily activities, length of marches, comments on the weather, personnel assignments, sicknesses, etc.

10. Dreese, *An Imperishable Fame*, p. 119; Robert E. Miller to "Dear Parents," June 19, 1863, Schoff Civil War Collection, William L. Clements Library, University of Michigan; Pension Records of John H. Vincent, NA. Miller spent nearly

four months recuperating in a brigade hospital near Union Mills and later at St. Paul's Church Hospital in Alexandria. Unlike many other Civil War hospital patients, Robert was highly complimentary of the care he received and of the facilities. Vincent was placed in Douglas Hospital in Washington. He remained here until the regiment was mustered out at Harrisburg, Pa.

11. Nevins, *A Diary of Battle*, p. 220.

12. Dreese, *An Imperishable Fame*, p. 120; Nevins, *A Diary of Battle*, p. 221; Pension Records of George L. Stone, NA.

13. Edwin B. Coddington, *The Gettysburg Campaign: A Study in Command* (New York: Charles Scribners' Sons, 1968), pp. 73–75.

14. Dreese, *An Imperishable Fame*, p. 120; Nathan Cooper to "My Dear Mary," May 17, 1863, Warren County Historical Society Collection.

15. George McFarland to "Dear Wife," June 18, 1863, and June 19, 1863, George McFarland Papers, PSA; Alexander Seiders to "Dear Wife," June 21, 1863, Sally Smith Collection.

16. Robert E. Miller to "Dear Parents," June 19, 1863, Schoff Civil War Collection, William L. Clements Library, University of Michigan.

17. George McFarland to "Dear Wife," June 19, 1863, George McFarland Papers, PSA.

18. Bessie Mell Lane, ed., *Dear Bet: The Carter Letters, 1861–1863: The Letters of Lieutenant Sidney Carter, Company A, 14th Regiment, South Carolina Volunteers, Gregg's — McGowan's Brigade, CSA, to Ellen Timmons Carter* (Clemson, S.C.: B. M. Lane, 1978), p. 95; Spencer Glasgow Welch, *A Confederate Surgeon's Letters to His Wife* (New York: Neale, 1911; reprint edition, Marietta, Ga.: Continental, 1954), pp. 55–56.

19. Chamberlin, *History of the One Hundred Fiftieth Regiment Pennsylvania Volunteers*, pp. 110–111; Dreese, *An Imperishable Fame*, p. 120; "The Diary of Alfred D. Staudt," *Historical Review of Berks County* 41 (Winter 1975–1976), p. 16; *Muster Rolls of the 151st Pennsylvania Volunteers*, PSA.

20. George McFarland to "Dear Wife," June 19, 1863, George McFarland Papers, PSA.

21. Nathan Cooper to "Dear Mary," December 27, 1862, June 21, 1863, and June 24, 1863, Warren County Historical Society Collection.

22. Robert E. Miller to "Dear Parents," June 19, 1863, Schoff Civil War Collection, William L. Clements Library, University of Michigan; George McFarland to "Dear Wife," June 18, 1863, and June 23, 1863, George McFarland Papers, PSA.

23. William O. Blodget to "Dear Brother," March 21, 1863, Rosemary McCorkel Collection; Robert E. Miller to "Dear Parents," May 21, 1863, Schoff Civil War Collection, William L. Clements Library, University of Michigan; *Pottsville Miners' Journal*, April 18, 1863; Chamberlin, *History of the One Hundred Fiftieth Regiment Pennsylvania Volunteers*, pp. 110–111.

24. Coddington, *The Gettysburg Campaign*, pp. 120–123.

25. George McFarland to "My Dear Wife," June 26, 1863, George McFarland Papers, PSA; Dreese, *An Imperishable Fame*, p. 121; Survivors' Association, *History of the 121st Regiment Pennsylvania Volunteers* (Philadelphia: Press of the Catholic Standard and Times, 1906), p. 50.

26. George McFarland to "My Dear Wife," June 26, 1863, George McFarland Papers, PSA; Dreese, *An Imperishable Fame*, p. 121.

27. Dreese, *An Imperishable Fame*, p. 121; Nevins, *A Diary of Battle*, pp. 224–225; Survivors' Association, *History of the 121st Regiment Pennsylvania Volunteers*, p. 49.

28. George McFarland to "My Dear Wife," June 26, 1863, George McFarland Papers, PSA.

29. Pension Records of Solomon Strause, NA.

30. George McFarland to "My Dear Wife," June 26, 1863, George McFarland Papers, PSA; Nevins, *A Diary of Battle*, p. 225.

31. Dreese, *An Imperishable Fame*, p. 121–122; Nevins, *A Diary of Battle*, p. 225.

32. Coddington, *The Gettysburg Campaign*, pp. 209, 214–216, 219–220.

33. Dreese, *An Imperishable Fame*, p. 123; Bates, *History of Pennsylvania Volunteers*, Vol. 4, p. 694.

34. William O. Blodget to "Dear Sister," June 28, 1863, Rosemary McCorkel Collection.

35. Chamberlin, *History of the One Hundred and Fiftieth Regiment Pennsylvania Volunteers*, p. 115.

36. Dreese, *An Imperishable Fame*, p. 123; Survivors' Association, *History of the 121st Regiment Pennsylvania Volunteers*, p. 49.

37. Dreese, *An Imperishable Fame*, p. 123.

38. Coddington, *The Gettysburg Campaign*, p. 127.

39. Dreese, *An Imperishable Fame*, p. 122.

40. Welch, *A Confederate Surgeon's Letters to His Wife*, pp. 57–58; J. F. J. Caldwell, *The History of a Brigade of South Carolinians Known First as "Gregg's," and Subsequently as "McGowan's Brigade"* (Philadelphia: King & Baird, 1866; reprint edition, Dayton, Ohio: Press of Morningside Bookshop, 1974), pp. 93–94.

41. Coddington, *The Gettysburg Campaign*, pp. 154–155; Caldwell, *The History of a Brigade of South Carolinians*, p. 94; Underwood, *History of the Twenty-sixth Regiment of the North Carolina Troops*, p. 40.

42. Coddington, *The Gettysburg Campaign*, pp. 180–182, 186; Richard Meade Bache, "Penned up in Gettysburg: A Surgeon's Experience During the Three Day's Battle," Gettysburg Newspaper Clippings, Vol. 6, Part 2, Gettysburg National Military Park Library.

43. Coddington, *The Gettysburg Campaign*, p. 195.

44. Caldwell, *History of a Brigade of South Carolinians*, p. 95; Welch, *A Confederate Surgeon's Letters to His Wife*, pp. 56, 58; Abner Perrin to Governor Bonham, July 29, 1863, *The Mississippi Valley Historical Review*, March 1938, p. 521.

45. Coddington, *The Gettysburg Campaign*, pp. 230–232.

46. Pension Records of Lafayette Westbrook, NA. Westbrook claimed that his right foot was crippled because he could not find a large enough pair of army shoes to fit his large feet.

47. Pension Records of William Michael, NA.

48. Robert E. Miller to "Dear Parents," June 30, 1863, Schoff Civil War Collection, William L. Clements Library, University of Michigan.

49. Morning Report Book, Company H, 151st Pennsylvania Volunteers, RG 94, NA; Nevins, *A Diary of Battle*, pp. 229–230.

50. Michael A. Riley, *"For God's Sake, Forward!," Gen. John F. Reynolds, USA* (Gettysburg: Farnsworth House Military Impressions, 1995), pp. 45–46; Coddington, *The Gettysburg Campaign*, pp. 233–234; *OR*, Vol. 27, Part 1, pp. 243–244.

51. Seward Osborne, *Holding the Left at Gettysburg, The 20th New York State Militia on July 1, 1863* (Hightstown, N.J.: Longstreet House, 1990), p. 3; Survivors' Association, *History of the 121st Regiment Pennsylvania Volunteers*, p. 127; Property Damage Claim of Jacob B. Brown, File #214—758, NA; Nicholson, *Pennsylvania at Gettysburg*, Vol. 2, p. 768. White's story that he served as a guide for the Third Division is

plausible considering the fact that there was a widespread scarcity of local maps among high-ranking Union officers throughout the campaign. William A. Frassanito, *Early Photography at Gettysburg* (Gettysburg: Thomas Publications, 1995), pp. 8, 10.

52. James Ashworth to George McFarland, May 4, 1866, George McFarland Papers, PSA.

Ashworth was born in Bury, Lancashire, England, on September 11, 1836. His parents immigrated to the United States in 1838, eventually settling in Frankford near Philadelphia. James received his education at the Philadelphia High School and afterwards obtained employment at a local shipping house. When the Civil War erupted, he accompanied General Patterson's command to Hagerstown as a civilian and later fought with these troops during a skirmish with Confederate forces near Williamsport, Maryland. Afterward, he was mistakenly arrested as a Confederate spy, but his comrades cleared him by their testimony. In August 1862, he raised a company of men from Frankford, which became Company I, 121st Pennsylvania Volunteers. He served with the regiment at the battles of Fredericksburg and Chancellorsville. Survivors' Association, *History of the 121st Regiment Pennsylvania Volunteers*, p. 139.

53. Osborne, *Holding the Left at Gettysburg*, p. 1.

54. John D. S. Cook, "Personal Reminiscences of Gettysburg," in McLean and McLean, *Gettysburg Sources*, 3 vols. (Baltimore: Butternut and Blue, 1986–1990), Vol. 2, p. 124.

55. *OR*, Vol. 27, Part 1, pp. 244, 312, 316. These changes were in effect throughout much of the army's northward movement. See also Riley, "*For God's Sake, Forward!*," p. 44.

56. "Extract from a Memoir of Chapman Biddle" in Survivors' Association, *History of the 121st Regiment Pennsylvania Volunteers*, pp. 236–239; Kevin O'Brien, "'Give Them Another Volley, Boys': Biddle's Brigade Defends the Union Left on July 1, 1863," *The Gettysburg Magazine*, no. 19 (July 1998), p. 37.

57. Morning Report Book, Company H, 151st Pennsylvania Volunteers, RG 94, NA.

Chapter 3

1. Coddington, *The Gettysburg Campaign*, pp. 237, 261.

2. H. T. Lee to Samuel P. Bates, February 6, 1871, Samuel P. Bates Papers, PSA. Lieutenant Harry T. Lee served as an aide-de-camp on General Doubleday's staff.

3. *OR*, Vol. 27, Part 1, pp. 246–247.

4. *Ibid.*, p. 244; David G. Martin, *Gettysburg July 1* (Conshohocken, Pa.: Combined Books, 1995), pp. 90–95; Riley, "*For God's Sake, Forward!*," pp. 46–47.

5. *OR*, Vol. 27, Part 1, p. 312.

6. *Ibid.*, p. 244.

7. George McFarland, undated account of the battle of Gettysburg, George McFarland Papers, PSA; Survivors' Association, *History of the 121st Regiment Pennsylvania Volunteers*, p. 127.

8. Thomas Rowley never returned to active field command following the Battle of Gettysburg. In April 1864, a court-martial found him guilty of conduct unbecoming of an officer and a gentleman, drunkenness while on duty, and conduct prejudicial to good order and military discipline. However, a number of Third Division officers testified on behalf of Rowley, and Secretary of War Edwin M. Stanton refused to cashier the general due to the conflicting evidence. Interestingly, Lieutenant Colonel McFarland, an avowedly firm temperance

man, thought highly of Rowley. Also, in a biographical sketch submitted to McFarland by James Onslow it was claimed that there was "no braver soldier or truer gentleman than General Thomas A. Rowley." However, during the Battle of Chancellorsville two months earlier, McFarland recorded the following in his diary entry for May 5: "... refusing a drink of whiskey offered me by Genl. Rowley..." Thomas returned to civilian life in late 1864 as a lawyer and peace officer in his native Pittsburgh. Stewart Sifakis, *Who Was Who in the Civil War, Vol. 1* (New York: Facts On File, 1988), p. 345; Lance J. Herdegen, "The Lieutenant Who Arrested a General," *The Gettysburg Magazine*, no. 4 (January 1991), pp. 25–32; O'Brien, "'Give Them Another Volley, Boys,'" pp. 40, 42; Dreese, *An Imperishable Fame*, p. 100; James Onslow, "Biographical Sketch of Thomas A. Rowley," May 26, 1866, George McFarland Papers, PSA.

9. Frances C. Harper to J. Horace McFarland, August 5, 1939, Personal Papers of George F. McFarland, Dr. Charles L. Eater, Jr., Collection; "Native of Adams County Writes of Experiences of Parents During '63 Battle," (Gettysburg) *Compiler*, April 26, 1941, Adams County Historical Society. The meeting between McFarland and Martha "Emily" Cunningham on July 1 and George's return visit some ten years later were recorded by Frances Cunningham Harper, Emily's niece. Frances Cunningham was born on November 6, 1864. She was the youngest child of John and Margaret Cunningham. Frances grew up steeped in stories of the battle from her family and friends. Cunningham Family File, Adams County Historical Society.

10. Cook, "Personal Reminiscences of Gettysburg" in McLean and McLean, *Gettysburg Sources*, Vol. 2, p. 125.

11. Osborne, *Holding the Left at Gettysburg*, p. 5; Chamberlin, *History of the One Hundred and Fiftieth Regiment Pennsylvania Volunteers*, p. 117.

12. "The Life Story of 'Blind Mike' Link," *Reading Eagle*, July 12, 1899; Pension Records of Michael Link, NA; Morton L. Montgomery, ed., *Historical and Biographical Annals of Berks County Pennsylvania*, 2 vols. (Chicago: J. H. Beers, 1909), Vol. 1, p. 1034.

13. Pension Records of Adam Heilman, NA; *Reading Daily Times*, July 11, 1863; Mary Haney Arnold to Author, April 8, 1998.

14. Cook, "Personal Reminiscences of Gettysburg," in McLean and McLean, *Gettysburg Sources*, Vol. 2, p. 125.

15. Osborne, *Holding the Left at Gettysburg*, p. 6; *OR*, Vol. 27, Part 1, p. 326.

16. "Judge Slagle at Gettysburg," undated newspaper clipping, Timothy H. Smith Collection. This newspaper article contained a lengthy letter from Slagle to his brother dated September 13, 1863, which detailed his activities during the Battle of Gettysburg.

17. Cook, "Personal Reminiscences of Gettysburg," in McLean and McLean, *Gettysburg Sources*, Vol. 2, p. 126; Dreese, *An Imperishable Fame*, p. 127; George McFarland, undated account of the Battle of Gettysburg, George McFarland Papers, PSA. The time of arrival of the Third Division was estimated by various officers from as early as 10 A.M. to as late as noon. Most of the evidence indicates that both the First and Second Brigade reached the field near 11 A.M. James Beale, "The Statements of Time on July 1 at Gettysburg, Pa. 1863," in McLean and McLean, *Gettysburg Sources*, Vol. 3, pp. 43, 59. It is important to note that there was no standardized time during the Civil War.

18. Riley, "*For God's Sake, Forward!*," pp. 47–49; Martin, *Gettysburg July 1*, p. 99.

19. Nicholson, *Pennsylvania at Gettysburg*, Vol. 2, p. 768. In his address of July 1, 1888, at the dedication of the 151st's regimental monument, McFarland stated that his regiment arrived "upon the field south of the Theological Seminary just in time to see our much-beloved Reynolds carried to the rear in a dying condition." Historian Richard Shue believes Reynolds was shot between 10:35 and 10:45 A.M. Richard S. Shue, *Morning at Willoughby Run, July 1, 1863* (Gettysburg, Pa.: Thomas Publications, 1995), pp. 113, 121. This time frame is fairly close to the approximate 11 A.M. arrival of the 151st.

20. H. T. Lee to Samuel P. Bates, February 6, 1871, Samuel P. Bates Papers, PSA. During a visit to the Gettysburg battlefield in 1866, George McFarland met General William Gamble, who commanded a brigade in General John Buford's cavalry division during the battle. McFarland recorded the following account from Gamble concerning the death of Reynolds: "Genl. Gamble, who opened the cavalry fight at 9 in the morning, informed me that Genl. Reynolds rode up to him on Seminary Ridge and after obtaining all the information he could from him said he would go and examine the line. Genl. Gamble told him the rebels were fighting his men (dismounted) at close range on this ridge and that he (Genl. R) would certainly be hit if he rode to the front. Genl. Reynolds dashed on however, and was borne back in a dieing condition within 15 minutes." Diary of George F. McFarland, June 30, 1866, Personal Papers of George F. McFarland.

Gamble was brevetted brigadier general on December 14, 1864. He held the rank of colonel at Gettysburg. Gamble served in the military for various periods following the Civil War. He died of cholera while on active duty in Nicaragua on December 20, 1866. Sifakis, *Who Was Who in the Civil War, Vol. 1*, p. 147.

21. For a full discussion of the topography and road network in the Gettysburg vicinity and its influence upon the battle see Martin, *Gettysburg July 1*, pp. 582–588, and Warren W. Hassler, Jr., *Crisis at the Crossroads: The First Day at Gettysburg* (University: University of Alabama Press, 1970; reprint, Gettysburg: Stan Clark, 1991), pp. 21–25. In an attempt to distinguish the two crests of McPherson's Ridge, historian John B. Bachelder named the eastern crest "Buford's Ridge" in his 1873 guidebook, *Gettysburg, What to See, and How to See It*. Another guidebook published in the 1950s referred to this ridge as "Reynolds' Ridge." J. Warren Gilbert, *The Blue & Gray: A History of the Conflicts During Lee's Invasion and Battle of Gettysburg* (Gettysburg: Bookmart, 1952), p. 43. Unfortunately, neither name became popular with historians and the confusion continues today.

Although the woodlot on McPherson's Ridge has been commonly referred to as McPherson's Woods since the time of the battle, the land was actually owned by John Herbst in 1863. The northern woodline served as the border between the Herbst and Edward McPherson properties. The woods has been officially designated Reynolds Woods. William A. Frassanito, *Early Photography at Gettysburg*, pp. 59–60. In the interest of historical accuracy, Herbst's Woods will be used throughout this text. This wood lot was more open at the time of the battle with much less understory than at the present, probably due to livestock grazing and the high demand for firewood. The volunteer group to which the author belongs, "Friends and Descendants of the 151st Pennsylvania," is currently working to restore this area more closely to its 1863 appearance.

22. *OR*, Vol. 27, Part 1, p. 244.

23. Nevins, *A Diary of Battle*, p. 234.

24. Gregory A. Coco, *A Vast Sea of Misery: A History and Guide to the Union and Confederate Field Hospitals at Gettysburg, July 1–November 20, 1863* (Gettysburg: Thomas Publications, 1988), p. 6. The Seminary has added numerous buildings since the battle and most of the trees comprising the original "seminary grove" have been removed.

25. Abner Doubleday, *Chancellorsville and Gettysburg* (New York: Charles Scribner's Sons, 1882; reprint, New York: Da Capo, 1994), Introduction by Gary W. Gallagher, p. xi; Nevins, *A Diary of Battle*, p. 233; D. Scott Hartwig, "The Defense of McPherson's Ridge," *The Gettysburg Magazine*, no. 1 (July 1989), p. 15; Larry Tagg, *The Generals of Gettysburg: The Leaders of America's Greatest Battle* (Campbell, Calif.: Savas, 1998), pp. 25–27.

26. William O. Blodget to "Dear Brother," March 21, 1863, Rosemary McCorkel Collection.

27. Hartwig, "The Defense of McPherson's Ridge," p. 15; Martin, *Gettysburg July 1*, pp. 186–190; H. T. Lee to Samuel P. Bates, February 6, 1871, Samuel P. Bates Papers, PSA.

28. *OR*, Vol. 27, Part 1, pp. 246–247.

29. Nevins, *A Diary of Battle*, p. 233.

30. *OR*, Vol. 27, Part 1, pp. 317, 320, 326–327; Martin, *Gettysburg July 1*, pp. 177–178.

31. Osborne, *Holding the Left at Gettysburg*, pp. 6–7.

32. *OR*, Vol. 27, Part 1, pp. 247, 327; John B. Bachelder, "Movements of the 151st Penn. Vols. of Biddle's Brigade: Notes of a Conversation with Colonel George F. McFarland, 151st Penn. Volunteers," in David L. and Audrey J. Ladd, eds., *The Bachelder Papers: Gettysburg in Their Own Words*, 3 vols. (Dayton, Ohio: Morningside House, 1994–1995), Vol. 1, p. 271.

33. Martin, *Gettysburg July 1*, pp. 180–181; Hartwig, "The Defense of McPherson's Ridge," p. 17; Hassler, *Crisis at the Crossroads*, pp. 57–58; Tagg, *The Generals of Gettysburg*, p. 28.

34. *OR*, Vol. 27, Part 1, pp. 312–313.

35. *Ibid.*, p. 247; Hartwig, "The Defense of McPherson's Ridge," p. 17; Doubleday, *Chancellorsville and Gettysburg*, p. 136; Varina D. Brown, *A Colonel at Gettysburg and Spotsylvania* (Columbia, S.C.: The State Company, 1931; reprint, Baltimore: Butternut and Blue, n.d.), p. 78.

36. Hartwig, "The Defense of McPherson's Ridge," p. 17.

37. Coddington, *The Gettysburg Campaign*, pp. 278–279; Martin, *Gettysburg July 1*, pp. 195–198. An interesting note regarding the selection of Cemetery Hill as a concentration point for the Union army is found in the memoirs of Henry Jacobs. Henry points out the fact that his father, Michael, a Pennsylvania College professor, may have played a key role in this vital decision. "[H]e accompanied a staff officer to the college cupola, and pointed out the strategic importance of Cemetery Hill. Whether his opinion ever reached Gen. Howard or Gen. Reynolds, we cannot tell. The strength of the position is such that it must have attracted any trained military eye. But when a battle begins where a general has not the opportunity to choose a field, in a country as yet entirely unknown, he is not in a position to exercise his judgment to the best advantage. We do not claim therefore, that my father's conversation with the staff officer had anything to do with the result. But there is such a possibility. His botanical and geological excursions had familiarized him with every acre of what became the battle-field, and his experience as an engineer gave him some of the advantages belonging to the military training." Henry E. Horn, ed., *Memoirs of Henry Eyster Jacobs*, 2 vols. (Huntingdon, Pa.: Church Management Service, 1974), Vol. 1, p. 54.

38. Doubleday, *Chancellorsville and Gettysburg*, pp. x, 134–135, 137. In response to this "baleful intelligence" Meade

assigned command of the First Corps to Major General John Newton, a division commander in the Sixth Corps, on the evening of July 1. As a result, Doubleday reverted to command of the Third Division for the remainder of the battle. After his request to be restored as First Corps commander was denied by Meade, Doubleday departed for Washington on July 7th and never returned to active duty during the remainder of the war.

39. *Ibid.*, p. 138; D. Scott Hartwig, "The 11th Army Corps on July 1, 1863," *The Gettysburg Magazine*, no. 2 (January 1990), pp. 33–35.

40. Hartwig, "The Defense of McPherson's Ridge," p. 19.

41. Walker, *Appointment at Gettysburg*, p. 91.

42. "The 151st Pennsylvania Regiment at Gettysburg," *Reading Eagle*, June 16, 1912; Kerry Lanza, "One Moment of Glory: 151st Pennsylvania Volunteers, With Five Berks Companies, Write History at Gettysburg," *Historical Review of Berks County* (Summer 1998), p. 107.

43. Pension Records of Peter Drumheller, NA. The exact location and timing of this incident are unknown.

44. *OR*, Vol. 27, Part 1, pp. 315, 317, 320, 327; "Judge Slagle at Gettysburg," Timothy H. Smith Collection.

45. *OR*, Vol. 27, Part 1, pp. 248–249.

46. Coddington, *The Gettysburg Campaign*, p. 307.

47. Underwood, *History of the Twenty-sixth Regiment of the North Carolina Troops*, p. 49.

48. *OR*, Vol. 27, Part 2, pp. 642–643; Martin, *Gettysburg July 1*, pp. 186, 349–350.

49. Underwood, *History of the Twenty-sixth Regiment of the North Carolina Troops*, pp. 41, 48–49, 57.

50. Transcript of an interview with John R. Lane, W. H. S. Burgwyn Papers, North Carolina Department of Cultural Resources, Division of Archives and History, Raleigh, North Carolina.

51. Nevins, *A Diary of Battle*, p. 235.

52. Chamberlin, *History of the One Hundred and Fiftieth Regiment Pennsylvania Volunteers*, p. 120.

53. Martin, *Gettysburg July 1*, p. 344; "Judge Slagle at Gettysburg," Timothy H. Smith Collection.

54. John B. Bachelder, "Movements of the 151st Penn. Vols. of Biddle's Brigade: Notes of a Conversation with Colonel George F. McFarland, 151st Penn. Volunteers," Ladd and Ladd, *The Bachelder Papers*, Vol. 1, p. 271.

55. *OR*, Vol. 27, Part 1, pp. 313, 315, 317.

56. *Ibid.*, p. 320.

57. Martin, *Gettysburg July 1*, pp. 342–343, 347, 356; Horatio N. Warren, *The Declaration of Independence and War History: Bull Run to the Appomattox* (Buffalo: Courier, 1894), p. 30.

58. Walker, *Appointment at Gettysburg*, pp. 91–92.

59. St. Clair A. Mulholland, *A Record of Human Sacrifice of Daring Deeds and Heroic Men: Percentage of Losses at Gettysburg Greatest in History* (Gettysburg: W. H. Tipton, 1903), in Ladd and Ladd, *Gettysburg Sources*, Vol. 1, p. 6.

60. Survivors' Association, *History of the 121st Regiment Pennsylvania Volunteers*, p. 127.

61. *Ibid.*, pp. 52–53; *OR*, Vol. 27, Part 1, p. 323.

62. *OR*, Vol. 27, Part 1, p. 323.

63. James Ashworth to George McFarland, May 4, 1866, George McFarland Papers, PSA; Sarah Sites Rodgers, *The Ties of the Past: The Gettysburg Diaries of Salome Myers Stewart, 1854–1922* (Gettysburg: Thomas Publications, 1996), p. 175. Remarkably, Ashworth returned to his regiment and rose steadily in rank, culminating with a colonel's commission on

January 10, 1864. A month later, however, he was honorably discharged for disability by special order. Ashworth was embittered by his forced departure and wrote McFarland: "Some people are discharged [from] the service for drunkenness, for cowardice, and other crimes. I, and I am sorry to say many more, have received the same treatment, was discharged 'on account of wounds received in action.'"

Ashworth's adventures did not end with the termination of his active military service. He immediately joined the Veteran Reserve Corps and served in New Orleans and Baton Rouge until the close of the war. While en route to New Orleans, the steamer he was aboard wrecked off the coast of Florida. The passengers finished the journey on a gunboat. Following the end of hostilities, James helped to discharge convalescents from hospitals located in Washington, Philadelphia, York, and Baltimore. He next took charge of the Freedmen's Bureau in Louisa Courthouse, Virginia. Ashworth finished his career as a revenue assessor in southeastern Pennsylvania, a position to which he was appointed by President Grant. He resigned in February 1882 and died one month later in Gainesville, Florida. Survivors' Association, *History of the 121st Regiment Pennsylvania Volunteers*, pp. 140, 289.

64. Charles Atlee to George McFarland, March 21, 1866, George McFarland Papers, PSA. Atlee recovered from his wounds and eventually attained the rank of captain. He was honorably discharged on December 21, 1864. Survivors' Association *History of the 121st Regiment Pennsylvania Volunteers*, p. 259.

65. *Ibid.*, pp. 55, 129.

66. Osborne, *Holding the Left at Gettysburg*, pp. 12–14.

67. Edwin R. Gearhart, *In the Years '62 to '65: Personal Recollections of Edwin R. Gearhart* (Stroudsburg, Pa.: Daily Record Press, 1901), pp. 34–35; Biographical Sketch of Andrew Gregg Tucker, George McFarland Papers, PSA.

68. Jeremiah Hoffman to George McFarland, undated account, Dr. Charles Eater, Jr., Collection; Pension Records of Jeremiah Hoffman, NA.

69. *Union County Star and Lewisburg Chronicle*, July 24, 1863, Union County Historical Society Archives, Lewisburg, Pa.

70. Warren, *The Declaration of Independence and War History: Bull Run to the Appomattox*, p. 30.

71. Survivors' Association, *History of the 121st Regiment Pennsylvania Volunteers*, pp. 53, 240, 242–243; Jordan and Manarin, eds., *North Carolina Troops, 1861–1865*, Vol. 11, pp. 241, 315. Davis was the captain of Company G. He was captured at Gettysburg on July 3 and confined at Johnson's Island, Ohio, until paroled on February 24, 1865. Chapman Biddle was honorably discharged on December 10, 1863, due to poor health. He returned to his law practice in Philadelphia, where he died in 1880 at the age of 59. Just prior to his death, Biddle delivered a highly detailed account of the first day's battle at Gettysburg before the Historical Society of Pennsylvania. "Extract from a Memoir of Chapman Biddle," in Survivors' Association, *History of the 121st Regiment Pennsylvania Volunteers*, pp. 240–246.

72. James W. Downey, *A Lethal Tour of Duty: A History of the 142d Regiment Pennsylvania Voluntary Infantry, 1862–65* (Masters thesis, Indiana University of Pennsylvania, 1995), p. 32.

73. "Pittston Man's Story of His War Experiences," *The Pittston Gazette*, May 4, 1912, courtesy of Robert Carichner.

74. Busey, *These Honored Dead: The Union Casualties at Gettysburg*, p. 283; Undated casualty list, George McFarland Papers, PSA.

75. Gearhart, *In the Years '62 to '65*, p. 35; Horatio Warren, *Two Reunions of the 142d Regiment, Pa. Vols.* (Buffalo, N. Y.: Courier, 1890), p. 10.

76. J. R. Balsley, "A Gettysburg Reminiscence," *National Tribune*, May 19, 1898; Gearhart, *In the Years '62 to '65*, p. 35.

77. Busey and Martin, *Regimental Strengths and Losses at Gettysburg*, p. 240.

78. "Report of Lt. Col. William W. Dudley," in Ladd and Ladd, *The Bachelder Papers*, Vol. 2, pp. 941–942.

79. Hartwig, "The Defense of McPherson's Ridge," p. 24.

80. Underwood, *History of the Twenty-Sixth Regiment of the North Carolina Troops*, p. 49.

81. Hartwig, "The Defense of McPherson's Ridge," p. 23; Charles H. McConnell, "First and Greatest Day's Battle of Gettysburg," Gettysburg Newspaper Clippings, Vol. 6, Part 4, Gettysburg National Military Park Library.

82. Underwood, *History of the Twenty-Sixth Regiment of the North Carolina Troops*, p. 50; Busey and Martin, *Regimental Strengths and Losses at Gettysburg*, p. 239; R. Lee Hadden, "The Deadly Embrace: The Meeting of the Twenty-fourth Regiment, Michigan Infantry and the Twenty-sixth Regiment of North Carolina Troops at McPherson's Woods, Gettysburg, Pennsylvania, July 1, 1863," *The Gettysburg Magazine*, no. 5 (July 1991), p. 32.

83. "Southern Soldiers in Northern Prisons," *Southern Historical Society Papers*, Vol. 23 (1895), p. 159, Robert Brake Collection, USAMHI; Underwood, *History of the Twenty-Sixth Regiment of the North Carolina Troops*, pp. 51–52; Charles H. McConnell, "First and Greatest Day's Battle of Gettysburg," Gettysburg Newspaper Clippings, Vol. 6, Part 4, Gettysburg National Military Park Library.

84. "William Ramsey to John B. Bachelder," May 7, 1883, in Ladd and Ladd, *The Bachelder Papers*, Vol. 2, p. 956.

85. Underwood, *History of the Twenty-Sixth Regiment of the North Carolina Troops*, p. 51; Transcript of an interview with John R. Lane, W. H. S. Burgwyn Papers, North Carolina Department of Cultural Resources, Department of Archives and History, Raleigh, North Carolina.

86. *OR*, Vol. 27, Part 1, p. 327.

87. R. D. Sayre, "A Day at Gettysburg," *National Tribune*, April 13, 1899.

88. *OR*, Vol. 27, Part 1, p. 327; George F. McFarland, "The 151st P. V. in the Battle of Gettysburg," *Juniata Tribune*, Mifflintown, Pa., 1888.

89. *OR*, Vol. 27, Part 1, p. 327; Nicholson, *Pennsylvania at Gettysburg*, Vol. 2, p. 769.

90. Nathan Cooper to "Dear Wife," July 2, 1863, Warren County Historical Society Collection.

91. *OR*, Vol. 27, Part 2, p. 643.

92. *Ibid.*, Part 1, p. 327.

93. George McFarland, "Notes to Report of the 151st Regt. Pa. Vols.," Ladd and Ladd, *The Bachelder Papers*, Vol. 1, p. 89.

94. Busey, *These Honored Dead*, p. 296; Mark W. Troup, "Snyder County's Role at the Battle of Gettysburg," *The Snyder County Historical Society Bulletin* (Middleburg, Pa.: Country Print Shop, 1996), pp. 38–39.

95. Pension Records of Abe C. Freet, NA.

96. Pension Records of Benjamin Armstrong, NA; Busey, *These Honored Dead*, p. 295.

97. Pension Records of Isaac Smith, NA.

98. Pension Records of Michael Bratton, NA.

99. Potts, "A First Defender in Rebel Prison Pens," p. 342.

100. R. D. Sayre, "A Day at Gettysburg," *National Tribune*, April 13, 1899.

101. Busey, *These Honored Dead*, pp. 296, 298.

102. Busey and Martin, *Regimental Strengths and Losses at Gettysburg*, p. 299; J. J. Young, Captain and Assistant Quartermaster, to Governor Zebulon B. Vance, July 4, 1863, Robert Brake Collection, USAMHI; Martin, *Gettysburg July 1*, p. 356. Colonel Collett Leventhorpe descended from a prominent English family. He served in the British army before he came to America, settling in western North Carolina during the late 1840s. His wounds were too severe to allow him to travel when Lee's army withdrew to Virginia. Leventhorpe was treated by Union surgeons, and after nine months of captivity, he was exchanged. President Jefferson Davis later commissioned Leventhorpe as a brigadier general. Michael C. Hardy, "England's Gift to the Confederacy: Brigadier General Collett Leventhorpe," *North & South*, Vol. 1, Issue 6, pp. 66–69.

103. George F. McFarland, "Report of Movements of 151st Pennsylvania," February 7, 1867, Ladd and Ladd, *The Bachelder Papers*, Vol. 1, pp. 300–301; M. C. Barnes to General W. W. Dudley, March 28, 1883, *ibid.*, Vol. 2, pp. 937–938. Barnes was later captured by the Confederates, but he reported, "I did not stay long with the rebs. They didn't feed me well enough, so I ran off."

104. Nicholson, *Pennsylvania at Gettysburg*, Vol. 2, p. 769.

105. George McFarland, "Correct List by Name of Killed, and Mortally Wounded, and Wounded, and of Captured Officers in the Battle of Gettysburg, Pa.," April 23, 1889, 151st Pennsylvania File, Gettysburg National Military Park Library. At the bottom of this list was attached the following endorsement by Governor James A. Beaver, a former Civil War general: "Col. McFarland is a reliable gentleman whose statements are entitled to the utmost confidence."

106. William O. Blodget to "Dear Wife," July 2, 1863, Warren County Historical Society Collection, Warren, Pa; Busey, *These Honored Dead*, p. 297; James L. Lott to George F. McFarland, October 4, 1864, George McFarland Papers, PSA. Frank, Lott, and Norris survived their wounds.

107. George McFarland, Undated casualty list, George McFarland Papers, PSA; Busey, *These Honored Dead*, p. 299.

108. Pension Records of Lewis Rentschler, NA.

109. Pension Records of Michael Link, NA; "The Life Story of 'Blind Mike' Link," *The Reading Eagle*, July 12, 1899.

110. Pension Records of Thomas Moyer, NA.

111. Pension Records of James Weida, NA; George McFarland, "Correct List by Name of Killed, and Mortally Wounded, and Wounded, and of Captured Officers in the Battle of Gettysburg, Pa.," April 23, 1889, 151st Pennsylvania File, Gettysburg National Military Park Library.

112. Simon J. Arnold to Mrs. Seiders, July 20, 1863, Sally Smith Collection.

113. Pension Records of Franklin Weaber, NA, including Franklin Weaber to "Dear Brother," February 27, 1863.

114. Pension Records of Franklin Wendling, NA.

115. George McFarland, Undated casualty list, George McFarland Papers, PSA.

116. Pension Records of William S. Strause, NA.

117. Bates, *History of the Pennsylvania Volunteers*, Vol. 4, pp. 692–694; Letters from Joe Smith, M.D., December 2, 1997, March 19, 1998, and April 29, 1998; Letter from Mike Straus, July 19, 1998. My heartfelt thanks to Dr. Smith and Mr. Straus for providing me with a wealth of material on the Strauses.

118. Pension Records of Solomon Strause, NA.

119. Walker, *Appointment at Gettysburg*, p. 109.

120. Philip Katcher, *The Civil War Source Book* (New York: Facts On File, Inc., 1992), p. 55.

121. Jordan and Manarin, *North Carolina Troops, 1861–1865*, Vol. 11, p. 241.

122. "The Diary of Alfred D. Staudt," *Historical Review of Berks County* 41 (Winter 1975–1976), p. 16; "The 151st Pennsylvania Regiment at Gettysburg," *Reading Eagle*, June 16, 1912.

123. *OR*, Vol. 27, Part 1, pp. 327–328; Nathan Cooper to "Dear Wife," July 2, 1863, Warren County Historical Society Collection.

124. R. D. Sayre, "A Day at Gettysburg," *National Tribune*, April 13, 1899.

125. Underwood, *History of the Twenty-Sixth Regiment of the North Carolina Troops*, p. 51; "The 151st Pennsylvania Regiment at Gettysburg," *Reading Eagle*, June 16, 1912.

126. *OR*, Vol. 27, Part 2, p. 643.

127. *Ibid.*, Part 1, p. 327.

128. Busey, *These Honored Dead*, pp. 296, 298, 300.

129. *OR*, Vol. 27, Part 2, p. 639.

130. "Valor of Pennsylvania Boys in the Civil War," copy in possession of author.

131. *OR*, Vol. 27, Part 2, pp. 638–639.

132. Underwood, *History of the Twenty-Sixth Regiment of the North Carolina Troops*, p. 55.

133. J. J. Young, Captain and Assistant Quartermaster, to Governor Zebulon B. Vance, July 4, 1863, Robert Brake Collection, USAMHI. It is difficult to ascertain the number of casualties the 26th lost in its separate engagements with the 24th Michigan and the 151st Pennsylvania. In contemporary articles and books dealing with the first day's action, the 24th Michigan has garnered much of the credit for inflicting heavy losses on the North Carolinians.

This was not always the case. An early historian of the battle wrote the following on this subject: "I was at Gettysburg a little over a year ago, and while there had a talk with some of the 151st Penn., who were dedicating a monument which was located on the site of the encounter.... The smaller loss of the 151st Penn. as compared with that of the 26th N.C., is due to the fact that it was a smaller regiment. It is not claimed that the 151st Penn. inflicted all of the loss sustained by the 26th N.C., but I am unable to decide as to whether the 19th Ind. or the 142nd Penn. contributed the balance." William F. Fox to Captain William H. S. Burgwyn, September 30, 1889, Robert Brake Collection, USAMHI. Fox, formerly of the 107th New York, was the author of *Regimental Losses in The American Civil War* and the editor of the three-volume *New York at Gettysburg*.

Similarly, in John M. Vanderslice's *Gettysburg Then and Now* appears the following passage: "[T]he 26th North Carolina, fighting its way up the woods, was penetrating a gap between the 142d Pennsylvania and the 19th Indiana, of Meredith's brigade, the left of which had been forced back. At this juncture the 151st Pennsylvania, which was in reserve near the seminary, rushed to the front and met the 26th North Carolina in one of the bloodiest struggles that took place on the field...."

John M. Vanderslice, *Gettysburg Then and Now* (New York: G. W. Dillingham, 1897), p. 95. Vanderslice served as a director of the Gettysburg Battlefield Memorial Association. In these early accounts the role of the 151st in the defense of McPherson's Ridge was emphasized and that of the 24th Michigan seemed to be neglected or even ignored.

134. "Unparalleled Loss of Company F, 26th North Carolina Regiment, Pettigrew's Brigade, at Gettysburg," *Southern Historical Society Papers*, Vol. 28 (1900), pp. 199–204, Robert Brake Collection, USAMHI.

135. Henry C. Kirkman to Dr. George Kirkman, August 6, 1863, and Chaplain W. Burton Owen to Dr. George Kirkman, December 8, 1863, Harrisburg Civil War Round Table, Gregory A. Coco Collection, USAMHI. Private Henry Kirkman was wounded in the foot and captured on July 3. He was hospitalized at Camp Letterman, but died of pneumonia on September 1, 1863. Captured during Lee's retreat from Gettysburg, Private Wiley Prentiss Kirkman was incarcerated at Point Lookout, Maryland, where he died of scurvy on March 10, 1865, less than a month before Lee's surrender. Jordan and Manarin, *North Carolina Troops, 1861–1865*, Vol. 7, pp. 554–555.

136. Timothy H. Smith, *The Story of Lee's Headquarters: Gettysburg, Pennsylvania* (Gettysburg: Thomas Publications, 1995), p. 17; J. Michael Miller, "Perrin's Brigade on July 1, 1863," *The Gettysburg Magazine*, no. 13 (July 1995), pp. 24–25; Nevins, *A Diary of Battle*, p. 235.

137. Brown, *A Colonel at Gettysburg and Spotsylvania*, p. 78.

138. Smith, *The Story of Lee's Headquarters*, pp. 16–17.

139. Doubleday, *Chancellorsville and Gettysburg*, p. 147.

140. Hartwig, "The Defense of McPherson's Ridge," p. 24; Chamberlin, *History of the One Hundred and Fiftieth Regiment Pennsylvania Volunteers*, pp. 132–135; *OR*, Vol. 27, Part 1, p. 328; *OR*, Vol. 27, Part 2, p. 643.

141. George McFarland, "Report of Movements of 151st Pennsylvania," February 7, 1867, in Ladd and Ladd, *The Bachelder Papers*, Vol. 1, pp. 301–302.

142. *OR*, Vol. 27, Part 2, p. 643; *OR*, Vol. 27, Part 1, p. 250.

143. Pension Records of William Gray, NA.

144. *OR*, Vol. 27, Part 2, pp. 638, 656.

145. Faust, ed., *Historical Times Illustrated Encyclopedia of the Civil War*, pp. 438, 569; Tagg, *The Generals of Gettysburg*, pp. 324–327. On July 2, 1863, Pender was struck in the thigh by a shell fragment. He died on July 8th following an amputation of the limb, which had become badly infected.

146. Caldwell, *The History of a Brigade of South Carolinians*, p. 96; Welch, *A Confederate Surgeon's Letters to His Wife*, p. 64.

147. Brown, *A Colonel at Gettysburg and Spotsylvania*, p. 78

148. Welch, *A Confederate Surgeon's Letters to His Wife*, p. 64; Caldwell, *The History of a Brigade of South Carolinians*, p. 97.

149. *OR*, Vol. 27, Part 2, pp. 656–657; Hassler, *Crisis at the Crossroads*, pp. 117–119.

150. Caldwell, *The History of a Brigade of South Carolinians*, p. 97; Abner Perrin to Governor Bonham, July 29, 1863, *The Mississippi Historical Review*, p. 522.

151. Brown, *A Colonel at Gettysburg and Spotsylvania*, p. 79.

152. *OR*, Vol. 27, Part 2, pp. 657, 661; Martin, *Gettysburg July 1*, p. 404.

153. Rufus R. Dawes, *Service with the Sixth Wisconsin Volunteers* (Marietta, Ohio: E. R. Alderman, 1890), p. 175.

154. Welch, *A Confederate Surgeon's Letters to His Wife*, p. 64.

155. Robert K. Beecham, *Gettysburg: The Pivotal Battle of the Civil War* (Chicago: A. C. McClure & Co., 1911), pp. 80–81.

156. Miller, "Perrin's Brigade on July 1, 1863," p. 27.

157. Caldwell, *The History of a Brigade of South Carolinians*, p. 97.

158. *OR,* Vol. 27, Part 2, pp. 661–662; Miller, "Perrin's Brigade on July 1, 1863," p. 27; Brown, *A Colonel at Gettysburg and Spotsylvania*, p. 80. Just before the Battle of Spotsylvania, Perrin vowed to emerge a live major general or a dead brigadier. On May 12, 1864, he led his brigade in a daring counterattack on the Bloody Angle. The law of averages, which Perrin had defied near the Lutheran Seminary, caught up with him when he fell from his horse pierced by seven bullets. Tagg, *The Generals of Gettysburg*, p. 332.

159. Caldwell, *The History of a Brigade of South Carolinians*, pp. 97–98.

160. Brown, *A Colonel at Gettysburg and Spotsylvania*, pp. 79–80; Nathan Cooper to "Dear Wife," July 2, 1863, Warren County Historical Society Collection.

161. *Maine at Gettysburg: Report of Maine Commissioners* (Portland, Maine: Lakeside Press, 1898), p. 84.

162. Nicholson, *Pennsylvania at Gettysburg*, Vol. 2, p. 909; Nevins, *A Diary of Battle*, p. 236.

163. Pension Records of Davis Meredith, NA; Pension Records of Adam Heilman, NA; *Reading Daily Times*, July 11, 1863.

164. Brown, *A Colonel at Gettysburg and Spotsylvania*, p. 80.

165. George McFarland, "Report of Movements of the 151st Pennsylvania," February 7, 1867, in Ladd and Ladd, *The Bachelder Papers,* Vol. 1, p. 302; Dreese, *An Imperishable Fame*, p. 143; Nathan Cooper to "Dear Wife," July 2, 1863, Warren County Historical Society Collection.

166. *OR,* Vol. 27, Part 1, pp. 657, 662.

167. John A. Leach to John B. Bachelder, June 2, 1884, in Ladd and Ladd, *The Bachelder Papers*, Vol. 2, p. 1046.

168. *OR,* Vol. 27, Part 1, p. 321; Survivors' Association, *History of the 121st Regiment Pennsylvania Volunteers*, p. 56.

169. Warren, *The Declaration of Independence and War History: Bull Run to the Appomattox*, p. 30.

170. Biography of Andrew Gregg Tucker, George McFarland Papers, PSA.

171. James W. Downey, *A Lethal Tour of Duty: A History of the 142d Regiment Pennsylvania Voluntary Infantry, 1862–65,* pp. 31–32.

172. *OR,* Vol. 27, Part 1, p. 328.

173. George McFarland, "Report of Movements of the 151st Pennsylvania," February 7, 1867, in Ladd and Ladd, *The Bachelder Papers*, Vol. 1, p. 302.

174. *OR,* Vol. 27, Part 1, p. 328.

175. Brown, *A Colonel at Gettysburg and Spotsylvania*, pp. 214–216; Nevins, *A Diary of Battle*, pp. 236–237; *OR,* Vol. 27, Part 1, pp. 250–251.

176. *OR,* Vol. 27, Part 1, p. 328; Dreese, *An Imperishable Fame*, p. 143; Nicholson, *Pennsylvania at Gettysburg*, Vol. 2, p. 770.

177. Nicholson, *Pennsylvania at Gettysburg*, Vol. 2, p. 770; Pension Records of William Gray, NA.

178. R. D. Sayre, "A Day at Gettysburg," *National Tribune*, April 13, 1899.

179. *OR,* Vol. 27, Part 1, pp. 328–329.

180. *Ibid.,* p. 328; Walker, *Appointment at Gettysburg*, p. 93; Samuel T. Allen to George McFarland, undated, George McFarland Papers, PSA.

181. Brown, *A Colonel at Gettysburg and Spotsylvania*, p. 81; Caldwell, *The History of a Brigade of South Carolinians*, p. 98.

182. For a detailed discussion of the retreat of the Federal First Corps, see Smith, *The Story of Lee's Headquarters*, pp. 26–36.

183. Pension Records of George Stone and Henry Patterson, NA.

184. Nathan Cooper to "Dear Wife," July 2, 1863, Warren County Historical Society Collection; Pension Records of William Gray, NA.

185. Walker, *Appointment at Gettysburg*, pp. 93–94.

186. Potts, "A First Defender in Rebel Prison Pens," p. 343.

187. Coco, *A Vast Sea of Misery*, pp. 20–21.

188. Martin, *Gettysburg July 1*, pp. 454–456. Nearly 2,400 chaplains were appointed to Federal regiments during the Civil War. Reverend Howell was one of thirteen chaplains who died in combat.

189. Pension Records of James Reber, NA; Bates, *History of Pennsylvania Volunteers*, Vol. 4, p. 693.

190. Coddington, *The Gettysburg Campaign*, p. 307.

191. Nevins, *A Diary of Battle*, p. 237.

192. Cook, "Personal Reminiscences of Gettysburg," in McLean and McLean, *Gettysburg Sources*, Vol. 2, pp. 131–132.

193. "Judge Slagle at Gettysburg," Timothy H. Smith Collection.

194. Walter L. Owens to George F. McFarland, August 6, 1866, in Ladd and Ladd, *The Bachelder Papers*, Vol. 1, p. 268; *OR,* Vol. 27, Part 1, p. 328.

195. Robert E. Miller to "Dear Brother," July 18, 1863, Schoff Civil War Collection, William L. Clements Library, University of Michigan. During his stay at St. Johns College Hospital in Annapolis, Maryland, Miller spoke with this unidentified member of Company K who had participated in the battle.

196. Bates, *History of Pennsylvania Volunteers*, Vol. 4, pp. 693, 694.

197. Pension Records of Albert Yost and Henry Merkle, NA.

198. George McFarland to Simon J. Arnold, February 24, 1864, Letter of Recommendation, Mary Haney Arnold Collection; Pension Records of Simon Arnold, NA.

199. David A. Murdoch, ed., "Catherine Mary White Foster's Eyewitness Account of the Battle of Gettysburg, with Background on the Foster Family Union Soldiers," *Adams County History*, Vol. 1 (1995), pp. 49 51, 63.

200. Letters from Joe Smith, M.D. to Author, December 3, 1997, and March 20, 1998; Pension Records of William S. Strause, NA.

201. Brown, *A Colonel at Gettysburg and Spotsylvania*, pp. 83–84; Busey and Martin, *Regimental Strengths and Losses at Gettysburg*, p. 292; Biography of Captain James Boatwright, 14th South Carolina File, Robert L. Brake Collection, USAMHI. Abner Perrin cited Boatwright for "uncommonly brave conduct" during the battle.

202. Lane, *Dear Bet, The Carter Letters: 1861–1863,* pp. xx, 95–96, 100, 107. Sidney's older brother, Private Giles Carter, was wounded and captured on July 3rd at Gettysburg. He was exchanged on September 16, 1863. Two of his younger brothers perished in the Confederate service prior to Gettysburg. One sibling died of disease and the other was killed at the Battle of Chancellorsville.

203. Brown, *A Colonel at Gettysburg and Spotsylvania*, p. 84.

204. William S. Whitney to "The M. E. High Priest and Companions of Mountain City N. R. A. Chapter, Pottsville, Pa.," November 2, 1863, Adams County Historical Society, Get-

tysburg, Pa.; Sheldon A. Munn, *Freemasons at Gettysburg* (Gettysburg: Thomas Publications, 1993), p. 30. Mr. Munn estimates that nearly 18,000 Masons were present at Gettysburg and that approximately 5,600 became casualties there.

205. Miller, "Perrin's Brigade on July 1, 1863," p. 30.

206. Martin, *Gettysburg July 1*, p. 499.

207. "The 151st Pennsylvania Regiment at Gettysburg," *Reading Eagle*, June 16, 1912.

208. Coddington, *The Gettysburg Campaign*, p. 315; Douglas Southall Freeman, *Lee's Lieutenants: A Study in Command* (New York: Charles Scribner's Sons, 1944), pp. 91–92; Hassler, *Crisis at the Crossroads*, p. 137.

209. Coddington, *The Gettysburg Campaign*, pp. 284–285, 296–299, 321; Martin, *Gettysburg July 1*, pp. 478–482; Hassler, *Crisis at the Crossroads*, pp. 135–137.

210. Coddington, *The Gettysburg Campaign*, pp. 321–322.

211. Hassler, *Crisis at the Crossroads*, p. 140.

212. Brown, *A Colonel at Gettysburg and Spotsylvania*, p. 84; *OR*, Vol. 27, Part 1, p. 328; E. P. Alexander, *Military Memoirs of a Confederate* (New York: Charles Scribner's Sons, 1907), p. 384.

213. William O. Blodget to "Dear Brother," July 5, 1863, Rosemary McCorkel Collection.

214. Busey and Martin, *Regimental Strengths and Losses at Gettysburg*, pp. 262, 264–266, 270, 272–273. The regimental casualty figures utilized by the authors for these rankings were taken directly from the *Official Records*, Vol. 27, Part 1, pp. 173–187.

215. Charles H. McConnell, "First and Greatest Day's Battle of Gettysburg," Gettysburg Clippings, Vol. 6, Part 4, Gettysburg National Military Park Library.

216. William F. Fox, *Regimental Losses in The American Civil War, 1861–1865*, p. 66.

217. Chamberlin, *History of the One Hundred and Fiftieth Regiment Pennsylvania Volunteers*, p. 140.

218. Doubleday, *Chancellorsville and Gettysburg*, p. 155.

219. Osborne, *Holding the Left at Gettysburg*, pp. 17–18. The camp site was probably located near the Catherine Guinn farm. "Katie" Guinn was in her 70s at the time of the battle and was said to physically "beat up" any soldiers she discovered lurking near her house. The farm no longer exists. The National Park Service employee parking lot is located on part of the site. Coco, *A Vast Sea of Misery*, pp. 61–62.

220. Cook, "Personal Reminiscences of Gettysburg," in McLean and McLean, *Gettysburg Sources*, Vol. 2, p. 132.

221. Osborne, *Holding the Left at Gettysburg*, p. 17.

222. William O. Blodget to "Dear Wife," July 2, 1863, Warren County Historical Society.

Chapter 4

1. Tagg, *The Generals of Gettysburg*, pp. 1, 4–5.

2. Coddington, *The Gettysburg Campaign*, pp. 323–324.

3. *Ibid.*, pp. 330–332; Hassler, *Crisis at the Crossroads*, pp. 23–24.

4. Tagg, *The Generals of Gettysburg*, p. 5; Doubleday, *Chancellorsville and Gettysburg*, p. 162.

5. Doubleday, *Chancellorsville and Gettysburg*, pp. 157–158.

6. Coddington, *The Gettysburg Campaign*, pp. 337–338.

7. Thomas L. Elmore, "A Meteorological and Astronomical Chronology of the Gettysburg Campaign," *The Gettysburg Magazine*, no. 13 (July 1995), p. 12.

8. Tagg, *The Generals of Gettysburg*, pp. 12–13, 27; Cook, "Personal Reminiscences of Gettysburg," in McLean and McLean, *Gettysburg Sources*, Vol. 2, p. 134.

9. Tagg, *The Generals of Gettysburg*, pp. 30–31; Tony Trimble, "Paper Collars: Stannard's Brigade at Gettysburg," *The Gettysburg Magazine*, no. 2 (January 1990), p. 75. For an excellent history of Stannard's Brigade, see Howard Coffin, *Nine Months to Gettysburg* (Woodstock, Vt.: Countryman, 1997). At Gettysburg, this brigade consisted of the 13th, 14th, and 16th Vermont. The 12th and 15th regiments were on detached duty as train guards and thus missed the battle.

10. Dreese, *An Imperishable Fame*, p. 62.

11. Busey and Martin, *Regimental Strengths and Losses at Gettysburg*, pp. 240–241.

12. *OR*, Vol. 27, Part 1, p. 328; Nicholson, *Pennsylvania at Gettysburg*, Vol. 2, p. 770.

13. Nathan Cooper to "Dear Wife," July 2, 1863, Warren County Historical Society Collection.

14. Elmore, "A Meteorological and Astronomical Chronology of the Gettysburg Campaign," p. 12.

15. Walter L. Owens to George McFarland, August 6, 1866, in Ladd and Ladd, *The Bachelder Papers*, Vol. 1, p. 268.

16. Cook, "Personal Reminiscences of Gettysburg," in McLean and McLean, *Gettysburg Sources*, Vol. 2, p. 133.

17. Coddington, *The Gettysburg Campaign*, pp. 343–356, 383–384; James McPherson, *The Atlas of the Civil War* (New York: Macmillan, 1994), pp. 120–121.

18. Coddington, *The Gettysburg Campaign*, pp. 427–428; "Judge Slagle at Gettysburg," Timothy H. Smith Collection.

19. Coddington, *The Gettysburg Campaign*, pp. 356–357; Garry Adelman, "The Third Brigade, Third Division, Sixth Corps at Gettysburg," *The Gettysburg Magazine*, no. 11 (July 1994), pp. 92–93.

20. McPherson, *The Atlas of the Civil War*, p. 121; Tagg, *The Generals of Gettysburg*, pp. 317–318.

21. Coddington, *The Gettysburg Campaign*, pp. 423–424; Tagg, *The Generals of Gettysburg*, pp. 13–14; *OR*, Vol. 27, Part 1, p. 321.

22. Walter L. Owens to George McFarland, August 6, 1866, in Ladd and Ladd, *The Bachelder Papers*, Vol. 1, pp. 268–269. The 36-year-old Gibbon commanded the Second Division of Hancock's Second Corps at Gettysburg, and on two different occasions during the battle, he commanded the corps. Gibbon was raised in North Carolina, but he remained loyal to the Union. He was widely recognized as one of the most able division commanders in the army. Tagg, *The Generals of Gettysburg*, pp. 44–45.

23. *OR*, Vol. 27, Part 1, p. 321; Theodore Gates to John Bachelder, October 26, 1865, in Ladd and Ladd, *The Bachelder Papers*, Vol. 1, p. 204; George R. Stewart, *Pickett's Charge: A Microhistory of the Final Attack at Gettysburg, July 3, 1863* (Boston: Houghton Mifflin, 1959), pp. 51, 58, 61. The position occupied by Gates' command on July 2nd and 3rd on Cemetery Ridge is marked today by a small monument commemorating the 20th New York State Militia. This monument was dedicated in 1981 by historian Seward Osborne. There is no monument in this area devoted solely to the 151st. Thus, this regiment was the only Northern unit present in the front lines during the Pickett-Pettigrew Charge that does not currently have a monument in the area to mark its position.

24. *OR*, Vol. 27, Part 1, p. 321.

25. Stewart, *Pickett's Charge*, pp. 52, 66–67.

26. *OR*, Vol. 27, Part 1, pp. 318, 321; Stewart, *Pickett's Charge*, p. 69.

27. Stewart, *Pickett's Charge*, pp. 61–62, 68; Abner Doubleday, "Report of the Operations of the Third Division of the First Army Corps, Army of the Potomac, from the 1st to the 7th of July 1863, including the 2nd and 3rd Days of the Battle of Gettysburg, Pa.," September 19, 1863, copy in George McFarland Papers, PSA.

28. McPherson, *The Atlas of the Civil War*, p. 121; Craig L. Symonds, *Gettysburg: A Battlefield Atlas* (Baltimore: Nautical & Aviation Publishing Company, 1995), pp. 59, 61.

29. Walter L. Owens to George McFarland, August 6, 1866, in Ladd and Ladd, *The Bachelder Papers*, Vol. 1, p. 269; "Judge Slagle at Gettysburg," Timothy H. Smith Collection.

30. Coddington, *The Gettysburg Campaign*, pp. 449–454.

31. *Ibid.*, pp. 454–456; Symonds, *Gettysburg: A Battlefield Atlas*, p. 67

32. Coddington, *The Gettysburg Campaign*, p. 455; Symonds, *Gettysburg: A Battlefield Atlas*, p. 67; James Miller to "Dear Sister," August 2, 1863, Schoff Civil War Collection, William L. Clements Library, University of Michigan.

33. Coddington, *The Gettysburg Campaign*, p. 489; Stewart, *Pickett's Charge*, p. 89; Cook, "Personal Reminiscences of Gettysburg," in McLean and McLean, *Gettysburg Sources*, Vol. 2, p. 135.

34. Coddington, *The Gettysburg Campaign*, pp. 489–490; Stewart, *Pickett's Charge*, pp. 86–88, 114; McPherson, *The Atlas of the Civil War*, pp. 122–123.

35. Coddington, *The Gettysburg Campaign*, p. 484; Stewart, *Pickett's Charge*, pp. 100–101; Nathan Cooper to "Dear Wife," July 3, 1863, Warren County Historical Society Collection.

36. Jacobs, *Memoirs of Henry Eyster Jacobs*, Vol. 1, p. 58.

37. Cook, "Personal Reminiscences of Gettysburg," in McLean and McLean, *Gettysburg Sources*, Vol. 2, p. 135.

38. *OR*, Vol. 27, Part 1, p. 318.

39. Walter L. Owens to George McFarland, August 6, 1866, in Ladd and Ladd, *The Bachelder Papers*, Vol. 1, p. 269.

40. Pension Records of Benjamin Oliver, NA.

41. William O. Blodget to "Dear Brother," July 5, 1863, Rosemary McCorkel Collection.

42. Cook, "Personal Reminiscences of Gettysburg," in McLean and McLean, *Gettysburg Sources*, Vol. 2, p. 136; Jacob Hardenburgh to Theodore Gates, October 9, 1878, Robert L. Brake Collection, USAMHI.

43. Stewart, *Pickett's Charge*, p. 143; Doubleday, "Report of the Operations of the Third Division."

44. "Judge Slagle at Gettysburg," Timothy H. Smith Collection.

45. Stewart, *Pickett's Charge*, pp. 131, 135–136, 149, 156–161; Coddington, *The Gettysburg Campaign*, pp. 495–500; Dr. Michael Jacobs, "Gettysburg Weather Reports," Gettysburg National Military Park Library.

46. Jacobs, *Memoirs of Henry Eyster Jacobs*, Vol. 1, p. 58.

47. Paul Andrew Hutton, ed., *Gettysburg: Colonel William C. Oates and Lieutenant Frank A. Haskell* (New York: Bantam, 1992), p. 213; Cook, "Personal Reminiscences of Gettysburg," in McLean and McLean, *Gettysburg Sources*, Vol. 2, p. 137.

48. Coddington, *The Gettysburg Campaign*, pp. 489, 505–506; Doubleday, *Chancellorsville and Gettysburg*, p. 193.

49. Coddington, *The Gettysburg Campaign*, pp. 503; Doubleday, *Chancellorsville and Gettysburg*, p. 193; Hutton, *Gettysburg: Colonel William C. Oates and Lieutenant Frank A. Haskell*, p. 215.

50. Doubleday, *Chancellorsville and Gettysburg*, p. 192; *OR*, Vol. 27, Part 1, pp. 318–319, 322; Coddington, *The Gettysburg Campaign*, p. 513; Jacob Hardenburgh to Theodore Gates, October 9, 1878, Robert L. Brake Collection, USAMHI.

51. Coddington, *The Gettysburg Campaign*, pp. 515, 519; Doubleday, *Chancellorsville and Gettysburg*, pp. 192–193.

52. Coddington, *The Gettysburg Campaign*, pp. 507–508; Doubleday, *Chancellorsville and Gettysburg*, p. 193.

53. Coddington, *The Gettysburg Campaign*, pp. 516–517; Stewart, *Pickett's Charge*, pp. 212–217; D. Scott Hartwig, "It Struck Horror To Us All," *The Gettysburg Magazine*, no. 4 (January 1991), p. 97; Wayne E. Motts, "*Trust in God and Fear Nothing*": *Gen. Lewis A. Armistead, CSA* (Gettysburg: Farnsworth House, 1994), p. 45.

54. Hutton, *Gettysburg: Colonel William C. Oates and Lieutenant Frank A. Haskell*, p. 217.

55. Coddington, *The Gettysburg Campaign*, p. 518; Stewart, *Pickett's Charge*, pp. 234–236.

56. Theodore Gates to Peter F. Rothermel, April 28, 1868, Peter Rothermel Papers, PSA; Walter L. Owens to George McFarland, August 6, 1866, in Ladd and Ladd, *The Bachelder Papers*, Vol. 1, p. 269.

57. *OR*, Vol. 27, Part 1, pp. 319, 322. The thought of naming the clump or copse of trees the High Water Mark of the Rebellion was conceived by Colonel John B. Bachelder, one of the most influential early historians of the battle. The site was memorialized in 1891 with a bronze tablet listing all of the Southern units which participated in the charge and the Union organizations that met the assault. See Frassanito, *Early Photography at Gettysburg*, pp. 238–240.

58. William O. Blodget to "Dear Sister," February 10, 1863, Rosemary McCorkel Collection.

59. *OR*, Vol. 27, Part 1, p. 319; Jacob Hardenburgh to Theodore Gates, October 9, 1878, Robert L. Brake Collection, USAMHI.

60. Cook, "Personal Reminiscences of Gettysburg," in McLean and McLean, *Gettysburg Sources*, Vol. 2, p. 137; Jacob Hardenburgh to Theodore Gates, October 9, 1878, Robert L. Brake Collection, USAMHI.

61. Walter L. Owens to George McFarland, August 6, 1866, in Ladd and Ladd, *The Bachelder Papers*, Vol. 1, pp. 269–270; *OR*, Vol. 27, Part 1, p. 322.

62. Nathan Cooper to "Dear Wife," July 9, 1863, Warren County Historical Society Collection.

63. George McFarland, "Report of Movements of 151st Pennsylvania," February 7, 1867, in Ladd and Ladd, *The Bachelder Papers*, Vol. 1, p. 304.

64. Pension Records of John T. Strause, NA; Pension Records of Valentine Painter, NA; Painter Family History Compiled by Stewart P. Biehl, Hamburg, Pa.

65. *OR*, Vol. 27, Part 1, p. 328.

66. William O. Blodget to "Dear Brother," July 5, 1863, Rosemary McCorkel Collection; Walter L. Owens to George McFarland, August 6, 1866, in Ladd and Ladd, *The Bachelder Papers*, Vol. 1, p. 270.

67. Walter L. Owens to George McFarland, August 6, 1866, in Ladd and Ladd, *The Bachelder Papers*, Vol. 1, p. 270.

68. *OR*, Vol. 27, Part 1, p. 322.

69. William Blodget to "Dear Brother," July 5, 1863, Rosemary McCorkel Collection.

70. Cook, "Personal Reminiscences of Gettysburg," in McLean and McLean, *Gettysburg Sources*, Vol. 2, p. 137.

71. Coddington, *The Gettysburg Campaign*, pp. 517–519, Stewart, *Pickett's Charge*, pp. 242–245.

72. Doubleday, *Chancellorsville and Gettysburg*, pp. 196–197.

73. Jacobs, *Memoirs of Henry Eyster Jacobs*, Vol. 1, p. 58.

74. *OR*, Vol. 27, Part 1, p. 322; Theodore Gates to Peter F. Rothermel, April 28, 1868, Peter Rothermel Papers, PSA.

75. Cook, "Personal Reminiscences of Gettysburg," in McLean and McLean, *Gettysburg Sources*, Vol. 2, p. 138.

76. James T. Miller to "Dear Brother," June 8, 1863, Schoff Civil War Collection, William L. Clements Library, University of Michigan.

77. Doubleday, *Chancellorsville and Gettysburg*, p. 197; Stewart, *Pickett's Charge*, pp. 251–252, 258–260.

78. John Michael Priest, "Lee's Gallant 6000?," *North & South*, Vol. 1, Issue 6, p. 55; Symonds, *Gettysburg: A Battlefield Atlas*, p. 79

79. Symonds, *Gettysburg: A Battlefield Atlas*, pp. 79, 96.

80. William Blodget to "Dear Brother," July 5, 1863, Rosemary McCorkel Collection.

81. Samuel T. Allen to George McFarland, undated letter, George McFarland Papers, PSA; Pension Records of Samuel Allen, NA.

82. Doubleday, *Chancellorsville and Gettysburg*, p. 196; Cook, "Personal Reminiscences of Gettysburg," McLean and McLean, *Gettysburg Sources, Vol. 2*, p. 141.

83. William Blodget to "Dear Brother," July 5, 1863, Rosemary McCorkel Collection.

84. Nevins, *A Diary of Battle*, p. 252.

85. Cook, "Personal Reminiscences of Gettysburg," pp. 138, 144; *OR*, Vol. 27, Part 1, p. 319. Gates stated that Hodges was killed within fifty feet of him. Theodore Gates to Peter Rothermel, April 28, 1868, Peter Rothermel Papers, PSA.

86. *OR*, Vol. 27, Part 1, pp. 319, 322.

87. Gregory A. Coco, *A Strange and Blighted Land, Gettysburg: The Aftermath of a Battle* (Gettysburg: Thomas Publications, 1995), pp. 58–60, 63.

88. Glenn Tucker, *High Tide at Gettysburg* (Indianapolis: Bobbs-Merrill, 1958), p. 383; Jacobs, *Memoirs of Henry Eyster Jacobs*, Vol. 1, p. 59.

Chapter 5

1. Chamberlin, *History of the One Hundred Fiftieth Regiment Pennsylvania Volunteers*, pp. 152–153.

2. Abner Doubleday, congratulatory order dated July 4, 1863, copy in George McFarland Papers, PSA.

3. Harry W. Pfanz, "The Gettysburg Campaign After Pickett's Charge," *The Gettysburg Magazine*, no. 1 (July 1989), p. 118; Coddington, *The Gettysburg Campaign*, p. 537.

4. Chamberlin, *History of the One Hundred Fiftieth Regiment Pennsylvania Volunteers*, p. 152.

5. Pfanz, "The Gettysburg Campaign After Pickett's Charge," pp. 118–119; Coddington, *The Gettysburg Campaign*, pp. 536–537.

6. Cook, "Personal Reminiscences of Gettysburg," in McLean and McLean, *Gettysburg Sources*, Vol. 2, p. 141.

7. William O. Blodget to "Dear Brother," July 5, 1863, Rosemary McCorkel Collection.

8. James T. Miller to "Dear Parents," July 6, 1863, Schoff Civil War Collection, William L. Clements Library, University of Michigan.

9. After his wounding on July 3, Samuel Allen spent the night in an ambulance behind the lines. The next morning he was transported to a nearby barn for treatment. The site of this field hospital was not identified by Allen, but it may have been the Peter Frey farm, which was located just behind the Union lines along the Taneytown Road. Samuel T. Allen to George McFarland, undated letter, George McFarland Papers, PSA.

10. Theodore Chase to "My Dear Brother," June 21, 1863, Warren County Historical Society Collection.

11. Pfanz, "The Gettysburg Campaign After Pickett's Charge," pp. 120–121; Coddington, *The Gettysburg Campaign*, pp. 549–550.

12. William O. Blodget to "Dear Brother," July 5, 1863, Rosemary McCorkel Collection.

13. Symonds, *Gettysburg: A Battlefield Atlas*, p. 83.

14. *OR*, Vol. 27, Part 1, p. 324; Doubleday, "Report of the Operations of the Third Division."

15. Nevins, *A Diary of Battle*, p. 254.

16. Warren, *The Declaration of Independence and War History: Bull Run to the Appomattox*, p. 32.

17. George S. Bisbee to "Mr. Babcock," September 23, 1863, in pension records of George H. Babcock, NA. Bisbee and sixteen others from the 20th New York State Militia performed various duties at the Seminary Hospital until they were relieved on August 16th. Affidavit by Surgeon Robert Loughran, 20th New York State Militia, dated August 16, 1863, Seward Osborne Collection.

18. Simon J. Arnold to "Mrs. Seiders," July 20, 1863, Sally Smith Collection.

19. Coco, *A Strange and Blighted Land*, p. 73.

20. Nathan Cooper to "Dear Wife," July 9, 1863, Warren County Historical Society Collection.

21. William O. Blodget to "Dear Brother," July 5, 1863, Rosemary McCorkel Collection.

22. Mark M. Boatner, III, *The Civil War Dictionary* (New York: Vintage Books, 1991), p. 339.

23. Warren, *The Declaration of Independence and War History: Bull Run to the Appomattox*, p. 32.

24. Doubleday, *Chancellorsville and Gettysburg*, Introduction by Gary W. Gallagher, p. x.

25. Pfanz, "The Gettysburg Campaign After Pickett's Charge," p. 122.

26. Nathan Cooper to "Dear Wife," July 9, 1863, Warren County Historical Society Collection.

27. James T. Miller to "Dear Brother," June 8, 1863, Schoff Civil War Collection, William L. Clements Library, University of Michigan; Pension Records of Lafayette Westbrook and George S. Mills, NA.

28. Coddington, *The Gettysburg Campaign*, p. 564; Nevins, *A Diary of Battle*, pp. 258–259.

29. Nevins, *A Diary of Battle*, p. 258; Nathan Cooper to "Dear Wife," July 9, 1863, Warren County Historical Society Collection.

30. Coddington, *The Gettysburg Campaign*, pp. 560–561, 565–566.

31. Nevins, *A Diary of Battle*, p. 259.

32. Warren, *The Declaration of Independence and War History: Bull Run to the Appomattox*, pp. 32–33.

33. *Ibid.*, pp. 33–34; Nathan Cooper to "Dear Wife," July 12, 1863, Warren County Historical Society Collection.

34. Pfanz, "The Gettysburg Campaign After Pickett's Charge," pp. 123–124.

35. Nathan Cooper to "Dear Wife," July 12, 1863, Warren County Historical Society Collection.

36. Nevins, *A Diary of Battle*, p. 260.

37. Pfanz, "The Gettysburg Campaign After Pickett's

Charge," p. 124; Coddington, *The Gettysburg Campaign*, pp. 570–571.

38. Nevins, *A Diary of Battle*, pp. 261–262.

39. Bates, *History of Pennsylvania Volunteers*, Vol. 4, p. 681; William J. Miller, *The Training of an Army: Camp Curtin and the North's Civil War* (Shippensburg, Pa.: White Mane, 1990), p. 265.

40. Pension Records of Charles Ammarell and George W. Briggs, NA; Inscription on Tombstone of Benjamin Naugle, Richfield Union Cemetery, Richfield, Pa.

Chapter 6

1. J. Howard Wert, "In the Hospitals of Gettysburg, July 1863," *Harrisburg Telegraph*, Harrisburg, Pa., July 2, 1907. Professor John Howard Wert was a well-known writer, educator, and Civil War veteran. In 1863, he was twenty-two years old and resided with his parents on a farm located south of Gettysburg along the Baltimore Pike. The Wert farmstead was used as a field hospital, and J. Howard witnessed firsthand the ravages of war. During the battle, he served as a scout for Union officers and later enlisted in the 209th Pennsylvania Infantry. Wert wrote a number of articles and books on Gettysburg and Adams County history before his death in 1920. Obituary of John Howard Wert, courtesy of G. Craig Caba, curator, Wert Gettysburg Collection; Coco, *A Vast Sea of Misery*, pp. 78–79.

2. Correspondence of the *Star and Chronicle*, Hereford, Maryland, July 9, 1863, in *Union County Star and Lewisburg Chronicle*, July 21, 1863.

3. Coco, *A Strange and Blighted Land*, p. 153.

4. Busey and Martin, *Regimental Strengths and Losses at Gettysburg*, p. 266.

5. Biographical Sketch of Amos C. Blakeslee, George McFarland Papers, PSA; Dreese, *An Imperishable Fame*, p. 59; *Muster Rolls of the 151st Pennsylvania Volunteers*, PSA.

6. Biographical Sketch of Warren J. Underwood, George McFarland Papers, PSA; Peter Hayward to "Mr. Editor," December 17, 1862, printed in the January 6, 1863, edition of the *Montrose Democrat*.

7. Biographical Sketch of Jonas Kauffman, George McFarland Papers, PSA.

8. Military Service Records of George Shivery, NA.

9. Coco, *A Strange and Blighted Land*, pp. 189–191.

10. Affidavit of George Decker in Pension File of Lafayette Westbrook, NA; Coco, *A Strange and Blighted Land*, p. 158.

11. *OR*, Vol. 27, Part 1, p. 329.

12. Dreese, *An Imperishable Fame*, p. 143.

13. George McFarland, "After the Battle: An Hour in the Hospital," George McFarland Papers, PSA.

14. Dreese, *An Imperishable Fame*, pp. 139–140.

15. Hoffman was promoted to captain on July 4, 1863. He was paroled by the Confederates, and by July 13th was at his home in Shaefferstown, Lebanon County, recuperating from his wounds. The projectile that lodged in his right hip greatly limited the flexibility of the joint, and he could not bear any weight on his right leg. As a consequence of his severe medical condition, Hoffman was honorably discharged from the service on November 21, 1863. Jeremiah took up the study of law and was admitted to practice in the several courts of Lebanon County on January 4, 1866. In 1865, Hoffman ran as the Democratic candidate for county treasurer, and in 1866 for State Senator, but he met with defeat in a strongly Republican district. Tragically, Hoffman died July 29, 1867, from the injuries he sustained after being thrown out of a carriage. Pension and Military Service Records of Jeremiah Hoffman, NA; *Franklin and Marshall College Obituary Record* (Lancaster, Pa.: The Franklin and Marshall College Alumni Association, 1900), pp. 199–200.

16. Dreese, *An Imperishable Fame*, p. 140–141. Cummins died on the morning of July 2, while Tucker passed away early on July 5.

17. Busey, *These Honored Dead*, pp. 298–299.

18. John B. Linn, "A Tourist at Gettysburg," *Civil War Times Illustrated* (September/October 1990), p. 62; Busey, *These Honored Dead*, p. 295.

19. Dreese, *An Imperishable Fame*, pp. 139, 142, 145, 146.

20. Pension File of George McFarland, NA.

21. Jeffrey B. Roth, "Civil War Medicine at Gettysburg," *The Gettysburg Hospital Quarterly* (Spring 1985), p. 3; Coco, *A Strange and Blighted Land*, pp. 163–164.

22. Surgeon's Certificate of Amos C. Blakeslee, Pension File of George McFarland, NA.

23. J. Howard Wert, "Little Stories of Gettysburg," *Gettysburg Compiler*, December 24, 1907, J. Howard Wert File, Adams County Historical Society, Gettysburg, Pa.

24. According to the 1860 census report, Elizabeth resided with her elderly parents, George and Mary; a twelve-year-old boy named Lester Burket; and John Roy, a carpentry apprentice. 1860 Census Report, Gettysburg, Pa., Adams County Historical Society, Gettysburg, Pa.

25. Joseph K. Barnes, ed., *The Medical and Surgical History of the War of the Rebellion, 1861–1865* (Washington, D.C.: Government Printing Office, 1870; reprint, Wilmington, N.C.: Broadfoot, 1990–1991, 12 vol.), Vol. 7, p. 92.

26. Dreese, *An Imperishable Fame*, pp. 141–142.

27. *Ibid.*, pp. 142, 148, note 11.

28. E. F. Conklin, *Women at Gettysburg 1863* (Gettysburg: Thomas Publications, 1993), pp. 186–188; Frank Moore, *Women of the War; Their Heroism and Self-Sacrifice* (Hartford, Conn.: S. S. Scranton, 1867), p. 176.

29. Mrs. Ellen Harris to "My Dear Mrs. McFarland," July 4, 1863, George McFarland Papers, Dr. Charles Lloyd Eater, Jr., Collection.

30. Conklin, *Women at Gettysburg 1863*, p. 189; Moore, *Women of the War*, pp. 176–177.

31. Dreese, *An Imperishable Fame*, p. 143.

32. "The Life Story of 'Blind Mike' Link," *Reading Eagle*, July 12, 1899.

33. Pension Records of James Weida, NA; Roth, "Civil War Medicine at Gettysburg," p. 3.

34. Lydia Catherine Ziegler Clare, "A Gettysburg Girl's Story of the Great Battle," and Hugh M. Ziegler, "Reminiscence of Hugh M. Ziegler of the Battle of Gettysburg Which Occurred on the First, Second and Third Days of July, 1863," Adams County Historical Society, Gettysburg, Pa. Lydia was thirteen or fourteen years old at the time of the battle, and her account was written about 1900. Hugh set down his recollections in 1933. He was only ten years old in 1863. In the 1860 census, Emanuel was listed as a 26-year-old lace weaver with no real estate. Mary was 25 at the time of this report. Besides Lydia and Hugh, the other children living in the Seminary at the time of the battle were most likely: William C., Jacob L., and George E. 1860 Census Report, Gettysburg, Pa., Adams County Historical Society, Gettysburg, Pa.

35. Lydia Catherine Ziegler Clare, "A Gettysburg Girl's

Story of the Great Battle," Adams County Historical Society, Gettysburg, Pa.

36. Busey, *These Honored Dead*, pp. 297–299.

37. Hugh M. Ziegler, "Reminiscence of Hugh M. Ziegler of the Battle of Gettysburg Which Occurred on the First, Second and Third Days of July, 1863," and "Lincoln's Gettysburg Address," Adams County Historical Society, Gettysburg, Pa.

38. Sarah M. Broadhead, *The Diary of a Lady of Gettysburg, Pennsylvania, from June 15 to July 15, 1863* (Gettysburg, Pa.: Privately published, 1864), p. 17, copy in Adams County Historical Society Collection, Gettysburg, Pa. Sarah Broadhead was born December 11, 1831, and died in Rathmill, N.J., at the age of 78. At the time of the battle Sarah resided at 217 Chambersburg Street with her husband, Joseph, and her three-year old daughter, Mary. Clair P. Lyons, Letter to Adams County Historical Society, May 12, 1992, Sarah Broadhead File, Adams County Historical Society, Gettysburg, Pa.

39. Broadhead, *The Diary of a Lady*, pp. 18–20.

40. *Ibid.*, p. 40; J. Howard Wert, "In the Hospitals of Gettysburg," *Harrisburg Telegraph*, July 27, 1907.

41. *Union County Star and Lewisburg Chronicle*, July 10, 1863.

42. Broadhead, *The Diary of a Lady*, p. 23.

43. J. Howard Wert, "In the Hospitals of Gettysburg," *Harrisburg Telegraph*, July 25, 1907.

44. Dreese, *An Imperishable Fame*, pp. 143–144; Paul L. Roy, "Colonel McFarland's Diary Reveals War-School Career," *Gettysburg Times*, June 27, 1941.

45. Dreese, *An Imperishable Fame*, p. 144; Paul L. Roy, "Colonel McFarland's Diary Reveals War-School Career," *Gettysburg Times*, June 27, 1941; Pension Records of James Weida, NA.

46. Theodore Chase to Miss I. M. Penfield, July 9 and July 16, 1863, Warren County Historical Society Collection.

47. "Recollections of Visitations at Gettysburg After the Great Battle in July, 1863" by the Rev. F. J. F. Schantz, in Ralph S. Shay, ed., *Reflections on the Battle of Gettysburg* (The Lebanon County Historical Society, 1963), Vol. 13, no. 6, pp. 295, 297.

48. Coco, *A Strange and Blighted Land*, pp. 162–167.

49. Biographical Sketch of Henry Chancellor, Jr.; Mrs. Henry Chancellor to George McFarland, November 29, 1863, George McFarland Papers, PSA.

50. Barnes, *The Medical and Surgical History of the War of the Rebellion*, Vol. 10, p. 774; Busey, *These Honored Dead*, pp. 296, 299; Coco, *A Strange and Blighted Land*, p. 164.

51. William S. Whitney to "The M. E. High Priest and Companions of Mountain City N.R.A. Chapter, Pottsville, Pa.," November 2, 1863, Adams County Historical Society, Gettysburg, Pa.

52. Coco, *A Strange and Blighted Land*, p. 225.

53. Pension Records of Michael Link, NA; Barnes, *The Medical and Surgical History of the War of the Rebellion*, Vol. 7, p. 92; Simon J. Arnold to Mrs. Seiders, July 20, 1863, Sally Smith Collection; Dreese, *An Imperishable Fame*, p. 145.

54. Dreese, *An Imperishable Fame*, p. 144; Obituary of S. Brady Caveny, *Harrisburg Patriot*, 1926 Newspaper Clipping, Richard H. Frecon Collection.

55. Dreese, *An Imperishable Fame*, p. 145. Loughran was born on July 4, 1835, in Hamden, Delaware County, New York. He graduated from the Albany Medical College in the fall of 1857. In 1860, Robert was elected to the state legislature and served as chairman of the Committee on Medical Societies and Colleges. On the 14th of January 1861, Dr. Loughran was commissioned assistant surgeon of the 20th N.Y.S.M. for a three-month enlistment. When the regiment reentered the service for three years, Loughran was commissioned as surgeon. Biographical Sketch of Dr. Robert Loughran, George McFarland Papers, PSA.

Dr. Andrew Jackson Ward was born in New Milford, Susquehanna County, Pa., March 1, 1824. He was educated at the University of Pennsylvania, graduating with the class of 1846. Immediately afterward, he entered the army as an assistant surgeon during the Mexican War. After the war, Ward moved to Madison, Wisconsin, and set up a practice. However, his adventurous spirit also led him to St. Louis and California, where he participated in the Pikes Peak gold rush. He joined the 2nd Wisconsin in 1861. Biographical Sketch of Dr. Andrew J. Ward, George McFarland Papers, PSA.

56. Dr. Charles Horner was born in Gettysburg on May 5, 1824. A graduate of Pennsylvania College and the University of Pennsylvania, Charles started a successful practice in the office of his father, Dr. David Horner. The government engaged his services on July 23, 1863. He was known as "a young man of excellent ability and popular manners." Biographical Sketch of Dr. Charles Horner, George McFarland Papers, PSA; John B. Horner, *Essential to a Nation's Life: The Story of Dr. Charles and Robert Horner of Gettysburg* (Gettysburg: Horner Enterprises, 1997), p. 84.

Dr. Henry Huber was originally from Philadelphia and practiced medicine in Chicago before coming to Gettysburg in 1849. Here, he established a large practice and upon his death was remembered as "one of our most successful physicians, justly esteemed for his professional skill and eminent personal worth." Obituary of Henry Huber, *The Star and Sentinel*, October 22, 1873.

Nicholas Kizer served as a nurse for McFarland during his stay at the Seminary and also for a period after his return home to McAlisterville. Kizer mustered out with his company on June 24, 1865. Benjamin F. Carr was captured at the Battle of the Wilderness on May 6, 1864. He died on March 11, 1865, at Camp Parole, Annapolis, Maryland, a center for returning prisoners of war. Richard E. Matthews, *The 149th Pennsylvania Volunteer Infantry Unit in the Civil War* (Jefferson, N.C.: McFarland & Company, 1994), pp. 10, 215, 239, 250.

57. Dreese, *An Imperishable Fame*, p. 145.

58. *Ibid.*, pp. 146–148. Shortly after the building was relinquished as a hospital, the board of directors of the institution began planning to repair the damages sustained to the property during the battle. The board did not solicit any compensation from the government for these damages. Instead, the directors made a public appeal for funds and the sum of $4,210.69 was raised. Of this amount, $2,346.18 was used for the renovation of the Seminary building and grounds. The remainder was set aside for repairs at the Pennsylvania College. However, $660.50 was later awarded to the Seminary as compensation for occupancy of the buildings for hospital use.

President Samuel S. Schmucker reported: "The injury done to the property of the Institution is considerable.... The Seminary edifice was perforated by several balls, and large portions knocked out of the N. East gable corner.... The fences around all the fields as well as those along the Seminary Avenue were destroyed, many of the rails and boards incorporated with the breastwork, others broken and burned." Before the summer of 1864, all repairs were completed and classes were resumed. Report of the Chairman of the Faculty, August 11, 1863, and August 8, 1864, and Abstract of Meeting Minutes, Board of Directors, Gettysburg Seminary, dated August 11,

1863, and August 9, 1864, Lutheran Theological Seminary File, Adams County Historical Society, Gettysburg, Pa. A copy of the appeal for funds appeared in the July 27, 1863, issue of the *Gettysburg Compiler* and the August 7, 1863, issue of the *Lutheran Observer*. For a detailed history of the Lutheran Theological Seminary see Abdel Ross Wentz, *Gettysburg Lutheran Theological Seminary, Vol. 1, History, 1826–1895* (Harrisburg, Pa.: Evangelical Press, 1965).

59. Coco, *A Vast Sea of Misery*, p. 20; W. C. Storrick, *Gettysburg: The Place, The Battles, The Outcome* (Harrisburg, Pa.: J. Horace McFarland, 1932), p. 149.

60. Potts, "A First Defender in Rebel Prisons," p. 343.

61. Pension Records of Frank Lyon, NA; James Miller to "Dear Brother," July 6, 1863 and to "Dear Sister," August 2, 1863, Schoff Civil War Collection, William L. Clements Library, University of Michigan.

62. Pension Records of Frank Lyon, NA; Frank Lyon to Theodore Putnam, November 23, 1862, Warren County Historical Society Collection, Warren, Pa.

63. Coco, *A Vast Sea of Misery*, p. 20; Martha Ehler, The Patriot Daughters of Lancaster, *Hospital Scenes After the Battle of Gettysburg, July 1863* (Philadelphia: Henry B. Ashmead, Book and Job Printer, 1864; reprint, Gettysburg: G. Craig Caba, 1993), p. 25.

64. Coco, *A Vast Sea of Misery*, p. 20.

65. *Ibid.*, pp. 20–21.

66. Martha Ehler, The Patriot Daughters of Lancaster, *Hospital Scenes After the Battle of Gettysburg*, pp. 23–24.

67. *Ibid.*, pp. 24–28.

68. Coco, *A Vast Sea of Misery*, p. 20.

69. Horner, *Essential to a Nation's Life*, pp. 40–41.

70. Henry S. Huidekoper, *Historic Church and Hospital on the Battlefield of Gettysburg*, copy of pamphlet in Gettysburg National Military Park Library.

71. Rodgers, *The Ties of the Past*, pp. 19, 150, 152.

72. *Ibid.*, pp. 152, 154–157. The dying soldier Sallie encountered just inside the church was Sergeant Alexander Stewart of the 149th Pennsylvania. Later, Sallie married Henry F. Stewart, Alexander's younger brother.

73. Conklin, *Women at Gettysburg 1863*, pp. 212, 213–214. The order from Emmitsburg numbered at least 232 sisters. These women served in hospitals throughout the North and South both during and after the war.

74. J. R. Balsley, "A Gettysburg Reminiscence," *National Tribune*, May 19, 1898.

75. Nelson Reaser to "Dear Father," July 18, 1863, Pension Records of Nelson Reaser, NA. Private Joseph A. Brickley escaped the battle unscathed. Private Levi Losey was wounded on July 1, but he mustered out with his company on July 27, 1863. As mentioned previously, George Decker served in the ambulance corps during the battle.

76. Busey, *These Honored Dead*, p. 298.

77. Pension Records of Albert Yost and Solomon Strause, NA.

78. Biographical Sketch of Dr. James Fulton, George McFarland Papers, PSA.

79. Linn, "A Tourist at Gettysburg," p. 59. In a footnote to his biographical sketch, McFarland wrote, "At Culpepper [*sic*] early in 1864 Surg. Fulton was ordered before a medical examining board together with Asst. Surg. Scott to stand an examination. Feeling assured that this order was intended to kill them, Drs. F. & S. refused to appear and handed in their resignations. Upon this both were dishonorably discharged. The sec. of war, however, when the facts were made known to him, issued an order removing the *dis* and honorably discharged them."

Dr. Fulton eventually married and had two daughters. Fulton ended his days as a complete invalid. At age 78, he was blind and helpless, suffering with dementia. Rodgers, *The Ties of the Past*, p. 174.

80. Coco, *A Vast Sea of Misery*, pp. 17–18.

81. Coco, *A Strange and Blighted Land*, p. 190.

82. *Ibid.*, pp. 191, 193; Coco, *A Vast Sea of Misery*, pp. 84, 88.

83. Walker, *Appointment at Gettysburg*, p. 90.

84. "The Diary of Alfred D. Staudt," p. 16.

85. Pension Records of Solomon Strause, NA.

86. Samuel T. Allen to George McFarland, undated letter, George McFarland Papers, PSA; Pension Records of John T. Strause, NA; Coco, *A Vast Sea of Misery*, p. 63.

87. Busey, *These Honored Dead*, pp. 296, 300.

88. Coco, *A Strange and Blighted Land*, p. 225.

89. *Adams Sentinel and General Advertiser*, Gettysburg, Pa., July 21, 1863.

90. Coco, *A Strange and Blighted Land*, p. 225; J. Howard Wert, "In the Hospitals of Gettysburg, July 1863," *Harrisburg Telegraph*, August 16, 1907.

91. Walker, *Appointment at Gettysburg*, p. 91; "The Diary of Alfred D. Staudt," p. 16.

92. Pension Records of Thomas Moyer, NA.

93. Walker, *Appointment at Gettysburg*, p. 92.

94. Pension Records of Thomas Moyer, NA.

95. Walker, *Appointment at Gettysburg*, p. 90; "The Diary of Alfred D. Staudt," p. 16.

96. Pension Records of Lewis Rentschler, NA.

97. Excerpt from Rentschler Family History compiled by Annette Friedberg, 1990–1993. The author wishes to express his heartfelt gratitude to Robert Carichner of Hughesville, Pa., for providing him with a copy of this fascinating account. Dr. Henry Diehl Rentschler was in his early 20s at the time of the battle. He died in 1921.

98. Barnes, *The Medical and Surgical History of the War of the Rebellion*, Vol. 8, p. 481.

99. Busey, *These Honored Dead*, p. 295.

100. Barnes, *The Medical and Surgical History of the War of the Rebellion*, Vol. 9, p. 214.

101. *Ibid.*, Vol. 5, pp. 394–395.

102. Frank H. Taylor, *Philadelphia in the Civil War, 1861–1865* (Philadelphia: Dunlap, 1913), p. 226.

103. *Ibid.*, p. 224.

104. Boatner, *The Civil War Dictionary*, p. 476.

105. Taylor, *Philadelphia in the Civil War*, pp. 224, 226–227.

106. *Ibid.*, pp. 230–231.

107. "The Diary of Alfred D. Staudt," p. 16; Walker, *Appointment at Gettysburg*, p. 90.

108. Taylor, *Philadelphia in the Civil War*, pp. 226–227.

109. Walker, *Appointment at Gettysburg*, pp. 90–91.

110. Taylor, *Philadelphia in the Civil War*, pp. 234–235.

111. Busey, *These Honored Dead*, pp. 299–300.

112. Taylor, *Philadelphia in the Civil War*, p. 228.

113. Busey, *These Honored Dead*, pp. 297–299.

114. Taylor, *Philadelphia in the Civil War*, p. 228.

115. Barnes, *The Medical and Surgical History of the War of the Rebellion*, Vol. 3, p. 92.

116. Pension Records of Davis Meredith and Solomon Strause, NA.

117. "The Diary of Alfred D. Staudt," p. 33.

118. Wert, "In the Hospitals of Gettysburg, July 1863," *Harrisburg Telegraph*, August 16, 1907.

119. Barnes, *The Medical and Surgical History of the War of the Rebellion*, Vol. 8, p. 523; Busey, *These Honored Dead*, p. 297.

120. Robert Miller to "Dear Brother," July 18, 1863, Schoff Civil War Collection, William L. Clements Library, University of Michigan.

121. Pension Records of George Stone, NA.

122. Pension Records of Franklin Weaber, NA.

123. Dr. Walter L. Powell, ed., *Camp Letterman: The Lost Legacy of Gettysburg's Hospital Woods* (Gettysburg: The Gettysburg Battlefield Preservation Association, 1997), p. 5.

124. Coco, *A Vast Sea of Misery*, p. 167; Powell, *Camp Letterman*, pp. 5–6; Coco, *A Strange and Blighted Land*, p. 227.

125. Powell, *Camp Letterman*, p. 6.

126. Coco, *A Strange and Blighted Land*, p. 230.

127. Powell, *Camp Letterman*, pp. 6–7.

128. *Ibid.*, p. 7.

129. *Adams Sentinel*, Gettysburg, Pa., August 17, 1863.

130. Busey, *These Honored Dead*, p. 299; Transcript of 1863 Diary of Salome Myers, Adams County Historical Society Collection, Gettysburg, Pa.; Joe Smith, M.D. to Author, September 5, 1998,

131. Busey, *These Honored Dead*, p. 298.

132. Coco, *A Strange and Blighted Land*, p. 236. The figure for the number of deaths at Camp Letterman was taken from the roster of Confederate dead at the camp compiled by Kathy George Harrison, Historian, Gettysburg National Military Park, and from John W. Busey, *These Honored Dead: The Union Casualties at Gettysburg*. A compilation of these lists, arranged by state, appears in the Gettysburg Battlefield Preservation Association's publication on Camp Letterman which has been cited above. Interestingly, the deaths were nearly equal between the opposing armies: 153 Union deaths as compared to 146 suffered by the Confederates. The November 16, 1863, issue of the Gettysburg *Compiler* stated that a total of 381 men died at this hospital.

Sadly, the Camp Letterman site is not located within the bounds of the Gettysburg National Military Park, and as of this writing (February 1999), it is currently threatened by development. A large area along both sides of the York Pike (U.S. Route 30) just outside of the borough has fallen prey to classic strip development. The Association is trying to acquire a small portion of the tract.

133. Busey, *These Honored Dead*, p. 296.

134. Coco, *A Strange and Blighted Land*, p. 306.

135. Note accompanying letter from Frank Lyon to Theodore Putnam, November 23, 1862, Warren County Historical Society Collection, Warren, Pa.; Tombstone Inscription, Nailor Family Plot at East Salem U. B. Church Cemetery.

136. Michael A. Dreese, "The Saga of Andrew Gregg Tucker," *Bucknell World*, Vol. 26, No. 6 (November 1998), p. 21.

137. *Revised Report of the Select Committee Relative to the Soldier's National Cemetery, Together with the Accompanying Documents, as Reported to the House of Representatives of the Commonwealth of Pennsylvania* (Harrisburg, Pa.: Singerly & Myers, 1865), pp. 20, 24–25, 29, 32–33. The final cost of the cemetery exceeded $80,000. Altogether 3,354 reinterments were completed here, of which 1,664 were unknown by name, and 979 were unknown by both name and state. Coco, *A Strange and Blighted Land*, p. 122. It is likely that the remains of many soldiers who served in the 151st now rest under these

unknown plots considering the decomposed condition of the dead later recovered from the first day's field of battle.

138. Coco, *a Strange and Blighted Land*, p. 122.

Chapter 7

1. Coco, *A Strange and Blighted Land*, p. 256; Coddington, *The Gettysburg Campaign*, p. 309.

2. Potts, "A First Defender in Rebel Prison Pens," p. 343.

3. Lonnie R. Speer, *Portals to Hell: Military Prisons of the Civil War* (Mechanicsburg, Pa.: Stackpole, 1997), pp. 4, 104. After it was discovered that numerous Union soldiers were allowing themselves to be captured in order to go home, Federal officials established parole camps.

4. *Ibid.*, pp. 9–13.

5. *Ibid.*, pp. 98, 101–103.

6. Robert H. Kellogg, *Life and Death in Rebel Prisons* (Hartford, Conn.: L. Stebbins, 1865), p. 360.

7. Speer, *Portals to Hell*, pp. 100, 102; Boatner, *The Civil War Dictionary*, p. 270.

8. Speer, *Portals to Hell*, pp. 103–105.

9. Coco, *A Strange and Blighted Land*, p. 258.

10. Frederick Trautmann, ed., *Twenty Months in Captivity: Memoirs of a Union Officer in Confederate Prisons* (Cranbury, N.J.: Fairleigh Dickinson University Press, 1987), p. 28. Prior to his enlistment in the Union army, Domschcke was an editor of German newspapers in Milwaukee. He became a captain in the all–German 26th Wisconsin to fight the slavery that he so hated. His account is one of the most complete, most balanced, and most authoritative Union memoirs of prison life. At Gettysburg, the 26th suffered 217 casualties from an engaged strength of 443 officers and men. Busey and Martin, *Regimental Strengths and Losses at Gettysburg*, p. 255.

11. Potts, "A First Defender in Rebel Prison Pens," p. 343; Trautmann, *Twenty Months in Captivity*, p. 29.

12. Potts, "A First Defender in Rebel Prison Pens," p. 344.

13. Trautmann, *Twenty Months in Captivity*, pp. 28–29, 135.

14. Coco, *A Strange and Blighted Land*, p. 259.

15. Edward A. Ross to Theodore B. Gates, July 6, 1863, Seward R. Osborne Collection.

16. Coco, *A Strange and Blighted Land*, p. 295; Potts, "A First Defender in Rebel Prison Pens," p. 344; Trautmann, *Twenty Months in Captivity*, p. 29.

17. Trautmann, *Twenty Months in Captivity*, p. 29.

18. *Ibid.*, pp. 29–30.

19. Potts, "A First Defender in Rebel Prison Pens," p. 344; William Gray to George McFarland, April 26, 1865, George McFarland Papers, PSA.

20. Potts, "A First Defender in Rebel Prison Pens," p. 344; Trautmann, *Twenty Months in Captivity*, p. 31.

21. OR, Vol. 27, Part 3, p. 514; Coddington, *The Gettysburg Campaign*, p. 541.

22. Trautmann, *Twenty Months in Captivity*, pp. 32–33; Chamberlin, *History of the One Hundred and Fiftieth Regiment Pennsylvania Volunteers*, p. 308.

23. Potts, "A First Defender in Rebel Prison Pens," pp. 344–345.

24. John W. Schildt, *Roads from Gettysburg* (Chewsville, Md.: John W. Schildt, 1979), pp. 43, 76, 79.

25. Trautmann, *Twenty Months in Captivity*, p. 33; Chamberlin, *History of the One Hundred and Fiftieth Regiment Pennsylvania Volunteers*, p. 308.

26. Trautmann, *Twenty Months in Captivity*, pp. 33–34; Chamberlin, *History of the One Hundred and Fiftieth Regiment Pennsylvania Volunteers*, p. 308.

27. Potts, "A First Defender in Rebel Prison Pens," p. 345.

28. Stewart Sifakis, *Who Was Who in the Civil War, Vol. 2* (New York: Facts On File, 1988), p. 140; Boatner, *The Civil War Dictionary*, p. 423; Coddington, *The Gettysburg Campaign*, pp. 17, 535.

29. Coco, *A Strange and Blighted Land*, p. 297.

30. Trautmann, *Twenty Months in Captivity*, p. 34.

31. Jerry W. Holsworth, "Quiet Courage: The Story of Winchester, Va., in the Civil War," *Blue & Gray* (December 1997), p. 7.

32. Trautmann, *Twenty Months in Captivity*, pp. 34–35; William Gray to George McFarland, April 26, 1865, George McFarland Papers, PSA.

33. Trautmann, *Twenty Months in Captivity*, p. 35.

34. *Ibid.*, pp. 35–36; Chamberlin, *History of the One Hundred and Fiftieth Regiment Pennsylvania Volunteers*, pp. 308–309.

35. Coco, *A Strange and Blighted Land*, pp. 298–299.

36. Trautmann, *Twenty Months in Captivity*, p. 36. Conversely, if a prison was located in a rural area, the transports usually arrived at night, which allowed for more control over the disoriented prisoners. Speer, *Portals to Hell*, p. 55.

37. Speer, *Portals to Hell*, pp. 89–90, 92. The main reason for separating enlisted men and officers originated from the belief that higher ranking prisoners deserved better quarters, increased privileges, and preferential treatment. It was also hoped that such arrangements would deprive the enlisted men of the leadership required to organize an escape. *Ibid.*, p. 59.

38. Kellogg, *Life and Death in Rebel Prisons*, pp. 364–365.

39. Speer, *Portals to Hell*, p. 90.

40. Trautmann, *Twenty Months in Captivity*, p. 38.

41. Kellogg, *Life and Death in Rebel Prisons*, p. 364.

42. Most of Streight's two–thousand man command was mounted on mules during the expedition. Colonel Streight was tricked into surrendering to a force almost three times smaller than his own. See Edward D. Longacre, *Mounted Raids of the Civil War* (Lincoln: University of Nebraska Press, 1994), pp. 66–90.

43. Trautmann, *Twenty Months in Captivity*, p. 37; Potts, "A First Defender in Rebel Prison Pens," p. 345.

44. William Gray to George McFarland, April 26, 1865, George McFarland Papers, PSA.

45. Speer, *Portals to Hell*, pp. 90–91; Trautmann, *Twenty Months in Captivity*, p. 149, note 9.

46. Speer, *Portals to Hell*, p. 90.

47. William Gray to George McFarland, April 26, 1865, George McFarland Papers, PSA.

48. Kellogg, *Life and Death in Rebel Prisons*, pp. 358–359.

49. Potts, "A First Defender in Rebel Prison Pens," p. 345.

50. Speer, *Portals to Hell*, p. 123; Trautmann, *Twenty Months in Captivity*, p. 38.

51. Potts, "A First Defender in Rebel Prison Pens," pp. 345–346; Trautmann, *Twenty Months in Captivity*, p. 39.

52. Trautmann, *Twenty Months in Captivity*, pp. 38, 40.

53. *Ibid.*, pp. 40–41, 47.

54. Potts, "A First Defender in Rebel Prison Pens," p. 346.

55. William Boltz to "Dear Wife and Children," July 27, 1863, Pension Records of William Boltz, NA.

56. Potts, "A First Defender in Rebel Prison Pens," p. 346.

57. Trautmann, *Twenty Months in Captivity*, pp. 43–44.

58. Speer, *Portals to Hell*, pp. 123–124; Trautmann, *Twenty Months in Captivity*, pp. 44–45, 57; Frederic F. Cavada, *Libby Life: Experiences of a Prisoner of War in Richmond, Va., 1863–64* (Philadelphia: King & Baird, 1864), p. 36.

59. Speer, *Portals to Hell*, p. 63.

60. Pension Records of William Gray, NA.

61. Trautmann, *Twenty Months in Captivity*, p. 49; Cavada, *Libby Life*, p. 128.

62. Trautmann, *Twenty Months in Captivity*, pp. 49–51, 55.

63. *Ibid.*, p. 56. At least ten Gettysburg civilians, mostly U.S. Government representatives, such as local postmasters, were marched south into captivity. These individuals eventually ended up at a holding camp in Salisbury, North Carolina. William Harper died during his confinement at Salisbury and George Codori died of pneumonia three days after his return in March 1865. Coco, *A Strange and Blighted Land*, pp. 257, 397–398, note 5.

64. Potts, "A First Defender in Rebel Prison Pens," p. 346; Trautmann, *Twenty Months in Captivity*, p. 51.

65. William Gray to George McFarland, April 26, 1865, George McFarland Papers, PSA; Pension Records of William Gray, NA.

66. Trautmann, *Twenty Months in Captivity*, p. 149, note 6.

67. William Boltz to "My Dear Wife," October 10, 1863, Pension Records of William Boltz, NA.

68. Trautmann, *Twenty Months in Captivity*, p. 52.

69. William Boltz to "My Dear Wife," December 2, 1863, and January 26, 1864, Pension Records of William Boltz, NA.

70. Trautmann, *Twenty Months in Captivity*, p. 53; Potts, "A First Defender in Rebel Prison Pens," p. 346.

71. Trautmann, *Twenty Months in Captivity*, p. 59.

72. Potts, "A First Defender in Rebel Prison Pens," p. 346.

73. Trautmann, *Twenty Months in Captivity*, p. 56.

74. Kellogg, *Life and Death in Rebel Prisons*, pp. 360, 366.

75. Speer, *Portals to Hell*, pp. 57, 122–123.

76. *Ibid.*, pp. 121–122.

77. At the time of his enlistment, Isaac Derr was 24 years old and listed his occupation as a carpenter. Stupp, a farmer, was four years younger. Young Ezra was plagued with misfortune throughout his brief service. Stricken with typhoid during the regiment's organization at Harrisburg, he was absent on a furlough from the end of November 1862 to near the end of February 1863. He rejoined his unit near Fredericksburg against the advice of his physician. During the march to Gettysburg, he fell ill once again.

There is conflicting evidence as to where the two men were captured. The company muster out roll lists both men as missing since June 25, 1863, on the march between Poolesville and Jefferson, Maryland. Indeed, Stupp later testified that he received permission from Lieutenant Yost to fall out of line during the march north. In a letter to his wife penned from Libby Prison in late July 1863, Captain Boltz stated that the two men were taken near Emmitsburg. Meanwhile, prisoner of war records indicate that Stupp and Derr were captured at Gettysburg on July 1st! Neither soldier specified where he was captured in his application for an invalid pension.

Stupp received a $35 monthly pension from the government for rheumatism and "soreness of the breast," which he attributed to his confinement at Belle Isle. Conversely, Derr applied for an invalid pension based on the injuries he sustained when his team of horses bolted away from him on a steep mountainside. Derr was thrown from a wagon during the incident. *Muster Rolls of the 151st Pennsylvania Volunteers*, PSA; William Boltz to "Dear Wife and Children," July 27, 1863,

Pension Records of William Boltz, NA; Pension Records of Isaac K. Derr and Ezra Stupp, NA.

On September 21, 1863, Private Frank Elvidge of the 150th Pennsylvania recorded in his diary that 720 prisoners left Belle Isle for City Point. A week later, Elvidge and about 400 others were paroled for release. Chamberlin, *History of the One Hundred and Fiftieth Regiment Pennsylvania Volunteers*, p. 311.

78. Trautmann, *Twenty Months in Captivity*, p. 49.

79. William Boltz to "My Dear Wife," January 26, 1864, Pension Records of William Boltz, NA.

80. Speer, *Portals to Hell*, pp. 231–233; Trautmann, *Twenty Months in Captivity*, pp. 62–66; Potts, "A First Defender in Rebel Prison Pens," pp. 346–347. As the senior officer involved with the tunnel project, Colonel Abdel Streight was given the honor of being the first to escape. He made it safely to Union lines. Colonel Rose was exchanged in July 1864 and went on to fight in the battles of Franklin and Nashville. He continued to serve in the military until 1894. Boatner, *The Civil War Dictionary*, p. 708.

81. Trautmann, *Twenty Months in Captivity*, pp. 67–68.

82. Longacre, *Mounted Raids of the Civil War*, pp. 225–257; Speer, *Portals to Hell*, p. 206. The scheme was masterminded by General Judson Kilpatrick who led nearly 3,600 cavalrymen during the expedition. Colonel Ulric Dahlgren led 500 additional troopers in support of Kilpatrick. On March 1, Dahlgren rode into a night ambush and was killed, while nearly 100 of his men were captured. The operation cost the Federals 340 men, 583 horses, and a large amount of equipment and accouterments. Boatner, *The Civil War Dictionary*, pp. 460–461.

83. Trautmann, *Twenty Months in Captivity*, p. 71.

84. Military Service Records of William Boltz, NA; William Boltz to "My Dear Wife," October 10, 1863, Pension Records of William Boltz, NA.

85. Trautmann, *Twenty Months in Captivity*, pp. 71–73.

86. Potts, "A First Defender in Rebel Prison Pens," p. 347.

87. Trautmann, *Twenty Months in Captivity*, p. 74.

88. *Ibid.*, pp. 74–75. Libby's notoriety survived the war. In 1889, the building was dismantled and reerected in Chicago by a group of Northern investors. Known as the "Libby Prison War Museum," the structure became a popular tourist attraction, but interest diminished with the coming of the Chicago World's Fair in 1893. By 1895, the museum was out of business, and four years later, the directors voted to tear down the building. Speer, *Portals to Hell*, p. 302.

89. Speer, *Portals to Hell*, pp. 126–128; Trautmann, *Twenty Months in Captivity*, 75–77.

90. Trautmann, *Twenty Months in Captivity*, pp. 78–79; Potts, "A First Defender in Rebel Prison Pens," p. 347.

91. Trautmann, *Twenty Months in Captivity*, pp. 79–90; Potts, "A First Defender in Rebel Prison Pens," pp. 347–348.

92. William Gray to George McFarland, April 26, 1865, George McFarland Papers, PSA.

93. Pension Records of William Gray, NA.

94. Trautmann, *Twenty Months in Captivity*, pp. 86–87, 90. From July 26th to July 31st, General George Stoneman led two divisions of cavalry on an expedition to destroy the railroad between Atlanta and Macon. Stoneman was granted permission to raid Macon and liberate the prisoners being held there and at nearby Andersonville after he completed his primary mission. Stoneman reached the outskirts of Macon on July 30th, but discovered that it was guarded by state militia troops. While he was attempting to circle south of the city, he

was cut off and surrounded by enemy cavalry. Stoneman and 700 of his men were captured while trying to extricate themselves from the trap. Boatner, *The Civil War Dictionary*, pp. 801–802.

95. Trautmann, *Twenty Months in Captivity*, pp. 98–100; Speer, *Portals to Hell*, pp. 213, 268; Chamberlin, *History of the One Hundred and Fiftieth Regiment Pennsylvania Volunteers*, p. 313.

96. Potts, "A First Defender in Rebel Prison Pens," p. 348.

97. Trautmann, *Twenty Months in Captivity*, p. 102; Speer, *Portals to Hell*, pp. 213–214.

98. Trautmann, *Twenty Months in Captivity*, p. 103; Potts, "A First Defender in Rebel Prison Pens," p. 348.

99. Trautmann, *Twenty Months in Captivity*, p. 103.

100. Potts, "A First Defender in Rebel Prison Pens," p. 349.

101. Speer, *Portals to Hell*, p. 214.

102. Potts, "A First Defender in Rebel Prison Pens," pp. 348–349.

103. Chamberlin, *History of the One Hundred and Fiftieth Regiment Pennsylvania Volunteers*, p. 312.

104. Trautmann, *Twenty Months in Captivity*, p. 104. Despite repeated Union efforts to capture the city, the Confederate garrison at Charleston held out until February 17, 1865. When Sherman passed west of the city during his northward march, he cut off its communications with the interior and rendered its further occupation useless. Faust, *Historical Times Illustrated Encyclopedia of the Civil War*, p. 131.

105. Trautmann, *Twenty Months in Captivity*, p. 105; Potts, "A First Defender in Rebel Prison Pens," p. 349; Chamberlin, *History of the One Hundred and Fiftieth Regiment Pennsylvania Volunteers*, pp. 314–315.

106. Trautmann, *Twenty Months in Captivity*, pp. 106–108; Speer, *Portals to Hell*, p. 270–271; Potts, "A First Defender in Rebel Prison Pens," pp. 349–350.

107. Trautmann, *Twenty Months in Captivity*, p. 108.

108. Speer, *Portals to Hell*, p. 271.

109. Trautmann, *Twenty Months in Captivity*, pp. 109–110.

110. William Gray to George McFarland, April 26, 1865, George McFarland Papers, PSA.

111. Speer, *Portals to Hell*, p. 272; Trautmann, *Twenty Months in Captivity*, pp. 110–112; William Gray to George McFarland, April 26, 1865, George McFarland Papers, PSA; Chamberlin, *History of the One Hundred and Fiftieth Regiment Pennsylvania Volunteers*, p. 316. Domschcke identified two of the shooting victims: Lieutenant Alvin Young, 4th Pennsylvania Cavalry, and a Lieutenant Turbane of the 66th New York.

112. Speer, *Portals to Hell*, p. 272.

113. Trautmann, *Twenty Months in Captivity*, p. 113.

114. *Ibid.*, pp. 113–114; Potts, "A First Defender in Rebel Prison Pens," p. 350.

115. Chamberlin, *History of the One Hundred and Fiftieth Regiment Pennsylvania Volunteers*, p. 315; Trautmann, *Twenty Months in Captivity*, pp. 114–116; Potts, "A First Defender in Rebel Prison Pens," p. 350.

116. Potts, "A First Defender in Rebel Prison Pens," pp. 350–351.

117. Trautmann, *Twenty Months in Captivity*, p. 119; Potts, "A First Defender in Rebel Prison Pens," p. 351; Chamberlin, *History of the One Hundred and Fiftieth Regiment Pennsylvania Volunteers*, p. 317.

118. William Gray to George McFarland, April 26, 1865, George McFarland Papers, PSA; Chamberlin, *History of the One Hundred and Fiftieth Regiment Pennsylvania Volunteers*, p. 317.

119. Potts, "A First Defender in Rebel Prison Pens," p. 352.

120. *Ibid.*; Pension Records of William Gray, NA.

121. Potts, "A First Defender in Rebel Prison Pens," p. 352.

122. Pension Records of Charles Potts, NA.

Epilogue

1. George B. McClellan to "Soldiers of the Army of the Potomac," March 14, 1862, original leaflet in author's collection.

2. *Muster Rolls of the 151st Pennsylvania Volunteers*, PSA.

3. J. S. Schenck, ed., *History of Warren County, Pennsylvania* (Syracuse, N. Y.: D. Mason & Co., 1887), pp. 295, 315, 683; W. F. Clinger, "Old English Family Famed in Chivalry Fades out in Warren," *Stepping Stones*, Warren County Historical Society, Vol. 12, No. 2 (May 1968), p. 348; Pension Records of Harrison Allen, NA; Sifakis, *Who Was Who in the Civil War, Vol. 1*, p. 80.

4. Schenck, *History of Warren County, Pennsylvania*, pp. 295, 315, 683–685; Pension Records of Samuel Allen, NA.

5. Dreese, *An Imperishable Fame*, pp. 10–16; newspaper clipping, *Juniata Sentinel and Republican*, May 11, 1881, Juniata County Historical Society, Mifflintown, Pa.; George McFarland, Final Report as Superintendent of Soldiers' Orphans, May 1871, George McFarland Papers, PSA.

6. Pension Records of John W. Young, NA; *Annual Report of the Pennsylvania Commission of Soldiers' Orphan Schools for the Year Ending May 31, 1902* (Harrisburg, Pa.: Wm. Stanley Ray, 1902), pp. 70–71.

7. Mary Haney Arnold to Author, March 31, 1998, and April 8, 1998; Simon Arnold to "My darling wife," November 27, 1882, Mary H. Arnold Collection; Letter of Recommendation from A. C. Bird, General Agent, Toledo, Wabash, & Western Railway, January 31, 1876, Mary H. Arnold Collection; Obituary of Simon J. Arnold, *St. Louis Globe Democrat*, July 26, 1889; Julian S. Rammelkamp, *Pulitzer's Post-Dispatch 1878–1883* (Princeton, N.J.: Princeton University Press, 1967), pp. 1–3; Pension Records of Simon Arnold, NA.

8. Stocker, *Centennial History of Susquehanna County, Pennsylvania*, p. 168.

9. *Ibid.*, p. 360; New Milford Township and Borough Historical Committee, *A New History of New Milford* (New Milford, Pa.: Campbell, 1959), p. 30-s; Pension Records of George Stone, NA.

10. Pension Records of Amos Tucker, NA.

11. Pension Records of Lafayette Westbrook, NA.

12. Pension Records of John Vincent, NA.

13. Kellogg Family History and Genealogy compiled by Robert Kellogg Crane, Williston, Tennessee; Robert Crane to author, January 31, 1999; Robert Crane, "Family Matters: Stephen Crane's Brother, Wilbur," A Talk Given Before the Stephen Crane Society at the Annual Meeting of the American Literature Association, San Diego, Calif., May 29, 1992; Stephen W. Sears, *Chancellorsville* (New York: Houghton Mifflin, 1996), pp. 509–511. Robert Kellogg Crane is the great-grandson of Robert Kellogg and the great-nephew of Stephen Crane.

14. Pension Records of Randal Sayre, NA.

15. Eric Michael to Author, January 6, 1999; Pension Records of William Michael, NA; *Annual Report of the Pennsylvania Commission of Soldiers' Orphan Schools for the Year Ending May 31, 1902*, pp. 70–71.

16. Pension Records of Walter Owens, NA.

17. Pension Records of Davis Meredith, NA.

18. Richard H. Frecon to Author, August 17, 1998; Obituary of S. Brady Caveny, newspaper clipping from 1926 issue of the *Harrisburg Patriot*, courtesy of Richard Frecon.

19. Pension Records of Henry Patterson, NA.

20. Pension Records of Thomas Moyer, NA.

21. "The Life Story of 'Blind Mike' Link," *Reading Eagle*, July 12, 1899; Pension Records of Michael Link, NA.

22. Pension Records of Lewis Rentschler, NA.

23. Rosemary McCorkel to Author, April 23, 1998, January 6, 1999, and January 8, 1999. All of the quotes in this section are derived from letters or documents in the possession of Mrs. McCorkel.

24. Robert Miller to "My Dear Son," July 4, 1863, and Harrison Allen to "Mr. Miller," August 2, 1864, Miller Brothers Letters, Schoff Civil War Collection, William L. Clements Library, University of Michigan; Schenck, *History of Warren County, Pennsylvania*, pp. 297, 300, 590–591, lxix; Pension Records of Robert E. Miller, NA.

25. Adah Sidon to Author, August 30, 1998; Schenck, *History of Warren County, Pennsylvania*, p. 437; Pension Records of Nathan Cooper, NA.

26. Mike Straus to Author, January 19, 1999; Pension Records of Adam G. Strause, NA.

27. "The Diary of Alfred D. Staudt," p. 14; Pension Records of Alfred Staudt, NA.

28. Obituary of William Boltz, *Reading Eagle*, May 4, 1906; Pension Records of William Boltz, NA; Morning Report Book, Company H, 151st Pennsylvania Volunteers, NA.

29. Pension Records of Albert Yost, NA.

30. Pension Records of William S. and Solomon Strause, NA; Cyrus T. Fox, *Reading and Berks County, Pennsylvania: A History*, 2 vols. (New York: Lewis Historical Publishing Company, 1925), Vol. 2, p. 127; Joe Smith, M.D. to Author, January 9, and January 10, 1999; Recollections of Mr. Robert Kunkle.

31. Walker, *Appointment at Gettysburg*, p. 109.

32. Pension Records of William Gray, NA; Obituary of William Gray, *Pottsville Republican*, January 27, 1890.

33. Pension Records of Charles Potts, NA.

34. Pension Records of James Weida, NA.

35. Pension Records of Adam Heilman, NA; Sauers, *Advance the Colors!*, Vol. 2, p. 453; Obituary of Adam Heilman, *Berks and Schuylkill Journal*, June 22, 1878.

36. Montgomery, *Historical and Biographical Annals of Berks County, Pennsylvania*, Vol. 1, pp. 1034–1035; Obituary of Charles Ammarell, *Reading Eagle*, March 5, 1923.

37. Pension Records of Franklin Wendling, NA.

38. George F. McFarland Diary, 1866, private collection. For details of the relationship between Bachelder and McFarland, see Dreese, *An Imperishable Fame*, pp. 9–10, 12, 170. Hayes was one of six Civil War soldiers to become president of the United States. He emerged from the war as a brevet major general of volunteers. Before his election to the presidency in 1876, Hayes served in the House of Representatives and for two terms as governor of Ohio. Sifakis, *Who Was Who in the Civil War, Vol. 1*, pp. 187–188.

39. Ladd and Ladd, *The Bachelder Papers*, Vol. 1, Introduction by Dr. Richard Sauers, pp. 9–14. For an excellent account of Bachelder's background and his numerous contributions to the interpretation and preservation of the Gettysburg battlefield, see Richard A. Sauers, "John Bachelder: Government Historian of the Battle of Gettysburg," *The Gettysburg Magazine*, no. 3 (July 1990), pp. 115–127.

40. "Reunion of First Day's Fight," undated newspaper clipping, George McFarland Papers, PSA.

41. Brown, *A Colonel at Gettysburg and Spotsylvania*, p. 88.

42. Nicholson, *Pennsylvania at Gettysburg*, Vol. 1, p. iii. Beaver was the colonel of the 148th Pennsylvania. He was later awarded a brevet to brigadier general.

43. George McFarland, "151st Regiment Pennsylvania Volunteer Infantry," George McFarland Papers, Dr. Charles Lloyd Eater, Jr., Collection.

44. Coco, *A Strange and Blighted Land*, p. 370; John M. Vanderslice, *Gettysburg: A History of the Gettysburg Battle-field Memorial Association with An Account of the Battle Giving Movements, Positions, and Losses of the Commands Engaged* (Philadelphia: The Memorial Association, 1897), pp. 199–201, 236–238; Harlan D. Unrau, *Gettysburg National Military Park and Gettysburg National Cemetery: Administrative History* (Gettysburg: National Park Service, 1991), pp. 41, 51, 53, 57. In 1866, the GBMA secured a contract to purchase about five acres of land comprising the eastern portion of Herbst's woods. This parcel was purchased when veterans of the First Corps announced plans to erect a monument in this vicinity in honor of their fallen commander. Later, it was decided to place this memorial in the more heavily visited Soldiers' National Cemetery. In 1886, the Commonwealth of Pennsylvania erected a small monument in Reynolds Woods to mark the site of Reynolds' death. Frassanito, *Early Photography at Gettysburg*, pp. 59, 64.

45. George McFarland to "Comrades," June 13, 1888, copy of original circular in 151st Pennsylvania File, Gettysburg National Military Park Library. The ad for the Eagle Hotel was found in James T. Long, *The 16th Decisive Battle of the World — Gettysburg* (Gettysburg: Gettysburg Compiler Print, 1906). Captain Long was a battlefield guide and lecturer who operated his business out of the hotel.

46. George McFarland to Major Samuel Harper, June 18, 1888, 151st Pennsylvania File, Gettysburg National Military Park Library.

47. George McFarland, "151st Regiment Pennsylvania Volunteer Infantry," George McFarland Papers, Dr. Charles Lloyd Eater, Jr., Collection; "The 151st P. V. Regiment at Gettysburg," *Democrat and Register*, Mifflintown, Pa., July 11, 1888.

48. Nicholson, *Pennsylvania at Gettysburg*, Vol. 2, pp. 767–770.

49. *Ibid.*, Vol. 1, pp. 1–19.

50. "The 151st P. V. Regiment at Gettysburg," *Democrat and Register*, Mifflintown, Pa., July 11, 1888.

51. The first evidence of the three bronze muskets appeared in a photograph in *Pennsylvania at Gettysburg*, which was published in 1904. In all earlier photographs of the monument that I have examined, including the one taken on Pennsylvania Day in 1889, the original design appears. An image of the first monument was also found in John M. Vanderslice's *Gettysburg Then and Now*, which was published in 1897. Therefore, it is likely that the new design appeared sometime between 1897 and 1904. It is quite possible that the monument was damaged during a major storm that swept through Gettysburg on September 30, 1896. High winds toppled a number of trees in Reynolds Grove at this time and one may have struck the monument.

The major difference between the two lists of casualties for the 151st is the number of killed vs. wounded. In the *Official Records* (Vol. 27, Part 1, p. 174), McFarland reported 51 killed and 211 wounded. His amended list shifted 30 of the wounded to the killed and mortally wounded category. For more information on the casualty figures of the 151st Pennsylvania, see

George McFarland to Major Samuel Harper, March 30, 1889 and George McFarland to John P. Nicholson, July 13, 1889, 151st Pennsylvania File, Gettysburg National Military Park Library, and Nicholson, *Pennsylvania at Gettysburg*, Vol. 2, 1132–1134. The board of directors of the GBMA acknowledged that the War Department records "may not be absolutely correct" and that "any changes furnished officially from the Adjutant General's office will be cheerfully adopted by the Association." Vanderslice, *Gettysburg: A History of the Gettysburg Battle-field Memorial Association*, pp. 238–239.

52. Martin B. Sloat, "Springs Hotel," *The Gettysburg Times*, October 20, 1984; Newspaper Clippings and Copy of 1881 Advertising Circular for the Gettysburg Springs Hotel, Springs Hotel File, Adams County Historical Society, Gettysburg, Pa; Map of the Battlefield of Gettysburg with the Locations of Monuments Erected by the Commonwealth of Pennsylvania, Nicholson, *Pennsylvania at Gettysburg*, Vol. 2, p. 1172; Gettysburg Convention and Visitors Bureau, *Gettysburg*, 1996, "Map of Gettysburg," pp. 24–25.

53. Coco, *A Strange and Blighted Land*, p. 371; *Annual Reports of the Gettysburg National Military Park Commission to the Secretary of War, 1893–1904* (Washington, D.C.: Government Printing Office, 1905), pp. 38, 51, 54, 85, 90–91, 95.

54. Gearhart, *In the Years '62 to '65*, p. 36.

Appendix I

1. George McFarland, "Teachers in the Army," *Pennsylvania School Journal* (March 1863), pp. 269–270.

2. George McFarland, "The Victory at Gettysburg, the Work of the Teacher," *Pennsylvania School Journal* (October 1866), pp. 95–96.

3. Nicholson, *Pennsylvania at Gettysburg*, Vol. 2, p. 768.

4. Bates, *History of Pennsylvania Volunteers*, Vol. 4, p. 677.

5. Dreese, *An Imperishable Fame*, pp. 14, 19; *Muster Rolls of the 151st Pennsylvania Volunteers*, PSA; McAlisterville Academy Attendance Books, J. Horace McFarland Collection, PSA; 1862 Diary of George McFarland, Dr. Charles Lloyd Eater, Jr., Collection.

6. Dreese, *An Imperishable Fame*, pp. 9–10, 23, 24.

7. Vanderslice, *Gettysburg Then and Now: The Field of American Valor*, p. 115.

8. St. Clair A. Mulholland, *A Record of Human Sacrifice of Daring Deeds and Heroic Men: Percentage of Losses at Gettysburg Greatest in History* (Gettysburg: W. H. Tipton, 1903), pp. 6–7. Mulholland commanded the 116th Pennsylvania of the "Irish Brigade" at Gettysburg. He was wounded four times during the war, and he received a brevet as major general of volunteers for his distinguished service. In 1895, Mulholland was awarded the Congressional Medal of Honor for his heroic conduct at the battle of Chancellorsville. Sifakis, *Who Was Who in the Civil War*, Vol. 1, p. 282.

9. "Valor of Pennsylvania Boys in the Civil War," undated newspaper clipping, copy in author's collection. This article was published sometime prior to April 12, 1912, the date of death for Walter Owens, who was interviewed for the story.

10. "Guiding Through the Twenties," *The Battlefield Dispatch: The Newsletter of the Association of Licensed Battlefield Guides, Inc.*, Vol. XV, No. 4 (April 1996), p. 6.

11. Storrick, *Gettysburg: The Place, The Battles, The Outcome*, pp. 38–39.

12. Coco, *A Strange and Blighted Land*, pp. 374–377. For a detailed account of the history of the Gettysburg licensed

battlefield guides, see Frederick W. Hawthorne, *A Peculiar Institution: The History of the Gettysburg Licensed Battlefield Guides* (Gettysburg: The Association of Licensed Battlefield Guides, Gettysburg, Pa., 1991).

13. Stewart, *Pickett's Charge*, p. 61.

14. Dreese, *An Imperishable Fame*, p. 5.

15. Biographical Sketches of Harrison Allen, Samuel Allen, and Warren Underwood, George McFarland Papers, PSA; Walker, *Appointment at Gettysburg*, p. 2.

Appendix II

1. This list was compiled by George McFarland and submitted to the War Department in 1889 to correct the original figures he had submitted with his official report. A copy of the list is in the 151st Pennsylvania File, Gettysburg National Military Park Library.

BIBLIOGRAPHY

Manuscript Collections and Official Documents

National Archives, Washington, D.C.
Pension Records, Casualty Reports and Military Service Records
Morning Report Book, Company H, 151st Pennsylvania Volunteers, Record Group 94

Pennsylvania State Archives, Harrisburg, Pa.
Samuel P. Bates Papers
George McFarland Papers, J. Horace McFarland Collection
Peter Rothermel Papers
Muster Rolls of the 151st Pennsylvania Volunteers, RG-19

Private Collections
Simon J. Arnold Papers, Mary Haney Arnold Collection
William O. Blodget Papers, Rosemary McCorkel Collection
Charles L. Eater, Jr., Collection
Seward R. Osborne Collection
Alexander Seiders Papers, Sally Smith Collection
Timothy H. Smith Collection

United States Army Military History Institute, Carlisle Barracks, Pa.
Lyman Beebe Letters
Robert L. Brake Collection
Gregory A. Coco Collection

Warren County Historical Society, Warren, Pa.
William Blodget to wife, July 2, 1863
Theodore Chase Papers
Nathan Cooper Letters
Frank Lyon to Theodore Putnam, November 23, 1862

Miscellaneous
W. H. S. Burgwyn Papers, North Carolina Department of Cultural Resources, Division of Archives and History, Raleigh, N.C.
Civilian Folders, Adams County Historical Society, Gettysburg, Pa.
151st Pennsylvania File, Gettysburg National Military Park Library, Gettysburg, Pa.
Robert E. Miller Papers, Miller Brothers Letters, Schoff Civil War Collection, William L. Clements Library, University of Michigan, Ann Arbor, Mich.

Newspapers

Adams Sentinel and General Advertiser, Gettysburg, Pa.
Berks and Schuylkill Journal
Compiler, Gettysburg, Pa.
Democrat and Register, Mifflintown, Pa.
The Gettysburg Times
Harrisburg Patriot
Harrisburg Telegraph
Juniata Sentinel and Republican
Juniata Tribune
Montrose Democrat
The Pittston Gazette
Pottsville Miners' Journal
Pottsville Republican
Reading Daily Times
Reading Eagle
The Star and Sentinel, Gettysburg, Pa.
Union County Star and Lewisburg Chronicle

Published Works

Annual Report of the Pennsylvania Commission of Soldiers' Orphan Schools for the Year Ending May 31, 1902. Harrisburg, Pa.: Wm. Stanley Ray, 1902.
Annual Reports of the Gettysburg National Military Park Commission to the Secretary of War, 1893–1904. Washington, D.C.: Government Printing Office, 1905.
Balsley, J. R. "A Gettysburg Reminiscence." *National Tribune,* May 19, 1898.
Barnes, Joseph K., ed. *The Medical and Surgical History of the War of the Rebellion, 1861–1865.* Washington, D.C.: Government Printing Office, 1870. Reprint, Wilmington, N.C.: Broadfoot, 1990–1991, 12 vol.
Bates, Samuel P. *History of the Pennsylvania Volunteers: 1861–1865.* 5 vols. Harrisburg, Pa.: B. Singerly, 1869–1871.
Boatner, Mark M., III. *The Civil War Dictionary.* New York: Vintage Books, 1991.
Broadhead, Sarah M. *The Diary of a Lady of Gettysburg, Pennsylvania from June 15 to July 15, 1863.* Gettysburg: Privately published, 1864.
Brown, Varina D. *A Colonel at Gettysburg and Spotsylvania.* Columbia, S.C.: The State Company, 1931. Reprint, Baltimore: Butternut and Blue, n.d.
Busey, John W. *These Honored Dead: The Union Casualties at Gettysburg.* Hightstown, N.J.: Longstreet House, 1996.

_____, and David G. Martin. *Regimental Strengths and Losses at Gettysburg.* Hightstown, N.J.: Longstreet House, 1994.

Caldwell, J. F. J. *The History of a Brigade of South Carolinians Known First as "Gregg's," and Subsequently as "McGowan's Brigade."* Philadelphia: King & Baird, 1866. Reprint, Dayton, Ohio: Press of Morningside Bookshop, 1974.

Cavada, Frederic F. *Libby Life: Experiences of a Prisoner of War in Richmond, Va., 1863–64.* Philadelphia: King & Baird, 1864.

Chamberlin, Thomas. *History of the One Hundred and Fiftieth Regiment Pennsylvania Volunteers, Second Regiment, Bucktail Brigade.* Philadelphia: F. McManus, Jr., 1905. Reprint, Baltimore: Butternut and Blue, 1986.

Coco, Gregory A. *A Strange and Blighted Land, Gettysburg: The Aftermath of a Battle.* Gettysburg: Thomas Publications, 1995.

_____. *A Vast Sea of Misery: A History and Guide to the Union and Confederate Field Hospitals at Gettysburg, July 1–November 20, 1863.* Gettysburg: Thomas Publications, 1988.

Coddington, Edwin B. *The Gettysburg Campaign: A Study in Command.* New York: Charles Scribners' Sons, 1968.

Conklin, E. F. *Women at Gettysburg 1863.* Gettysburg: Thomas Publications, 1993.

"The Diary of Alfred D. Staudt." *Historical Review of Berks County* 41 (Winter 1975–1976): 14–16, 32–33.

Doubleday, Abner. *Chancellorsville and Gettysburg.* New York: Charles Scribner's Sons, 1882. Reprint, New York: Da Capo, 1994.

_____. "Report of the Operations of the Third Division of the First Army Corps, Army of the Potomac, from the 1st to the 7th of July 1863, including the 2nd and 3rd Days of the Battle of Gettysburg, Pa." Sept. 19, 1863. Copy in George McFarland Papers, PSA.

Downey, James W. *A Lethal Tour of Duty: A History of the 142d Regiment Pennsylvania Voluntary Infantry, 1862–65.* Master's thesis, Indiana University of Pennsylvania, 1995.

Dreese, Michael A. *An Imperishable Fame: The Civil War Experience of George Fisher McFarland.* Mifflintown, Pa.: Juniata County Historical Society, 1997.

_____. "The Saga of Andrew Gregg Tucker." *Bucknell World,* Vol. 26, No. 6 (November 1998): 20–21.

Ehler, Martha. *The Patriot Daughters of Lancaster. Hospital Scenes After the Battle of Gettysburg, July 1863.* Philadelphia: Henry B. Ashmead, 1864. Reprint, Gettysburg: G. Craig Caba, 1993.

Elmore, Thomas L. "A Meteorological and Astronomical Chronology of the Gettysburg Campaign." *The Gettysburg Magazine,* No. 13 (July 1995): 7–21.

Faust, Patricia, ed. *Historical Times Illustrated Encyclopedia of the Civil War.* New York: Harper & Row, 1986.

Fox, William F. *Regimental Losses in the American Civil War, 1861–1865.* Albany, N.Y.: Albany Publishing Company, 1889.

Frassanito, William A. *Early Photography at Gettysburg.* Gettysburg: Thomas Publications, 1995.

Gearhart, Edwin R. *In the Years '62 to '65: Personal Recollections of Edwin R. Gearhart.* Stroudsburg, Pa.: Daily Record Press, 1901.

Hartwig, D. Scott. "The Defense of McPherson's Ridge." *The Gettysburg Magazine,* No. 1 (July 1989): 15–24.

Hassler, Warren W., Jr. *Crisis at the Crossroads: The First Day at Gettysburg.* University: University of Alabama Press, 1970. Reprint, Gettysburg: Stan Clark, 1991.

Horner, John B. *Essential to a Nation's Life: The Story of Dr. Charles and Robert Horner of Gettysburg.* Gettysburg: Horner Enterprises, 1997.

Hutton, Paul Andrew, ed. *Gettysburg: Colonel William C. Oates and Lieutenant Frank A. Haskell.* New York: Bantam, 1992.

Jacobs, Henry E. *Memoirs of Henry Eyster Jacobs, Notes on a Life of a Churchman.* 3 vols. Ed. by Henry E. Horn. Huntington, Pa.: Church Management Service, 1974.

Jordan, Weymouth T., Jr., and Louis H. Manarin, eds. *North Carolina Troops, 1861–1865.* 12 vols. Raleigh, N.C.: Division of Archives and History, 1971–1996.

"Judge Slagle at Gettysburg," Timothy H. Smith Collection.

Kellogg, Robert H. *Life and Death in Rebel Prisons.* Hartford, Conn.: L. Stebbins, 1865.

Ladd, David L., and Audrey J. Ladd, eds. *The Bachelder Papers: Gettysburg in Their Own Words.* 3 vols. Dayton, Ohio: Morningside House, 1994–1995.

Lane, Bessie Mell, ed. *Dear Bet: The Carter Letters, 1861–1863: The Letters of Lieutenant Sidney Carter, Company A, 14th Regiment, South Carolina Volunteers, Gregg's — McGowan's Brigade, CSA, to Ellen Timmons Carter.* Clemson, S.C.: B. M. Lane, 1978.

"The Life Story of 'Blind Mike' Link," *Reading Eagle,* July 12, 1899.

Longacre, Edward D. *Mounted Raids of the Civil War.* Lincoln: University of Nebraska Press, 1994.

Linn, John B. "A Tourist at Gettysburg." *Civil War Times Illustrated* (September/October 1990): 26, 57–65.

McClean, James L., and Judy W. McLean. *Gettysburg Sources.* 3 vols. Baltimore: Butternut and Blue, 1986–1990.

McFarland, George F. "Teachers in the Army." *Pennsylvania School Journal* (March 1863): 269–270.

_____. "The Victory at Gettysburg, the Work of the Teacher." *Pennsylvania School Journal* (October 1866): 95–96.

McPherson, James. *The Atlas of the Civil War.* New York: Macmillan, 1994.

Martin, David G. *Gettysburg July 1.* Conshohocken, Pa.: Combined Books, 1995.

Matthews, Richard E. *The 149th Pennsylvania Volunteer Infantry in the Civil War.* Jefferson, N.C.: McFarland & Company, 1994.

Miller, J. Michael. "Perrin's Brigade on July 1, 1863." *The Gettysburg Magazine,* No. 13 (July 1995): 22–32.

Miller, William J. *The Training of an Army: Camp Curtin and the North's Civil War.* Shippensburg, Pa.: White Mane, 1990.

Montgomery, Morton L., ed. *Historical and Biographical Annals of Berks County Pennsylvania.* 2 vols. Chicago: J. H. Beers, 1909.

Moore, Frank. *Women of the War; Their Heroism and Self-Sacrifice.* Hartford, Conn.: S. S. Scranton, 1867.

Mulholland, St. Clair A. *A Record of Human Sacrifice of Daring Deeds and Heroic Men: Percentage of Losses at Gettysburg Greatest in History.* Gettysburg: W. H. Tipton, 1903.

Munn, Sheldon A. *Freemasons at Gettysburg.* Gettysburg: Thomas Publications, 1993.

Murdoch, David A., ed. "Catherine Mary White Foster's Eyewitness Account of the Battle of Gettysburg, with Background on the Foster Family Union Soldiers." *Adams County History,* Vol. 1 (1995): 45–67.

Nevins, Allan, ed. *A Diary of Battle: The Personal Journals of Colonel Charles S. Wainwright, 1861–1865.* New York: Harcourt, Brace, & World, 1962.

Nicholson, John P., ed. *Pennsylvania at Gettysburg: Ceremonies at the Dedication of the Monuments Erected by the Commonwealth of Pennsylvania to Mark the Positions of the Pennsylvania Commands Engaged in the Battle.* 3 vols. Harrisburg, Pa.: William Stanley Ray, State Printer, 1914.

O'Brien, Kevin. "'Give Them Another Volley, Boys': Biddle's Brigade Defends the Union Left on July 1, 1863." *The Gettysburg Magazine,* No. 19 (July 1998): 37–52.

Osborne, Seward. *Holding the Left at Gettysburg, The 20th New York State Militia on July 1, 1863.* Hightstown, N.J.: Longstreet House, 1990.

Pfanz, Harry W. "The Gettysburg Campaign After Pickett's Charge." *The Gettysburg Magazine,* No. 1 (July 1989): 118–124.

Potts, Charles P. "A First Defender in Rebel Prison Pens." *Publications of the Historical Society of Schuylkill County,* Vol. 4 (1914): 341–352.

Powell, Walter L., Ph.D., ed. *Camp Letterman: The Lost Legacy of Gettysburg's Hospital Woods.* Gettysburg: The Gettysburg Battlefield Preservation Association, 1997.

Riley, Michael A. *"For God's Sake, Forward!," Gen. John F. Reynolds, USA.* Gettysburg: Farnsworth House Military Impressions, 1995.

Rodgers, Sara Sites. *The Ties of the Past: The Gettysburg Diaries of Salome Myers Stewart, 1854–1922.* Gettysburg: Thomas Publications, 1996.

Roth, Jeffrey B. "Civil War Medicine at Gettysburg." *The Gettysburg Hospital Quarterly* (Spring 1985): 2–4.

Roy, Paul L. "Colonel McFarland's Diary Reveals War–School Career." *Gettysburg Times,* June 27, 1941.

Sauers, Richard A. *Advance the Colors!* 2 vols. Lebanon, Pa.: Sowers, 1987–1991.

Sayre, R. D. "A Day at Gettysburg." *National Tribune,* April 13, 1899.

Schenck, J.S., ed. *History of Warren County, Pennsylvania.* Syracuse, N. Y.: D. Mason & Co., 1887.

Schildt, John W. *Roads from Gettysburg.* Chewsville, Md.: John W. Schildt, 1979.

Shue, Richard S. *Morning at Willoughby Run, July 1, 1863.* Gettysburg: Thomas Publications, 1995.

Sifakis, Stewart. *Who Was Who in the Civil War.* 2 vols. New York: Facts On File, 1988.

Smith, Timothy H. *The Story of Lee's Headquarters: Gettysburg, Pennsylvania.* Gettysburg: Thomas Publications, 1995.

Speer, Lonnie R. *Portals to Hell: Military Prisons of the Civil War.* Mechanicsburg, Pa.: Stackpole, 1997.

Stewart, George R. *Pickett's Charge: A Microhistory of the Final Attack at Gettysburg, July 3, 1863.* Boston: Houghton Mifflin, 1959.

Stocker, Rhamanthus M. *Centennial History of Susquehanna County, Pennsylvania.* Baltimore: Regional Publishing Company for the Susquehanna County Historical Society and Free Library Association, 1974.

Storrick, W. C. *Gettysburg: The Place, The Battles, The Outcome.* Harrisburg, Pa.: J. Horace McFarland, 1932.

Survivors' Association. *History of the 121st Regiment Pennsylvania Volunteers.* Philadelphia: Press of the Catholic Standard and Times, 1906.

Symonds, Craig L. *Gettysburg: A Battlefield Atlas.* Baltimore: Nautical & Aviation Publishing Company, 1995.

Tagg, Larry. *The Generals of Gettysburg: The Leaders of America's Greatest Battle.* Campbell, Calif.: Savas, 1998.

Taylor, Frank H. *Philadelphia in the Civil War, 1861–1865.* Philadelphia: Dunlap, 1913.

Thompson, Heber S. *The First Defenders.* First Defenders' Association, 1910.

Trautmann, Frederick, ed. *Twenty Months in Captivity: Memoirs of a Union Officer in Confederate Prisons.* Cranbury, N.J.: Fairleigh Dickinson University Press, 1987.

Tucker, Glenn. *High Tide at Gettysburg.* Indianapolis: Bobbs-Merrill, 1958.

Underwood, George C. *History of the Twenty-sixth Regiment of the North Carolina Troops in the Great War, 1861–'65.* Goldsboro, N.C.: Nash Brothers, 1901. Reprint, Wendell, N.C.: Broadfoot's Bookmark, 1978.

"Valor of Pennsylvania Boys in the Civil War," undated newspaper clipping, author's collection.

Vanderslice, John M. *Gettysburg: A History of the Gettysburg Battle-field Memorial Association with An Account of the Battle Giving Movements, Positions, and Losses of the Commands Engaged.* Philadelphia: The Memorial Association, 1897.

_____. *Gettysburg Then and Now: The Field of American Valor.* New York: G. W. Dillingham, 1897.

Walker, John Hunt, M.D. *Appointment at Gettysburg.* Seattle: ARS OBSCURA, 1994.

The War of the Rebellion: A Compilation of the Official Records of the Union and Confederate Armies. 79 volumes in 128 parts. Washington, D.C.: Government Printing Office, 1880–1901.

Warren, Horatio N. *The Declaration of Independence and War History: Bull Run to the Appomattox.* Buffalo: Courier, 1894.

_____. *Two Reunions of the 142d Regiment, Pa. Vols.* Buffalo: Courier, 1890.

Welch, Spencer Glasgow. *A Confederate Surgeon's Letters to His Wife.* New York: Neale, 1911. Reprint, Marietta, Ga.: Continental, 1954.

Wentz, Abdel Ross. *Gettysburg Lutheran Theological Seminary, Vol. 1, History, 1826–1895.* Harrisburg, Pa.: Evangelical Press, 1965.

Wert, J. Howard. "In the Hospitals of Gettysburg, July of 1863," *Harrisburg Telegraph,* Series of 12 articles printed between July 2 and October 7, 1907.

_____. "Little Stories of Gettysburg," *Gettysburg Compiler,* December 24, 1907.

Index

187